The Modern World since 1870

Second edition

L.E. Snellgrove

LONGMAN

PEARSON EDUCATION LIMITED
*Edinburgh Gate, Harlow, Essex, CM20 2JE, England
and Associated Companies throughout the world.*

First published 1968
Second edition 1981
40 39 38 37 36

ISBN 978-0-582-22299-1

Set in 10/12 Times Roman, Linotron 202

Printed in Malaysia, VVP

Contents

1	Telegrams and Timetables *The Franco-Prussian War*	1
2	The Old Order *Habsburg and Ottoman Empires*	10
3	Meeting at Fashoda *Imperialism and the 'Scramble for Africa'*	18
4	Subjects of the Queen *British Empire in the Nineteenth Century*	25
5	Two New Giants *USA and Japan*	35
6	Kaiser William Steams Ahead *Causes of the First World War (I)*	44
7	Murder at Sarajevo *Causes of the First World War (II)*	52
8	Defeat at the Marne *The First World War (I)*	59
9	From Ypres to the Somme *The First World War (II)*	67
10	Revolution and Victory *The First World War (III)*	78
11	Woodrow Wilson's Peace *The Versailles Treaty*	88
12	Greek, Turk, Jew and Arab *The Middle East 1918–1938*	97
13	Communism and Fascism *Russia and Italy 1918–1938*	107
14	Depression and New Deal *USA 1918–1939*	119
15	From Empire to Commonwealth *The British Overseas 1900–1947*	128
16	The World of Adolf Hitler *Germany 1918–1933*	143
17	Swastikas over Europe *Causes of the Second World War*	152
18	Rehearsal in Spain *The Spanish Civil War*	163
19	The Road to Pearl Harbour *The Far East 1917–1941*	171
20	Blitzkrieg *The Second World War in Europe*	180
21	From Midway to Hiroshima *The Second World War in the Far East*	193
22	The Troubled Peace *The United Nations and the Cold War*	203
23	Sun, Chiang and Mao *China until 1953*	216
24	War and Peace *North Africa and the Middle East since 1945*	226
25	The Impossible Dream *Africa since 1900*	240
26	From Stalin to Détente *Russia since 1945*	262
27	Revolutions Lost and Won *The Far East since 1945*	275
28	The Search for Justice *USA since 1945*	288
29	Democracy and Dictatorship *Latin America*	303
30	After Empire *The Dominions, India and Ireland since 1945*	320
31	Defeat and Victory *Europe since 1945*	332
	Index	344

1
Telegrams and Timetables
The Franco-Prussian War

During January 1871 an important ceremony took place near Paris. Five months previously France had been invaded and the French armies defeated by the Germans. Now, in the square before the palace of Versailles, hundreds of German soldiers stood motionless in the cold. Inside, their officers, dressed in blue and carrying their spiked helmets, mounted the long stairway between ranks of troops and walked to the famous hall whose walls are lined with mirrors. At one end a platform had been erected, decorated with German regimental flags. Nearby stood an altar.

At twelve o'clock a stir of excitement went through the crowded assembly. It died quickly to a hushed silence as the King of Prussia, William I, entered, escorted by German princes and dukes. There was a rustle of hymn books, a clink of swords as men knelt. A military choir sang 'Let all the world rejoice in the Lord', followed by the congregation joining in 'Praise and honour unto the Lord'. A clergyman conducted prayers and gave a sermon. The simple service was soon over. Then the King walked to the platform and read a short statement,

Proclamation of the German Empire at Versailles, January 1871

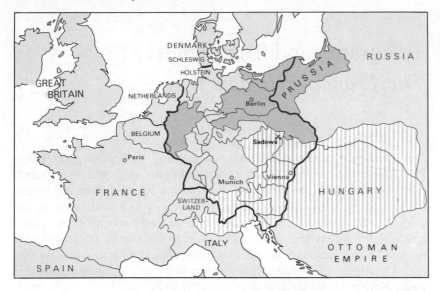

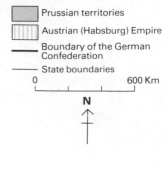

Europe, showing the German states before unification

saying that he was ready to be Emperor of the new German Reich (Empire) which would be formed by uniting the German kingdoms of the North German Confederation and the South German States. His Chancellor, **Otto von Bismarck**, a large man dressed in the blue tunic and high boots of a Prussian cavalryman, stepped forward and proclaimed that the Second Reich existed from that moment. One of the dukes shouted, 'Long live His Majesty the Emperor!' He was answered by a mighty cheer. Swords were drawn and waved. Bands played the German National Anthem. The scene was reflected and multiplied in the mirrors so that there seemed to be thousands, not hundreds, of men present. It was 18 January 1871, a day of sorrow for France, of rejoicing for Germany.

Otto von Bismarck – founder of the new Germany

Enter Bismarck

Following the end of the Napoleonic Wars (1815) four large nations, Russia, France, Prussia and Austria, had been of roughly equal power in Europe. Consequently there was a 'balance of power' between them, which helped to maintain peace in Europe. But in 1862 William I of Prussia appointed Bismarck as Prime Minister and gave **Helmuth von Moltke** the task of reorganising his army. Bismarck was not interested in a balance of power. His aim was to unite most of the German states under the leadership of Prussia, if necessary by war. To do this he needed to overcome the opposition of two powerful countries, Austria and France (see map above). Austria's German royal family, the Habsburgs, looked upon themselves as the leaders of some of these states. They were certain to resent any attempt to deprive them of such a privileged position. France's rulers had always regarded a disunited Germany as essential for their safety. They feared a powerful, united Germany bordering France's eastern frontier.

Bismarck's solution to this problem was to fight each country separately. At first few people realised what he was doing. In 1864 the new

Helmuth von Moltke – organiser of the German victory against France

Prussian army was tried out in a war against Denmark. The quarrel concerned the ownership of two border territories called Schleswig and Holstein (see map on page 2). Austria was persuaded to join Prussia. Little Denmark stood no chance, and after the war Prussia took Schleswig and Austria swallowed Holstein. Bismarck, however, knew that Austria would never be able to defend a territory almost encircled by Prussia. In June 1866 Prussian troops occupied Holstein as well and war with Austria followed.

What happened then astonished everyone. Moltke's carefully planned invasion overwhelmed the Austrians. After only a few weeks the Austrian commander sent a desperate telegram to his Emperor:

> Your Majesty most urgently requested to make peace at any price. Catastrophe inevitable.

The young ruler, Franz Joseph, could hardly understand what had happened. He replied:

> Impossible to conclude peace. I order – if unavoidable – retreat in best order. Has there been a battle?

By the time this message arrived the slowly retreating Austrians had been forced to fight at **Sadowa** (also called Konnigratz). Prussian soldiers, armed with a new kind of rifle, were firing five shots to their enemy's one. Battling bravely the Austrian ranks were shot to pieces. The **Seven Weeks' War** was over.

This short war had long-term results. At one blow Austria ceased to be the leading German power in Europe. German states north of the River Main joined Prussia in a **North German Confederation**; the South German States became free of Austrian influence (see map on page 5). At home Bismarck was treated as a hero. Previously he had made enemies because he had defied the Prussian parliament. Now the happy Prussians passed a law pardoning him for this! Abroad, the French regarded the war as a great disaster. Sadowa was looked upon as a French defeat simply because it had increased Prussia's power and influence. It was now clear what Bismarck intended. It was only a matter of time before war broke out between France and Prussia.

War with France, 1870–1871

An excuse was soon found. In 1869 the Spanish forced their Queen to leave the country, and began to look for a new monarch. One candidate was Prince Leopold of Hohenzollern, of the Prussian royal family. Bismarck and his King felt flattered that a Prussian might rule Spain. The French were horrified. On 6 July 1870 the French ambassador told William that, should Leopold become King of Spain, France would declare war on Prussia. Six days later Leopold decided not to seek the throne. The crisis seemed to be over, but the French were excited and warlike. Prussia's King was asked to promise that Leopold would never again be a candidate for the Spanish throne. William firmly refused.

Bismarck was in Berlin when he received a telegram from the King, who was on holiday at Ems, telling him of this interview. Sitting at dinner with Moltke, Bismarck wrote a shortened version and arranged for it to be published. As he explained later, the difference between his version and the King's 'was not the result of stronger words but of the form'. The King's message stated that the ambassador's request had been refused but he hoped that negotiations would continue. Bismarck's was more abrupt, suggesting a quarrel.

When the **Ems telegram**'s contents became known there was uproar in both countries. The Prussians felt sure that a Frenchman had insulted their King; the French that the Prussian King had insulted their ambassador! A French minister exclaimed, 'They wish to force us into war.' He was right. Bismarck wanted the war at that moment because Moltke had assured him that the army was ready. Afterwards he used to boast that he had started it. Actually his trick would not have succeeded had the French been less keen to fight. With crowds parading the Paris streets shouting 'On to Berlin', the French Government had little choice. War was declared on 19 July 1870.

The French troops who started to mobilise were thought to be among the best in the world. They were equipped with a good rifle, the *chassepot*, and a machine-gun, the *mitrailleuse*, which was a bundle of barrels fixed together and worked by a handle. They despised the Germans as soldiers. Their generals, Bazaine and Macmahon, were experienced, brave men. Their Emperor, Napoleon III, bore a name likely to inspire French soldiers, for he was the nephew of the great Napoleon Bonaparte who had crushed the First German Empire sixty-four years before. Compared with Bazaine and Macmahon, Moltke seemed more like a professor than a soldier, He was not a sword-waving hero, charging at the head of his cavalry, but a thoughtful man who spent his time working out troop movements with the aid of railway timetables.

Unfortunately for France, Moltke knew what he was doing, whereas Bazaine and Macmahon did not. He understood that railways and the mass-production of goods in factories had changed warfare. To fight bravely and skilfully was no longer enough. Now there was the technical problem of how to call up, say, a million men in a few days; how

Napoleon III – defeated French Emperor

The French mitrailleuse, an early type of machine-gun

to transport them swiftly to the battlefield; how to feed them and their guns; above all, how to organise a whole nation so that everyone contributed to the war effort. The Austrian Emperor's pathetic telegram before Sadowa had shown just how good Moltke was at solving such problems. Now his army was poised for an even bigger invasion: his railways pointed like pistols at the heart of France.

Only careful planning could prevent the huge armies then available from becoming mere hungry mobs, stranded somewhere on a railway line blocked with carriages and trucks. This is what happened to the French army. Whereas all German reservists recalled to the army reported to the barracks nearest to their homes, some Frenchmen had to cross France, or even sail from Algiers, in Africa, to reach their regimental depots. The Prussian railway system had been built for war. The French system was inadequate for the traffic which now began to struggle along it. Three movements in different directions soon brought mobilisation almost to a standstill. As regiments tried to reach the front, reservists tried to join their regiments and supplies and ammunition followed the army. Matters were made worse by the civilians who were still allowed to travel. After twenty-six days the French army was far from mobilised. One group of men who left Lille on 18 July had still not reached their regiment when fighting ceased.

All this would not have mattered had the Germans been in the same state. It soon became obvious that they were not. Most of their movements went smoothly and by early August Moltke's armies were across the French frontier. To make supplies easy to obtain they advanced in widely spaced groups which only concentrated for battle. There was no need to send food and ammunition for, say, 200,000 men, up one road or railway line. Ahead rode scattered cavalry units, sometimes of as few as three or four riders, who penetrated deeply into French territory, damaging railway lines and cutting telegraph wires. This added to the French confusion. Like the tentacles of an octopus, the Germans seemed to be all around them.

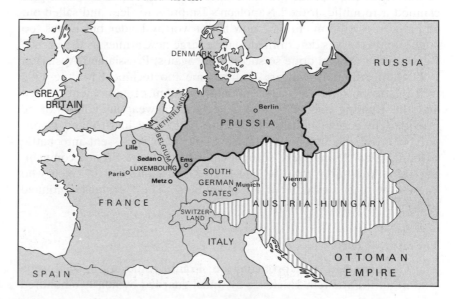

Europe before the Franco-Prussian War

Sedan and Metz

The first big clash occurred on 6 August. The French were beaten. Their *mitrailleuse* had been kept so secret that few soldiers knew how to use it. Their rifles were very good but the Germans tended to stay out of range and shatter them with heavy artillery fire. Fearing he would be surrounded, the French commander, Macmahon, ordered a retreat. Slowly his army was herded together into a huge, unwieldy mass. This time there was no need to send telegrams to the Emperor. Napoleon was with his army but he was so ill that he had little idea what to do. By late August 170,000 French soldiers were crushed together in the fortress of **Sedan** (see map on page 5), pounded day and night by heavy guns and short of food. For them the war was nearly over.

On 2 September Napoleon sent a message to the Prussian King, who was also with his armies, saying that he wished to surrender. Bismarck met him on a quiet country road, and they went into a little cottage. Sitting in a tiny room they talked across a rough wooden table. Even Bismarck felt sorry for the unfortunate man, broken in spirit, sick in body, whom he had last seen in magnificent surroundings at the Tuileries palace in Paris. Napoleon surrendered his army, knowing that by doing so he would lose his throne as well. Meanwhile, Bazaine's forces retreated so slowly that they too were surrounded, and driven into **Metz**. For six weeks they grew hungrier and hungrier until men searched the fields for potatoes and horses nibbled each other's tails. On 27 October his army of 200,000 men also surrendered. Every French regimental flag was captured except that of the Imperial Guard, which was burnt by its commander.

Before this, on 20 September, the victorious Germans had encircled Paris. A week later, when they dredged up the telegraph cable from the bed of the Seine, the French capital ceased to have any effective contact with the outside world. France's new leader, Gambetta, proclaimed a republic, forced Napoleon's Empress to flee, and sailed out of Paris in a balloon. France now had a worthy leader but it was too late. Gambetta was determined to raise large new armies as the French Revolutionaries had done so successfully against Prussia and Austria in 1792. Unfortunately warfare had become too technical for the 1792 victories to be repeated. The enormous amount of equipment needed and the training necessary to handle modern weapons could not be provided in a few months. Desperate battles by half-trained troops only delayed the inevitable defeat. Some men were sent into battle without rifles. Many were so undisciplined that one French commander remarked sadly that he had been given command of 'men who knew how to get killed, but not of soldiers'. The Germans continued to spread over the country.

The siege of Paris

The Germans had their problems too. France could not be said to be beaten until Paris fell. Enclosed by walls, guarded by nearly a hundred

A balloon is prepared for Gambetta's flight during the siege of Paris, 1870–1

Battles between French and German troops near Paris, 1870

forts as well as fortified villages, its defences stretched for 60 kilometres. A vast army was needed even to surround it. To attack such a sprawling maze of buildings and streets defended by an armed population would have been madness. Nor was this the only problem. All over occupied France guerrilla fighters, called *franctireurs*, were attacking German outposts. When caught they were executed instead of being treated as prisoners of war. Foreigners began to feel sorry for the French. The Germans grew angry and began to behave badly. One German officer wrote home, 'We are learning to hate them [the French] more every day.' At the Versailles Headquarters quarrels broke out between Bismarck and his generals. The ceremony on 18 January looked very grand but, actually, William was reluctant to be crowned Emperor until the war was over. At home, as the New Year came, people asked why, if the war was won, the soldiers had not returned? On 5 January 1871 Bismarck agreed to the bombardment of Paris, hoping this would cause the population to surrender. Large Krupps guns started firing 300 to 400 shells a day. People abroad were appalled at this attack on civilians. Bismarck started to worry in case Britain or Austria decided to intervene.

Fortunately for the Prussians, the situation inside Paris saved them. Rich people were still well fed. One restaurant owner raided the zoo and produced meals made from zebra, elephant, yak and buffalo. But hunger was widespread amongst the poor and, as revolutionaries played upon their discontent, France's generals began to fear a Paris rebellion. To prevent this they surrendered on 28 January 1871, thus ending the fighting. That they had cause to be afraid of rebellion was shown a few months later when some Parisians revolted, forming a rebel government called the Commune. French troops who had surrendered

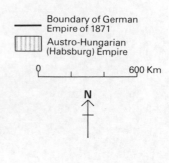

Boundary of German
Empire of 1871

Austro-Hungarian
(Habsburg) Empire

0   600 Km

N

*Europe, showing the new
German Empire, 1871*

at Metz and Sedan were brought home to crush this rising. They
did so savagely, killing 20,000 in a few weeks. Even whilst this slaughter was taking place, the **Treaty of Frankfurt** was signed between
France and Germany on 10 May 1871. By its terms France lost the two
provinces of Alsace and Lorraine (see map above), and had to pay 200
million francs compensation to the Germans.

A new age

The Franco-Prussian War showed that a new age had dawned.
Germany, not France, was now the greatest military and industrial
power on the Continent. To the Germans it seemed a miracle. After
centuries of disunity, with each small German state at the mercy of
France or Austria, they had achieved nationhood by two quick wars.
The result was worship of the army by the German people, which
allowed its leaders to become more important than they should have
been. Worse still, Bismarck's dazzling success made his ruthless
methods, such as the trickery with the Ems telegram, seem right.
Right or wrong no longer mattered; only the good of the 'Fatherland'.
Any deed was justified if it led to greater power for Germany. This
belief was called **Realpolitik**.

The other 'miracle man', Moltke, also gave people dangerous ideas.
The defeats of Austria and France seemed to indicate that all future
wars would end quickly. Victory would go to the nation which got its
army moving first. Few people asked themselves what would have happened if the French had been as well-organised as the Germans. The
American Civil War, in which equally matched armies slaughtered
each other for five years, was ignored. Germans were so dazzled by
Moltke's tricks that they forgot they could be imitated. Between 1914
and 1918 an astonished world saw what happened when most armies
were well-prepared and the nations involved organised for total war.

Finally, the Frankfurt peace treaty made a future war between France and Germany almost certain, providing the French could find an ally to fight with them. The loss of Alsace and Lorraine was an insult few Frenchmen could bear. Moltke realised this and said, 'What our sword has won in half a year, our sword must guard for half a century.' Bismarck attempted to solve the problem without further war. He tried to form alliances which would leave France without friends. During his time as Chancellor he succeeded. King William once said to him, 'You seem to me at times to be like a rider who juggles on horseback with five balls, never letting one fall.' This was true. Unfortunately, the German leaders who followed Bismarck after 1890 were not so expert. They began to make mistakes. When the First World War started France had two allies whereas Germany had only one. Moltke's methods were copied and the German Empire, created in the winter of 1871, crashed to ruin in 1918.

Timeline

1862 Bismarck appointed Prussian Prime Minister.
1864 Prussia defeats Denmark and takes Schleswig. Austria takes Holstein.
1866 Prussia defeats Austria and takes Holstein. North German Confederation formed.
1869 Prince Leopold of Hohenzollern candidate for Spanish throne.
1870 War between German states and France (Franco-Prussian War). French army surrenders. Napoleon III abdicates. Siege of Paris begins.
1871 German Empire proclaimed. Siege of Paris ends. Treaty of Frankfurt signed.

Questions

1. 'They wish to force us into war.'
   a) Why did Bismarck want to force the French to fight a war against Prussia?
   b) What did Prussia gain at the end of the war?
   c) Describe in your own words the event that is being celebrated in the picture on page 1.

2. 'Any deed was justified if it led to greater power for Germany. This belief was called Realpolitik.'

   Give examples of Bismarck's use of 'Realpolitik'. What is your opinion of policies based on such principles?

3. Write short paragraphs on each of the following:
   a) the Ems telegram
   b) von Moltke
   c) Sedan
   d) the Treaty of Frankfurt

2
The Old Order
Habsburg and Ottoman Empires

The German nation before 1870 had been one people divided into separate states. Two other European countries were the opposite. Both the Austrian (Habsburg) Empire and the Turkish (Ottoman) Empire consisted of many peoples united under foreign rule.

The Habsburg 'patchwork'

Of the two, the Habsburg was the strangest. Most empires have been created by one nation conquering others. But this one had been formed mainly through the marriages of the Habsburg family. A son or daughter would wed the child of another prince and their descendants would inherit a dukedom or kingdom. The result was a 'patchwork' empire of bits and pieces whose subjects were linked not by race or religion but by a similar way of life and loyalty to a Habsburg.

During the nineteenth century the Habsburg Empire consisted of no less than eleven nationalities: Germans, Hungarians (Magyars), Czechs, Poles, Ruthenians, Romanians, Croats, Serbs, Slovaks, Slovenes and Italians. Of these, two, the German and Hungarian, were masters of the others. The Habsburg Empire was very large, spread like a fatherly hand across southern Europe. Half of it was

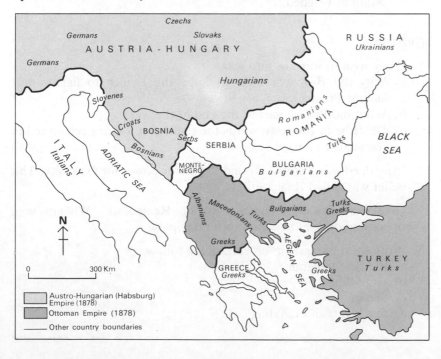

Balkan races at the frontiers of the Habsburg and Ottoman Empires. Ruthenians, Czechs, Poles, Croats, Serbs, Slovaks and Slovenes were all Slavs

*Unlucky Emperor, Franz
Joseph of Austria-Hungary*

controlled directly by imperial officials whose speech was German and religion Catholic. German literature, German architecture and German music gave it a distinct flavour. By 1867 the other, Hungarian, half had become semi-independent. Magyar nobles paid no taxes to the central government; only duties on goods coming from Austria. They ruthlessly held down the races within their territory. During the Napoleonic Wars **nationalism**, the desire of a nationality to rule itself, arose to menace Habsburg power. Patriots wrote books to show that their own people were separate and distinct. Usually they contrasted their past freedom with their present sad state. Sometimes their tales were true. The Czechs and Serbs, for example, really had been independent. Some Serbs had even gained their freedom from the Turks in 1829. Their state, Serbia, bordered Austria itself. At other times writers invented an independent history. But, true or false, when the Empire's subjects began to believe such stories the Habsburgs were in trouble. Loyalty to a family was replaced by loyalty to a nation. For this reason the Habsburg Empire was doomed long before it collapsed.

From 1848 until 1916, the Emperor of these territories was **Franz Joseph**. His long reign saw one disaster after another. Sadowa (see page 3) could have ended his rule. Moltke and the Prussian generals wished to crush Austria completely. Franz Joseph was saved by Bismarck, who ordered the advance to stop for a surprising reason. If the Habsburg Empire broke up, large numbers of Catholic Germans would wish to join Prussia. The dominant position of Protestant Prussia in the new Germany would then be threatened, because there would be more Catholics than Protestants. Bismarck's aim was a German Empire controlled by Prussia; a larger version of Prussia in which the Prussian ruling class, the Junkers, would be firmly in control. Although he believed that Austria's power needed to be limited he preferred the Habsburg Empire to remain intact.

Hardly had the Prussian guns stopped firing than poor Franz Joseph was faced by another danger. If Bismarck did not want to destroy the Empire, many of its subject nationalities did. The Hungarians, for example, saw the Empire's weakness as an opportunity to gain more freedom. They demanded a freer hand, forcing Franz Joseph to divide the Empire into two parts so that it became Austria-Hungary (1867). Franz Joseph remained ruler of both but with control only of the army and foreign affairs. This scheme, called the **Dual Monarchy**, weakened his independence. The Emperor's only ally against more blackmail by the Hungarians was Germany. The Germans realised that they had only to threaten greater friendship with Hungary to force Franz Joseph to do their bidding. Defeated in war, Austria-Hungary's monarch was now tied to the new Germany.

The Ottoman Empire

The Ottoman Empire was of the old type. Like the Romans or Assyrians, the Turks had won it all by military conquest. These fierce warriors first burst upon the Arab Empire in the seventh century. They quickly adopted the Muslim faith because its few strict rules and promise of heavenly rewards if killed in battle appealed to them. Early waves of Turkish invaders, called Seljuks (after one of their chiefs), were followed in later centuries by even fiercer men called Ghazis, or Warriors of the Faith. A Ghazi chief named Osman gave his name to the Empire for it was mispronounced as Ottoman. His successors ruled in two capacities: as Sultan, or political leader; and also as Caliph, or spiritual guardian of the Muslim faith.

By the seventeenth century Ottoman Turks had conquered the Crimea (later part of Russia), Iraq, Syria, Palestine, western Arabia, Egypt, Libya, Tunisia and Algiers. They had also crossed into Europe and conquered many Christian peoples in what are now the Balkan countries of Yugoslavia (a combination of Serbia and Croatia), Bulgaria, Romania and Greece. In 1645 their Empire reached its greatest extent. Then the tide turned. In 1683 a Turkish army which seemed poised to capture Vienna, capital of the Habsburg Empire, was defeated by an army of Polish and Habsburg troops.

This defeat was a turning point in Ottoman history. From that time the Turks began to fall behind in technical development. Turkish soldiers were still some of the best in the world but they were not equipped with the new inventions which were changing warfare. Turkish education was still unscientific, consisting mainly of a study of the Muslim holy book, the Koran. The Turks became old-fashioned and inefficient. Between 1826 and 1830 the Greeks rebelled successfully against the Sultan, helped by British and French fleets which destroyed the ships supplying the Turkish armies in Greece (**Battle of Navarino 1827**). In 1839 the Sultan's Pasha (governor) in Egypt, **Mehemet Ali**, defied his master, and defeated the Turks sent against him.

The problems caused by the slow decline of the Ottoman Empire were known as the **Eastern Question**. Two great powers, the Habsburg and Russian Empires, competed for control of the Balkan lands. Millions of people living in the area were Slavs whose language and religion were similar to those of the Russians. It was natural that they should look towards Russia for help in their fight for independence. The Russian leaders, whether they believed in Slav freedom or not, could use these desires as an excuse to extend their influence in the region. The Habsburg rulers, on the other hand, had many Slavs living within their own territories, plus a Slav country, Serbia, on the border (see map on page 10). Dreams of Slav freedom were just as likely to break up the Habsburg as the Ottoman Empire. Consequently, the Habsburgs preferred the area to be ruled by the Turks. They also wanted to conquer Serbia because its very existence as an independent state made their own Serbs discontented and anxious to throw off Habsburg rule.

Russia's drive to the sea

At most times the Eastern Question involved stopping Russia from conquering areas ruled by the Turks. The quarrel involved Britain and France as well as Austria. Both the French and British had much influence and many trading interests in the eastern Mediterranean. The

Eastern Europe, area of conflict during the Russo-Turkish War of 1877–8

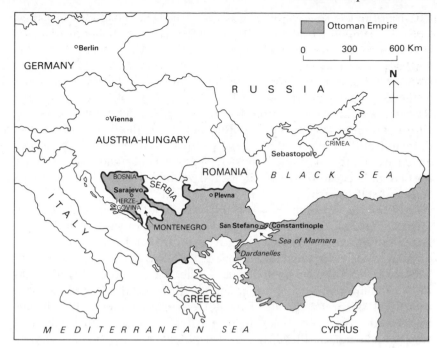

Russian drive towards Constantinople was as much geographical as political. Russian clergymen of the Orthodox Christian faith might talk of Constantinople as their 'holy' city. Russian politicians might complain of the Turkish ill-treatment of Christians and say they wanted a free Slav 'Empire'. But Russia wanted an outlet to the Mediterranean which could not be throttled by the Turks.

Russia is a land power which at first had no coastline at all. For two hundred years Russian armies struck both north and south to find ways to the sea. By 1724 Russia had succeeded in establishing St Petersburg (now Leningrad) on the northern, Baltic coast. Leningrad is a great port but it is often icebound in winter. So, later in the eighteenth century, Russian armies pushed south, hoping to gain control of a warm water port. They overran the Crimea and built Sebastopol on the Black Sea.

This port had disadvantages from the Russian point of view. The Black Sea is almost a lake. Its only outlet to the Mediterranean is by way of the Sea of Marmara and the Straits of the Dardanelles (see map above). Through these narrow waters Russian grain ships sailed, carrying their cargoes west to help pay for Russia's factory development. This 'lifeline' ran through Turkish territory. The Turkish Sultan could throttle Russia's trade if he wished. So could any other country which might invade the region, or even a newly-independent country set up by a power hostile to Russia. Russia therefore became deeply interested in the Christian parts of the Ottoman Empire, arguing that she had a right to protect them against Turkish cruelty. She also tried to get her warships allowed into the Mediterranean by international agreement. Both these aims brought her into conflict with Britain.

Britain and France went to war with Russia in 1854, claiming they were determined to save the Ottoman Empire from being overrun by Russia. French and British troops attacked, and eventually captured, Sebastopol and destroyed its defences. This so-called **Crimean War (1854–6)** checked any Russian threat to French and British influence in the Eastern Mediterranean, which, by the terms of the peace treaty, Russian warships were forbidden to enter. Within twenty years the European situation encouraged Russia to defy this ban. France was defeated and weak after the Franco-Prussian War. Britain was governed by a Liberal Prime Minister, William Gladstone, who disliked the Turks because of their cruelty and wanted the Slav peoples to be free and self-governing.

In 1877 the Russians saw an opportunity to intervene in Turkish affairs. The Bulgars staged an unsuccessful rebellion against the Sultan. After their victory the Turks began to torture and murder Christians on a large scale. In one district alone 12,000 Christians were massacred. This was all the Russians needed. The Tsar sent his armies into the Ottoman Empire, saying he intended to free the Christians from the Turks once and for all. Turkish troops fought well although outnumbered. After very fierce fighting Russian forces captured the fortress of **Plevna** (or Pleven). The Turks fell back as Russian soldiers pushed through the snow-covered mountains towards Constantinople.

Benjamin Disraeli

In Britain a new, Conservative Prime Minister took a different view from Gladstone. **Benjamin Disraeli** was determined that the Russians should not spread their power to the Mediterranean. Thoroughly alarmed, he sent a British fleet into the Dardanelles. Advancing Russians sighted the minarets of Stamboul, near Constantinople, only to see the masts of British warships as well. The Tsar was in a dilemma. He could not be sure his men would be allowed to cross without fighting and his exhausted troops were in no condition to risk a new war with Britain. The Tsar ordered them to stop.

Nevertheless, Russia had broken the power of the Turks single-handed. She was determined to enjoy the prizes of a costly and hard-fought war. The Turks were forced to sign the **Treaty of San Stefano, March 1878**. By its terms a large triangular area between the Danube, the Black Sea and the Aegean Sea was formed into a country called Bulgaria (see map on page 16). It was supposed to be independent, but no one believed it would be. The Bulgars had the same religion and spoke the same language as the Russians. They would be free only in name, taking their orders from the Tsar. At one stroke 'Big Bulgaria' put the Russians astride two seas, one of which led directly into the Mediterranean. It seemed that they had gained what they desired.

Congress of Berlin, 1878

Few European governments were prepared to accept this situation. Germany feared such an increase in Russian power. Britain saw Russian warships challenging her naval supremacy in the Mediterranean and threatening her new lifeline to the Far East – the Suez Canal (opened in 1869). Habsburg ministers knew that San Stefano had

*'Disraeli's Secret Agreements'.
A cartoon of 1878 illustrates
Disraeli's cunning methods of
diplomacy*

ignored Austrian claims to two Balkan territories called Bosnia and
Herzegovina (see maps on page 16). They also disliked the idea of an
empire like their own splitting into separate nations. How long would
their people remain quiet if this happened? Bismarck had treaty links
with both Russia and Austria. He wanted them to remain friends, not
quarrel over control of the Balkans. He decided to intervene, and in
1878 he called a conference of European nations at Berlin.

The Congress of Berlin, June 1878 was the largest gathering of European leaders since the 1815 meetings at Vienna after Napoleon's
defeat. The fact that it was held in Berlin, not Vienna, showed how
important the new Germany had become. However, in some ways the
Congress was dominated by Disraeli, the British Prime Minister. This
cunning politician went to Berlin having already made three secret
agreements. The first was with Russia. Disraeli had no intention of
going to war but he kept this secret from the Russians! The Russian
Tsar, Alexander II, decided to play safe. Even before the conference
began he had agreed to a reduction in the size of 'Big Bulgaria'.
Second, the British persuaded the Turks to let Russia keep some of
her conquests in return for a guarantee that Britain would come to her
aid in any future war with Russia. This agreement was unpopular with
Turkey, especially as she had surrendered Cyprus to Britain as a base
for use against Russia. Finally, Austria-Hungary was promised Bosnia-
Herzegovina. She wanted this province in order to hamper the development of a strong Serbia. The people of the region resented this
and Austria's 'peaceful protection' turned into a major military
operation, involving a battle to get into the town of Sarajevo.

At the Congress itself such secret agreements became open. On
every point the Russians and Turks were forced to give in. 'Big

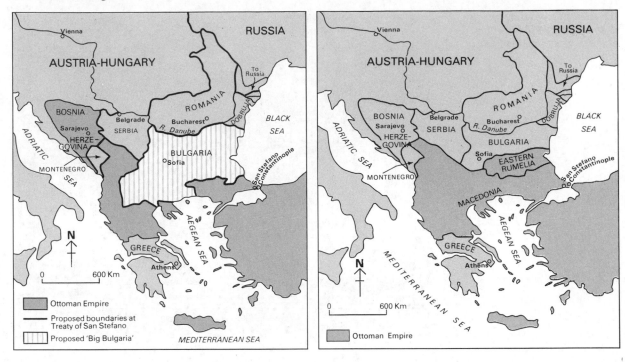

Balkan crisis: the boundaries proposed by the Treaty of San Stefano (left) and the actual frontiers after the Congress of Berlin (right)

Bulgaria' was divided into two parts, a smaller independent Bulgaria and an independent Macedonia (see maps above). The province of Eastern Rumelia was returned to the Turks on condition they allowed it a Christian governor. Even Bismarck was impressed by Disraeli's bluff and said admiringly, 'The Jew, he's the man.' When Disraeli reached home he told the British people he had brought back 'Peace with Honour'. In fact, the men at Berlin sowed the seeds of the First World War.

The alliance between Germany and Russia was never as strong after this Congress. The Russians had expected the British and Austrians to be against their Balkan schemes. They had expected their ally, Germany, to support them. After all, Russia had made no move whilst the Germans fought Austria in 1866 and France in 1870–1. Had she done so, Bismarck might not have been so successful and the German Empire might never have been formed. Bismarck claimed he was the 'honest broker', the umpire, if you like, of the Congress. Actually, he wanted to remain friends with both Austria and Russia and their quarrels were making this difficult. In the end Germany had to choose, and she chose Austria. By 1900 Russia was in an alliance with France against Germany.

The Turks were angry at seeing their 'friends', Britain and Austria-Hungary, take almost as much territory from them as their enemy, Russia. They were bitter and decided to seek friendship from the one country which had not benefited directly from the Congress, Germany. Bismarck himself did not wish to enter the quarrel about the Balkans. But his successors after 1890 sent German men and money to help modernise Turkey and to re-equip the Turkish army. In 1898 the new German Emperor, William II, visited Constantinople and made a speech about the 'undying friendship' between the two peoples. Not surprisingly, the Turks fought on the German side during the First World War.

Finally, Austria-Hungary's control of Bosnia-Herzegovina led the Serbs of the area to keep up a constant struggle against Habsburg rule. The Serbs who lived within the Empire were encouraged to demand independence by the independent state of Serbia. In later years serious attempts were made by Austrian and Russian groups to take over the government of Serbia. In 1903 a Russian group won this particular 'battle' and Austrian generals began to talk of a 'limited' war to conquer or control Serbia. Such a limited war was unlikely because Russia would almost certainly come to Serbia's rescue. If this happened a war between the great powers was very likely.

Timeline

1683   Turks defeated before Vienna.
1826   Greeks rebel against Turks.
1839   Mehemet Ali, Pasha of Egypt, rebels against Sultan.
1854–6   Crimean War.
1877   Russo-Turkish War.
1878   Treaty of San Stefano (March). Congress of Berlin (June).

Questions

1. Look at the cartoon on page 15.
   a) Which countries are represented by the lion and the bear?
   b) To what conference of European countries does this cartoon refer?
   c) The cartoon was called 'Disraeli's Secret Agreements'. What were these agreements?

2. a) Name the Balkan lands which belonged to Turkey before the Treaty of San Stefano (1878).
   b) Why was Turkey called the 'Sick man of Europe' at this time?

3. a) Why did Russia want to intervene in Turkish affairs in 1877?
   b) Why did other European countries dislike the terms of the Treaty of San Stefano (1878)?

4. a) What do you understand by the term 'nationalism'?
   b) Explain in your own words why the Habsburg Empire is called 'a patchwork empire of bits and pieces'.
   c) Which nationalities were most likely to want to break away from the Habsburg Empire and why?

5. Write short paragraphs on each of the following:
   a) the Dual Monarchy
   b) the Battle of Navarino
   c) the Crimean War, 1854–6
   d) 'Big Bulgaria'

3
Meeting at Fashoda
Imperialism and the 'Scramble for Africa'

On 19 September 1898 a British and a French officer faced each other on board a steamer near the fort at Fashoda on the banks of the Nile in Africa. The Frenchman, Captain Marchand, was small and dark with flashing eyes and a black beard. The Englishman, Lord Kitchener, had the straight back and moustache of a typical British soldier of the day. Each had arrived at that spot after many adventures. Marchand had travelled for nearly a year. His 7 officers and 120 native troops had tracked through thousands of kilometres of wilderness. They had carried the pieces of a small river steamer all the way, rolling its boiler on logs through the jungle. Kitchener had brought an army through the Sudan, laying a railway line as he went. He had defeated a large force of Dervishes at **Omdurman**, reconquered the Sudan and crushed the power of the men who had killed the British General Gordon 13 years before. Now he had come on to Fashoda with 5 gunboats and 2,000 men. Marchand had been there since July. His men had repaired a ruined fort, occupied the small village and triumphantly hoisted the French flag.

Each soldier had clear orders. Britain's Prime Minister had said to Kitchener, 'We claim the Sudan by right of conquest because it is the simplest and most effective.' On no account was he to recognise the right of another power 'to occupy any part of the Nile Valley'.

Marchand on the way to Fashoda, 1898

Marchand had been told by his government, 'You are going to fire a pistol shot in the Nile; we accept all its consequences.' Some British statesmen dreamed of a band of British territory stretching the length of Africa, south from Cairo to Cape Town (see map on page 22). The French wanted a line of colonies extending from Dakar in the west to the Gulf of Aden in the east. Both claimed Fashoda as their own, because it guarded the Upper Nile, on whose waters the Egyptians relied to irrigate their crops.

Fortunately, the men on the spot proved less aggressive than their political masters. Kitchener, for example, decided it would be safer to act on behalf of Egypt. He wore an Egyptian uniform and his ships flew Egyptian flags. In this way France would not be directly involved with Britain. Both soldiers took an instant liking to each other and after a good dinner discussed the matter frankly. Kitchener protested at the flying of the French flag on Egyptian territory. Marchand pointed out that he was obeying orders. Kitchener replied that he, too, had orders and, unlike Marchand, he had the force to carry them out. Marchand knew that his pitiful little army stood no chance in a fight. Bravely he insisted that he and his men would die rather than submit to force. Kitchener admired his toughness; obviously he was not bluffing. Eventually, Marchand agreed that he need not fight if the Egyptian flag was put up and the French flag left alone. To the thunder of a twenty-one gun salute this was done. Then both leaders thankfully referred the matter to their governments.

France, Britain and Egypt

In France the politicians began to have second thoughts. At one time the French had seemed about to occupy Egypt. It was a Frenchman, Ferdinand de Lesseps, who had designed the **Suez Canal**. French money had helped to finance the digging and, when the Canal opened in 1869, half the shares in the Canal company were French-owned. Yet, when Egypt's ruler, Khedive Ismail, went bankrupt in 1875 and Frenchmen were considering buying his shares, Disraeli had acted swiftly. Realising the value of controlling a shorter sea route to Australia, New Zealand and India, he had borrowed £4 million and bought the Khedive's shares. Britain became part-owner of the Canal and Disraeli wrote joyfully to Queen Victoria: 'It is settled; you have it, Madam. Four million sterling! and almost immediately . . . the entire interest of the Khedive is now yours.'

In 1882 France lost another opportunity. When Arabi Pasha rebelled against Tewfik, Ismail's son, his fight for independence was ended by a British fleet which bombarded Alexandria and an army which defeated him at **Tel-el-Kebir**. Britain then occupied Egypt, although not the Sudan. There, a religious fanatic, the Mahdi, forced a British withdrawal and killed their commander, General Charles Gordon. It was this defeat which Kitchener had just avenged - when he reached Fashoda.

Early French inactivity was due mainly to fear of Germany. After 1870 the thought of another German invasion was like a nightmare to

A contemporary cartoon of the Fashoda incident

Lord Kitchener. He met Marchand at Fashoda

most French politicians. They certainly feared to become involved in any other quarrels in case Germany attacked again. This was why the French fleet was ordered to sail away when the British guns opened fire on Alexandria, and why no French troops fought at Tel-el-Kebir. The preparations made by the British government after the Fashoda meeting convinced the French that Britain would fight if necessary. As neither Russia nor Germany could be relied on for help the French gave way. Marchand retreated and the British tactfully changed the name from Fashoda to Kodok so that no Frenchman would ever be reminded of it. An agreement, the **Anglo-French Convention**, signed in March 1899, fixed a limit to each country's expansion. From a line drawn between the rivers Nile and Congo the French promised not to move east and the British west. The 'Fashoda incident' was over.

Imperialism

The founding of colonies, **imperialism**, had been a European habit for centuries. In the sixteenth century the Spanish took most of South America and Mexico and the Portuguese the East Indies. In the eighteenth century Britain and France fought for control of North America and India. Nowhere had the natives resisted successfully. With his cannon and warships, his superior discipline and organisation, the European always managed to master non-European races. Robert Clive defeated hordes of Indians with a few thousand European-trained troops. French and British troops reduced the fierce Red Indian to little more than a dangerous nuisance. Whole tribes were wiped out by a few regiments armed with flintlock muskets.

The effect of this might have been less if the European had not insisted upon bringing his way of life with him. Rarely did he copy the ways and customs of those he conquered. In earlier times he built churches, houses and roads. In the nineteenth century he laid railways, erected factories and dug mines. Usually he tried to reproduce his homeland. He surrounded himself with objects and names which reminded him of home, with New South Wales in Australia, Canterbury in New Zealand and Birmingham in Alabama. All this helped to create a barrier between him and the native people. Usually he despised their ways. Americans never wore feathers; few Britons wore turbans or became Hindus. To subject races imperialism became a dirty word. It indicated not only that they had been conquered but that their way of life had been rejected at the same time.

Imperialism was only one reason for the spread of European ways of life. During the nineteenth century migration played a significant part as numbers of Europeans left their homes for various reasons. Between 1815 and 1914 Europe's population rose from one-fifth of the world's total to one-quarter. Other continents increased their populations, but not so quickly, because in Europe better medical care lowered the death rate. During this time, also, 40 million Europeans went abroad to seek their fortunes. By 1914, 700 million people living outside Europe were of European descent. The USA, in particular, became a gigantic extension of Europe, a large child rapidly growing bigger and stronger than its parents. Europe was an octopus, spreading its tentacles all over the world.

At the same time Western technical skill and knowledge grew even more superior. Cannon and musket had been terrible enough. By 1800 Europeans had the steam-engine. Production was no longer limited by the number of men employed. Power-driven machines could equal the work of thousands of craftsmen in a few hours. Later locomotives and power-driven ships could send men and armies speeding across continents and oceans. European factories produced goods at an astonishing rate. They gave European forces guns which made the old cannon seem like pea-shooters, warships which could have destroyed the old fleets in a few minutes.

European industry began to expand so fast that it created new problems. In a hundred years, 1770 to 1870, production of coal increased 30 times. During the next 10 years it increased 20 times again. Iron production doubled in 20 years. Steel production was multiplied by 7 in the same period. Goods were mass-produced so fast and profits made so quickly that businessmen looked for new places to sell their goods and invest their money. Imperialism had often been profitable. Now it seemed to be essential if the steel-mills, textile factories and coal-mines were to be kept going at full blast. An American, Ralph Waldo Emerson, summed up the situation when he said, 'Things are in the saddle and ride mankind.'

African scramble

Most of this extra colonisation took place in the last thirty years of the nineteenth century. During this time 26 million square kilometres of land and 150 million people were taken over by European states; the

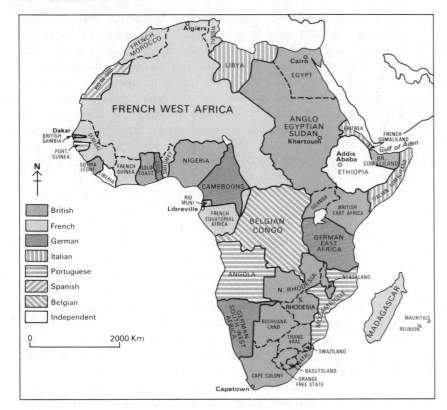

The 'Scramble for Africa': European colonies in 1875 (above) and in 1914 (left)

British Empire was nearly doubled. Most of this expansion was in two areas, Africa and South East Asia. Africa, in particular, with her vast empty spaces inhabited by comparatively defenceless peoples, seemed a tempting prize. The result was a rush for land so great that it was labelled by journalists 'the Scramble for Africa'.

Look at the two maps on this page. In 1875 only one-tenth of Africa was ruled by European countries. Twenty years later nine-tenths belonged to the Europeans and the only independent powers south of the Sahara were Ethiopia (Abyssinia), Liberia and the Boer states in South Africa. The 'scramble' soon resembled a race. One French writer decided it was a disease which he called Kilometritus or Milomania! In 1885 the larger European nations even signed the **Treaty of Berlin** which laid down the rules by which the scramble was to be conducted. Any power which 'effectively' occupied an African territory was to notify other governments immediately. This would give it the right of possession. In addition the rivers Niger and Congo were to be free to all and slavery was to be abolished.

The question has often been asked, why at this particular time? One reason, increased production of goods and surplus profits, has already been mentioned. Possibly an even more important one was the Congress of Berlin (see Chapter 2) which settled the map of Europe in such a way that only war could change it. The most powerful nation, Germany, was controlled by Bismarck who desired peace, and a precarious balance of power existed. Nations were forced to look elsewhere to add to their possessions. Weak, undefended Africa offered a few easy wars against spear-throwing tribesmen, 'sporting wars' Bismarck called them, but nothing as nasty as a European conflict between equals. Three less important factors assisted the scramble. Explorers, like Henry Morton Stanley and David Livingstone, had collected enough information to make the so-called 'dark continent' less unknown. Steamships and railways had speeded up travel. Finally, heavy artillery and machine-guns made European victory in battle almost certain.

Individual countries joined in the race for different reasons. Britain, as we have seen, originally took control of Egypt to guard her trade route with the Far East. Some states never did have African colonies, notably Austria-Hungary and Russia. The latter preferred to expand into Asia. Others went for trade or raw materials, for territory in which to invest spare money in profitable enterprises, for more land, or just because other nations did. This last was a strong motive. Just as today one man buys an expensive car which he can hardly afford because the man next door has one, so then nations conquered colonies because another nation had done so. Certainly Germany's East African colonies cost her more than they were worth. They were seized mainly because she felt that a great power should have colonies.

The men who landed and took the risks, who died of disease or sunstroke, varied as much as their governments. There were men who went as missionaries because they felt they had a duty to teach Christianity to pagans. Typical of these were groups like the French Catholic Fathers, or individuals like Livingstone. There were administrators who went to serve their country, believing they were bringing order into the lives of unfortunate natives. Typical of these were Evelyn Baring (Lord Cromer) in Egypt, Frederick Dealtry Lugard in Nigeria, Alfred Milner in South Africa and Louis Hubert Lyautey in Morocco. There were men who went for love of adventure, like Stanley and the German, Karl Peters. There were those who desired influence and power, like Cecil Rhodes and the Belgian King Leopold who owned the Congo and treated it as his 'farm'. Probably there were unknown thousands who went for several of these reasons. Even the best men did not pretend that it was all for the benefit of the natives. Lugard once said:

> It is well then to realise that it is for our advantage – and not alone at the dictates of duty – that we have undertaken responsibilities in East Africa. It is in order to foster the growth of trade of this country, and to find an outlet for our manufactures and our surplus energy, that our far-seeing statesmen and our commercial men advocate colonial expansion.

The Fashoda incident was typical of the quarrels between the European imperialists. Like greedy dogs they snapped and snarled over the available bones. Fortunately for world peace, the chances of war breaking out were not as great as they seemed because no colonial quarrel really threatened a nation's safety. Indeed, the African scramble was a safety-valve which let off European steam where it could do relatively little harm to Europeans. It was at Sarajevo not Fashoda, that an incident led to general war. The powerful world of that time was doomed to destroy itself because of a European, not a colonial quarrel.

Timeline

1869   Opening of Suez Canal.
1875   Khedive of Egypt bankrupt. Britain buys shares in Suez Canal.
1882   British occupy Egypt after Battle of Tel-el-Kebir.
1885   Treaty of Berlin.
1898   Fashoda incident.
1899   Anglo-French Convention.

Questions

1. Look at the cartoon on page 19.
   a) Which point of view of the 'Fashoda incident' does this cartoon represent, the British or the French?
   b) What is the flag flying above the fort?
   c) Who is the man who seems to be running away?
   d) How far is this cartoon an accurate portrayal of what actually happened?

2. 'To subject races "imperialism" became a dirty word.'
   a) Who were the 'subject races' of the French, British and Spanish mentioned on page 20 at the beginning of the section on imperialism?
   b) Explain in your own words the meaning of 'imperialism'.
   c) Why did 'imperialism' become a 'dirty word' to the subject races?

3. Which European countries took part in the 'Scramble for Africa'? What were their reasons for taking part?

4. Write short paragraphs on each of the following:
   a) Omdurman
   b) the Suez Canal
   c) the importance of the River Nile
   d) the Anglo-French Convention, 1899
   e) the Treaty of Berlin, 1885

4

Subjects of the Queen
British Empire in the Nineteenth Century

The British people had not always been enthusiastic about their Empire. The American Revolt (1775) had come as a great shock to the home country. In the years which followed many politicians looked upon colonies as expensive and often rebellious nuisances. Only a minority were imperialists like Disraeli. Consequently Britain gained her second empire slowly. Although landings were made in Australia in 1788 the whole continent was not declared British until 1829. New Zealand was claimed eleven years later. In both cases it was fear of French occupation which drove the government to act.

Canada, Australia and New Zealand

With Canada Britain showed a similar reluctance. In 1791 the territory had been divided into two provinces, Ontario (English) and Quebec (French). The two were very different. French Canada had few towns, its trappers and farmers lived in cabins strung out along the banks of the St Lawrence in what was described as 'one continuous white cottaged street'. Their life was lonely, cut off from both France and their English neighbours. By contrast, Ontario consisted of busy thriving towns, inhabited in many cases by Empire loyalists whose fathers and grandfathers had crossed the border rather than live in an independent USA. Neither really liked the other. The English-speaking Canadians complained that their trade was being hampered by French control of the St Lawrence. The French feared that their way of life would be swamped by their more numerous neighbours.

In 1837 there were riots in both provinces so Britain sent Lord Durham to report on the situation. He stayed only seven months and annoyed most Canadians he met. Yet, back home he wrote a report, the **Durham Report, 1839**, which became a blueprint for the Commonwealth type of empire we know today, with each part a separate, self-governing unit loyal to the Queen. Durham made two suggestions. First, he thought Ontario and Quebec should be united so that the French would be outnumbered. Second, he suggested that Canadians should be allowed to govern themselves in all home affairs in order to prevent another war of independence. This he called '**Dominion status**'. His superiors accepted the first suggestion immediately. The second was made law in 1867. By the **British North America Act** four provinces, Ontario, Quebec, New Brunswick and Nova Scotia, were formed into one country with Dominion status.

Dominion status did not mean independence until the twentieth century (see Chapter 15). But it helped Canadian development in four

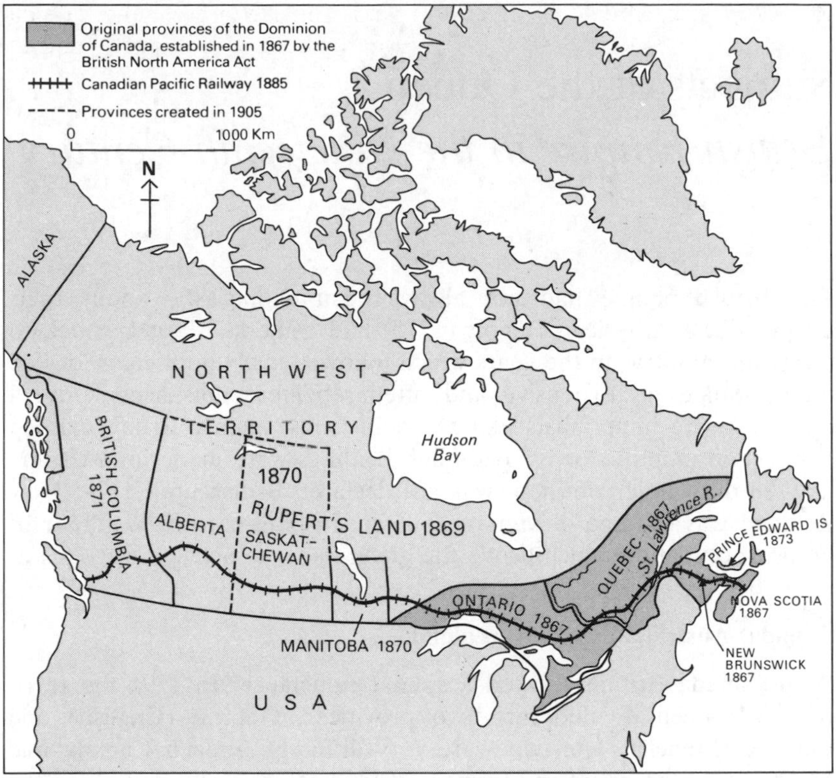

Original provinces of the Dominion of Canada, established in 1867 by the British North America Act

++++ Canadian Pacific Railway 1885

----- Provinces created in 1905

0   1000 Km

N

ALASKA

NORTH   WEST   TERRITORY

1870

Hudson Bay

BRITISH COLUMBIA 1871

ALBERTA

RUPERT'S LAND 1869

SASKAT-CHEWAN

QUEBEC 1867

St. Lawrence R.

PRINCE EDWARD IS 1873

ONTARIO 1867

NOVA SCOTIA 1867

MANITOBA 1870

NEW BRUNSWICK 1867

U S A

ways. Trade could move about the country without duties. Defence could be planned on a national scale. The government could often bargain with foreign countries in trading matters on an equal basis. Soon railways helped to bind the continent together even more securely. In 1869–70 Rupert's Land and Manitoba joined the Dominion, followed soon afterwards by British Columbia, Prince Edward Island and North West Territory. The final link came in 1885 when railways spanned the continent and reached the Pacific coast (see map above). Across lonely prairies and mountains unknown even to Indians, the engineers built a line which united Canada more surely than Acts of Parliament. Settlers followed the engineers and soon the empty prairies of Saskatchewan and Alberta were transformed into vast farms supplying Europe with wheat.

Durham's 'home rule' idea was applied to Australia also. Like Canada the isolated Australian states were unconnected for many years. At first progress was slow. The crossing of the Blue Mountains (1817) had opened up land for sheep farming. The discovery of gold in 1851 had caused prospectors to swell the small population. Even so, it was 1862 before Charles Sturt made the first north to south crossing of the interior, and 1882 before the first refrigerated ship, *Strathleven*, managed to bring fresh meat from Australia to Europe. In a way this voyage was more important than all the discoveries. Before it happened Australian and New Zealand sheep and cattle had been bred for hides and fat only. Enormous quantities of meat were wasted because there was too much to eat. Refrigerated ships, on the other hand, meant that carcases could be sent to Europe. Two new farming industries were born.

By 1900 Australia was a relatively small British colony spread sparsely over a vast continent. Around were overcrowded territories whose people thought enviously of Australian open spaces. Germans controlled nearby Papua. The French were in Tahiti. Japan was beginning to build an overseas empire. Obviously only a single government would be able to organise the defence of such a territory. The time was ripe for another dominion. **The Commonwealth of Australia Act, 1900** joined the six states in a federal system similar to that of the USA. Each kept its own assembly but it also sent representatives to a parliament which controlled defence and foreign affairs.

Landing frozen meat from Australia, 1890

South Africa

Most of the new British Empire developed peacefully, although Maori Wars did occur in New Zealand. In one area only was there serious trouble. South Africa's story is one of disputes and war.

Britain captured the Dutch Cape Colony during the Napoleonic wars and bought it afterwards for £14 million. Before the Suez Canal was cut such a base at the tip of Africa (see map on page 22) seemed valuable for the Royal Navy. Britain also took over a number of Dutch farmers (Boers), tough, religious folk who disliked all government and used African natives as slaves. Living a lonely life, such men learned to be self-reliant, to read their Bibles and to shoot very accurately. They owned large farms: 2,500 hectares was quite common. They also reared families of ten, twelve or more children. As each son usually wanted a similar-sized farm to that of his father, the Boers gobbled up more land and moved steadily inland. This habit irritated the British, who saw their responsibilities growing heavier each year. The Boers, for their part, hated paying taxes and thought the British attitude to Africans soft. When natives were given voting rights in 1828 they were disgusted. When talk of freeing the slaves reached their ears they were horrified. However, it was the desire for more land and more freedom which caused some of them to clamber into their ox-waggons and start the **Great Trek** inland in 1836.

The clue to much later trouble is contained in a statement made by these first **Voortrekkers**, as they were called. They wrote, 'We quit this colony under the full assurance that the English Government has nothing more to require of us, and will allow us to govern ourselves without interference in future'. In other words the Boers felt they were going off to found a new land. The British government, however, disliked such people marching off into the interior. They foresaw that wars with natives would result and British troops would have to come to the rescue. As expected, the advancing Boers soon clashed with the Bantu people who lived inland. Fighting, massacres and ambushes followed until the Boers won a victory at Blood River in 1838.

The next few years saw history repeat itself. Boer pioneers would occupy a new region and set up an independent state. There would be

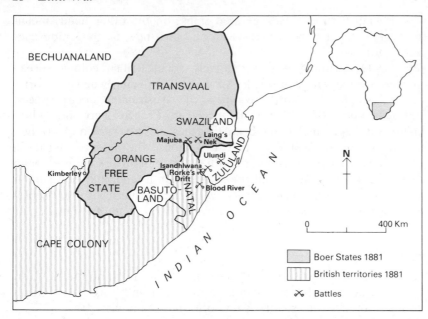

South Africa in 1881

fighting with the natives and the British would move in to restore
order. The British took over Natal in this way in 1843. At first the
Boer republics of the Transvaal and Orange Free State were given a
limited amount of freedom by the terms of the **Sand River Convention,
1852**. Then, when diamonds were found in the Orange Free State in
1867, British troops moved in to administer the disorderly boom town
of Kimberley. Finally, in 1877, the bankrupt and weak Transvaal
appeared such an easy conquest for the Zulus on its border that the
British felt compelled to occupy it. They found the prisons empty because there was no food for the convicts and a state treasury which
contained 12s 6d (62½p). Within two years their worst fears concerning a spread of Boers inland were justified. Forty thousand Zulu spear-
men led by their King, Keshwayo, slaughtered a British force at
Isandhlwana. Only the heroic defence of a medical station at **Rorke's
Drift** halted their advance. It was six months before the enemy was
defeated at **Ulundi** (see map above).

*Diamond mines at Kimberley,
1895*

   The end of the Zulu menace had an unexpected result. Just as the
removal of French armies from America had left the Americans free to
rebel against Britain, so the destruction of Zulu power encouraged the
Transvaal Boers to do the same. For some time they had known that
Liberal politicians in Britain were in favour of their independence, particularly the Liberal leader, William Gladstone. When he won the 1880
election and became Prime Minister the Boers felt optimistic. Unfortunately, some of Gladstone's Liberals did not agree with him. Whilst
the English politicians argued the Boers lost patience. Shouldering
their rifles and mounting their horses they declared war.

   To such expert shots the red-coated British infantry offered wonderful targets. At Laing's Nek a British force led by Sir George Colley
was driven off easily. It retreated to a high mountain called **Majuba**,
the Zulu word for wild pigeons. Here, nearly 2,000 metres up, the men

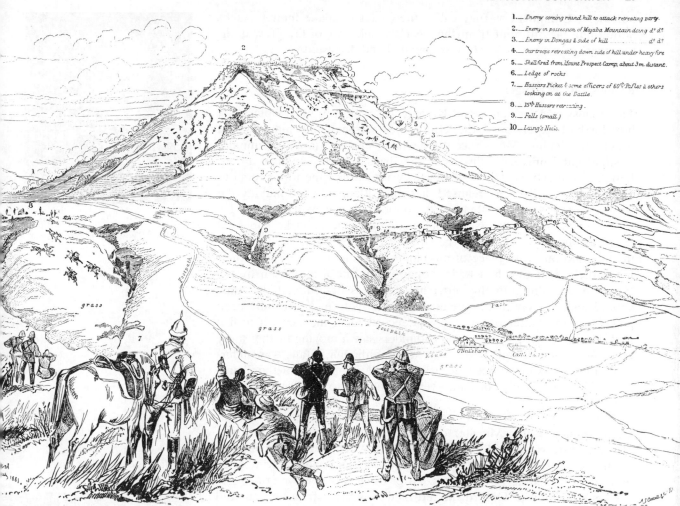

1.— Enemy coming round hill to attack retreating party.
2.— Enemy in possession of Majuba Mountain doing d° d°
3.— Enemy in Dongas & side of hill .... d° d°
4.— Our troops retreating down side of hill under heavy fire
5.— Shell fired from Mount Prospect Camp, about 3 m. distant.
6.— Ledge of rocks
7.— Hussars Picket & some officers of 60ᵗʰ Rifles & others looking on at the Battle.
8.— 15ᵗʰ Hussars retreating.
9.— Falls (small.)
10.— Laing's Nek.

A drawing of the Battle of Majuba Hill, 1881

felt safe. The Boers climbed Majuba by paths hidden from the defenders. Then they rose up and opened fire at close range. A British survivor wrote, 'the attack advanced so rapidly we could only see their rifles through the smoke as they crept up'. All Colley's force of 354 men were either killed, wounded or captured. Most of the dead were shot above the chest. Some had as many as six bullets through their heads.

Even before Majuba Gladstone had intended to make the Transvaal independent. Now he did so by the terms of the **Pretoria Convention, 1881**, the agreement which ended what is now known as the **First Boer War**. After this agreement South Africa contained four provinces of mainly Boer settlers: Cape Colony and Natal ruled by Britain; and two semi-independent states, the Orange Free State and Transvaal (see map on page 28). Whether permanent peace would now have come is doubtful. But in 1885 rich seams of gold were discovered in the Transvaal. Settlers poured in, creating a thriving town, Johannesburg, around the diggings. Boer farmers watched contemptuously as these outsiders, **Uitlanders** as they called them, dug to make their fortune. Something far different from the Boer's simple way of life grew up in the heart of his country. He was appalled and disgusted.

Rhodes versus Kruger

The Transvaal President, **Paul Kruger**, was typical of his people. As a boy he had experienced the Great Trek. As a young man he had fought the Zulus. More recently he had been at Majuba. Cunning, obstinate and brave, he distrusted the British and dreamed of an all-Dutch South Africa. His first thought was to throw the foreigners out of his country. Then he realised that the Uitlanders were making the Transvaal the richest, instead of the poorest, South African state. He therefore planned a two-sided policy. On the one hand he squeezed every available penny out of the Uitlanders. They were taxed on their income and on every piece of machinery or equipment they imported. Even their dynamite had to be bought from one firm chosen by the Boer government. On the other hand he was determined that they should have no say in the government. The vote had originally been given to a man after one year's residence. Kruger increased it to five and then to fourteen years. The Uitlanders saw it moving further away the longer they stayed. Kruger's attitude, although unfair, was understandable. Uitlanders made up half the male population of the Transvaal. 'I am not ready to hand over my country to strangers', Kruger remarked.

Cecil Rhodes – he dreamed of a British African Empire

The atmosphere was now explosive, made worse by the activities of **Cecil Rhodes**, Prime Minister of Cape Colony. Rhodes, the son of a Hertfordshire vicar, had been sent to South Africa as a young man for health reasons. During this 'convalescence' he had gone to Kimberley and made a fortune in diamonds. After using this new wealth to pay for his education at Oxford, he returned to South Africa and entered politics. His money and his powerful personality made a tremendous impact. Politically Rhodes's aim was exactly opposite to that of Kruger. 'Oom Paul' (Uncle Paul), as his people called him, wanted a truly Dutch South Africa, with the British no longer in control. Rhodes resented the fact that the two Boer republics were semi-independent, and aimed to overthrow them. By 1895 he had managed to conquer the Matabele and Mashona tribes and take over Bechuanaland (now Botswana). This vast area encircled the Transvaal's northern borders with British-controlled territory (see map on page 32).

Inside a Johannesburg gold mine around 1900

A clash between the two men gradually became inevitable. To Rhodes the Uitlander problem seemed the lever to open a way into the Transvaal. In Johannesburg discontented mine-owners were often threatening to rebel. If they did so British troops could move in, claiming they had come to restore order. With this in mind, Rhodes stationed units of his own British South Africa Company police on the border, commanded by his friend, Dr Starr Jameson. Week after week during 1895 Jameson and his men impatiently patrolled up and down. Week after week rumours of Uitlander revolts gave them hope. Week after week plots were hatched, complaints were heard, but nothing

Paul Kruger – he saw the Boers' life-style threatened by the Uitlanders

happened. Unlike Jameson, however, the Uitlanders were surrounded by Boer riflemen. They remembered Majuba and did nothing.

Tired of waiting Jameson lost his head. He crossed the border with 470 men, hoping his arrival would stir the Uitlanders into activity. The result of the **Jameson Raid** was complete disaster. The horsemen needed to dash 290 kilometres to Johannesburg. Secrecy was essential if they were to succeed. Unfortunately, although they cut most of the telegraph wires, they left the one to Pretoria, the Transvaal capital, intact. As a result the enemy were the first to learn of their movements. Boer commandos assembled swiftly and ambushed the invader. At Doornkop, Jameson's force surrendered after losing sixteen men. The plan to 'open' the Transvaal had failed.

Drift to war

No event in South African history had such tragic results. Both Rhodes and the British government were against the Raid. Joseph Chamberlain, the British Colonial Secretary, had actually sent a telegram to Jameson ordering him to stop. Afterwards Rhodes and Chamberlain always claimed that they knew of a possible rebellion but nothing else. To the outside world this seemed unlikely. Foreigners condemned a 'British invasion' of a small country. In South Africa itself, Boers who had previously thought Kruger too extreme, now joined him, and he won the 1898 election with a majority which made him almost a dictator. The Orange Free State had taken little part in the quarrel up to this time. Now Marthinus Steyn, a Kruger supporter, was elected President and he at once signed an alliance with the Transvaal. Rhodes's own political career was never the same. He lost the support of the Dutch voters in Cape Colony and resigned. Kruger began to buy German weapons and to fortify Johannesburg.

At first many British people disapproved of the Jameson action. This attitude changed, however, when the German Emperor, William II, sent a telegram congratulating Kruger on defeating the raiders. This **Kruger telegram** infuriated many Britons and made them rally patriotically to Jameson's defence. When the doctor was handed over to the British and brought to England he was given a short prison sentence which he never served.

Meanwhile, the Uitlander trouble grew worse. At first it had been mine-owners who grumbled most. After the killing of a British workman by a Boer policeman the miners took up the cry for better treatment. Crowds chanting 'franchise' (the right to vote) to the tune 'Rule Britannia' became a common sight in Johannesburg. Matters were not improved when Britain sent Lord Milner to South Africa to negotiate. Milner, a well-educated man, was disgusted by Kruger's obstinacy and ignorance. At successive conferences the old Boer refused to consider better treatment for the Uitlanders. Rhodes and Jameson had both lost patience with him in the past. Now Milner did the same.

Kruger did not care. He remembered Majuba and thought that the British Liberal Party would be against a war as they had been then. He knew his young soldiers were eager to fight. He imagined Germany

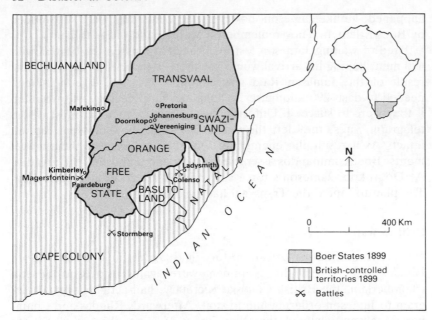

South Africa during the Second Boer War, 1899–1902

could help. In 1899 he demanded complete independence. Milner refused and reinforcements of British troops were shipped from India. Kruger saw his opportunity. He demanded their immediate withdrawal. When Britain refused Transvaal and Orange Free State troops invaded British South Africa.

Second Boer War, 1899–1902

The spring rains had already fallen. Green grass covered the *veldt* (plains), providing the food without which the Boers' horses would have starved. Later a British officer wrote,

> Oh why, oh why did we fight the Boers at this time of year when the grass is plentiful all over the country? What a different story it would have been had we taken him on in May when there is no grass and he can't feed his ponies and cattle.

In fact the Boers attacked on 11 October 1899 in the middle of the southern spring. The few British troops were swept back by fast moving commandos. They retreated to three towns, Ladysmith, Kimberley and Mafeking, where they were besieged. When the British commander, Sir Redvers Buller, arrived from England he attempted to relieve them. The result was three defeats at **Stormberg**, **Magersfontein** and **Colenso** (see map above). At Colenso a long line of British troops advanced slowly through the tall grass at an enemy they could not see. One thousand were shot down and ten guns captured.

Many Liberals felt the war had been forced upon the Boers and fierce arguments raged in Britain. But this time there was no Gladstone to sign a quick peace. The Queen set the mood when she said: 'We are not interested in the possibilities of defeat; they do not exist.'

Buller was replaced by Lord Roberts; recruits poured in; troopships sailed crowded with men. Roberts, whose son had been killed at Colenso, arrived in a sad, determined mood. Already the situation was not so favourable to the Boers as it had been. Instead of driving deep into Cape Colony, and perhaps conquering it before reinforcements arrived, they had wasted time besieging unimportant towns. A golden opportunity to drive the British into the sea had been lost.

Open warfare lasted five months. Roberts sent a cavalry force to relieve Kimberley whilst he moved east with the infantry to surround the enemy. Knowing he was fighting swift troops he, too, moved fast; when his wagons were captured in a surprise raid he cut down his men's rations and kept them marching. By 27 February 1900 the Boers' main army was encircled and forced to surrender at **Paardeburg**. The rest was easy. **Mafeking** was relieved after 217 days of siege and its defender, **Robert Baden-Powell**, became world famous. On 31 May Roberts reached Johannesburg. Five days later he was in Pretoria. After Kruger's last defeat at Bergendal on 27 August he left the country he had led to disaster.

The war seemed to be over. Roberts returned triumphantly to Britain. The Boers felt differently. They fought on for seventeen months, raiding, ambushing, destroying equipment and railway lines. Today we should say they organised an 'underground' movement. Lord Kitchener, who took over from Roberts, was forced to conquer every inch of the country, erecting blockhouses and fences as he did so, destroying farms that sheltered raiders, killing cattle which might be used as food. It was slow and terrible. Boer families were rounded up like herds of cattle and placed in large, hastily built concentration camps. These were overcrowded and lacked proper sanitation. Twenty thousand men, women and children died of disease in them. Britain had rarely been so unpopular on the Continent. At last, on 31 May 1902, at **Vereeniging**, the Boer dream of a Dutch South Africa ended with a peace treaty which put the Transvaal and Orange Free State firmly under British control. It made English the first language to be taught in all schools and allowed the farmers £3 million to rebuild their homes and buy new stock.

The Boer War marked the high tide of Britain's imperialist fever. Never again were her people so enthusiastic about their Empire. A few farmers had held them at bay for three years, causing the deaths of 22,000 men and costing the British taxpayers £220 million. The only pleasing sign from the British point of view was the way the other dominions had sent troops to help. Otherwise the war had split the nation, caused her people to be hated abroad and given birth to a bitterness in South Africa which has continued to the present day.

Timeline

1815	Britain takes possession of Dutch Cape Colony.
1836	Boer farmers begin Great Trek.
1838	Boer victory at Blood River.
1839	Lord Durham reports on Canada (Durham Report).

1852   Sand River Convention. Limited freedom for Orange Free
        State and Transvaal.
1867   British North America Act makes Canada a Dominion.
1877   Transvaal annexed by Britain.
1879   Zulu War.
1881   British force defeated at Majuba in First Boer War. Trans-
        vaal given freedom by Pretoria Convention.
1895–6 Jameson Raid.
1898   Kruger telegram.
1899   Second Boer War begins.
1900   Commonwealth of Australia Act.
1902   Treaty of Vereeniging.

Questions

1. a) Who were the Boers? Why did they clash with the British in
      1880?
   b) Which South African states became independent of British rule,
      after the Pretoria Convention of 1881?
   c) Who were the Uitlanders? Why was Kruger considered to have
      treated them badly?
   d) How did Rhodes and Kruger disagree about the future of
      Africa?

2. Outline the main causes and events of the Boer War of 1899–1902.

3. What problems and opportunities faced the Dominions of Canada
   and Australia by 1900?

4. Write short paragraphs on each of the following:
   a) the Treaty of Vereeniging
   b) the Kruger Telegram
   c) the Jameson Raid
   d) the Durham Report and 'Dominion status'

5

Two New Giants
USA and Japan

Americans who read the *New York Journal* in the 1890s were used to sensational events because the paper's owner, <u>William Randolph Hearst</u>, believed in exaggerated stories. Seldom did he disappoint them with a dull or boring tale. Even so, they must have been surprised at a news item dated 16 February 1898. Apparently the US

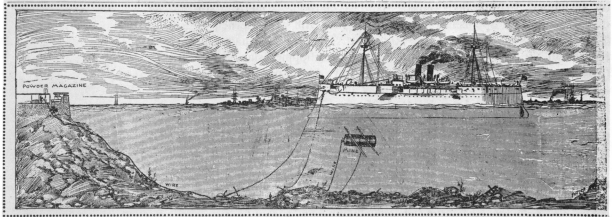

THI$50,000 REWARD.—WHO DESTROYED THE MAINE?—$50,000 REWARD.

NEW YORK JOURNAL
AND ADVERTISER.

The Journal will give $50,000 for information, furnished to it exclusively, that will convict the person or persons who sank the Maine.

The Journal will give $50,000 for information, furnished to it exclusively, that will convict the person or persons who sank the Maine.

NO. 5,572.   Copyright, 1898, by W. R. Hearst.—NEW YORK, THURSDAY, FEBRUARY 17, 1898.—16 PAGES.   PRICE ONE CENT In Greater New York | Elsewhere and Jersey City. | TWO CENT

DESTRUCTION OF THE WAR SHIP MAINE WAS THE WORK OF AN ENEMY

$50,000!

$50,000 REWARD!
For the Detection of the Perpetrator of the Maine Outrage!

The New York Journal hereby offers a reward of **$50,000 CASH** for information, **FURNISHED TO IT EXCLUSIVELY**, which shall lead to the detection and conviction of the person, persons or government criminally responsible for the explosions which resulted in the destruction, at Havana, of the United States war ship Maine and the loss of 253 lives of American sailors.

The **$50,000 CASH** offered for the above information is on deposit with Wells, Fargo & Co. and will be paid upon the production of the convicting evidence.

No one is barred, be he the humble but misguided seaman eking out a few miserable dollars by acting as a spy, or the attache of a government secret service, plotting, by any devilish means, to revenge fancied insults or cripple menacing countries.

This offer has been cabled to Europe and will be made public in every capital of the Continent and in London this morning.

The Journal believes that any man who can be bought to commit murder can also be bought to betray his comrades. **FOR THE PERPETRATOR OF THIS OUTRAGE HAD ACCOMPLICES.** life.

     W. R. HEARST.

Assistant Secretary Roosevelt Convinced the Explosion of the War Ship Was Not an Accident.

The Journal Offers $50,000 Reward for the Conviction of the Criminals Who Sent 258 American Sailors to Their Death. Naval Officers Unanimous That the Ship Was Destroyed on Purpose.

$50,000!

$50,000 REWARD
For the Detection of the Perpetrator of the Maine Outrage!

The New York Journal hereby offers a reward of **$50,000 CASH** for information, **FURNISHED TO IT EXCLU-**SIVELY, which shall lead to the detection and conviction of the person, persons or government criminally responsible for the explosion which resulted in the destruction, at Havana, of the United States war ship Maine and the loss of 253 lives of American sailors.

The **$50,000 CASH** offered for the above information is on deposit with Wells, Fargo & Co. and will be paid upon the production of the convicting evidence.

No one is barred, be he the humble, but misguided, seaman, eking out a few miserable dollars by acting as a spy, or the attache of a government secret service, plotting, by any devilish means, to revenge fancied insults or cripple menacing countries.

This offer has been cabled to Europe and will be made public in every capital of the Continent and in London this morning.

The Journal believes that any man who can be bought to commit murder can also be bought to betray his comrades. **FOR THE PERPETRATOR OF THIS OUTRAGE HAD ACCOMPLICES.** life.

     W. R. HEARST.

POWDER MAGAZINE   MAINE   WIRE

NAVAL OFFICERS THINK THE MAINE WAS DESTROYED BY A SPANISH MINE.

George Eugene Bryson, the Journal's special correspondent at Havana, cables that it is the secret opinion of many Spaniards in the Cuban capital, that the Maine was destroyed and 258 of her men killed by means of a submarine mine, or fixed torpedo. This is the opinion of several American naval authorities. The Spaniards, it is believed, arranged to have the Maine anchored over one of the harbor mines. Wires connected the mine with a powder magazine, and it is thought the explosion was caused by sending an electric current through the wire. If this can be proven, the brutal nature of the Spaniards will be shown by the fact that they waited to spring the mine until after all the men had retired for the night. The Maltese cross in the picture shows where the mine may have been fired.

battleship, *Maine*, had been blown up off Cuba by Spaniards using a 'secret infernal machine'. Two hundred and fifty-eight American sailors had died. The *Journal* offered $50,000 to anyone who could give information leading to the capture of those responsible. This story caused a wave of fierce indignation to sweep across the USA. Americans, particularly those who supported the Republican Party, demanded war with Spain. President McKinley hesitated until the uproar grew too great. A leading Republican, Theodore Roosevelt, told him scornfully that he had no more backbone than a chocolate éclair! Reluctantly McKinley gave way. So began the Spanish-American War.

Theodore Roosevelt

The Spanish-American War

As usual with Hearst's 'news', the tale he told his readers was not strictly true. Since 1895 Cuban rebels had been fighting to free themselves of Spanish rule. The American people took a keen interest in the struggle. Most of the businessmen would have preferred the Spaniards to remain in control. However, the ordinary American favoured the Cubans. Here was a small country fighting for independence even as they themselves had fought against Britain in 1775. Hearst encouraged this attitude. By 1898 there seemed to be a stalemate, with rebels holding the countryside and Spaniards the towns. Day by day Hearst told his readers of the terrible deeds of the Spanish commander, although he was silent about the equally cruel Cuban general. When the *Maine* was destroyed his newspaper claimed that the Spanish had done it. There was no evidence to prove this. In fact, the last thing Spain wanted was a war with the USA. Experts failed to discover why the *Maine* blew up and it has remained a mystery. Yet the *New York Journal*'s announcement that the Spaniards were responsible did more than anything else to cause the Spanish-American War.

The Americans rushed into battle with much enthusiasm but little organisation. Their army sailed to the tropics in thick woollen uniforms, with out of date equipment. Fortunately for them, the Spaniards were as badly organised. The entire American force landed without resistance, although the enemy had known of a possible invasion for six weeks. Fighting was soon over. American ships sank the old-fashioned Spanish fleet outside Santiago harbour. American soldiers stormed the Spanish defences at **San Juan Hill** with the help of 'Rough Riders' led by Theodore Roosevelt. Their success made him famous in the USA. In the Pacific, Spain's Philippine Islands were invaded and her navy destroyed in **Manila Bay**. At the peace the USA took the Philippines, Guam and Hawaii in the Pacific (see map on page 37). By the **Platt Amendment, 1905** she gained the right to interfere in Cuban affairs, and to have coaling depots and a naval base on Cuban soil. Afterwards the whole affair was described as 'a splendid little war'. It seemed most satisfactory from the American point of view.

The truth was a little different. The Cuban rebels were far from happy. They had wanted to beat the Spanish themselves. Now the Americans took all the credit. Cuba's general was not even invited to

The Far East – area of conflict between Japan and the USA

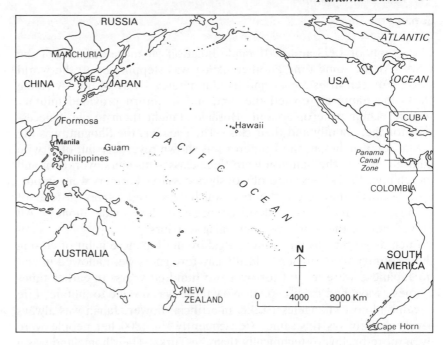

Cuba: the chief battle areas during the Spanish-American War, 1898

the final surrender ceremony. Furthermore, although fighting losses were small, thirteen American soldiers died of yellow fever for every one killed in battle. Even worse casualties occurred in the Philippines. Here, rebels who had been fighting against the Spanish now turned upon the Americans. A grim two-year campaign followed in which the US army suffered heavily. At home Americans were worried by their losses. They wondered why their country had suddenly become an imperialist power.

Certainly events moved at bewildering speed. As a result of this unexpected war the USA gained 3,141 islands in the Pacific. She had to rule a native population of 7 million. Six months earlier most Americans did not know whether the Philippines were islands or canned fruit! Now they had an empire. And once on the path of imperialism the USA found it difficult to stop. One thing tended to lead to another. With an Atlantic and a Pacific coastline, the USA needed a two-ocean navy. Since a dangerous voyage round Cape Horn was necessary to reinforce one or the other, Americans became interested in a possible **Panama Canal** across the Isthmus, the narrow strip of land connecting North and South America (see map opposite). When the Panamanians rebelled against their country, Colombia, in 1901, the USA assisted them. Once free, the new government rewarded the USA by allowing her a strip of land from coast to coast. Before long US engineers had driven a canal across this, whilst US troops fortified the zone. Not everyone was happy about these developments. South Americans felt they were being bullied by their giant neighbour. US citizens who wanted their country to remain isolated from world affairs were worried. A few realised that the USA was about to become a power with world responsibilities.

Japan

The events of 1898 and 1901 made isolation far more difficult for the USA. At the same time another nation was stepping on to the world stage. For centuries Japan had lived a medieval way of life. A ruling class, the Samurai, owned the land and in return provided military service. Their code of honour, Bushido, taught them to die if necessary for their family and their class. Their leader, the Shogun, was the actual ruler of Japan; the Emperor was shown reverence but otherwise ignored. Below the Samurai were three classes: farmers, workmen and merchants. Workmen were obviously necessary. Farmers were important because they grew the rice which was used as tax instead of money. Merchants were despised because they made money. All bowed before the grim sword-swinging warriors.

Commodore Perry. He opened up Japan at gun point

Such a system was made more rigid by the Japanese habit of closing their country to foreigners. Hardly any foreigners were allowed in and no Japanese were let out for over two hundred years. In earlier times Chinese ways had been copied. Now there was no one to imitate. Life became almost changeless. Like an artificial flower, Japan was always lovely yet always the same. Consequently, in 1800 her people were even more backward technically than the Turks. Their homeland was a solitary, beautiful prison off the coast of Asia.

The sleeping beauty was revived by a kiss from a loving prince. Japan had no such pleasant awakening. One after the other the Russians (1804), the British (1842) and the Americans (1853), arrived and demanded trade. When the Japanese refused they were threatened with war. To the Americans Japan's refusal to trade or establish diplomatic relations seemed obstinate and stupid. Between 1853 and 1854 **Commodore Perry** appeared with larger and larger US fleets. Finally he ordered the decks of his warships to be cleared for action. A medieval people found themselves gazing down the muzzles of modern guns. They were forced to give way. Their country was 'opened up' at gun point.

US ships and men arrive in Japan, 1854

Samurai warrior in traditional dress

Nearby China showed thoughtful Japanese what might happen as a result of this. Between 1840 and 1860 many Chinese ports were occupied by European soldiers and merchants. Her laws were ignored, her people humiliated, her Emperor's palace burned. Japan was a smaller and more organised country than China. Her warlike Samurai did not waste time complaining about such treatment, even though they resented it bitterly. Instead they realised that Western superiority was a matter of better ships, better guns and better trained armies. Many started to experiment with European military tactics; one warrior even built a foundry and began to cast cannon. Japan's first steamer was launched in 1855. Her navy was founded the following year. In 1868 the Shogun was overthrown. New rulers, the Meiji government, set about the task of bringing Japan into the nineteenth century.

Changes followed at amazing speed. In 1873 the Western (Gregorian) calendar took the place of the Chinese lunar calendar; seven years later Western education was introduced. In 1890 a style of government modelled on the Prussian, which emphasised the power of the monarch, was adopted, and a tax system based on money replaced rice payments. Everywhere the Japanese looked for the best and copied what they saw. Britons designed their navy; Germans reorganised their army. Telegraph wires, railways and factories crossed and scarred the lovely Japanese landscape. Samurai like Iwasaki Yataro founded the Mitsubishi shipyards. Others built silk, cement and mining works. The government started businesses and then handed them over to private enterprise. Japan exported as much as she could, particularly textiles, to pay for all this development.

The Japanese did not copy the foreigner because they admired him. They did so in order to beat those who had treated them so rudely. No European was ever asked to stay longer than necessary. As soon as a foreign expert had taught them enough, he was sent away. Consequently Japan never became a colony; she kept control of all her new power. In addition priority was given to warlike development. By 1894 Japan possessed twenty-eight modern warships, one fully equipped dockyard and machinery to make quick-firing guns and torpedoes. One-third of the national budget was spent on the army and navy. In schools children sang songs like 'Come, foes, come'. As adults all men had to do military service. Patriotism was encouraged by teaching absolute obedience to the Emperor. An old religion, Shinto, was revived because it taught that the Emperor was descended from a god. In this way Samurai fighting traditions were taught to a whole nation.

China was first to suffer from these preparations. In 1894 the two countries quarrelled over control of Korea (see map on page 40). In the short war which followed Japan's modern army easily defeated the Chinese. Not only Korea but Manchuria and part of China were overrun by the Japanese troops. When Peking, the Chinese capital, seemed threatened China surrendered. By the **Shimonoseki Treaty, 1895**, Japan received Formosa (now Taiwan) and Port Arthur on the Liautung peninsula. Korea was declared independent of Chinese influence. To Japan's surprise France, Russia and Germany refused to accept these terms. Russia in particular resented the arrival of

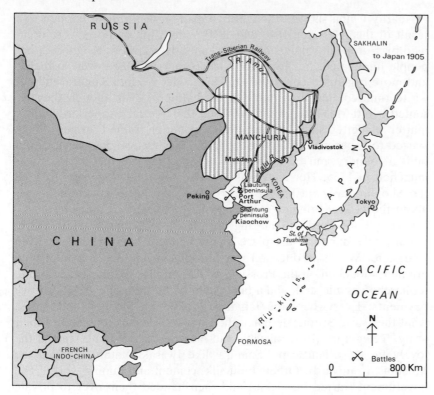

Japanese expansion, 1895–1905

Japanése in areas like Manchuria. The three countries forced the Japanese to give Port Arthur to Russia. This **Triple Intervention** infuriated the Japanese. They realised they were being robbed by people who were eager to seize Chinese territory themselves. Their answer was to build many more warships and wait for a chance to settle scores with Russia.

Russo-Japanese War

The opportunity and excuse came quite soon because Russia's Far Eastern expansion continued. In 1900, for example, she occupied the whole of Manchuria. Britain became alarmed and, partly because of this, signed an alliance with Japan (1902). This was a great triumph for the Japanese who were thus recognised for the first time as partners with a great Western nation. Japan now felt strong enough to demand a settlement which would recognise Russian rights in Manchuria and Japanese rights in Korea. The Russians refused to discuss the matter with people they called 'little apes' and their troops invaded Korea. Japan's reaction was devastating. On 9 February 1904 Japanese destroyers steamed into **Port Arthur** after dark. The Russians were unprepared. Their ships were lit up as it was peacetime. Guns on shore were wrapped in tarpaulins. The Japanese had no difficulty in torpedoing two battleships and one cruiser. After only forty years of modernisation the Japanese were at war with one of the great powers.

Actually all the advantages lay with the Japanese 'David' not the Russian 'Goliath'. Provided she gained control of the seas, Japan's troops could sail quickly to the war area. Russia, on the other hand, depended on a single 8,000-kilometre railway running across a wilderness. This advantage was soon pressed home. Japanese ships beat the Russians outside Port Arthur, whilst Japanese soldiers crossed the Yalu River and invaded Manchuria (see map opposite). With command of the seas established it was possible to land other armies in Liautung. Soon Port Arthur itself was besieged. The Russian position could hardly have been worse. Her troops had spent six weeks travelling across Asia in open cattle trucks. To them the war meant nothing except separation from their homes. Even some of the officers were discontented: one wrote home, 'The aims of this war, its causes and even its conduct are deeply repulsive to me.' The Japanese fought with much more enthusiasm. They were determined to beat the Westerners.

By autumn Port Arthur had fallen, forcing the Russians to retreat on **Mukden**. Winter came, a severe one which caused sentries to freeze to death at their posts. Fierce winds scoured the ploughed fields, making the dust rise in great clouds which obscured the sun, filled men's eyes, noses and throats, and jammed their rifles. All equipment had to be carried by horse or man because no wheeled vehicles could move across such desolate country. In such fearful conditions nearly a million men fought a long battle. By day the guns roared almost continuously. By night compact masses of silent Japanese would rush upon the enemy, eager to fight hand to hand. After three months victory went to the Japanese.

Russia's final disaster came at sea. When war broke out her much larger navy was dispersed round the world. One fleet had already been defeated by the Japanese. Another in the Black Sea was not allowed out under the terms of the agreement reached at the Congress of Berlin (see page 15). A third, Baltic force, was over 17,000 kilometres from the scene of action. In desperation the Russians decided to send their Baltic fleet round the world. German firms offered to supply coal at various points on the route.

The long voyage nearly ended at the beginning. As the Russians passed down the Channel they steamed through some English fishing boats, mistook them for warships and opened fire. The actual damage was slight, one fishing boat sank and a Russian cruiser was hit by a Russian shell. Nevertheless, there was uproar in England, where Japan was popular. For some time the Russian ships were shadowed by the vastly superior British fleet. Fortunately, no shots were fired. Later, coaling became a nightmare. In tropical climates sailors worked with cotton-waste pads in their mouths to help breathing, slaving for twenty-four hours at a time in high temperatures. The ships were loaded until their main armour belts were submerged. Coal was even piled loose on the decks. At Madagascar came the longest delay when the Russian government decided to send a second fleet to join them. By the time the whole armada arrived in Far Eastern waters it was 1905 and Port Arthur had fallen. Only a sea victory could make the trip worthwhile.

On 27 May 1905 the weary Russians met the Japanese fleet in the Straits of **Tsushima**. Their slow-moving vessels stood little chance against modern warships. Admiral Togo, the Japanese commander, was able to steam across the top of the Russian line, his guns blazing. This 'crossing the T' was the most effective form of attack, generally making victory almost certain. Japanese shells tore the Tsar's warships to pieces. After only an hour eight Russian battleships had been sunk. Togo had won the most devastating sea victory since that of Nelson at the Nile in 1798.

With their army and navy defeated, a revolution broke out in Russia in 1905. Men at the Putilov steelworks in St Petersburg went on strike. The sailors of the Black Sea fleet mutinied. When a procession of 150,000 marched peacefully to protest to the Tsar, Nicholas II, on Sunday, 22 January 1905, soldiers shot them down ruthlessly. But **Bloody Sunday** forced the Tsar to offer his people a parliament and convinced him he must make peace with the Japanese. Helped by the US government, a treaty was signed at **Portsmouth (New Hampshire, USA)**. Japan was recognised as overlord of Korea and South Sakhalin was given to her (see map on page 40). Russia's influence in Manchuria and Liautung was ended. But the Russians refused to pay any financial compensation. The Japanese, who had hoped to force the Russians to pay for the war, were furious, but they were too exhausted to go on fighting.

Russian battleships sinking at Tsushima. A picture painted soon after the event

The effect of these victories upon the Japanese people was similar to that of the Franco-Prussian War upon the Germans (see Chapter 1). In forty years Japan had modernised herself to a point where she could defeat a large European power. She became at one stroke an imperial nation with overseas territories and the obvious champion of Asian peoples against the West. Her people began to dream of a great future. They worshipped the armed forces which had been so successful. Japan faced the twentieth century in a dangerous mood. Europe had awakened a giant, not a beauty.

Timeline

1854	Commodore Perry (US Navy) visits Japan.
1868	Meiji government begins modernisation of Japan.
1895	China defeated by Japan. Shimonoseki Treaty. Triple Intervention. Cubans rebel against Spanish rule.
1898	Spanish-American War.
1901	US intervention in Panama.
1904–5	Russo-Japanese War.
1905	Platt Amendment. End of Russo-Japanese War (Treaty of Portsmouth). First Russian Revolution.
1914	Panama Canal completed.

Questions

1. Look at the front page of the *New York Journal* for 17 February 1898 on page 35.
   a) If you assume that the *Maine* was not destroyed by accident, whom do you think is most likely to have blown it up?
   b) What did the newspaper owner hope the effect of this news item might be upon American readers?
   c) Did the newspaper's owner, William Randolph Hearst, achieve his objective?

2. How did the Spanish-American War of 1898 change the rôle of the United States in the world?

3. Write short paragraphs on each of the following:
   a) the Panama Canal
   b) the modernisation of Japan, 1850–1905
   c) the Treaty of Shimonoseki, 1895
   d) the Russo-Japanese War, 1904–5

6

Kaiser William Steams Ahead
Causes of the First World War (I)

From 1871 the dominant nation in Europe was Germany and the dominant statesman Bismarck. His policy was to keep the peace. After Sadowa (see Chapter 1) he had said: 'Let us work quickly. Let us set Germany in the saddle. She will be able to ride all right.' After 1871 he felt this had been done. France and Austria-Hungary had been defeated. Germany was in the saddle. Only a combination of states could beat her. Bismarck owed his success to taking on his opponents one by one. Now he knew France would be looking for allies so that if she fought Germany again she would not be alone. To prevent this Bismarck decided to isolate her.

France's most suitable military ally was Russia because then Germany would be threatened on her eastern and western frontiers (see map opposite). The next best was Austria-Hungary for then Germany would also be threatened from two directions. To stop either alliance Bismarck signed treaties with both Russia and Austria-Hungary. His **Three Emperors' League, 1872** (*Dreikaiserbund*) bound the rulers of Germany, Austria-Hungary and Russia together in friendship. For a time this arrangement worked. Unfortunately, Russia and Austria-Hungary could never agree about the Ottoman Empire. Russia wanted it to split into separate states which she could control; the Habsburgs were determined to prevent the collapse of a multinational empire like their own. After the **Congress of Berlin, 1878** (see Chapter 2), when Austria-Hungary helped to stop Russian expansion in the Balkans, quarrels between the two increased. Bismarck did his best to keep them friends. It was no use. 'I am holding these two powerful, heraldic beasts apart by their collars', he grumbled. The old Prussian had to choose between them. He decided on Austria-Hungary because, as he said, 'If I must choose I will choose Austria; a constitutionally governed, pacific state which lies under Germany's guns; whereas we can't get at Russia.' The Three Emperors' League gradually faded away, leaving only a **Dual Alliance** between Germany and Austria-Hungary.

The solid wall against France had cracked. Nevertheless, Bismarck still tried to paper over the gaps. In 1887 he signed a special **Reinsurance Treaty** with Russia which guaranteed neutrality between the two in any war, providing Germany did not attack France or Russia attack Austria. It made the best of a bad job but it still meant that a two-front war was now possible. The fact that Italy had joined the Dual Alliance, making it the **Triple Alliance, 1882**, because she was angry over the French seizure of Tunis, did not really make up for the loss of Russia. Italy was not a first-class power. Neither was she really likely

Rival European alliances in 1914

to support her traditional enemy, Austria-Hungary. In fact she fought against Germany and Austria-Hungary in the First World War. By 1890, therefore, Bismarck's policy of isolating France had failed.

Kaiser William

If a statesman as clever as Bismarck was unable to prevent alliances against Germany his successors stood no chance at all.[1] William II, the German Emperor (Kaiser) from 1889,[2] was a vain, boastful man who loved pomp and ceremony and longed to be popular.[2] At least one German statesman thought he was insane.[3] Certainly he was an hysterical person, moody and liable to sudden changes of mind.[4] William II was not a clever politician.[5] Bismarck's achievements dazzled him so much that he failed to understand the difficulties which the Chancellor had overcome.[6] The new German Empire was powerful but not as powerful as William imagined.[7] Bismarck had seen the dangers which lurked all around. He had tried to isolate France.[8] He was against German overseas conquests which might annoy Britain.[9] He believed in keeping Austria-Hungary firmly under German control in case she started trouble in the Balkans.[10] He played down German interest in Turkey because this would unite both Russia and Britain against him.[11] And although his success had been founded on military power, he was against rousing hostile alliances which might threaten Germany's dominant rôle in Europe. After all, Bismarck had fought Germany's rivals one by one, not altogether.[12]

William was less cautious. First he quarrelled with Bismarck and dismissed him (1890). Then he chose less able ministers. The Reinsurance Treaty was allowed to lapse; an error of judgement which caused Russia to sign a **Dual Entente** (understanding) with France (1893) and therefore made a two-front war a possibility should hostilities begin.

An American cartoon making fun of Kaiser William II

He encouraged friendship with Turkey and so brought Russia and Britain together for the first time on the Eastern Question. Within four years of coming to power William made nearly all Bismarck's fears into reality. After the old Chancellor's dismissal he had announced, 'The ship's course remains the same. Full steam ahead is the order.' By 1898, when he decided to build a large navy, some Germans had realised it was full steam ahead to war.

William had always loved the sea. As a boy he had liked nothing better than to play with boats. As a man he longed to own a navy and even wished to design battleships himself. Every time he visited his grandmother, Queen Victoria, he was thrilled by the sight of British warships. To him a fleet was a way of increasing his own importance. Once he said, 'All ... my reign ... the Monarchs of Europe have paid no attention to what I have to say. Soon, with my great Navy to endorse my words, they will have to be more respectful.' His naval chief, Admiral Tirpitz, wanted a big navy for more sensible reasons. In 1870–1 German ports had been blockaded by French warships, a fact which could have had serious consequences had the war been a long one. Germany, he believed, needed a navy to protect her ports, merchant fleet and colonies.

As the two men planned a High Seas Fleet, Germany's naval weakness became obvious. She would have liked to help the Boers, but the British fleet made this impossible. Consequently, in 1900 a **German Navy Law** allowed for the building of forty-one battleships and sixty cruisers. Meanwhile a Naval League founded by Tirpitz encouraged a rather land-minded people to take an interest in a navy. Lectures about the fleet were given all over Germany. Men and women who had never seen the sea were taken on tours of German ports. A nation with the best army in the world was about to have one of the best navies.

A threat to Britain? The German High Seas Fleet at sea, 1914

Anglo-German naval rivalry

The effect upon Britain was startling. Since 1805, when Nelson won his victory at Trafalgar, no power had dared to challenge Britain's naval supremacy. Behind a shield of warships Britons had colonised a new empire, and North and South America had been able to develop without European interference. In 1900 the British Empire comprised one-quarter of the world's population and earth's surface. To protect it the British maintained a war fleet which was equal to any other two navies of the great powers. Continentals regarded armies as essential for their safety. Britain was an island. Her giant navy seemed vital if she was to be safe.

Until the German Navy Law, Britain had been friendly towards the new Germany. Despite the Crimean War, when they had been allies, most Britons still looked upon France as the traditional enemy. As late as 1904 some English novels described a French, not a German, invasion of Britain. William himself was fond of Queen Victoria although he did not like her successor, Edward VII (1901–10). Indeed, one of his many ideas was an alliance with Britain. If this happened, he once remarked with typical exaggeration, 'Not a mouse could stir in Europe without our permission'. Even the Kruger telegram and Germany's hostile attitude during the Boer War (see Chapter 4) did not stop some British statesmen from considering an Anglo-German alliance.

Actually Britain had taken little part in European affairs since the Congress of Berlin. What she wanted was a peaceful Europe so that she could continue her overseas expansion without interruption. Bismarck's policy seemed to promise this so Britain had remained free from European politics. In 1896 a Canadian remarked, 'the great Mother Empire stands splendidly isolated in Europe'. His words were reduced to a slogan, **Splendid Isolation**, which aptly described Britain's position. German naval shipbuilding changed all this. In Britain's opinion such a fleet had scarcely anything to defend. It could concentrate in the North Sea in overwhelming force, whereas British ships were spread round the world. Partly to deal with this threat and partly to get Japanese help in any clash with Russia over India, Britain signed the **Anglo-Japanese Alliance, 1902**. By its terms Japan's fleet would protect British Far Eastern possessions in any war. Meanwhile, Britain's naval chief, Admiral Fisher, imitated Tirpitz. More battleships were built. A **Navy League** was formed which published propaganda stressing the German danger. And in 1906 a new age in naval history dawned with the launching of the British super-battleship, the **Dreadnought.**

Symbol of a new age in naval warfare. HMS 'Dreadnought' in 1914

Tsushima (see page 42) had shown that improved gun-control systems and more accurate range-finders increased the distance at which ships could fight to 7 or 8 kilometres. The Dreadnought was faster, more powerful and more heavily armoured than any previous warship. She was 160 metres long, 25 metres wide, with a displacement tonnage of 18,100 tonnes. She had 279-millimetre thick armour, ten 305-millimetre guns set in moving turrets, 5 torpedo tubes and turbine engines which could drive her at a speed of 11 metres per second. On the day she was finished every battleship in the world was out of date!

Such a striking answer to the German challenge led to an expensive contest in which both sides built dreadnoughts. Near panic seemed to affect some people in England. In 1909, when Britain's Cabinet was debating whether to build four or six warships, Navy League members paraded the streets with placards reading, 'We want eight and we won't wait.' Eight were constructed. Occasionally conferences were called to try to limit each navy. They failed because neither side trusted the other and because William believed that his navy would frighten the British into greater friendship with Germany.

Entente Cordiale

Actually the opposite happened. Britain's reactions did not stop at building warships. She ceased to be proud of her 'splendid isolation' and began to look for allies. The 1902 alliance with Japan was the first move. Next came increased co-operation with France. In 1903 secret talks took place between French and British officials. News of the talks leaked out but William's ministers were convinced that the two would never be friends. Once again they were wrong. When Edward VII visited France angry crowds did shout 'Vivent les Boers' and 'Vive Fashoda'. But Edward continued to smile and wave to such good effect that when he left the crowds shouted, 'Vive notre roi'. It was a small, significant incident.

Sure enough, in April 1904 the 'impossible' happened. An **Entente Cordiale** (Friendly Agreement) was signed between Britain and France. Officially it was not a war alliance. Its pages dealt with matters like French supremacy in Morocco and British supremacy in Egypt. Unofficially, however, it indicated many things which were not written down. It showed, for example, that Britain, France and Russia might well be on the opposite side from Germany and Austria-Hungary in a future war. It suggested possible British intervention if Germany attacked France and meant that Britain could leave the Mediterranean to French warships if there was a war. However, it was not certain that Britain would be involved in a possible conflict.

The danger of war was made worse by two factors. First, since 1892, the German General Staff planned to attack France first should Germany be threatened by Russia. This was because they knew France to be the greater danger. Knowing of the French desire to retake Alsace and Lorraine (see Chapter 1), they expected a massive assault in this region. They were right. The French army's 'Plan 17' made arrangements for an offensive along a 332-kilometre front which would drive

THE HAGGERSTON ELECTION.

Poster exhibited by the Navy League in Haggerston, July 31 and August 1, 1908.

THE NAVY LEAGUE

THE NAVY PROTECTS YOUR **FOOD**

THE NAVY PROTECTS YOUR **WAGES**

THE NAVY INSURES **PEACE**

THE NAVY PREVENTS **INVASION**

MR. BURROWS WANTS

TO CUT DOWN THE NAVY

The Navy League urges you to put

THE NAVY FIRST

AND

BURROWS LAST.

British Navy League propaganda.

Count Alfred von Schlieffen, German Chief of Staff who planned to knock out France within weeks

the German army back to the Rhine. The German answer was a knockout blow through an entirely different area, Belgium (see map on page 45).

The author of this plan was **Count Alfred von Schlieffen**, German Chief of Staff. The 'Schlieffen Plan' was meant to knock France out within weeks, before the slow-moving Russian army was ready. To do this effectively it was necessary to attack through Belgium because the Franco-German border was hilly and well-defended. A large army was to cross the flat Belgian countryside and descend on Paris from the north. Shaped liked a hammer, its head was designed to swing behind the French who were expected to advance east on Germany. It was a clever scheme but everything depended on the hammer head, the right wing of the army, being so powerful that it could crush all opposition. On his deathbed, Schlieffen is reported to have said, 'It must come to a fight. Only make the right wing strong'.

The second factor increasing the risk of war was that in those days details of alliances, even the alliances themselves, were kept secret. Bismarck had set an example when he wrote out the Reinsurance Treaty by hand and put it away in a secret file. The Dual Alliance was completely unknown to outsiders for several years; Italy did not know of its existence when she signed her agreement with Germany and Austria-Hungary. France did not know the exact terms of the Triple Alliance, neither did Germany know those of the Dual Entente until 1918. As a result politicians and the ordinary man in the street could never be sure of the dangers which faced them. Each side found it easy to believe that there was a conspiracy against them. Wild rumours were accepted without question. Both Germany and Austria-Hungary thought they were being encircled by their enemies. Britain feared an attack on her Empire and trade. Russia saw a German threat developing against Constantinople. France awaited another German invasion.

France's fear was the most justified of all. Locked away in Plan 17 and the Schlieffen Plan were the seeds of a major war. Both plans were very detailed. The German officers even knew how many railway trucks would pass over the main Rhine bridges during the first days of their knockout blow. Both sides were eager for war. A German officer, after reading the Schlieffen Plan, remarked, 'Good, now we are ready. The sooner it starts, the better for us!' And a French general said of the same plan, 'Let them try it, it will make our task easier. As the Boche [Germans] advance, we will strike up through Belgium and cut them in half!' It was in such a mood that two of the most powerful nations faced each other at this time.

Algeçiras and Agadir

Franco-British friendship was the greatest mystery of all from the German point of view. Would Britain, they asked themselves, fight by France's side against Germany? After the Russo-Japanese War (see Chapter 5) had revealed Russian weakness, the German government became less anxious about a two-front war. They began to put pressure upon France to test British friendship. Between 1905 and 1911

William and his advisers deliberately provoked quarrels with France about Morocco. The result were crises which made Germany unpopular and strengthened the *entente* against her.

In 1905 Germany complained that her interests in Morocco were being flouted. William paid a visit to Tangier (see map opposite) where he made a speech suggesting that the Moroccan Sultan was independent of France. French politicians wondered what to do. Some believed they could rely on Britain. They favoured standing firm against Germany. Others were less sure of their new friend. They gave way to German demands for an international meeting to settle the problem. The result of the **Algeciras Conference** was disappointing for William. Most countries agreed that although Morocco was independent, France had a special right to act as 'policeman' in the area. Only Austria-Hungary, who had no interest in colonies anyway, stood by Germany. It was a remarkable example of how isolated Germany had become under the leadership of William and his ministers.

The Algeciras Conference showed that Britain would stand by France. It led to secret talks between British and French generals concerned with sending 100,000 British troops to France's aid if she were attacked. Even in Morocco itself it had the opposite effect from that intended by the Kaiser. The French began to take firmer control and to extend their possessions, spreading inland, 'like an oil stain', as one angry German described it. Clearly a new crisis was brewing. It came in 1908 when French soldiers forced their way into the German Consulate in Casablanca to arrest three Foreign Legion deserters. It was a trivial incident but the Germans made a fuss to divert attention from the Bosnian Crisis (see Chapter 7). Eventually it was settled by an International Court sitting at The Hague (Holland).

In 1911 occurred the worst crisis of pre-war years. French troops had occupied Fez to help the Sultan in his struggle with rebels. Germany protested at this 'invasion' of Morocco and demanded compensation. The matter could have been settled by appealing to the International Court. Instead the Kaiser sent a warship, the *Panther*, to **Agadir**, Morocco. Such threatening behaviour annoyed almost everybody, particularly Britain who disliked this show of force at sea. In London a Cabinet Minister, Lloyd George, made a speech in which he told Germany that Britain would fight if she or her allies were bullied in this way. To show he was not bluffing the British fleet was put on a war footing. William found himself facing a world war because of his foolish action. Hurriedly he agreed to French supremacy in Morocco. In exchange he received a worthless piece of territory in the French Congo. Afterwards one German wrote of this crisis, 'Like a damp squib, it startled, then amused the world, and ended by making us look ridiculous.'

No German statesman had looked ridiculous in Bismarck's time. By 1911 the Chancellor's worst fears had come true. Germany faced the possibility of a two-front war and a sea fight with Britain. And, whereas after Sadowa Austria-Hungary had been dependent upon Germany, by 1908 she was beginning to drag Germany along behind her in a policy which was to lead to disaster in the Balkans.

Morocco, scene of pre-war clashes between the Germans and the French

Timeline

1872   Three Emperors' League (*Dreikaiserbund*).
1879   Dual Alliance.
1882   Triple Alliance.
1887   Reinsurance Treaty.
1889   William II begins reign.
1890   Bismarck's dismissal by William II.
1893   Dual Entente.
1900   German Navy Law.
1902   Anglo-Japanese Alliance.
1904   Entente Cordiale.
1906   Algeçiras Conference.
1911   Agadir Crisis.

Questions

1. Look at the photograph of the British super-battleship HMS *Dread-nought* on page 47.
   a) Explain why, following its launching in 1906, 'every battleship in the world was out of date'.
   b) Why did Britain regard the building of such battleships as important at this time?
   c) In what way did the building of this and other dreadnoughts lead to 'an expensive contest' between Britain and Germany?

2. Describe two quarrels between France and Germany which nearly led to war before 1914. What part did Britain play in these crises?

3. 'The great Mother Empire stands splendidly isolated in Europe.' (Sir George Foster, in the Canadian House of Commons, 1896)

   a) Do you think 'splendid isolation' is an accurate description of British foreign policy at this time?
   b) What were the risks of such a policy?
   c) What were the reasons which led to a change in this policy within the next ten years?

4. Write short paragraphs on each of the following:
   a) the Dual Alliance
   b) Kaiser William II
   c) the Schlieffen Plan
   d) the Entente Cordiale, 1904

7

Murder at Sarajevo
Causes of the First World War (II)

Three empires, the Habsburg, Russian and Ottoman, clashed in the Balkans. The Ottoman Turks wanted to hold on to their remaining Christian (European) territories. They found it increasingly difficult to do so because Greece and a free Serbia (now part of Yugoslavia) made their own Greek and Serbian subjects want independence also. Russia wished these peoples to be independent of the Turks so that she could control them. This would make it easier for her to establish a port on the Mediterranean Sea (see map on page 54). The Habsburg rulers of Austria-Hungary thought that any Turkish break-up might encourage their own subject peoples to revolt. In particular, the Habsburgs disliked a free Serbia on their border. Serbian patriots were constantly urging the six million Serbs ruled by the Habsburgs to revolt. The Habsburg rulers feared that the knowledge that there was a free Serbia so near might encourage their own Serbs to do just that.

In July 1908 a movement began to make the Ottoman Empire strong once more. A group of young patriots led by **Enver Bey** persuaded a section of the Turkish army to revolt against the Sultan, Abdul-Hamid. After some fighting, Enver's men were successful. They overthrew the Sultan, placed his brother, Mohammed V, on the throne and established a free parliament. Enver's political party, the Committee of Union and Progress, is usually known as the **Young Turks**. The Committee set out to modernise and reform the government. The thought of a strong Turkey alarmed Austria-Hungary. Since 1878 the Habsburgs had run the Serbian province of Bosnia-Herzegovina but officially the region still belonged to Turkey. What if these young, energetic soldier-politicians demanded Bosnia back?

Enver Bey – leader of the Young Turks

Bosnian take-over

At a meeting of Russian and Austrian representatives held at **Buchlau** in Austria in September 1908 Austria's Foreign Minister explained that his country proposed to 'solve' the Bosnian problem by taking over the region completely. Later the Russian minister was to claim that he had been tricked by a promise that if Russia allowed the Bosnian take-over Austria-Hungary would, in return, support Russia in her old claim to have Russian warships allowed through the Dardanelles (see Chapter 2). In fact, only three weeks after this meeting Austria-Hungary took over Bosnia without consulting any other country. The Russian, Turkish, French and Serbian governments were furious.

The Tsar of Russia, Nicholas II, tried to call a conference of the great powers, similar to the Congress of Berlin, to discuss the take-over, but nobody was interested. Reluctantly, therefore, since Russia was in no condition for a major war so soon after her defeat by Japan, the Tsar advised the Serbs to accept the take-over. In the end the Turks received financial compensation from Austria-Hungary for their loss. However, what seemed a victory for the Habsburgs had an unfortunate result from their point of view. Serbia and Russia were not likely to forgive the Austrians for what they had done. The Russians decided to strengthen their army and stand firm next time their interests were threatened in the Balkans. The Serbs became even more bitter enemies of Austria-Hungary, for they looked upon Bosnia, with its largely Serbian population, as a province of their own country.

The Balkan League

The Young Turk rule of the Committee of Union and Progress was a failure. The Ottoman Empire continued to fall apart. Britain had Egypt, France had Algeria, Tunis and Morocco. In 1911 the Italians took Tripoli after a short war. The Turk seemed unable to defend himself. Yet, strangely enough, it was in Macedonia (see map on page 54), where Young Turk rule began to have an effect, that disaster struck. All the Balkan countries were a patchwork of quarrelling nationalities but in Macedonia the mixture reached crazy proportions. Wedged together in this small, hilly area were Greeks, Serbs, Albanians, Bulgars and Arab Muslims. Most disliked each other at this time and the result was a disorganised country, plagued with bandits, family feuds and killings.

The old Sultan, Abdul, had liked this situation, because so long as the inhabitants fought each other they had no time to turn on his government. The Young Turks took a different view. They decided to restore order, to force a single language and law upon the inhabitants and to call up all fit young men for military service. The effect inside Macedonia was bad enough. Slavs and Arab Muslims were proud of their own languages; the Greeks were devoted to their laws. All were against military service in an army they hated. Outside Macedonia, the suggested 'reforms' united the other Balkan states for the first time. Serbia, Greece and Bulgaria had long wanted an excuse to throw the Turks out of Europe. Only their own quarrels had prevented an alliance. Now, led by **Eleutherios Venizelos**, the Greek Prime Minister, they formed a **Balkan League** and declared war on Turkey (**First Balkan War, October 1912**).

The Turks were faced by three large and comparatively well-equipped armies, aided by good telegraph and telephone communications. Even at sea Sultan Mohammed's navy was outclassed by the small but efficient Greek fleet. After several battles and a fierce defence of the Babuna Pass, the Turks were driven out of Europe. Three weeks after the war started only Adrianople, Scutari and Janina remained in Turkish hands (see map on page 54). Such a swift change alarmed the major European powers. Austria-Hungary was against the sudden collapse of the Ottoman Empire. Her politicians also disliked the fact that as a result of the fighting Serbia, a landlocked country

The Balkans after the wars of 1912–13

before, had now gained a coastline on the Adriatic. An international conference was called in London and a peace treaty, the **Treaty of London, May 1913**, was forced upon the victorious Balkan League.

This Treaty proved useless. Just one month after its signing Bulgaria attacked her former allies because she had not received the port of Salonika. In this, the **Second Balkan War**, the Bulgarians were at first successful. Then at the Battle of Stip they suffered a complete defeat. As the exhausted Bulgarians retreated even worse happened. Romania, a Balkan but non-Slav country which had taken no part in the first war, saw a chance to gain some more territory cheaply. Four hundred thousand Romanian troops assaulted what was left of the Bulgarian army. Within a week most of Bulgaria was overrun and the Romanians were less than 80 kilometres from Sofia, the capital (see map above). There was nothing for the Bulgarians to do but surrender.

Again, the great powers intervened and forced a second treaty upon the Balkan countries. By the **Treaty of Bucharest, August 1913**, Greece took over southern Macedonia, Serbia received only northern Macedonia and Romania a strip of the Black Sea coast in South Dobruja. Adrianople, given to Bulgaria by the Treaty of London, was now taken away and returned to the Turks, who had staged a counter-attack when Bulgaria was collapsing. The big nations felt satisfied, particularly Austria-Hungary who had stopped Serbia's thrust to the sea. Serbia had a fresh reason to hate the Habsburg government. Her troops had captured part of the Adriatic coastline and had then had it taken away under pressure from Austria-Hungary at the treaty conference.

The fears of Austria-Hungary

Habsburg pleasure at the outcome of the Balkan Wars did not last long. An empire similar to their own had been broken up by a Balkan League. Austrian ministers began to worry in case a similar league attacked them. Had not Nikola Pašić, the Serbian Prime Minister, said after the fighting, 'The first round is won and now for the second round against Austria'? Some Austrian politicians could see no answer to the problem. Others, influenced by General Conrad von Hotzendorf, suggested the destruction of free Serbia as a possible solution. Austria-Hungary, they argued, had hostile powers on at least half her borders. Conrad possessed a good army which would be ideal for a short war. He did not have the trained reserves for a long one. Consequently he favoured attacking first so as to win a swift victory. Day by day he urged Emperor Franz Joseph to go to war with Serbia.

Actually, Conrad's advice was bad for several reasons. First, no combination of Balkan armies was likely to beat the Austrian forces on their own. Austria-Hungary was therefore in less military danger than Conrad supposed. Second, Russia was certain to come to Serbia's aid and, if she did, the existing European alliances would involve Germany and France in the fighting. Most important, Conrad's 'solution' ignored the real problem. If Austria-Hungary was in any danger it was from within. Sooner or later, not only the six million Serbs, but all the subject peoples, would demand their independence from Habsburg rule. In any case another Balkan League was unlikely after Bulgaria's treachery.

Serbia, after the two Balkan Wars, was in no military condition to wage war. Unfortunately, within Serbia's borders were fanatics whom Prime Minister Pašić could not control. Organisations like the 'Union or Death' (Black Hand Society) led by Colonel Apis, Head of Serbian Military Intelligence, believed that the Bosnian Serbs must be freed from Austrian rule. Their methods were violent, involving murder and sabotage. It was always likely that such dangerous men might give Conrad and his 'war party' the excuse they needed. This was what they did on 28 June 1914 in Sarajevo, Bosnia. On that day Archduke Franz Ferdinand, heir to the Austrian throne, and his wife, Sophia Chotek, came to the town on an official visit. Also present in Sarajevo that Sunday morning were six young conspirators, armed with pistols and bombs. Their mission was to kill the Archduke. One of them was a serious, determined young man named Gavrilo Princip.

Murder at Sarajevo

The news that the Archduke intended to watch army manoeuvres near Sarajevo had worried Pašić, who did his best to prevent trouble by trying to stop the conspirators crossing the border and by privately warning the Austrian government. Some young Serb, the Habsburgs were told, might slip a live cartridge into his rifle instead of a blank and fire it. The Archduke took no notice. He felt it was his duty to attend these manoeuvres.

The conspirators were little more than boys. They knew very little about European politics. They wanted Bosnia-Herzegovina to be part of Serbia, and believed that this could only be done with pistols and bombs. Most of them were very frightened on that June morning; some were to prove inefficient murderers. Princip had seen the Archduke and his wife a few days before, shopping in the bazaar at Sarajevo. He had done nothing because he wanted the Archduke's 'execution' to be a public one. Now he and the others were spread out along a riverside road called Appel Quay, covering the route to be used by the Archduke on his official visit to the town.

Franz Ferdinand arrived by train at 9.28 a.m. After inspecting a military camp opposite the station, he and his wife climbed into a dark green Graf and Stiff four-cylinder limousine. This car was second in a motorcade which carried soldiers and officials including the town's governor, General Potiorek, and the owner of the car, Franz, Count Harrach. Countess Sophia looked beautiful in a high-collared white dress and a white hat. The Archduke was in uniform, a light blue tunic, black trousers and a cocked hat topped with large, green, ostrich feathers. As the cars rolled slowly into the town they were cheered by people lining the Quay. Without knowing it, the imperial visitors passed two conspirators who were so terrified they did nothing. Then they reached Nedjelko Cabrinovic. Jumping forward to avoid hurting the spectators, this man knocked his bomb's cap off against a fire hydrant and threw it at the Archduke's car.

Franz Ferdinand saw it coming and, with great presence of mind, he deflected it into the road. It burst with a loud explosion, wrecking the car behind and injuring its occupants. The Archduke remained very cool. 'I threw it and then noticed how calmly Ferdinand turned towards me and looked at me with a cold, stiff glare', Cabrinovic remembered later. The Serbian swallowed poison and jumped into the river. This poison failed to work. Within minutes he was dragged out

The Archduke Franz Ferdinand and his wife at Sarajevo, 28 June 1914

The dead Archduke and his wife lie in state

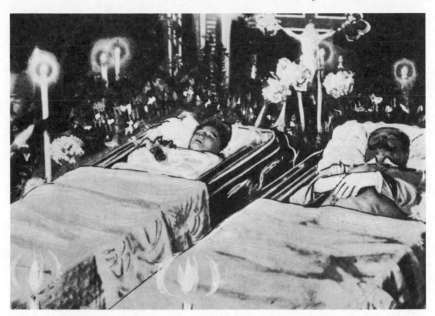

and arrested. Meanwhile the Archduke's car accelerated and drove to the Town Hall where the Mayor stood ready to welcome his famous visitors. By this time Franz Ferdinand had recovered sufficiently to be angry. He brushed the Mayor aside and cancelled the rest of his tour.

It was decided to leave Sarajevo as soon as Franz Ferdinand had seen his wounded officers in hospital. In case there was another murder attempt, it was thought best to leave by the Appel Quay instead of the advertised route. Franz Ferdinand wanted his wife to stay behind but she insisted on remaining with her husband. Since there seemed little chance of trouble now, Ferdinand agreed. The party climbed aboard once more. Count Harrach decided to stand on the running-board so that he could jump at any attacker. As it turned out he chose the wrong side of the car. And in the confusion nobody told the driver of the change of plan.

The car started back along the Appel Quay but at Franz Joseph Street the driver turned right. He should have gone straight on so Potiorek told him to turn round. This was fatal because Princip was standing nearby. As the car reversed towards him he stepped forward and fired two shots. The first struck the Archduke's throat. The second hit Sophia in the stomach. Franz Ferdinand, blood pouring from his mouth, saw that his wife was hit. 'Sopherl! Sopherl!' he cried out, 'Don't die! Keep alive for our children.' It was too late. His wife died even as he shouted. By the time the car reached the Governor's residence Franz Ferdinand was dead also. Princip meanwhile swallowed poison. Like Cabrinovic's it was useless and only made him sick. He was arrested and beaten up by the police.

It was 10.15 a.m. on the anniversary of the Archduke's wedding day. A friend of the conspirators sent a message to Belgrade, the Serbian capital. It read, 'Excellent sale of both horses'. The plotters in Serbia knew what this meant.

Timeline

1908	Young Turk rebellion in Ottoman Empire. Buchlau Conference. Austria-Hungary takes over Bosnia-Herzegovina (Bosnian Crisis).
1912	Formation of Balkan League. First Balkan War.
1913	Treaty of London (May). Second Balkan War. Treaty of Bucharest (August).
1914	Archduke Franz Ferdinand assassinated at Sarajevo.

Questions

1. Describe the main causes of dispute in the Balkans between 1870 and 1914. How did they affect relations between the great powers?

2. 'My policy is a policy of peace.'
   (Emperor Franz Joseph of Austria-Hungary)
   a) In what way did Franz Joseph and Conrad von Hotzendorf disagree on what should be Austria's policy towards Serbia?
   b) What was the real threat to the Habsburg Empire?

3. Write short paragraphs on each of the following:
   a) the Bosnian Crisis, 1908
   b) the Young Turks
   c) the Balkan League
   d) the murder of Archduke Franz Ferdinand

8

Defeat at the Marne
The First World War (*I*)

At first very little happened. For years Austrian statesmen had been complaining of the danger from Serbia. Now Serbians had murdered the heir to their throne. Everybody expected a swift reply, possibly an invasion of Serbia. Actually day followed day without Austria-Hungary seeming to do much at all. Franz Ferdinand and his wife were buried quietly. A leisurely investigation began to trace those responsible for the crime. Few foreign newspapers made much of the story. Europe continued to enjoy a hot summer.

Behind the scenes, however, much was happening. In Vienna Conrad's supporters argued with the Emperor who still feared that any war with Serbia would involve Russia. In case this happened it was essential to be sure of German support. On 5 July the Austrian ambassador told Kaiser William that the murder conspiracy had been planned in Serbia. His government, he said, intended to present Prime Minister Pašić with very severe demands. If these were rejected they proposed to occupy the country. William had sometimes advised his Austrian allies to be patient with Serbia. Now he told the Austrians that Germany would support them all the way, mainly because he felt certain Russia was not ready for war.

The pace now quickened. On 23 July the Habsburg government presented their ultimatum. In it they insisted that Serbia should stop encouraging nationalist propaganda, allow Austrian officials into Serbia to help crush revolutionary movements, punish all those involved in the murder plot and prevent arms and explosives crossing the Bosnian border. Pašić agreed to all these conditions except one. He refused to let Austrians into his country. Austria-Hungary took this as a complete refusal and declared war on 28 July. Russia's reply was immediate. She began to mobilise her troops.

Germany was now in a dilemma. Since 1892 her generals had expected a war with both Russia and France. Obviously France was the more dangerous of the two so **Count Alfred von Schlieffen**, German Chief of Staff, had suggested a massive attack against her before the slow-moving Russian army was ready (see page 49). The present situation made this difficult; if Russia was allowed to mobilise in peacetime the whole plan might fail. Alarmed, the Germans ordered Russia to demobilise within twelve hours. The Tsar's government refused. On 31 July 1914 the German Chancellor, Theodore von Beth-mann-Hollweg, sent for Schlieffen's successor, Helmuth von Moltke, a nephew of the victor of the Franco-Prussian War (see Chapter 1). 'Is the Fatherland in danger?' he asked. 'Yes', replied Moltke. In any case the time seemed ripe for action. The Kaiser's army was still better than the Russian and French forces but there were signs that both were catching up. The Kiel Canal had just been deepened to allow Germany's dreadnoughts to steam swiftly from the Baltic to the North Sea (see map on page 65). <u>Consequently Germany declared war on Russia (1 August) and France (3 August). And, because of the Schlieffen Plan, her troops attacked France first.</u>

The Schlieffen Plan had many snags. The most important was political, not military. **Belgium's neutrality** in any war had been guaranteed by the Treaty of London (1839). Britain, as well as Prussia, had signed this document. Indeed a neutral Belgium had been Britain's idea because she had always wished to keep an area so near the English coast out of hostile hands. Twice before, in 1702 and 1793, she had gone to war to prevent an enemy conquering the area. For this reason the Plan might lead to an unwanted conflict with Britain. Germany, of course, knew this. Unfortunately, her generals could think of no other way of planning a two-front war. Nor were they particularly worried. Being soldiers, they underestimated the danger from the British navy. Certainly in the short war they planned it mattered little who controlled the seas. The politicians, on their side, hoped that Britain would agree to German troops occupying Belgium provided they promised to evacuate it afterwards. On 2 August the Germans asked Belgium for permission to cross her borders. When this was refused they marched in, overrunning tiny Luxembourg as well (see map on page 62).

The war begins

Until that moment at least half the British Cabinet had been against fighting, especially as the German fleet had promised to stay out of the Channel. The invasion of Belgium changed Britain's attitude completely and she demanded that the Kaiser's troops withdraw. When they refused to do so she declared war on Germany (4 August 1914). The Kaiser and Bethmann-Hollweg were surprised. 'Just for a scrap of paper Great Britain is going to make war on a kindred nation', complained the Chancellor. Actually more than a treaty, more than a country's safety, was involved. Germany herself, or at least Prussia, had guaranteed Belgian neutrality. Now she had broken her promise. How could one country trust another if written promises were treated as mere 'scraps of paper'? Bismarck's belief that might was right now led Germany to disaster. By midnight on 4 August all the countries in the two great power groupings (see map on page 45) were at war except Italy.

The majority of people welcomed the war. Only a few realised that a great disaster was brewing. Sir Edward Grey, the British Foreign Minister, stood at the windows of his office, watching the lamps being lit, and said, 'The lamps are going out all over Europe; we shall not see them lit again in our lifetime.' Even so, he did not find many to agree with him. In most European capitals cheering crowds greeted the news. People had been taught that a modern war would be swift. A few lightning marches and a great battle would settle the matter.

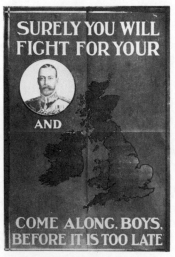

A call from King and Country. Of all the countries at war in 1914 only Britain had no military conscription

British troops arriving in Belgium, October 1914. Many of the crowd had never seen a British soldier before

To young Germans and Frenchmen, war between their two countries seemed unavoidable. Since 1871 the French had longed for revenge. Now the day of reckoning had come. This time there would be no easy German victory. Alsace and Lorraine would be liberated, the memories of Sedan and Metz would be wiped away (see Chapter 1). The Germans felt that war was necessary to save their Fatherland from encirclement. They believed they were about to give Germany back the dominant position she had enjoyed in Bismarck's day.

On all sides there was tremendous excitement. German troops were applauded all the way from their homes. One young man wrote, 'Such enthusiasm! – the whole battalion with helmets and tunics decked with flowers – handkerchiefs waving untiringly – cheers on every side – and over and over again the ever-fresh and wonderful reassurance of the soldiers. This hour is one such as seldom strikes in the life of a nation...'. Their enemies felt the same. One French soldier exclaimed, 'Thirty years of life would not be worth all that we are going to accomplish within the next few weeks... I wish you could share in some measure the peace we experience here!' Both were dead within a month.

Certainly it was a dramatic moment. The Schlieffen Plan was one of the great gambles of military history. It was so risky that Moltke had modified it even before the war. Ignoring Schlieffen's words (see page 49), he had strengthened the left wing, the handle or hinge of the swing, because he feared a French breakthrough in the east. When the invasion started other errors appeared. The Belgians put up a far better fight than the Germans had imagined. Liège held off attacks for nearly ten days; Antwerp did not fall until October. The Russians, too, mobilised far quicker than expected and invaded East Prussia.

[handwritten margin note: German chief of staff took over Schlieffen]

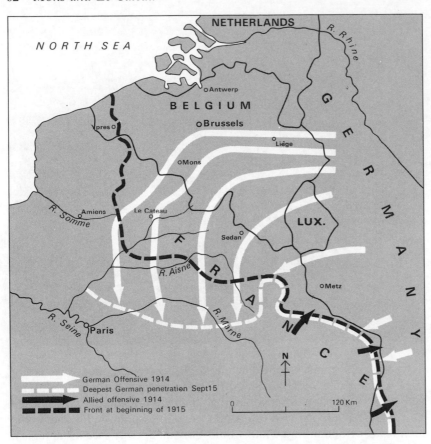

Map legend:
- German Offensive 1914
- Deepest German penetration Sept 15
- Allied offensive 1914
- Front at beginning of 1915

This forced Moltke to send two divisions back to the Russian Front. Even more unexpected, 125,000 British troops landed in France and marched south. The Germans mocked the size of the British force, William was supposed to have called it a 'contemptible little army'. Yet on 23 August 1914, at **Mons** (see map above), British rifle fire shot the advancing German lines to pieces. At **Le Cateau** five days later they staged another successful rearguard action. Afterwards the survivors were proud to call themselves 'Old Contemptibles'.

The 'miracle' of the Marne

Nevertheless, the sheer weight of the Schlieffen 'hammer' broke all resistance. Even the weakened German army numbered 1,125,000 men. Like a sea of grey uniforms, they rolled across Belgium and down into France. The French, like the British, fought well but their main offensive had been in the east. Here they had attacked against well-defended trenches and machine-gun posts. Dressed in blue and red, the cavalry still wearing the shining breastplates and helmets of past days, their brave ranks had been swept away. Now the remains of these armies had to stumble north to meet a new threat as the Germans approached Paris.

The French capital presented a problem. With millions of men clogging the supply routes, the Germans had no troops to spare for a siege. Their hammer thrust must either split and go round either side of the city, or swing inwards and pass to the east. Both moves were dangerous. The first would divide the whole army. The second would crush it into a small space. Whilst French cavalry, aircraft and balloons tried to find out which route the Germans had chosen, a German car was surprised on 1 September and its passengers killed. On one dead man the French found a card which marked the route of the extreme northern army, commanded by General von Kluck. These pencilled lines confirmed what air reconnaissance had already suggested. Von Kluck had chosen the second alternative. His men had swung east and then south. The German army was marching into the narrow space formed by Paris on one side and the retreating Allies (Britain and France) on the other (see map on page 62).

By this time both sides were exhausted. For nearly a month the soldiers had marched, in blazing hot weather, distances of anything up to 64 kilometres a day. Their feet were bruised, blistered and caked with dried blood, their shoulders cut by pack and rifle straps, their clothes stuck to their bodies with sweat. Clouds of dust raised by their boots covered the trees. At night they just collapsed and slept where they lay. One of General von Kluck's officers described a march like this, 'The men stagger forward, their faces coated with dust, their uniforms in rags, they look like living scarecrows.' Already the war had ceased to be a matter of throwing flowers and waving handkerchiefs.

On 6 September General Joffre, the French commander, decided to counter-attack. The **Battle of the Marne** which followed is one of the most important in history. Although named after the French river, it was really a number of battles fought on a front of 249 kilometres by nearly two million men. It took place in lovely weather. 'I do not remember ever to have seen such a long succession of beautiful days', wrote a French survivor. All over the autumnal countryside, great masses of men clashed in confused combat. They struggled in open fields, they charged up and down wooded slopes, they came to grips in old-fashioned villages. The Germans found themselves assaulted from Paris and from the south. The Paris attack came as a surprise. On the first day of the battle 250 taxis full of troops left the French capital. All through the night more followed. These 'taxis of the Marne' represented the first large-scale use of motor transport in war. They brought fresh men to fight the tired Germans, causing more and more of von Kluck's army to be diverted to deal with them. This in turn caused a gap to develop between von Kluck's men and the rest of the army.

This was Joffre's opportunity. The French and British drove forward into the space; at one time advance parties were 64 kilometres behind the actual front. In this crisis the German High Command, far away in Luxembourg, lost contact with operations. The same thing had happened in 1870 but then Bazaine and Macmahon had made so many mistakes that it did not matter (see Chapter 1). Now the

'The bodies lay in thick dark patches'. German dead at the Marne, September 1914

French army was better equipped and better led. Throughout these terrible days, when the fate of his country hung in the balance, Joffre kept calm. As he methodically assessed every piece of information he received, there were times when he knew more of the German army's movements than Moltke himself! By 11 September the German flow had been turned back. Their hopes of victory faded even as the weather turned to clouds and rain. Over many kilometres of countryside the bodies lay in thick dark patches. German grey beside French blue and British khaki, dead horses beside smashed guns, abandoned rifles, helmets and packs. Slowly and doggedly the German survivors retreated to the River Aisne. Joffre announced, 'The Battle ... is an incontestable victory for us'. Moltke told the Kaiser, 'Your Majesty, we have lost the war.' The great gamble had failed.

Stalemate in the West

Germany had not lost the war. But her failure to end it quickly turned it into a kind of war neither Schlieffen nor any other general had imagined. It was the Germans who first dug trenches and set up machine-gun posts. Victorious Allied (British and French) soldiers

*First World War, 1914.
Germany won victories on the
Western Front and at
Tannenberg and the Masurian
Lakes in the east*

were met by a hail of bullets which mowed them down. When the Germans themselves tried to break through down the Belgian coast they too were stopped in the same way at **Ypres.** For a month both sides poured men into this new battle. Thousands died to gain a few metres. When the Germans did make a gap fresh reserves were rushed in trains to block it. Here was the pattern of war for the next four years. Any assault could be slowed down by barbed wire and broken up with rifle and machine-gun fire. Big shells did not help. They merely tore up the ground, making an attack more difficult. If there was a breakthrough fresh troops were sent to the danger spot by rail. It became a war in which men attacked at walking pace but defended at railway speed. The Germans won victories during 1914. They conquered all Belgium, most of the French coal-mines and all her iron-fields. They destroyed two Russian armies at **Tannenberg** and the **Masurian Lakes** (see map opposite). But the 'quick war' scheme had failed. Germany had taken on a large part of the world in combat. She was outnumbered in a war which was to become an arithmetical exercise in killing.

The armies in the West were now locked together immovably, like frozen masses pressing against each other. The trench system gradually grew more elaborate until it became a spider's web disfiguring the landscape. Shallow, water-filled holes in fields became underground honeycombs, guarded by lines of barbed wire, with their own tramways, water-pipes, shell-proof dugouts and fire-steps. Against such

*Germans and French fight in
'no-man's-land'* (see page 69)
*The Frenchman in the centre
has just been hit*

defences there could be no encirclement, no smashing breakthrough, no stunning victory. Courage alone was not enough. Of the machine-gun one soldier wrote: 'I know of nothing more depressing in the midst of battle ... but the steady tac-tac-tac of that deadly weapon. It spreads suffering in a precise and methodic fashion.' Of barbed wire another said: 'The barbed wire terrified and obsessed the infantry-man. All his daring and courage came to naught when he came up against an incompletely destroyed network. He knew that he would get caught and lacerated ... His would be a slow, agonising death.'

Grey had spoken the truth. The lights of civilisation had gone out. A new 'Dark Age' of killing had begun.

Timeline

1914   Austrian ultimatum to Serbia (23 July).
Austria-Hungary declares war on Serbia (28 July).
Russia mobilises her army (30 July).
Germany declares war on Russia (1 August).
Germany declares war on France. Belgium invaded (3 August).
Britain declares war on Germany (4 August).
Battle of Mons (21 August).
Battle of Tannenberg (26–30 August).
Battle of the Marne (6–11 September).
Battle of the Masurian Lakes (9–14 September).
First Battle of Ypres (14 October–13 November).

Questions

1. 'Just for a scrap of paper Great Britain is going to make war on a kindred nation.'
   (German Chancellor, Bethmann-Hollweg, August 1914)

   a) Which nation was the German Chancellor referring to as 'a kindred nation'?
   b) What was the 'scrap of paper'?
   c) Why did Britain consider this 'scrap of paper' to be of vital importance?

2. What problems confronted the German army as it advanced on Paris in August to September 1914? What course did the generals decide to take? What were the results?

3. Write short paragraphs on each of the following:
   a) the Battle of the Marne
   b) the 'contemptible little army'
   c) the Treaty of London, 1839
   d) trench warfare

9

From Ypres to the Somme
The First World War (II)

The war which began in August 1914 at the start involved seven countries; at the end, thirty. A quarrel between Austrians and Serbs spread until Japanese and Americans fought Germans, Italians and Romanians fought Austrians, Turks killed Arabs, black troops campaigned in African jungles, Indians fought on the Western Front and Australians in the Holy Land. Nothing quite like it had happened before. It was the first war in which men were poisoned with gas and towns bombed from the air; the first in which women worked in armament factories; the first in which the world's entire industrial resources were used to produce death and destruction. Its results were far reaching. Four empires collapsed. Britain and France were weakened as world powers. Russia emerged as the first Communist state, the USA as the richest nation on earth. A dozen small countries were created out of the ruins. It was as though the world was heated until molten and then poured into a different mould.

Japan was the first non-European nation to join in. Because of the 1902 alliance with Britain (see page 47), her government ordered Germany to surrender Kiaochow on the Shantung peninsula (see map on page 40). When this was ignored Japan declared war on Germany (23 August 1914), captured Kiaochow and occupied German islands in the Pacific. By November 1914 her forces had finished active operations except for protecting Allied convoys and sinking German submarines. Japanese politicians used the war as an excuse to extend their influence in China. Japanese businessmen benefited from the removal of European competition. The war proved a boom time for Japan and she emerged stronger than ever before.

The same could not be said of the Ottoman Empire. Her Young Turk ruler, Enver Bey, admired Germany and felt sure she would win. He also wished to conquer the Caucasus from Russia (see map on page 79). The arrival in Turkish waters of two German warships, the *Goeben* and *Breslau*, increased Enver's confidence and Turkey declared war on Britain, France and Russia (12 October 1914). In the long run this drew the Middle East into the conflict because the Turks attacked Egypt and the British oil-fields in Persia (Iran). In the short run it led Enver to an invasion of the Caucasus which ended in disaster at **Sarikamish**. Most of his men who did not die in battle were frozen to death. Only one-eighth of the original army returned. This little-known defeat affected Turkish military strength. When her troops invaded Egypt (February 1915) they were beaten.

The only dominion which hesitated to join Britain actively was South Africa. Here bitterness against the British was so strong that some Boers rose in rebellion rather than fight Germany. They were defeated and early in 1915 South Africa entered the war in earnest. A former Boer leader, Jan Smuts, conquered German South West Africa but German East Africa (see map on page 22) was skilfully defended by General Lettow-Vorbeck. With a force of about 20,000 he held out until twelve days after his country had surrendered. Elsewhere the British navy swiftly disposed of the German Empire. Togoland in Africa, and Samoa and New Guinea in the Pacific, were all in Allied hands before 1915.

At first it seemed the Germans might hold their own at sea. On 1 November 1914 Admiral Craddock's Far Eastern Squadron was destroyed off **Coronel** (Chile) by a German force commanded by Admiral Graf von Spee (see map opposite). Craddock's ships were old and slow. They were caught silhouetted against the sunset and pounded to pieces within an hour. In Britain the news was received with grim determination. Two new battleships and five cruisers were detached from the British Grand Fleet. Their commander, Admiral Sturdee, was ordered not to return until the German ships were sunk. What could have been a long job was made easy by a stroke of luck for the British. On 7 December 1914 Sturdee's ships were coaling in the **Falkland Islands** when von Spee arrived to attack the base. The horrified German saw the distinctive tripod masts of the British battleships when it was too late. He swung away but after a chase four German warships were sunk and 2,300 sailors, including von Spee and his sons, were killed.

Apart from this the British navy's war work passed almost unnoticed. The army was engaged in dramatic battles. The fleet's real value lay in what did not happen. No German invasion of Britain was ever possible. Not a single troopship was lost through enemy action in the Channel. The dominions and colonies sent their soldiers to France without difficulty. Even the tight blockade of Germany did not hit the headlines. Yet by 1915 it was forcing the Germans to retaliate. On 4 February they announced a counter-blockade of Britain. Since they would have to use U-boats (submarines) this raised serious problems. Submarines could only sink ships. They were too small to stop them, send boarding-parties and destroy the cargo. As a result neutral ships, particularly American, were in danger. Ominously the US government warned the Germans not to touch their merchantmen. Despite this an

Naval battles between British and German fleets took place at Coronel and the Falkland Islands in 1914

German U-boat of the First World War

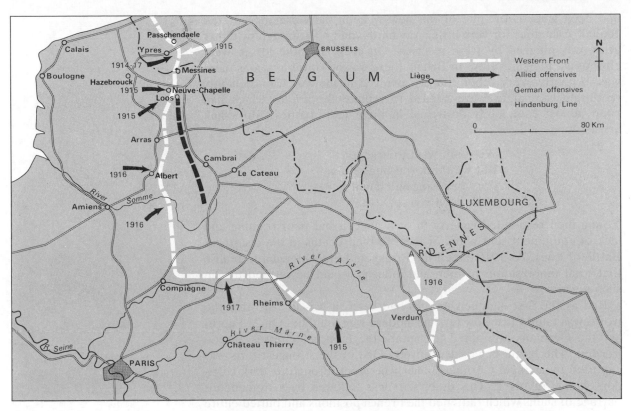

The Western Front, 1914–18

American tanker was torpedoed on 1 May 1915. Six days later a British liner, the *Lusitania*, was sunk off Ireland. Of the 1,200 passengers drowned, 118 were Americans. The uproar in the USA was so great that Germany feared she might declare war. Her U-boat campaign was then restricted to enemy ships until 1917.

Western Front, 1914–16

The Western Front established after the Marne hardly moved more than a few kilometres throughout the war. It ran from Ostend (Belgium), through Ypres, Loos, Arras and Albert, across the River Somme and round in a wide half-circle to Rheims and Verdun before ending at the Swiss border (see map above). Two salients (corners) jutted into the German defences at Ypres and Verdun. Like a great scar, this wilderness of ruins, mud, puddles, wire and corpses, disfigured the countryside for four years. Into it the great powers poured millions of men and millions of pounds of equipment. Here in misery and agony generations of French, German and British died or were crippled. Soldiers called it 'no-man's-land'.

Early in 1915 the French attacked near Compiègne, suffering 90,000 casualties. In March the British won at **Neuve-Chapelle** and gained a few square kilometres of land. Next month, during a German offensive, greenish-yellow clouds drifted from their lines, turning slowly to a white haze. Men ran back in panic, coughing and spluttering. They had been gassed. In spite of this new weapon the Germans suffered 100,000 casualties for very little. Any hard-won breakthrough by either army was plugged by fresh reserves. On every side the losses were enormous, the gains tiny. In Britain there was no conscription as there was in nearly every other country involved in the war. Consequently recruiting campaigns were needed to replace the armies which had been almost completely destroyed in these early battles. Music-hall artists sang:

> We don't want to lose you
> But we think you ought to go
> For your King and country
> Both need you so.

Young men responded eagerly to such appeals but poor training and lack of equipment sent many of them to their deaths in the disastrous Battle of **Loos**. As 1915 ended the British and French began to realise that total mobilisation of men and industry would be needed to win such a war.

Bad as the first eighteen months had been, it was in 1916 that the world was taught just how terrible modern war could be. On 21 February the Germans attempted to capture the French fortresses around **Verdun**. The battle began deceptively. One of the strongest forts was captured by a single German soldier who crept through its dark corridors with a revolver. This quiet start was followed by a tremendous barrage of shells which flattened the French positions and buried entire trench systems. The Germans seemed about to break through until General Pétain took charge and inspired his men. The French slogan was simply 'They shall not pass'. All their hatred of the Germans, all their patriotism, became concentrated in the desire to hold Verdun. Along the only road leading to the town lorryloads of soldiers and supplies passed, night and day, at intervals of fifteen seconds. This lifeline, called the 'Sacred Way' because so many men passed along it to their deaths, was like an open artery, draining away the young blood of France.

The German generals had planned to draw the French to Verdun and destroy them. Unfortunately, the German people became just as determined that Verdun should fall. They, too, were tempted to go on fighting. They, too, fed thousands of men into this tiny salient less than 8 kilometres wide. Outside the forts the land became an awful wilderness, churned up by explosives and poisoned with chemicals and gas. Inside them men lived like animals or fought hand to hand in dark tunnels. The bombardments were on a vast scale: on one day 100,000 gas shells fell on the defenders. A French soldier described how it felt to live in such a hell:

> We instantly recognise the shell that is coming to bury us. As soon as we pick out its mournful howl we look at each other in agony . . . . Our helmets clang together, we stagger about like drunks. The beams tremble, a cloud of choking smoke fills the dugout, the two candles go out.

The British go 'over the top' at the Somme, 1 July 1916

After five months the battle had resulted in 700,000 casualties but the French still held Verdun. To those who survived the battle it remained a horrible memory. To future Frenchmen it became an example of their national courage.

The French army was very close to breaking point. Clearly some other offensive would have to be launched before the Germans realised its weakness. The British commander, General Haig, was training a new volunteer army with which he hoped to attack at the **Somme**, in August 1916. Now he decided to launch his offensive a month earlier. For eight days nearly 2,000 British guns pounded the Germans. Then on 1 July an enormous British army began to move slowly across 'no-man's-land' towards the German defences. The soldiers had been told the enemy trenches would be smashed. They had expected shell-shocked soldiers ready to surrender. In fact the very deep German trenches were often unharmed and many kilometres of barbed wire stood undamaged. Everywhere they met a hail of accurate machine-gun fire. Before dark that day 47,000 British troops had been killed or wounded and hardly any ground had been captured. For months a similar slaughter was repeated each day. No amount of courage, no sacrifice, seemed able to bring success. Even a new weapon, the tank, merely ended up stuck in the mud or hoisted on tree-stumps. When a blizzard finally blotted out the battlefield on 18 November 1,250,000 casualties had been suffered by both sides and the British had captured 325 square kilometres of shell-torn mud and rubble.

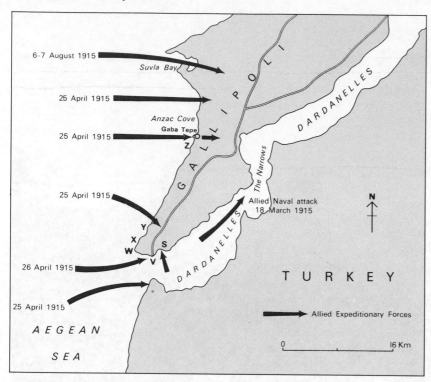

6-7 August 1915

Suvla Bay

25 April 1915

Anzac Cove
Gaba Tepe

25 April 1915

Z

The Narrows

25 April 1915

Allied Naval attack
18 March 1915

N

Y

X

S

W

V

26 April 1915

DARDANELLES

T U R K E Y

25 April 1915

Allied Expeditionary Forces

A E G E A N

S E A

0   16 Km

Main Allied attacks on the Turkish positions at Gallipoli, 1915

In Britain people were horrified and disillusioned. A brave volunteer army had marched to its death whilst others stayed safely at home. It seemed unfair. Soon after the battle the British government decided to start conscription. Meanwhile fierce arguments raged over the causes of the massacre. Many blamed Haig, others blamed the politicians who had started such a war. In France, too, men were losing confidence in their leaders. Many soldiers wondered why they were fighting. To them the real enemy was not the Germans or the Austrians, but war itself. They felt cut off from civilians who could never understand the horror of trench warfare. One soldier poet wrote bitterly:

> You smug-faced crowd with kindling eye
> Who cheer when soldier lads go by
> Sneak home and pray you'll never know
> The hell where youth and laughter go.

Gallipoli

Actually the Allied governments had been trying to find a way out of the deadlock on the Western Front since the first months of the war. Enemy territory was strongly defended to the east and west. It was less securely held in southern Europe where weak Austrian and Turkish armies had to protect difficult country and a long coastline. Here, it was thought, was the 'soft underbelly' of the Central Powers (Germany, Austria-Hungary, Turkey). If the Allies (Britain and France) could establish a bridgehead in Turkey or the Balkans they could

Anzac Cove, 1915. A photograph which shows how cramped the Allied position was at Gallipoli

link up with Russia and drive into the heart of Europe. It seemed the easiest way to win the war.

Two spots were suggested for an invasion, **Salonika** (Greece) and the **Dardanelles** in Turkey (see map opposite). The Dardanelles was attacked first. It proved far more difficult than expected. The 64-kilometre stretch of almost landlocked water formed by the Sea of Marmara and the Dardanelles presented many problems. Its coasts were bare and windswept with few bays and many steep cliffs. The land itself was well-defended by 84,000 troops commanded by a German, Liman von Sanders. The sea was infested with explosive mines. Any hope that the Dardanelles could be forced by warships alone was destroyed when naval attacks were abandoned after several battleships hit mines. Consequently an Allied army containing a large number of Australians and New Zealanders (**Anzacs**) landed on the **Gallipoli** peninsula on 25 April 1915. This date is still known as Anzac Day.

The chosen spots had been labelled S, V, W, X, Y and Z beaches by the British generals. Some were occupied easily because the Turks were unprepared. Others were fiercely defended. At V Beach the men came ashore from an old ship, the *River Clyde*. As they ran down the gangways, or came out of special holes in the side, they were massacred. Whining bullets whipped the sea into a turmoil. Boatloads of soldiers were wiped out. Those wading through the water often became entangled in barbed wire and were shot where they stood. High above, a British pilot reported that the sea was 'absolutely red with blood'. Through the blood-stained surf, over the bodies of their comrades, the survivors fought their way up the beach and drove the Turks back.

Numerous footholds were gained on that first day. Unfortunately for the Allies, the determined leadership of Mustafa Kemal, the local Turkish commander, stopped the Anzacs from capturing their real objective, the hills which run like a backbone down the peninsula. Thanks to him and his brave soldiers the Allied expedition was trapped between steep hillsides and open beaches. Repeated attacks up such bare ridges led to awful losses; thousands died capturing a few hundred metres. As the summer came the fighting increased in intensity. When a second landing was made, at **Suvla Bay** (see map on page 72) in August, 5,000 Turks were killed in one morning. In between offensives the men lived surrounded by their dead, sweating in a heat which caused disease to spread like wildfire. Even so, a friendly feeling grew up between the two armies, who admired each other as fair fighters. British troops threw tinned beef at enemy trenches, the Turks hurled grapes and sweets back. Meanwhile the Allied High Command began to have doubts about the whole scheme. In November 1915 Lord Kitchener was sent to investigate. He realised it was hopeless to fight on and ordered a withdrawal. By January 1916 no Allied troops were left at Gallipoli.

The Dardanelles invasion had ended in tragedy. When another expedition landed at **Salonika** in October 1915 the affair became a farce. From the start this particular scheme had one big drawback. Greece was not at war with Germany. Nevertheless her government was anti-German and it was hoped she would join the Allies. Such hopes were ruined by Russia. She was against Greece entering the war in case Greek troops captured Constantinople before the Russians. Accordingly Greece was 'persuaded' to remain neutral. Two hundred and fifty thousand Allied troops found themselves condemned to inactivity for three years. The Germans were amused at this. The British were not. One officer wrote home angrily: 'The German spies sit in rows on the quays at Salonika smoking large cigars and note down every man, horse, gun and ton of stores landed. This is a nice way to make war!'

Jutland

No sooner was Britain at war with Germany than everyone expected a great sea battle. In fact the Kaiser was anxious not to risk his expensive warships because his navy was not large enough to fight the whole British fleet. Consequently, the High Seas Fleet usually remained safe in port, protected by minefields. Admiral Tirpitz was not happy about this. He wanted a large-scale engagement which he was sure would cripple the British fleet even if the Germans were beaten. Admiral von Scheer, who took command in 1916, decided to try to lure part of the British Grand Fleet to destruction. He began to make regular sweeps in the North Sea, hoping to catch a few British ships on their own. He actually stood little chance of doing so because the British had the key to the German navy's signal code. Therefore they always knew when Scheer was at sea.

On 31 May 1916 Scheer steamed into the North Sea with his main fleet and sent Admiral Hipper's battlecruiser squadron ahead as a decoy. Admiral Jellicoe, commander of the British Grand Fleet, knew what the Germans were doing because of intercepted signals. He decided to send his own battlecruisers ahead, also to act as bait. Consequently, when the two squadrons made contact off the **Jutland** peninsula (see map opposite) in mid-afternoon, each was trying to lure its opponent into a trap.

Admiral Reinhard von Scheer, German commander at Jutland, 1916

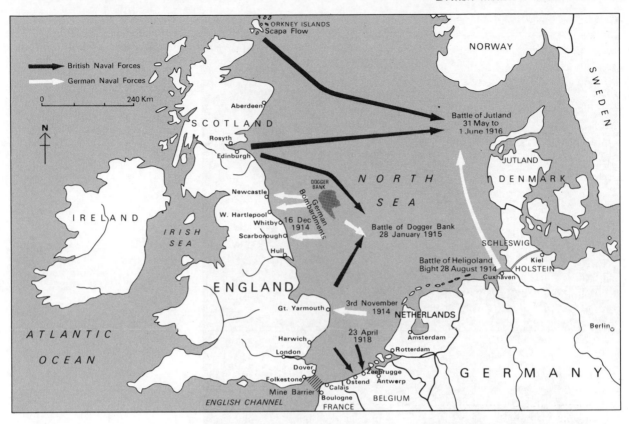

British Naval Forces
German Naval Forces

0   240 Km

N

ORKNEY ISLANDS
Scapa Flow

NORWAY

SWEDEN

SCOTLAND

Aberdeen

Rosyth

Battle of Jutland
31 May to
1 June 1916

Edinburgh

JUTLAND

DENMARK

Newcastle

DOGGER
BANK

N O R T H
S E A

German
Bombardments

W. Hartlepool
Whitby   16 Dec
1914
Scarborough

Battle of Dogger Bank
28 January 1915

SCHLESWIG

Hull

Kiel
HOLSTEIN

IRELAND

IRISH
SEA

E N G L A N D

Battle of Heligoland
Bight 28 August 1914
Cuxhaven

ATLANTIC

OCEAN

Gt. Yarmouth

3rd November
1914

NETHERLANDS

Berlin

Harwich

London

Dover

Folkestone
Mine Barrier
Boulogne

23 April
1918

Amsterdam

Rotterdam

G E R M A N Y

Calais
Ostend
Zeebrugge
Antwerp

BELGIUM

ENGLISH CHANNEL
FRANCE

*The Sea War, 1914–18,
showing the main battles
between British and German
fleets*

Admiral Beatty, who led the British battlecruiser squadron, was a bold officer who had made his name in 1914 when he sank three German cruisers and a destroyer off the Heligoland Bight. His opponent, Hipper, was a similar personality. When the two sighted each other they closed swiftly for the kill. From the start the fight went in Hipper's favour. British warships of the time had weak armour, particularly round their turrets, whilst the German gunners proved better marksmen. Within half an hour two British battleships were utterly destroyed by direct hits which exploded their magazines. The *Indefatigable* disappeared in a mighty cloud of smoke, its 17-metre long picket boat spinning high into the air. There were no survivors. A few minutes later the *Queen Mary* was enveloped in flames and sank in two pieces. Beatty, standing on the bridge of his flagship *Lion*, was amazed. 'There seems to be something wrong with our bloody ships', he remarked. Almost as he spoke a shell smashed into *Lion*'s own magazine. Although dying, Major Harvey (Royal Marines) managed to telephone an order to flood the area with water. His bravery saved Beatty's ship from a similar disaster.

Each minute brought the great fleets nearer. At 4.33 p.m. the look-out cruiser *Southampton* signalled Jellicoe, 'Have sighted enemy battle fleet'. Over 250 warships were speeding towards each other at a combined speed of 64 kilometres an hour. At 6.23 p.m. they came within range. Only then, as the whole horizon became alive with gun-flashes,

Germany's 'jailer'. The commander of the British Grand Fleet, Admiral John Jellicoe seen on his flagship 'Iron Duke'

did Scheer realise that he was almost surrounded by the British Grand Fleet. His only hope was to run. Fortunately, it was a misty evening, made denser by the smoke of gun-fire. As his battleships steamed round in huge arcs German gunners blew up the *Invincible*. Suddenly its silhouette was lit up by enormous flames. Twisted pieces of armour-plating whirled upwards. Then the tall mast collapsed and the ship broke in two. Of a crew of 1,062 only 6 survived.

Darkness came on to aid Scheer's attempts to escape. Meanwhile, Jellicoe was not kept well-informed by his cruiser captains. He had little idea of exactly where the enemy was situated. Even so he was too near for the Germans' liking. Desperately Scheer ordered his torpedo boats to launch suicide attacks against the Grand Fleet. Jellicoe was a cautious man. Although he was anxious to give battle he knew that the destruction of his fleet could mean Britain's defeat in the war. He turned away and took evasive action, leaving his destroyers and cruisers to fight a confused battle. Red gun-flashes, searchlight beams, the noise and the dreadful glare of burning ships continued all night. Both navies showed great bravery. Sixteen-year-old John Cornwall stood by his gun on HMS *Chester*, even when dying. German gun crews continued to fire as their ships sank.

Jellicoe placed his ships between the Germans and their home ports, hoping to destroy them next day. By dawn, however, it was clear that Scheer had passed through the Grand Fleet in the confusion. Afterwards each country claimed a victory. The German High Seas Fleet had inflicted far more damage than it received. Fourteen British ships, including 3 battleships, had been sunk and over 6,000 sailors were killed, whereas the German losses were 11 smaller ships and 2,500 men. On the other hand its result was clearly a British victory. The Kaiser's navy never attempted another voyage in force. Britain commanded the seas until hostilities ended, carrying soldiers and supplies and blockading Germany without interference. An American journalist summed up the Battle of Jutland well when he wrote, 'The German Fleet has assaulted its jailer but it is still in jail'.

Timeline

1914   Japan declares war on Germany (23 August).
       Turkey declares war on Britain, France and Russia (12 October).
       Battle of Coronel (1 November).
       Battle of the Falkland Islands (8 December).
1915   Second Battle of Ypres (20 April–24 May).
       Gallipoli expedition (25 April–20 December).
1916   Battle of Verdun (21 February–16 December).
       Battle of Jutland (31 May–1 June).
       Battle of the Somme (1 July–18 November).

Questions

1. 'After crawling out through the bleeding remnants of my comrades, and through the smoke and debris, wandering and running in the midst of the raging gunfire in search of refuge, I am now awaiting death at any moment.' (Letter found on dead German officer)

   'Mourn certainly for those who fell, but remember men moaning and weeping in an artillery barrage, men gibbering in a shell-shock ward, men drowning in the mud, men fixedly concentrating on holding their guts in their ripped bodies...' (From a book about the First World War by John Ellis, called *Eye-Deep in Hell*)

   Remembering what you have read about the First World War in chapters 8 and 9, what do these two extracts tell you about the kind of battles that the soldiers fought?

2. What was the exact purpose of the landings at Gallipoli in April 1915? How far were they successful?

3. Explain the importance of the British navy's work during the war. What was the significance of the Battle of Jutland in the struggle?

4. Write short paragraphs on each of the following:
   a) the German U-boat campaign   b) the Battle of Verdun
   c) the landings at Salonika   d) the Battle of the Somme

10

Revolution and Victory
The First World War (III)

Whereas on the Western Front too many soldiers were compressed into a comparatively small space, in the East there was too much front even for the large numbers involved. No permanent trench line was ever established. Instead the fighting swayed to and fro over immense distances. The Russians were ill-equipped by Western standards but they had three advantages. First, they were helped by the sheer size of the battlefield. As in the days when Napoleon invaded Russia, they could retreat until the German supply system was stretched too far. Second, the Russian army was easily the largest in the world at that time. No matter how terrible its losses it could usually replace them. Finally, there were the fearful winters which frequently stopped all fighting.

The Russian defeats at Tannenberg and the Masurian Lakes in 1914 (see Chapter 8) were followed by confused battles in which the Tsar's armies tried to encircle the Austrians and Germans and failed. Next year Germany mounted an offensive on the Eastern Front with all available men and weapons. The result was a massacre. Before a hurricane of shells and bullets a Russian army of nearly two million men was either killed, wounded or captured. Not even the Western Front had seen such losses. German soldiers grew tired of killing. One officer described the advance like this, 'Here and there lone grey figures jumped up and ran back weaponless in grey fur caps and fluttering, unbuttoned greatcoats, until there was not one remaining'. The Central Powers were left free to punish Serbia, assisted by Bulgaria who now joined the side she felt certain would win. Until then the gallant Serbs had held the Habsburg armies back, often inflicting severe defeats. Now they were attacked on two sides at once. Sarajevo was avenged in a dreadful way. Serbia's soldiers were either killed or driven into exile; her sick King, Peter, was carried from his country on a stretcher. Only old men, widows and orphans remained in a ruined and devastated countryside.

By this time Italy was fighting against Austria. France and Britain could offer her enemy territory if she fought for them. Germany and Austria-Hungary could promise very little. In April 1915 her government signed a secret **Treaty of London** with Britain, France and Russia, by which she was to receive the Trentino, South Tyrol, Istria, Trieste and some Dalmatian islands after the war (see map opposite). It seemed a good bargain until the actual campaign started. The Italian advance into Habsburg territory was barred by mountain ranges whose passes were well-defended. To attack meant fighting through thick snow, across ravines and up sheer cliff faces against carefully

The Italian Front

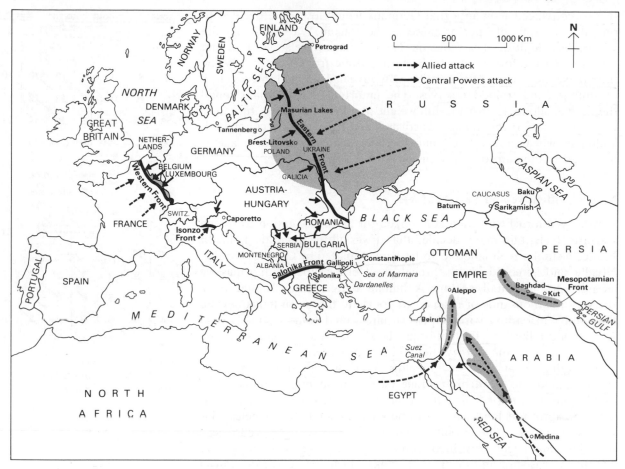

Main European battle fronts during the First World War

hidden machine-guns and artillery. The normal dangers of war were increased in such conditions. A slightly wounded man often fell to his death immediately; rocks splintered by shell-bursts made fearful wounds.

The Italians advanced bravely, often roped together or sliding on skis. Every time they were beaten back with heavy casualties. Few of them had been interested in the war anyway. These defeats caused thousands of troops to desert or surrender. On the Isonzo Front (see maps above and opposite), the Austrian army broke through and swung round behind the Italians. As the shattered Italian units fell back it seemed as though the enemy would break out of the mountains into the plains of northern Italy. So serious was the situation that Russia launched an offensive to ease the pressure and British troops had to be sent to help.

At first the Russians did as badly as ever. In heavy fighting they lost five times as many dead as the Germans. A few weeks later the Russian **General Brusilov** decided to attack on the Austrian sector in Galicia (see map above) without any of the usual artillery bombardments. To everyone's surprise his men broke through easily, taking 250,000 prisoners. This victory broke the spirit of the Austrian armies.

It also convinced Romania that Germany would lose. She decided to repeat her profitable performance in the Balkan Wars and join the victorious side at the last moment. The Germans were so worried that they rushed reinforcements to Eastern Europe from Verdun. By the time these men arrived the **Brusilov Offensive** had stopped through lack of supplies and trained reserves. The unfortunate Romanians found themselves alone against the full weight of a German army. In a matter of weeks their resistance was crushed and their country conquered. Valuable wheat and oil fell into German hands, but British agents managed to blow up the oil-wells.

Nivelle's offensive and Passchendaele

On the Western Front men still looked for an easy solution to trench warfare. In Britain many decided that it was all the generals' fault. In France a similar feeling led to Joffre being replaced by General Nivelle. Nivelle said he could smash through the German lines with a massive assault on one small sector. A human battering-ram would open the way for thousands of reserves to pour into the green fields beyond the mud and barbed wire. Open warfare would come again. Nivelle was a good talker. To the politicians he seemed like a magician whose wand would give the victory they so often promised.

Expecting an attack, the Germans suddenly retreated to new defences called the **Hindenburg Line** (see map on page 69). Nivelle's whole plan was tipped off balance; he had made careful preparations for the capture of land which was now undefended. Nevertheless, his first waves took some ground from the Germans. Then well-placed machine-guns began to thin the French ranks. Entire battalions were caught in cross-fire and destroyed. Tanks which crawled to the rescue were blown up by shells. Really the offensive was no better or worse than any other. But Nivelle had raised hopes too high. The magician had waved his wand but nothing had happened. Another battle had ended in the deaths of thousands of brave men. The survivors lost heart. A great number of soldiers mutinied and marched back to Paris demanding an end to the war. Some ran away and became robbers. Others stayed at their posts although they refused to advance. In this crisis Pétain took charge. Discipline was restored by ruthless methods. Over 23,000 men were punished. The Germans did not seem to know what was happening. Perhaps they had suffered too severely to take advantage of the mutiny. One German sent this message home: 'I send you greetings from my grave in the earth. We shall soon become mad in this awful artillery fire.' Another recorded: 'Hans is dead. Fritz is dead. Wilhelm is dead. There are many others. I am now quite alone in the company'!

Once again the British prepared to take the offensive. Early in the morning of 7 July 1917 German trenches at **Messines** were blown up by mines containing over half a million kilograms of explosives. As a tall cloud of smoke rose into the sky, the roar was heard as far away as London. German positions on the ridge ceased to exist. When Haig attacked on 31 July this area was occupied without difficulty. Else-

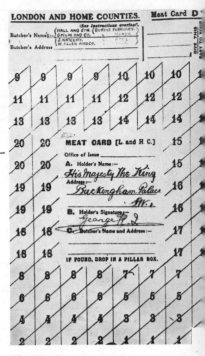

The King's ration card – everybody was rationed in Britain during the war

where the British were successful until their advance reached the old battlefield of **Ypres**. Here the extensive drainage system necessary to keep such low-lying land dry had been destroyed by shells. More bombardment and heavy rain churned the land into a sea of mud. Around the village of **Passchendaele** this slime swallowed guns and tanks, and drowned thousands of men. Like Verdun to the French, this battle became to the British the worst horror. 'Passchendaele is courage and sacrifice beyond understanding', wrote one survivor. 'Passchendaele is mud, sleet, ice, mud, noise, jagged steel, horror piled on reeking horror, men and animals torn to pieces...'.

There seemed no answer, no end to the slaughter. Even tanks proved less successful than expected. At the Somme they had been stuck in the mud. Some experts said this was because only a few had been used. So at Cambrai, in November 1917, 381 of these ugly monsters attacked across firm ground without warning. At first a hole 7 kilometres wide was punched in the German line. Later the weary infantrymen could not follow them swiftly enough. Gradually the machines suffered engine failures or were destroyed by shell-fire. A German army corps arrived unexpectedly by train and counter-attacked. Within days the Front was restored to its original position.

Russian revolutions

Although her armies were still unbeaten, Germany's failure to master the Grand Fleet meant a blockade which was slowly starving her people. Early in 1917 the Kaiser's government decided to gamble on a counter-blockade which would starve the British into surrender quickly. Their U-boats were ordered to sink all ships on sight. This deadly scheme nearly succeeded. In April, for example, 914,400 tonnes of British shipping were sunk. Unfortunately for Germany, so many US ships were destroyed that the **USA declared war on Germany, 1 April 1917**. The American fleet immediately swung into action against U-boats, helping the British convoy their merchantmen safely across the Atlantic. Worse still, from the German point of view, the American army prepared to train the millions of men who would make victory certain for the Allies. The Kaiser and his generals realised that their only hope was to win a smashing victory in the West before this 'blood transfusion' arrived.

US President Wilson's declaration of war came just as events in Tsarist Russia were leading to revolution. Two years of unbelievable slaughter had left the country very weak. Russia's industries had been strained to cope with a modern war. Her people were tired of the endless killing. The promises made after the 1905 Revolution (see page 42) had not been kept. Tsar Nicholas II had dissolved the Duma (parliament) established at that time and returned to ruling as a dictator. Real power was in the hands of himself and the Tsarina, his wife, a lady who relied upon the advice of a bogus 'holy man', **Gregori Rasputin**. Under these circumstances discontent grew rapidly. In 1916 a group of patriotic noblemen murdered Rasputin because of his evil influence on the Tsarina. That winter riots turned into revolution.

Gregori Rasputin – bogus 'holy man' of Russia

It all began simply enough when workers gathered in Petrograd (formerly St Petersburg, now Leningrad) to demonstrate against a bread shortage. This shortage was caused by peasants refusing to sell grain in exchange for almost worthless paper money. At first nobody took this demonstration very seriously. Bolshevik (Communist) agitators like Vladimir Ilyich Lenin and Gregory Zinoviev, who had criticised the government, had been driven abroad. None of the moderate political leaders were likely to start a rebellion. In any case there seemed plenty of soldiers available to protect the Tsar's government. The Tsarina, in particular, was not worried. 'This is a hooligan movement,' she wrote, 'young people run and shout that there is no bread simply to create excitement.' Rarely have words been so wrong. Most Russian factories were big; sometimes as many as a thousand men worked under one roof. It was easy to organise such large groups for serious action. Throughout the bitter winter of 1916–17, more and more workers went on strike, more and more mobs shouted in the snowy streets. And the soldiers sent to disperse these crowds frequently did nothing. Some even joined the troublemakers.

Deposed Emperor, Tsar Nicholas II of Russia

Like ripples on a pool, this disorder gradually spread throughout European Russia. At the front troops were still loyal but no sooner were they home on leave than they joined the agitators. Tsar Nicholas, meanwhile, seemed unaware of the danger. As Alexander Kerensky and other moderate politicians struggled to control the unexpected rising, as the workers formed councils called **Soviets**, he was sad because there was no time to play cards! When the Tsar did decide to crush the revolts his train was stopped on its way to Petrograd by armed rebels. On 15 March 1917 he was forced to abdicate (resign) the throne of Russia. This rising is known as the March Revolution because it took place in March.

A new government, led by Kerensky, decided to continue the war. Kerensky was very popular with the front line soldiers. Indeed, it was due to their influence that he had gained power. Imagining that greater freedom and the end of Tsarism would inspire them to win victories, he ordered another offensive. At first the Russians carried all before them. Then, as the bravest were killed, those following began to desert. Many were peasants who knew that under the new government the large estates were being taken from the landowners. They were anxious to return home and get some of the land. Soon the roads leading from the front were filled with deserters who marched along quite openly. In some cases complete armies returned to Russia. Officers who tried to stop them were shot. It was obvious the Russian people had finished with the war.

This was the Bolshevik Party's opportunity. Their leader, **Vladimir Ilyich Lenin**, was a Communist. To him and his supporters the war was just a useless slaughter about matters which did not concern the ordinary man. The real war, in their opinion, was between factory owners and workers, landowners and peasants. Russia must be given peace so that this other 'class war' could be won. Lenin believed that German, British and French workers would follow Russia's example, overthrow their governments and make peace. Because of these views he had

Alexander Kerensky. He ruled Russia for a few months in 1917 before the Bolsheviks took over

been driven into exile in Switzerland by the Tsar. Because of them the Germans cunningly allowed him to cross their territory and re-enter Russia at the time of the March Revolution. It was a wise move from their point of view. Lenin was to prove far more useful to the Germans on the Russian front than all their guns, shells and soldiers.

Kerensky was not an extremist. During his brief rule he tried to crush the powerful Bolshevik group in Petrograd and he forced Lenin to flee abroad again. But Kerensky had not started the Revolution in the first place. Thousands of workers and soldiers had done that. The failure of the July offensive and the collapse of the army deprived him of his only support. After another defeat the people were prepared for the peace Lenin promised them. Almost as important was the fact that the Bolshevik leader offered the peasants their land through nationalisation – something Kerensky's government had not done. Lenin returned secretly to Petrograd from Finland and on 7 November 1917 his small group seized power. Although it happened in November this second, Communist, rising of 1917 is called the **October Revolution**. This is because until it occurred Russia had used the Julian Calendar which was then thirteen days behind the Gregorian one followed by the rest of the Christian world.

From the start Lenin meant to set up a one-party state. At an election (the only free one ever held in Russian history) the Bolshevik Party won only 168 seats out of a total of 703. When this assembly met it was broken up by Bolshevik soldiers. Lenin now ordered a truce whilst his representatives went to discuss terms with the Germans. At **Brest-Litovsk**, Poland (see map on page 79), the aristocratic German generals sat down to bargain with a murderer just out of jail, two ordinary servicemen and a peasant who could not read. This strange scene illustrated the most important change caused by the First World War. Out of the ruins of Tsarist tyranny there arose a Communist dictatorship. In March 1918 a peace treaty was signed. The German terms were very harsh. Russia lost all the European lands she had conquered since the seventeenth century, including Poland and the Ukraine, but Lenin was free to consolidate his power. The Allies had already suffered a shattering defeat in October 1917 when the Italian armies had been completely destroyed at **Caporetto** (see map on page 78). Now they would have to fight the large German forces no longer needed on the Eastern Front.

Arabian campaigns, 1915–18

The Russian Empire had gone. The Habsburg Empire was falling apart. A third empire, the Ottoman, was being overrun. Initially the Turks had been successful. A British expedition which attempted to occupy Mesopotamia was surrounded and forced to surrender at **Kut-el-Amara** (April 1916). A year later massive British reinforcements and a new general, Edmund Allenby, altered the situation entirely. Turkish factories were unable to make enough ammunition and weapons; Turkish troops were poorly equipped and outnumbered. At the Battle of Beersheba (Palestine), 36,000 Turks faced 100,000 British

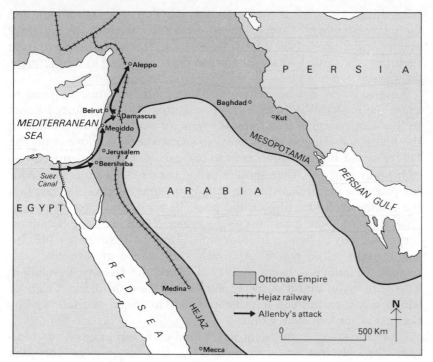

and Australian soldiers. Using cavalry, Allenby swung round behind
the enemy defences, forcing them to retreat. On 9 December 1917 he
was able to enter **Jerusalem**, walking humbly through the gates like a
pilgrim. Meanwhile, an Arab revolt had broken out inside the Ottoman Empire, led by **Colonel T.E. Lawrence** and Emir Feisal. Lawrence
was a scholar who spoke Arabic, translated Homer's stories and wrote
books about his experiences. Lawrence of Arabia, as he became
known, loved the desert and thought the Arab way of life romantic.
He was also a man of action, a soldier and an expert camel rider. Even
the tough tribesmen were impressed by his strength and endurance as
he led them on daring raids against Turkish barracks, ports and railways. In particular his men repeatedly blew up sections of the Hejaz
railway, the Turks' only supply route across the desert.

When Allenby started his final offensive (September 1918) he was
assisted by Feisal's Arab 'underground' movement, and also by the
newly formed Royal Air Force (RAF) which carried out many bombing raids. This time he did not attempt an encircling movement. Instead his men struck suddenly at the enemy's strongest point, cutting it
to pieces with a series of bayonet charges. Then Australian cavalry
swept through the gap and seized the narrow pass near the ancient
fortress of **Megiddo** (see map above). It was a battle in the old style,
with lancers charging to the sound of bugles. Success followed success.
Damascus fell on 1 October, Beirut a week later, and Aleppo by the
end of the month. On all fronts the Turks were defeated. At 9.40 p.m.
on 30 October 1918 Ottoman delegates signed an armistice aboard the
British warship *Agamemnon* lying off Lemnos island in the Mediterranean. A war which had been sparked off by the arrival of two German
battleships ended on a British one.

Haig's order to his troops during the final German attacks of the war, 1918

SPECIAL ORDER OF THE DAY
By FIELD-MARSHAL SIR DOUGLAS HAIG
K.T., G.C.B., G.C.V.O., K.C.I.E
Commander-in-Chief, British Armies in France.

To ALL RANKS OF THE BRITISH ARMY IN FRANCE AND FLANDERS.

Three weeks ago to-day the enemy began his terrific attacks against us on a fifty-mile front. His objects are to separate us from the French, to take the Channel Ports and destroy the British Army.

In spite of throwing already 106 Divisions into the battle and enduring the most reckless sacrifice of human life, he has as yet made little progress towards his goals.

We owe this to the determined fighting and self-sacrifice of our troops. Words fail me to express the admiration which I feel for the splendid resistance offered by all ranks of our Army under the most trying circumstances.

Many amongst us now are tired. To those I would say that Victory will belong to the side which holds out the longest. The French Army is moving rapidly and in great force to our support.

There is no other course open to us but to fight it out. Every position must be held to the last man: there must be no retirement. With our backs to the wall and believing in the justice of our cause each one of us must fight on to the end. The safety of our homes and the Freedom of mankind alike depend upon the conduct of each one of us at this critical moment.

General Headquarters,
Thursday, April 11th, 1918.

Commander-in-Chief,
British Armies in France.

Final battles

For three and a half years, ever since their retreat from the Marne, the Germans had defended on two fronts. Only at Verdun had they attacked. In the spring of 1918 they changed their tactics. With Russia out of the war and the USA in, Germany's leaders realised that the crisis had come. In the long run they could not hope to defeat the Americans. Food supplies were running short, Allied bombing raids were becoming frequent, unrestricted submarine warfare had failed. Austria-Hungary and Turkey were near collapse. The only hope seemed to be a quick devastating blow which would defeat Britain and France before the US army arrived in force. All through the winter of 1917–18 the troop trains rumbled across Germany from Russia. Another Schlieffen-like gamble was about to take place.

On 21 March 1918 a mighty German offensive developed from the Somme to Cambrai. At dawn, helped by thick fog, smoke and gas, massed German battalions achieved what had been thought impossible. They drove through, first, the advance machine-gun posts, then the Allied line itself. The French prepared to fall back on Paris; the British on the Channel Ports. It looked as though the two Allies would be divided for the first time since 1914. Wisely, Marshal Ferdinand Foch, the newly appointed Supreme Commander of the Franco-British armies, decided to retreat as far as possible without losing contact and then to counter-attack when the German thrust slowed. These were Joffre's tactics at the Marne and they now proved equally successful. A large reserve army was assembled near **Amiens** (see map on page 69)

German wounded after the Battle of Amiens, 1918

as many German soldiers stopped advancing and spent their time raiding houses. This was no longer the wonderfully disciplined force which
had crossed into Belgium in 1914.

Worried by this, the German High Command switched its point of
attack. Two more offensives, one at **Hazebrouck** in April and one on
the **Aisne** in May, smashed through the British defences. The second
assault came within 90 kilometres of Paris. But again the troops were
exhausted by their swift advance, again the supplies failed to keep up,
again soldiers became undisciplined. On 8 August Foch decided the
time was ripe for his counter-attack. Supported by nearly 500 tanks,
French, British and American units began an onslaught which continued until the Germans surrendered. Like the Russian soldier, the
ordinary German had suffered enough. He had made the supreme
effort and it had failed. He still fought well but he fell back steadily,
first over the ground conquered in the spring, then out of the Hindenburg Line altogether. By 26 September the Allies were fighting the last
campaign of the war.

Such efforts were not confined to the Western Front. Greece had at
last declared war and the army in Salonika went into battle so swiftly
that Bulgaria was knocked out in two weeks. On the River **Piave** in
Italy (see map on page 78) British and Italian troops broke up the last
Habsburg army. In France itself losses on each side were still about
equal but the German casualties could not be replaced. Desperately,
the German government ordered the High Seas Fleet to leave port and
fight. Two years of inactivity in port had ruined the fine fighting spirit
so obvious at Jutland (see page 74). Many sailors mutinied and their
example was copied all over Germany. On 9 November Kaiser William

*A defeated army. German
prisoners, August 1918*

abdicated and fled to Holland. Austria-Hungary had already collapsed into chaos and confusion with many of the separate nationalities proclaiming their independence. In Vienna, on 11 November 1918, the last Habsburg Emperor, Charles, wrote his abdication in pencil on a scrap of paper. Nobody was interested. His power had disappeared weeks before.

On the same day, in a railway carriage near **Compiègne (France)** the new German republican government agreed to an armistice. Fighting was to cease at 11 a.m. All over Europe the guns fell silent. A war which had cost the lives of 2,290,000 Turks, 3,000,000 Russians, 1,800,000 Germans, 1,300,000 French, 1,200,000 Austrians, 950,000 British, 460,000 Italians and 116,000 Americans, was over.

11,116,000 → total amount.

Timeline

1915   Serbia overrun. Italy enters war (Treaty of London).

1916   Brusilov Offensive. Romania declares war on Germany and is conquered. Italians defeated on the Isonzo.

1917   Failure of French offensive. French army mutiny. Third Battle of Ypres (Passchendaele). Russian (March) Revolution. USA declares war on Germany (April) following unrestricted submarine warfare. Russian (October) Revolution.

1918   Russia leaves war (Treaty of Brest-Litovsk). German offensive (March–July). Allied counter-attack (Battle of Amiens). Turks defeated by Allenby in Middle East. War ends (November).

Questions

1. Read Field-Marshal Douglas Haig's 'Special Order of the Day' on page 85.
   a) Why had the Germans begun 'terrific attacks' at this particular stage of the war?
   b) How successful were these attacks?
   c) Why is this document known as the 'backs to the wall' order?
   d) Some fighting soldiers were disheartened by this Order because they did not realise how serious the situation had become. Do you think the issuing of this Order was a good idea at this time?

2. a) Describe the events in Russia which led to (i) the March Revolution and (ii) the October Revolution of 1917?
   b) What part did Lenin play in these events?

3. 'In 1902 in *What is to be done?* Lenin had written "Give us an organisation of revolutionaries, and we shall overturn the whole of Russia."' (Merle Fainsod)

   Was the existence of 'an organisation of revolutionaries' the only reason for Lenin's success in seizing power in November 1917?

4. Write short paragraphs on each of the following:
   a) the Treaty of London, 1915   b) Cambrai
   c) Lawrence of Arabia   d) the US declaration of war, 1917

11

Woodrow Wilson's Peace
The Versailles Treaty

Exactly five years after the murder at Sarajevo delegates at Versailles, near Paris, met to sign the peace treaty in that same Hall of Mirrors where the German Empire had been proclaimed forty-eight years before (see Chapter 1). This time there were no Germans present, although the room was packed with nearly 2,000 men and women. At a central table sat Georges Clemenceau, the French Prime Minister, together with President Woodrow Wilson of the USA and David Lloyd George, Britain's Prime Minister. Outside, on the stairs once climbed by Bismarck, the tallest men of the French Republican Guard, magnificent in blue uniforms, steel breastplates and plumed helmets, stood with drawn sabres at the salute. This time their army had won.

At three o'clock Clemenceau signalled for silence. The chattering, the rustling of papers, the movements and coughing, died away. 'Bring in the Germans', snapped the old Frenchman. There was a sharp clash as each soldier replaced his sword in its scabbard. In the silence which followed all eyes turned towards the doorway. Through it came, not a general or an admiral, not one of the great men who had led Germany in war, but two civilians, one a violin player, the other an ex-private soldier. Both looked pale and uncomfortable as their footsteps echoed across some parquet flooring and died away on thick carpet. Quickly they seated themselves at the table on which lay the treaty document.

Clemenceau rose and announced in a clear voice, 'We are in complete agreement. I have the honour to ask messieurs the German Plenipotentiaries to sign.' The Germans rose to their feet, bowed, and scratched their names on a document which blamed Germany for the war. Cine cameras whirred quietly as they recorded the historic moment, people craned their necks to see the Allied leaders sign. Outside a salute of guns was fired, causing pigeons to whirl excitedly into the sky. Crowds could be heard cheering far away across the park. It was a terrible moment for Germany.

German signatures on the Versailles Treaty

Wilson's Fourteen Points

Only one of the agreements which made up the Paris Peace Settlement, the **Versailles Treaty** concerning Germany, had been signed that day. Three others were sealed during 1919, each named after a Paris suburb: Saint Germain with Austria; Trianon with Hungary and Neuilly with Bulgaria. In all of them the more important matters were decided by Woodrow Wilson, David Lloyd George and Georges Clemenceau. Neither Russia, Germany, Austria nor Turkey were consulted. Even Italy, an Allied country, was generally ignored.

Peace-makers gather at Versailles near Paris, 1919

The story behind the Versailles peace began in November 1917 when Lenin appealed for an end to the fighting. Let us have no demands for compensation, no stealing of land from another country, he proclaimed. Let us have a Europe in which all races can govern themselves. His message had no effect. Soon afterwards the Germans made a peace at Brest-Litovsk which confiscated large tracts of Russian territory (see page 83). They followed this with Western offensives aimed at winning the war quickly. The Allies also took no notice. They were furious that Russia had surrendered and afraid in case a Bolshevik-type revolution broke out in their own countries.

In the USA, however, President Wilson decided to show the world that other people besides the Bolsheviks wanted a fair peace. One Saturday morning he sat down in his White House office in Washington and typed out fourteen rules which he thought should guide future

treaty-makers. These became famous as **Wilson's Fourteen Points.**
Like Lenin's proposals they were ignored by Germany and Austria-
Hungary. After all, in the spring of 1918, it was not certain that they
would lose! Late in October, when faced with complete defeat, they
hurriedly accepted Wilson's Points because these seemed to offer better terms than France and Britain were likely to give. So it came about
that fair conditions offered originally to a powerful opponent were
brought forward as a basis for peace with an utterly defeated one.

When the Conference delegates first assembled in January 1919,
Raymond Poincaré, President of France, said to them: 'We are here to
repair the evil that it [the war] has done, and to prevent a recurrence
of it. You hold in your hands the future of the world.' Unfortunately,
he spoke to men who wanted to punish Germany more than they
wished to found a new world. Such feelings were natural in the circumstances. Everywhere German soldiers had fought on other people's land. The French, in particular, were determined to see that Germany was left too weak to attack again. An American visitor to Paris
wrote, 'It is impossible to comprehend the extraordinary obsession felt
in this country lest Germany within the next few years repeat the
action which she took in 1914.' It might have been difficult for an
American to understand. It was not hard for the French, nor for their
leader, Clemenceau.

*'We are here to repair the evil
the war has done'. Three
peace-makers, Georges
Clemenceau (France),
Woodrow Wilson (USA), Lloyd
George (Britain)*

To a certain extent Clemenceau was supported by the British. Lloyd George had just won a general election in a bitter Britain still mourning her million dead. He had promised that he would make Germany pay. Other politicians, although not so frightened of Germany, were anxious to gain more territory. The Poles had at last freed themselves from German and Russian rule. They wished to reoccupy land owned by Poland in the eighteenth century. The Czechs and Yugoslavs were busy forming states out of the Habsburg Empire. They were likely to quarrel over frontier lines. The Italian Prime Minister, Vittorio Emmanuele Orlando, arrived determined to get everything promised in the secret Treaty of London (see page 78).

Into this revengeful and greedy atmosphere came Woodrow Wilson with his Fourteen Points. With Europe exhausted, the USA was the most powerful nation in the world. Whether the British, French, Czechs, Poles or Italians liked it or not, they had to listen to the American leader. Yet the USA had suffered less than any other. Wilson himself was not interested in vengeance or more territory. Rather, he was an idealist who believed this was his opportunity to make a better world. Even at home he had had little political experience. Before becoming President in 1913 he had been a lawyer, an historian and Head of Princeton University. Of foreign affairs he knew little. He did not, for example, fully understand the very complicated problem of the Balkans and Eastern Europe. Finally, the cheering crowds he met convinced him that the ordinary man in the street was on his side. 'I had been listening to the heart of the world which comes to me with a very authentic throb', he remarked. Actually Europeans were often as greedy and selfish as their leaders.

More important than these failings was the fact that Wilson did not fully represent the government of the USA. Just before he sailed his Democratic Party had lost control of the Senate. As he crossed the Atlantic a political opponent, Theodore Roosevelt, warned Europe, 'Our allies and our enemies and Mr Wilson himself should all understand that Mr Wilson has no authority to speak for the American people at this time'. Very few Europeans understood this. Wilson was looked upon as the man who spoke for his country just as Clemenceau represented France and Lloyd George, Britain. It was to become a tragic misunderstanding.

Wilson was a good man and his Points represented noble ideals. He wanted no more secret treaties such as had helped to cause the war, no trade restrictions between countries, complete disarmament and freedom of the seas for all ships. He wished Russia to be free to choose her form of government, Belgium to be evacuated by foreign troops, Alsace and Lorraine to be returned to France. His allies did not always agree, and the Fourteen Points were disputed from the start. Britain objected to freedom of the seas so this was dropped. Only the defeated nations were disarmed, not the victorious ones. Trade barriers actually increased as the new nations erected frontiers. Russia was not left free to choose her government. She was invaded by British and other troops who helped in a civil war against the Bolsheviks (see Chapter 13). Italy demanded the land promised her by a secret treaty.

Even the Conference itself soon turned into private meetings between three men. On all sides Wilson found his Points ignored or altered. He became very frustrated.

Self-determination

Wilson believed that the frontiers of Europe should be redrawn so that all races ruled themselves. This right to choose one's own government he called **self-determination.** In a crude way this had begun to happen because nine new states had already been created out of the old empires (see map opposite). Four countries: Czechoslovakia, Yugoslavia, Austria and Hungary, had been carved from the Habsburg lands. Five others: Poland, Finland, Estonia, Latvia and Lithuania, had emerged from Russia and Germany. Unfortunately, there were practical difficulties in the way of self-determination. First, it was hard to say exactly what indicated a separate race or nation. The only possible guide was the language they spoke. This was the test chosen by Wilson but it was not a good one since many subject peoples used the tongue of their conquerors. Second, in many parts of Europe, particularly the Balkans, races were too mixed up to be divided without large-scale movements of population. Third, real countries cannot be created by drawing lines between racial groups. A country needs industries and railways, ports and agricultural land, frontiers which are protected by seas, rivers or mountains. Had Czechoslovakia not kept its 3,000,000 Germans she would have lost much industry. As it was, the Czech railway system, designed for the Habsburg Empire, now ran across the infant state in the most awkward directions.

For these reasons the post-war map of Europe was a strange patchwork which was often unfair to minorities. Yugoslavia, supposed to consist of Serbs and Croats, actually contained Slovenes, Bosnian Muslims, Magyars, Germans, Albanians, Romanians and Macedonians. Czechoslovakia, apparently the country of the Czechs and Slovaks, had Germans, Russians, Magyars, Poles and Jews as well. A worse example was Poland. Point thirteen had suggested that Poland, divided in the eighteenth century between Prussia, Russia and Austria, should be restored to independence. The idea seemed fair. There is no doubt that the Poles had been badly treated. However, their eighteenth-century lands had really been an empire comprising conquered peoples. Consequently only about two-thirds of the new Poland was inhabited by Poles. Furthermore its Russian border, the **Curzon Line** (see map opposite), was drawn without consulting Russia at all. And because Wilson believed Poland should have an outlet to the sea, a 'corridor' of land (the 'Polish Corridor') was driven across East Prussian territory, dividing it from the rest of Germany. The port at the end of it, **Danzig**, was made a free city under international, not Polish, control. The whole arrangement was very unsatisfactory. The Poles themselves did not help matters when they crossed the Curzon Line (1921) and seized more Russian land.

In two cases, self-determination was ignored altogether. First, the German-speaking population of Austria contained many who wanted

A restored and independent Poland showing the Curzon Line and the area taken by Poland in 1921

— Curzon Line

▦ Area gained by Poland in 1921 (Treaty of Riga)

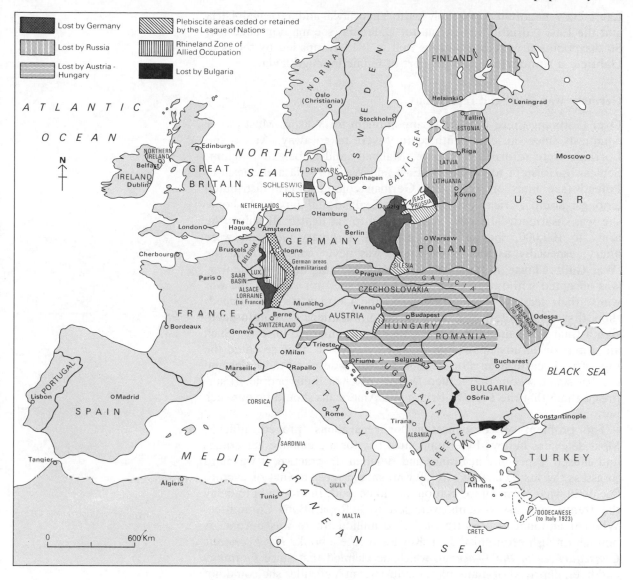

Lost by Germany		Plebiscite areas ceded or retained by the League of Nations		
Lost by Russia		Rhineland Zone of Allied Occupation		
Lost by Austria - Hungary		Lost by Bulgaria		

Europe after the First World War, 1920

union (**Anschluss**) with Germany. France was horrified at a suggestion which would make the German population larger than in 1914. Austria remained independent but a minority of Austrians were left with a grievance. Second, when Orlando, Italy's Prime Minister, demanded the rewards guaranteed by the Treaty of London, Wilson objected. He disliked the fact that these promises had been made in a secret agreement. He also thought Yugoslavia had a better claim to some of the lands. No other matter caused quite so much argument at the Conference. In the end Wilson appealed directly to the Italian people. To his surprise the Italians were furious at losing their due. To them it seemed disgraceful that their claims as an ally were being passed over in favour of Yugoslavia. The American President became the most unpopular man in Italy. His portraits were torn down by angry mobs or decorated with German helmets. The matter was left undecided.

Later Italy negotiated privately with Yugoslavia and received Istria
and the East Adriatic islands but not Dalmatia (see map on page 78).
So disappointed were her patriots that in 1919 groups led by the poet
Gabriele d'Annunzio seized the port of Fiume in Yugoslavia.

German 'war guilt' and reparations

Over Germany there was less disappointment for Wilson. Most of her
conquests since the eighteenth century were taken away. Alsace and
Lorraine were returned to France, Malmédy and Eupen to Belgium,
Schleswig-Holstein to Denmark, East and West Prussia and Silesia to
Poland (see map on page 93). German colonies were distributed
amongst South Africa, Australia, New Zealand and Japan. At home
she was disarmed. The navy was reduced to six light battleships; the
army to 100,000; the air force destroyed. Ordinary Germans were
angry, especially as their government was never consulted and the
'War Guilt' Clause in the Versailles Treaty, blaming them for the war,
was accepted without argument. To be punished for starting the war
whilst their leaders went free amazed the German people. Indeed,
their first representative, Count Brockdorff-Rantzau, had refused to
sign a treaty containing such a statement and remarked bitterly, 'Such
an admission on my lips would be a lie'. Above all, they resented the
loss of their eastern territories. Most Germans despised the Poles and
the Russians, whom they called *Dungervölker* or dung people. It surprised them that the French, British and Americans should favour such
nations.

The problem of compensation, or **reparations**, proved difficult.
Most delegates believed Germans must pay for the damage her armies
had caused, especially in France and Belgium. In practice, it was hard
to assess the losses exactly, to say who should receive what or even to
decide in what form compensation should be paid. In order not to delay
the treaty final assessments were left to a Reparations Committee.
When it announced a figure of £6,600 million, there was uproar. A
famous English economist, J.M. Keynes, wrote a book, *The Economic
Consequences of the Peace*, in which he claimed that since Germany
had been deprived of many of her industries at Versailles she could not
afford such vast repayments. His book became very popular. It was
translated into eleven languages and sold 140,000 copies. Since that
time Keynes's opinion has been contradicted by experts who believe
that Germany could have paid had she been forced to do so. They
have pointed out, for example, that Hitler's Germany spent three
times as much each year as the annual sum demanded in 1919. Nevertheless, whether right or wrong, most people agreed with Keynes at
the time. His book was praised by those who thought the whole Settlement a bad one.

Wilson's Fourteenth Point suggested a **League of Nations**. Really it
should have been number one because to him it was the most important. It proposed that each nation send representatives to a permanent
world assembly which could settle disputes between countries and alter
the Settlement if necessary. Allied leaders welcomed the idea. The

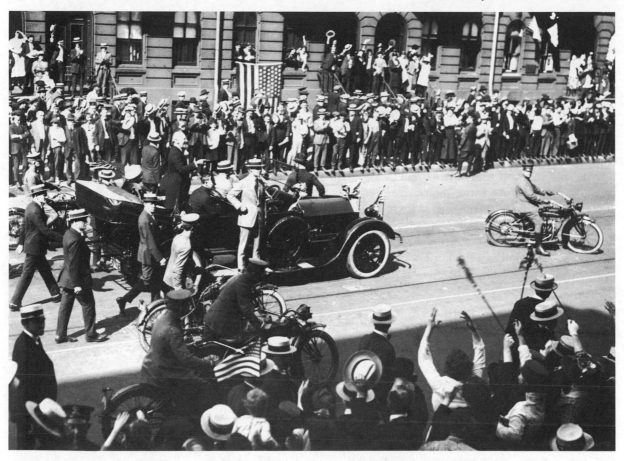

President Wilson returns to the USA, hoping to persuade his countrymen to join the League of Nations

League was established with headquarters at Geneva (Switzerland). Wilson was very pleased and returned home determined to persuade the American people to join. Providing this happened weaknesses in the peace treaties would not matter. The Settlement could be improved as the years passed. European peace would be guaranteed by the USA and Britain.

It was here that all Wilson's Paris disappointments faded away beside the tragedy awaiting him. Theodore Roosevelt's warning proved true. The average American voter, the average American politician, had no desire to be mixed up in European affairs. Irish Americans, in particular, disliked a treaty which left Ireland as part of the British Empire (see Chapter 15). The United States Congress refused either to accept the Settlement or to join the League. Wilson travelled 13,000 kilometres round the USA, making speech after speech, to try to change people's minds. If they did not join the League, he prophesied, 'I can predict with absolute certainty that within another generation there will be another world war'. He was not believed. Just as the Italian people had rejected his appeals, so now his own countrymen did the same. Tired and miserable, he suffered a stroke which left him paralysed for the rest of his life. The American people turned their backs upon Europe.

The rejection of the League and the Settlement was more than a personal tragedy for Wilson. Its effects were disastrous for the whole world. None of the decisions taken at the Peace Conference were likely to last long unless backed by the USA and Britain. With the USA out, Britain lost interest in European affairs and continued to disarm. France was left to face Germany alone. Before 1914 Imperial Germany had been encircled by three great powers: Austria-Hungary, Russia and France (see map on page 8). Now she faced only a weakened France, a Russia torn by civil war, and a number of small states. Being bitter about the Versailles Treaty, it was only a matter of time before her people realised their own strength and defied at least some of the peace terms. Before long, aggressive Germans were demanding their 1914 frontiers back. And one at least was claiming that even this line was not enough. In 1924 he wrote: 'State boundaries are made by man and changed by man ... Germany will either be a world power or there will be no Germany.' His name was Adolf Hitler.

Timeline

1917   Lenin appeals for peace.
1918   Woodrow Wilson announces Fourteen Points.
1919   Paris Peace Settlement (Treaties of Versailles, Saint Germain, Neuilly and Trianon).
1920   USA rejects Paris Peace Settlement and League of Nations.

Questions

1. 'Wilson was a good man and his Points represented noble ideals.'
   a) In what ways did the Fourteen Points represent 'noble ideals'?
   b) How successful was President Wilson in getting his Points accepted by the other powers represented at Versailles?
   c) Which Point did Wilson regard as the most important and why?

2. a) Name the Allied leaders and their countries who were at the Paris Peace Conference in 1919.
   b) What were the reasons which made it unlikely that the Allied leaders, apart from President Wilson, would treat Germany leniently or make a lasting peace?
   c) What were the main provisions of the Treaty of Versailles?

3. Write short paragraphs on each of the following:
   a) Reparations
   b) Self-determination
   c) *Anschluss*
   d) the Polish Corridor

12
Greek, Turk, Jew and Arab
The Middle East 1918–1938

As a result of the First World War Turkey had been deprived of North Africa, Syria, Iraq (Mesopotamia), Arabia and the Dardanelles. The area south of Anatolia was divided between the British and the French (see map below). To lose such a large, rebellious Empire might not have been a bad thing. Unfortunately, it soon became obvious that the Turkish homeland (Asia Minor, or Anatolia) was also threatened. During the war different governments had been promised not only parts of the old Empire but also portions of Turkey. The peace terms increased the danger because they allowed an Allied country to occupy any part of Turkey should she feel her safety threatened. Here was an open invitation to invasion. The new Sultan, Mohammed VI, felt helpless. British warships lay in Constantinople harbour; British soldiers surrounded him. His only hope was to make friends with his ex-enemies.

The Middle East after the First World War

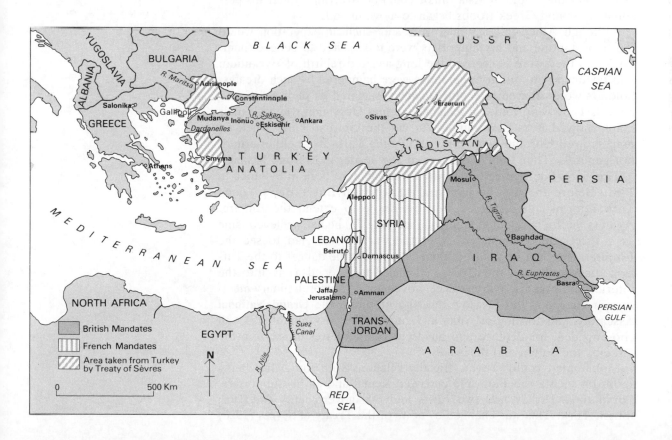

Greek invasion of Turkey

Although British, French and Italians seemed interested in Turkish territory, the real danger to Asia Minor came from the Greeks. Most of modern Turkey had been Greek until the Turks finally overran their Byzantine Empire and captured Constantinople in May 1453. Few Greeks had ever accepted this. Most dreamed of returning and conquering 'their' land. Legends and customs kept this hope alive through the centuries. Constantinople, not Athens, was referred to as 'The City'. Tuesday, the day Constantinople had fallen, was an unlucky day for all Greeks. Within the walls of St Sophia church in Constantinople, so they said, sat a Greek priest waiting to finish the service interrupted on that sad day. The large number of Greeks still living in Turkey were regarded as the advance-guard of this reconquest.

Greece's famous Prime Minister, Eleutherios Venizelos, shared these feelings, but he was realistic. He would have liked to restore the Greek Empire in Asia Minor but he did not believe his country had the resources to do so. Nevertheless, both President Wilson and Lloyd George encouraged a limited Greek occupation of Turkish territory. Accordingly, Venizelos used the excuse given in the peace terms and sent Greek soldiers to Smyrna (see map on page 97) in May 1919. This might not have mattered; Smyrna was very much a Greek city. But this was not all. King Constantine of Greece, unlike Venizelos, believed that the whole of Asia Minor could be overrun. Under his personal command Greek troops began to move inland.

Although Allied military men were sure such an expedition would fail, Constantine and his supporters were too excited to believe them. So far as they were concerned the long-awaited rebirth of Byzantium had begun. Even military operations were hampered by such dreams. Soldiers were ordered to capture towns designated by their old Greek names. They were told, for example, to find Dorylaion when all their maps showed it as Eskisehir, or 'to cut the Gordian knot' when no map showed Gordium any more. At first the Turks had neither armies nor generals. Then they found a great new leader in **Mustafa Kemal**.

This fierce, determined man was a Macedonian, born in Salonika in 1881. Before the war he had sympathised with Enver Bey's Young Turk reforms but disagreed with his desire to extend the Empire. Against the Italians and at Gallipoli (see page 73) he had achieved fame as a successful commander. After the war he was glad to see the Empire gone. Yet he realised sooner than most the danger to the Turkish 'heartland'. As the Greeks advanced he slipped away into the interior and organised a resistance movement. After preliminary meetings at Erzerum and Sivas, a rebel government, the **Grand National Assembly**, was formed at Ankara (January 1920). Its capital was well chosen, ideal for defence and hundreds of kilometres away from the Greeks, the Sultan and the Allies.

Mohammed could see his friendly relations with the Allies being spoilt by such a rebellion. He outlawed Kemal and all his supporters. For a time Turkey had two rulers and two governments and Turk fought Turk. This was changed by news of the **Treaty of Sèvres** (1920)

Atatürk (Mustafa Kemal), ruler of the new Turkey, reviewing some of his troops, September 1922

by which the victorious powers virtually divided Turkey between Kurdistan, Greece, Italy and France. Sèvres is a French town famous for its delicate china. Now its treaty was to prove as easily broken. The decision taken there was too much for most Turks. They saw they must either join Kemal or cease to exist as a nation. Consequently they deserted the Sultan in large numbers and his only army was defeated by Kemal's best general, Ismet, at **Inönü** (January 1921). This setback caused the Allies to wonder whether they had done the right thing at Sèvres. Hastily they offered Kemal and his Nationalists better terms. When these were rejected they washed their hands of the whole affair and proclaimed their neutrality. The Turkish 'bull' had broken the treaty made in a china shop! Greek and Turk were left to fight it out alone.

Meanwhile, Sèvres or no Sèvres, the Greeks continued to advance, marching through a lonely land of burnt villages and ruined harvests. By June 1921 they had almost encircled Ismet's army, so Kemal ordered a further retreat of 161 kilometres to the river Sakarya. The National Assembly was dismayed. They demanded that Kemal himself should take personal charge of the war. He agreed, providing he was made a dictator. Most members realised this was necessary if the new Turkey was to be saved. Kemal was allowed to organise the entire country for war. Half the available food, clothing, bedding, petrol, oil

Smyrna burns as the defeated Greek army flees from Turkey, 1922

and car spares was taken from the civilian population for military use. Grimly Kemal told his troops: 'There is no defence-line. There is a defence-area which is the whole country. Not an inch of it is to be given up until it is wet with Turkish blood.' With these words the Turks prepared to give battle on the **Sakarya**.

For twenty-two days the Greek army attacked and the Turks defended a 97-kilometre line of hills. Constantine's men gained ground but at too great a cost. Just as at Gallipoli, the Turkish troops responded to Kemal's leadership with suicidal bravery. If a hill was lost it was nearly always retaken by soldiers who charged heroically over piles of their own dead. On 13 September 1921 the Greeks gave up and withdrew. The new army had won the Battle of the Sakarya. From that moment Kemal was the unquestioned leader of his people. The National Assembly gave him the title *Gazi*, or Conqueror, and he was known by this name until his death. More important, France recognised his government as the legal ruler of Turkey.

After Sakarya Kemal's armies grew stronger whilst the Greeks became disorganised. Finally, in August 1922, the Turks launched a sudden offensive after a heavy artillery barrage. The ferocity of the attack was irresistible; whole regiments offered to fight to the death and did so. Soon the victorious chanting of the Muslim holy men all along the enemy lines told of victory. Four days later there was only a ragged mob of Greeks fleeing across country, killing peasants and destroying villages as they went. On 9 September Kemal entered Smyrna in triumph to find half the city burning. Many unfortunate Greeks who lived there jumped into the water to escape. Entire boat-loads were drowned, leaving a few miserable survivors to be picked up by British sailors. On land the Turks killed all they could find. It was a terrible end to Constantine's dream.

Kemal's victory had many repercussions. The British could see that their plan for the partition of Turkey had failed. The **Mudanya Agreement** recognised the Nationalist Government. Back in Greece there was national mourning, and Constantine was forced to abdicate. In Turkey, too, the old leaders disappeared. On 17 November 1922 Mohammed VI, last Sultan of the Ottoman family, left for Malta on a British warship. Turkey became a republic with its saviour, Kemal, as leader.

The Sèvres Treaty was replaced by a much fairer settlement negotiated at **Lausanne** (Switzerland) in 1923. By its terms the River Maritsa was declared to be the frontier between Greece and Turkey (see map on page 97). Gallipoli was given back to the Turks, although the Dardanelles had to be left without defences. The custom known as Capitulations, whereby foreign people were allowed to live in Turkey without having to pay taxes or obey the laws, was abolished. Finally, arrangements were made to send home all Greeks living in Turkey and all Turks living in Greece. This was particularly tragic for the Greeks, many of whose families had been in Turkey since the eighteenth century. Altogether just over a million Greeks and 450,000 Turks were uprooted in this way.

Modernisation of Turkey

Kemal was an unusual dictator in two ways. First, he never wished to extend the boundaries of his country, indeed he had fought to do the opposite. Second, he regarded victory in war as the beginning, not the end, of his work. All his life he had been irritated by Turkey's old-fashioned ways and customs. He wanted to modernise his country so that her people were no longer laughed at by Europeans. Consequently, he went about this peaceful task with all the energy he had shown in war. In some ways this proved more difficult than in Japan because Turkey's Muslim holy men were against nearly all changes, even small ones involving dress. Kemal himself was quite irreligious. To him the faith of Islam, which had inspired so many of his soldiers to die in battle, was merely a nuisance. He was determined that it should not stop any of his reforms.

In 1924 he abolished the position of Caliph, or leader of the faith, which had been held by a Muslim even after its usual holder, the Sultan, had gone. The holy men were appalled. In Kurdistan (see map on page 97), a particularly religious area, there were serious revolts. Kemal crushed this rebellion and executed many Kurds, including some of his supporters in the National Assembly. Two years later he decided to introduce an alphabet of twenty-eight letters to make reading and writing easier. Again the holy men protested, this time because the daily recitations from the Koran are supposed to be read in Arabic. Kemal ignored them. He ordered all his members of parliament to learn the new language or lose their seats. He even toured the

streets of Ankara demonstrating the alphabet on a blackboard and easel. The new language was learnt quickly. Soon after this success he appeared in public wearing a panama hat. Holy men reminded him that the red fez was the traditional headgear of the Turk. Kemal replied that it looked silly and made a law forbidding its use. Some holy men preached against this law. They were executed. Kemal even tried to discourage Turkish women from wearing the veil, although he never dared to make a law about it.

Nothing was too important or too trivial to be left unchanged. Women were given equal rights with men in 1926. By 1935 there were thirteen women members in the National Assembly. The Gregorian Calendar replaced several old and inaccurate methods of dating and metric weights were introduced in the same year. All Greek names were abolished: for example, Constantinople became Istanbul, Smyrna became Izmir, Adrianople, Edirne. Foreigners who still addressed letters to the old names had them returned. All Turks were ordered to adopt the European habit of having a surname. Kemal set an example by calling himself '**Atatürk**' or 'father Turk'. Ismet chose 'Inönü' after his successful battle. Some Turks had fun choosing a name which suited them. A dairyman called himself 'Ozsüt' which means 'pure milk'.

In spite of the new alphabet, Persian and Arabic phrases still made Turkish long-winded. Such words were pruned from the tongue. As a result a Turk no longer wrote, for example, 'Your slave has been engaged in the exercise of cogitation in respect of the proposals vouchsafed by your exalted person.' Instead he wrote, 'I have been thinking about your suggestion.' When Kemal died in November 1938 he had

The new alphabet which Atatürk forced his people to learn (left), and (right) a Turkish tradesman tries to learn the new characters

changed an old-fashioned Empire into a modern Republic. Probably no nation in recent times has owed so much to one man. Yet his greatest achievement was possibly not one of his famous reforms. Above all, he gave a proud, brave people back their self-respect. Under the Ottomans, the Turks had been despised as cruel and dishonest oppressors of other races. Under Atatürk they were admired all over the world.

Theodore Herzl – founding father of Zionism

Zionism and the Arabs

While Atatürk was winning his victories, two other races, the Jews and Arabs, were quarrelling over lands once ruled by the Sultan. In this case the problem went even further into the past. Just as Byzantium had been overrun by the Turks, so the ancient Jewish kingdom in Palestine had been conquered, first by Romans and then by Arabs. After the capture of Jerusalem in A.D. 70 the Jews had become wanderers, scattered across the Middle East and Europe. In most European countries they were disliked, first as the enemies of Christ, later from habit and prejudice. Some medieval governments expelled them from their territory altogether. Others made them live apart, usually in special suburbs called ghettos. In certain countries, particularly Russia, they were often massacred by mobs. Since they were not allowed to be lawyers, doctors or soldiers, and since Christians were forbidden to make excessive profits, Jews often became traders and bankers. The power which such work often gave them increased still further their unpopularity. Everywhere the Jew was feared, hated or despised.

In such circumstances it was natural that Jews should begin to think of re-establishing themselves in the Holy Land. This scheme, called **Zionism**, seemed a way of escape which might please those who hated the Jews. In the 1890s Theodore Herzl tried to interest Kaiser William II and Tsar Nicholas II in the idea, hoping they might use their influence with the Sultan to give permission for such a kingdom. Both monarchs were impressed with this answer to the 'Jewish problem'. Encouraged, Herzl organised the **First Zionist Conference** in 1897. Its objective was declared to be 'to create for the Jewish people a home in Palestine secured by public law'. Not every Jew was in favour; some even feared that a Zionist state might increase anti-Semitism (hatred of Jews). Nevertheless, enough were keen to get the movement off to a good start. In 1900 Herzl formed the **Jewish Colonial Trust**, a bank to provide money for settlers to go to Palestine. There were already a few Jewish farmers growing citrus fruits on a coastal strip north of Jaffa (see map on page 97). By 1914 the Jewish population in this area had increased by 12,000.

The outbreak of the First World War changed the situation. Jews sided with the country to which they belonged. German and Austrian Jews fought for the Central Powers; Palestinian Jews were forced into the Turkish army. In France, Britain and the USA Zionists saw the possible defeat of the Ottoman Empire as a wonderful opportunity to found their state. They persuaded both Lloyd George and President Wilson that their scheme was a good one. Britain, for her part, looked for a way to keep both Russia and the USA in the war. She decided that some sort of promise would please the many Jews living in both countries. On 2 November 1917, when the Allies were doing very badly on most fronts, a British minister, Arthur Balfour, sent a letter to the Zionist leaders assuring them his government would work for 'the establishment in Palestine of a national home for the Jewish people'. This became known as the **Balfour Declaration**. Even Balfour himself looked upon this 'promise' as mere propaganda. To the Zionists it seemed far more important; rarely can mere propaganda have had such devastating long-term effects.

Actually the Jews were not the only people who could help the Allies. From 1915 onwards British officials were trying to interest certain Arab chieftains, particularly the Sheriff of Mecca, in a rising against the Turks. As a reward they promised the Arabs independent kingdoms in Syria and Arabia (see map on page 97). One letter listed the boundaries of such territories. Owing to vague phrasing the Arabs assumed that it included the part of Syria which is Palestine. They were overjoyed. Only five days after the Balfour Declaration the British government promised the Arabs 'complete and final liberation of the peoples who have for so long been oppressed by the Turk'. Despite the words 'complete and final' no British statesman intended to include Palestine. Unfortunately, no Arab doubted that it was theirs, especially as it had a large Arab population and Jerusalem was a holy city for the Muslims. They revolted (see Chapter 10), and, after the defeat of the Turks, waited for their reward. So did the Jews!

The Arabs would never have agreed to a Jewish state anyway. But the situation was made worse in their opinion by the flow of European Jews coming to Palestine. They feared their land would be taken from them by a wave of immigrants. At the Paris Peace Conference the Arab chieftains made this clear. Apart from claiming that Palestine had been promised to them, they asked what was to happen to the Arab population if a Jewish state was set up. Surely, they argued, this was against the Wilsonian idea of self-determination? The Jews replied that they could see no reason why the two races could not live happily side by side. There was in their opinion ample room for all. The Arabs were not satisfied. The Jews would not give up their dream of a national state. Both demanded that Britain keep her wartime promises.

At first the Jews and Arabs just protested. Then violence became frequent as the two races clashed in street and countryside. In 1929 a quarrel developed about the **Wailing Wall** in Jerusalem (see picture opposite), which is sacred to both religions. When the Jews fixed a screen on it to separate men and women for prayer the Arabs decided their holy place was in danger of becoming a Jewish possession. Encouraged by a religious leader, the Mufti of Jerusalem, they began to murder Jews. Six years later similar riots grew into a full-scale war. For some time Jews had continued to enter the country. Some were allowed to settle. Others pretended to be 'tourists' and stayed for good or were smuggled in. Whichever way they came it irritated the Arabs. The terrible persecution of Jews which started in Germany following Hitler's rise to power (see Chapter 16) increased the flow. The Arab

The Wailing Wall, Jerusalem. It was here that a quarrel developed between Jews and Arabs in 1929

reply was to recruit rebel armies which attacked the British and the Jews. Bridges were blown up, trains derailed, outposts destroyed. Whilst British troops were hurried in to restore order, the Jews, too, took up arms. Their leader, Chaim Weizmann, did not believe in violence. Even so, some of his young men formed themselves into groups of gun-men, like Irgun Zwei Leumi, Haganah and the Stern Gang. Palestine became a land of bloodshed and terror.

By 1938, the British government was tired of the whole problem. When their suggested partition of the country between Arabs and Jews was rejected by the Arabs, they decided that a national state for the Jews was impossible. Jewish immigration was restricted even more and Jews were not allowed to buy land in certain areas. Most Zionists were infuriated by these restrictions. So were some British statesmen. Winston Churchill said of the Jews: 'They have made the desert bloom. They have started a score of thriving industries... They have harnessed the Jordan and spread its electricity through the land... Now... all this is to end'. Soon afterwards he was made Prime Minister of a Britain fighting for her life against Germany. A problem caused by the First World War was submerged in the Second.

Timeline

1897   First Zionist Conference.
1900   Jewish Colonial Trust formed.
1917   Balfour Declaration and promise to Arabs.
1919   Greeks occupy Smyrna.
1920   Atatürk forms Nationalist government (Grand National Assembly). Treaty of Sèvres. Battle of İnönü.
1921   Battle of the Sakarya.
1922   Greeks defeated by Turks. Mudanya Agreement.
1923   Treaty of Lausanne. Turkey officially declared a Republic.
1929   Jew-Arab riots in Palestine.
1938   British abandon idea of Jewish National State.

Questions

1. 'But for Mustafa Kemal [Atatürk] the proclamation of the [Turkish] Republic was only a first step. He wanted to change not only the régime, but society itself.' (Metin Toker, Turkish Historian)

   a) Who was Atatürk?
   b) Why did he want to change the way of life in Turkey? Describe what you think were the most important changes he made.

2. What was the Balfour Declaration of 1917? What were the reasons which made it difficult to carry out?

3. 'Most [Greeks] dreamed of returning and conquering "their" land.'
   a) Why did the Greeks regard parts of Turkey as 'their' land?
   b) How successful were their efforts to regain this land in 1921?

4. Write short paragraphs on each of the following:
   a) the Treaty of Sèvres, 1920
   b) the Mudanya Agreement
   c) Zionism
   d) the Wailing Wall incident, 1929

13

Communism and Fascism
Russia and Italy 1918–1938

Karl Marx, author of 'Capital' and co-founder with Engels of communism

The communist theories put into practice in Russia after 1917 had been born quietly in the Reading Room of the British Museum, London. Here, in the 1850s, librarians often saw a bearded man 'with a thick black mop of hair on his head, with hairy hands, and crookedly buttoned frock coat'. He was a German, **Karl Marx**, who sat day after day reading and making notes for his very long book called *Capital*. In this famous work Marx tried to analyse Western European history during the previous thousand years, to discover a pattern in the way events had happened and to suggest a solution to the misery of the poor.

Marx decided that change in historical terms was the result of a struggle between the 'haves' and the 'have-nots', between those who controlled the resources of trade and industry and those who were forced to work for them. These struggling social groups he called 'classes'. In most cases a small, powerful group controlled the lives and work of the rest. The political system was made to suit this class, whilst the majority remained oppressed and exploited. In the Middle Ages, lords, knights and merchants had, literally, 'lorded' it over the peasants. In Marx's own time, industrial Britain was creating a small, capitalist class who owned or controlled trade and industry – what Marx called 'the means of production, distribution and exchange' – and a proletariat (the ordinary wage-earners) who lacked resources and whose lives were controlled by these capitalists.

Marx and his friend, **Friedrich Engels**, saw class conflict as the main theme of history. The first words of their famous *Manifesto*, issued in 1848, were, 'The history of all past society is the history of the struggle between classes.' In particular, both Marx and Engels thought that capitalists and workers had such sharply opposed interests that they must clash. Large factories would produce well-organised working-class movements which would overthrow the capitalists, seize the means of production and redistribute wealth more evenly among the whole community. Such a revolutionary reorganisation they called communism because under it goods and wealth would be owned 'in common' and available to all as needed. Society would be organised more fairly under the slogan 'From each according to his ability, to each according to his need'.

Marx suggested that Western society had gone through a series of revolutionary struggles. Feudalism, for example, had been overthrown by capitalism in the sixteenth and seventeenth centuries. He also hoped that his 'dictatorship' of the workers would lead in the end to a truly 'classless' society. Certainly he believed that an industrialised, capitalist system would need to be created before communism could be introduced. The quarrel between capitalist and worker would provide the revolutionary 'spark'. Marx knew that Russia was not at such a stage, although towards the end of his life he stated that a communist revolution might succeed in Russia if it took place at the same time as similar revolutions in more advanced Western European states. Lenin was faced from the beginning by this problem. Indeed, some of his followers had been against the October Revolution (see page 83) simply because the time was not ripe according to Marxist theory. Lenin was more flexible. He argued – wrongly as it turned out – that Europe was ready for successful revolution after such a fearful war. He decided to seize power whatever the situation or the consequences.

So it came about that the first successful communist revolution occurred in a country with relatively few factories and a large majority of peasants. The vital 'spark' was not a battle between capitalist and worker but appalling suffering and bitter hatred born of centuries of oppression.

Lenin and Marxism

The Russian Communist leader, **Vladimir Ilyich Lenin**, was a man of outstanding personality. When he and his Bolsheviks took over in 1917 the majority of the Russian people were country peasants. They and their ancestors had suffered for centuries at the hands of invaders and landowners. They had been starved, beaten, overworked, and killed in wars far from home. They had just been slaughtered by the million in the worst war of all. All the survivors wanted was more food, better treatment and a little land of their own. What they did not want was another revolution. Indeed, only a minority wanted the Bolsheviks at all. At the only free election held in Russia the Bolsheviks gained only a small proportion of the seats (see Chapter 10).

Lenin knew this so he adapted Marxist theory to suit the situation. First, he decided to force the people to accept communism, relying on his well-disciplined Bolsheviks for success. Second, he realised that in Russia there must be two almost simultaneous revolutions instead of one. The workers and the middle classes would overthrow the ruling classes, but later the workers and peasants would turn upon the middle classes.

At first the odds against this happening seemed enormous. Although Bolshevik Soviets controlled many cities, most of the countryside was in the hands of their enemies. In the north, at Murmansk and Archangel (see map opposite), British troops had arrived to protect the large Allied ammunition dumps left after the war. In the south, anti-Bolshevik armies, called Whites, to distinguish them from the Communist Reds, were driving towards Moscow. In the east, a Czech legion, which during the war had surrendered to the Russians rather than fight for the Habsburgs, was now against the Bolsheviks. Led by Admiral Kolchak, it had established a government at Omsk which ruled more of Russia than Lenin's government. In the west the Poles

Founder of Communist Russia, Vladimir Ilyich Lenin

Russia, 1917–22

Railway

Land lost after World War I

Boundary of USSR by 1922

had crossed the Curzon Line (see page 92). Elsewhere peasant armies marched about attacking both sides. Finally, Japanese, American, French and Italian troops were based in different parts of Russia, usually as a result of agreements made with the Tsar.

The Communists won this Civil War because they were better disciplined and more determined than their opponents. Allied leaders could not make up their minds what to do. Some, like Winston Churchill and Marshal Ferdinand Foch, wanted a full-scale invasion of Russia so that communism could be wiped out. President Wilson, on the other hand, had a natural sympathy for revolutionaries which arose out of America's own successful revolution against Britain. French politicians were worried in case Marshal Foch became a military dictator.

Most governments feared that soldiers sent to Russia might be infected with Bolshevik ideas. Had not the French sailors stationed in the Black Sea hoisted red flags on their ships?

Trotsky speaking to Red soldiers from one of the cars carried on his war train, 1920

For these reasons foreign units were gradually withdrawn from Russia at the very moment when White armies were nearing Moscow. A new Red Army created by Leon Trotsky began to win. This brilliant organiser travelled to the fighting lines in a train so large that it had to be pulled by two engines. He rallied troops with a mixture of clever propaganda and terror; once he shot ten per cent of a regiment which looked like mutinying. At Tsaritsyn (see map on page 109) the White armies were driven back by General Tukhachevsky, although another Bolshevik, Joseph Stalin, took the credit and the city was renamed Stalingrad. Kolchak's Czechs revolted against their own leader and he was shot by his enemies. Petrograd was successfully defended by Communist workers whilst the Poles were driven out by patriotic peasants. By 1922 the Red Army was victorious and Lenin, as head of the new government, the Council of People's Commissars, was the master of Russia. Russia became the first Communist state in the world and was renamed the **Union of Soviet Socialist Republics** (the USSR or the Soviet Union).

Russia under Lenin

Even before 1922, Lenin's government had taken a tight grip on Russian life under a system named 'War Communism'. Most factories were nationalised, all political parties except the Communist Party were banned and their leaders imprisoned or shot. Russians could be arrested without reason and put in prison without trial. The secret police, the *Cheka*, did this so often that a new saying became popular, 'Every Russian has been, is, or will be in prison'. The Church's power was destroyed completely. Its schools, colleges, monasteries and shrines were closed. Christians could still attend church if they wished but a 'Godless League' printed propaganda against religion. Sunday was abolished and a six-day week instituted for a time. The Tsarist monarch who had been so devotedly supported by the Church had gone also. At Ekaterinburg (now Sverdlovsk) Nicholas and his family were shot in a cellar (1918). Their bodies were burned, thrown down a mineshaft, taken up and spread in a swamp. Nothing was left which a superstitious people might worship.

Lenin thought that all these crimes were justified in such desperate circumstances. What did it matter if 50,000 died so long as future generations enjoyed the benefits of communism? Had he lived the USSR might have become a happier country, even if not a democratic one. However he died in 1924. Three men succeeded him: **Stalin**, **Trotsky** and **Zinoviev**. In time, by careful control of the Communist Party, Stalin became sole dictator. This son of a shoemaker from the Russian province of Georgia was not intellectually brilliant like Lenin or Trotsky but he was more ruthless and violent. As a young man he had led murderous bank raids to obtain Party funds. For this he was imprisoned. After the Civil War he took control of the Party organisation, appointing men who would obey him without question. Lenin disliked Stalin and in a last testament (will) he described him as 'rude'. He also warned the other leaders against him. Zinoviev and Trotsky took no notice. They felt sure they could handle the rough Georgian.

Slowly but surely they were proved wrong. To Stalin, power was more important than anything else – even communism. Lenin's terror methods were now used, not to save the revolution, but to keep Stalin on top. A bitter quarrel with Trotsky developed gradually during the 1920s. Trotsky was a brilliant speaker and writer. He was a fanatical Marxist and a believer in world revolution. He had even condemned the **New Economic Policy (NEP)**, introduced in 1921 by Lenin himself, because it allowed private enterprise on a limited scale. For example, peasants could own their own land and keep any surplus food produced to sell at a profit. Trotsky knew that Lenin had only done this because of strikes and a peasant revolt in a province near Moscow. But he was no man for half-measures. Now he found that Stalin had abandoned the idea of stirring up workers' revolutions abroad. Stalin believed the Soviet Union's problems were so great that the government's efforts must be concentrated on modernising industry and agriculture at home. 'Socialism in one country' became his motto, and, when Trotsky disagreed, he was gradually stripped of his offices and, finally, in 1929, forced to leave the country. He became an exile, eventually settling down in Mexico where he was killed by one of Stalin's agents (1940).

Joseph Stalin. Disliked by Lenin, he lived to become dictator of Russia

Stalin – the Five Year Plans

Stalin summed up his policies when he said, years later, 'We are fifty or a hundred years behind the advanced countries. We must make good the lag in ten years. Either we do it or they crush us'. In 1928 he announced what he called his 'Second Revolution'. This involved the

transformation of the USSR from a mainly agricultural to an industrial nation. At the time seventy-five per cent of all Russians worked on the land. Under Stalin's **First Five Year Plan (1929–33)** there was to be a three-fold increase in coal, iron, steel, oil and machinery production. The key was a vast increase in electric power. Hydro-electric plants, like the one on the River Dneiper, were built for this purpose. In all, ninety new towns, including a steel centre at Magnitogorsk, car factories at Gorki and tractor plants at Rostov and Kharkov (see map on page 109), were established as a result of this Plan. The work was hasty and often inefficient. It was achieved by ruthless methods. The trade unions became little more than agents of the government. Even a day's absence by a worker led to instant dismissal. By 1932 the government was able to announce that the Plan's targets had already been met. The USSR was beginning to develop its heavy industry, although little effort was made to produce goods for the people.

Building of the Dneiper dam during the First Five Year Plan, 1932

During the **Second Five Year Plan (1933–7)** even more emphasis was placed upon hard work. Each man was paid according to whether or not he did a 'normal' amount of work each day. In fact, this 'normal' output was often the maximum which could be achieved by an exceptional worker. For example, in 1935 a miner named Aleksei Stakhanov was given some easy coal seams to work, equipped with the finest tools and allowed the best men as assistants. In one day he cut 104 tonnes of coal. This was then declared 'normal production' and miners who could not achieve it were paid less. Such schemes made the workers into slaves, often living close to starvation. Russia was being modernised the hard way. Stalin knew that with such industrialisation plans the food needed for extra factory workers could only be produced by more efficient farming methods. At the time of the Revolution the large estates of the landowners had been broken up and given to the peasants. Under Lenin's NEP peasant farmers had been allowed to sell surplus food for profit. Stalin wanted a more socialist scheme with farms working together in collectives. In these the peasants pooled all their land and animals, and shared out their work, their produce and their profits.

Such **collective farming**, as it was called, caused bitter resentment. Richer peasants, called *kulaks*, had their farms collectivised first. Most peasants realised that in time every farm would be collectivised so they began a sort of underground war against Stalin's policy. In some provinces they killed their cattle rather than join a collective; in others they even murdered the officials sent to supervise the scheme. Stalin ordered all who resisted to be sent to labour camps or shot. When even this failed to break the resistance he sent the army to attack rebellious communities. At times villages were bombed and machine-gunned by air force planes. Stalin got his way, but much livestock was destroyed and it was years before the countryside produced even the amount of food it had before collectivisation began.

Stalin – the Great Purges

Stalin had gained and strengthened his power by defeating Civil War heroes like Trotsky. Perhaps because he was afraid of losing his dominant position – or even his life – he began to destroy anybody who might criticise or rival him. And because he aimed to wipe out men whom communists regarded as heroes, he used the method of the well-publicised **show trial** at which the accused were put under pressure to 'confess' their 'crimes'. One of the first show trials occurred in 1928 when fifty engineers were accused of sabotaging a mine. Then, in December 1934, Sergey Kirov, First Party Secretary (Governor) of Leningrad, was murdered. Nobody knows who killed Kirov, although later it was suggested that Stalin arranged the assassination. Whether this was true or not, the death of Kirov was used as an excuse to first imprison and then try and execute some of the most powerful men in the Soviet Union.

The outside world watched in astonishment as the number of trials and executions grew. Between 1936 and 1938 nearly all the older Bolsheviks, including Zinoviev, were accused of the most extraordinary crimes, including plotting Stalin's death, spying for foreign governments and even trying to re-establish a capitalist system in the USSR. There was little truth in these charges yet all the accused were forced to 'confess'. Some were questioned for weeks without a break, or put in solitary confinement under glaring electric lights. Others had their bones broken or their families threatened. All confessed their 'guilt' publicly at their trials. Altogether 17 men who had helped to start the 1917 Revolution, half of the 139 members of the Party Central Committee and 23 of Russia's senior generals were shot. Millions of less important victims were killed or sent to labour camps. During the war Stalin boasted to Churchill that he had killed 10,000,000!

Purges on such a scale caused industry to slow down and farms to produce less. When somebody was brave enough to tell Stalin this, he calmly blamed the police. Soon afterwards, most of the secret police, including its chief, Nikolai Yezhov, were shot. Today few young Russians know the full extent of Stalin's terror. The older people know but they sometimes forget his crimes and mistakes and talk about him as the 'strong master' who made the Soviet Union modern and great.

Stalin – the Popular Fronts

Most of the early Bolsheviks had believed that revolution would break out all over Europe after the First World War. In some countries such risings did take place and were suppressed. This happened in Germany. Nevertheless, some leading Communists did not give up hope. Trotsky preached world revolution until the day he died. In 1919 Zinoviev founded an organisation, the **Comintern** (Communist International), to encourage communist revolutions abroad. Stalin, as we have seen, did not agree with this policy. During his early years of power he preached isolation from a hostile capitalist world.

But many of Stalin's policies were based on the belief that one day the advanced capitalist nations, including possibly Germany, would attack the Soviet Union and try to crush the Revolution. The rise of Hitler in the 1930s alarmed Stalin so much that he gave up the idea of non-intervention abroad. Instead, he began to advise foreign communists to join with socialist and liberal parties in their countries to form alliances, called **Popular Fronts**. The policy worked for a short time in France where there was a Popular Front government in 1936–7 led by Léon Blum. In Spain another Popular Front government was overthrown by a military rebellion led by General Franco (see Chapter 18). Stalin made a half-hearted attempt to save this government, sending advisers and military equipment. However, when it became clear that Germany was helping Franco to win, the Russian leader abandoned the Spanish communists and their allies.

In 1939, with German troops threatening Poland and clear danger of a war in Europe, Stalin desperately signed a treaty with his arch enemy, Adolf Hitler (see Chapter 17).

Mussolini and Fascism

The greatest evils of Stalin's régime were largely unknown both outside and inside the Soviet Union, and some foreigners remained enthusiastic about communism. One man returned from a conducted tour of the USSR and remarked, 'I have seen the future and it works'. Others, however, were filled with horror at such strange goings-on. Out of this fear grew **fascism**, partly as a reaction against communism, although also as a political movement with distinctive ideas. Its first political success was in Italy, helped by the writings of Gabriele d' Annunzio and the actions of **Benito Mussolini**. Born at Dovia in 1883, Mussolini was a violent and headstrong boy. He qualified as a teacher but soon turned to journalism. At first he was a communist, often leading strikes and ending up in prison as a result. Generally he preferred force to settle an argument: once he led a march on a town hall and threatened to throw the mayor out of the window if the price of milk was not reduced. By 1914 he was talking of an armed rising by a few determined 'superior' men. Two essentials of fascism, rule by a small superior group and violence, were firmly fixed in his head.

The First World War led Mussolini to give up communism. Most Italian socialists were against the war which they believed was being fought to make rich capitalists even richer. Mussolini, on the other hand, realised that a war against Austria-Hungary could give Italy the Trentino and Trieste areas (see page 78). This desire to enlarge Italian territory led him to justify the war and even to glorify fighting. Repeatedly, in speeches and articles, he clamoured for action. Most Italians wished to avoid the conflict but the King, too, was filled with dreams of glory. Eventually the government gave in and declared war on the Allied side (1915). As Mussolini rushed to join up he must have noticed how easy it had been for a noisy minority to get its own way.

Benito Mussolini, Fascist dictator of Italy

Mussolini was a brave soldier, serving at the front until he was injured by an accidental explosion. Returning home, he posed as a wounded hero. Long after they were necessary he hobbled about on crutches. In speeches he referred to himself as a 'survivor'. Meanwhile he decided that what Italy needed was a dictator 'energetic enough to make a clean sweep'. All the essentials of fascism: violence, dictatorship, glorification of war, were now in Mussolini's mind. It only remained to invent the name and organise the party. On 23 March 1919 Mussolini formed a **Fascio di Combattimento** (Fighting Group) in Milan. Here were the first band of Fascists, 'superior' men who boasted that they were bound as closely together as the rods and axes of the *Fascinae* which had symbolised the power of ancient Rome.

Like most European countries, Italy had been temporarily ruined by the war. She was deeply in debt, there were millions of unemployed and over 150,000 deserters who roamed about causing trouble. In such conditions, communist ideas spread quickly. Red (Communist) flags fluttered from town halls and local Soviets were set up. Now matters were made worse as the blackshirted Fascists (*Squadristi*) set about restoring 'order'. Mob battles with Communists became common. Men were killed or beaten up. They were filled with castor oil or made to eat live toads. Normal life was disrupted as strikes, riots and attacks on barracks, railway stations and banks filled the newspaper headlines. Altogether nearly 3,000 people died in street fighting in two years. Only the Communist leaders condemned Fascist violence. Others found plenty to approve of in Mussolini's party. Industrialists and landowners who wanted to keep their factories and their land; Catholics terrified in case their religion was destroyed by godless communism; middle-class people who loved law and order, supported them. Fascist brutality was ignored by the King, the army and the police. Only Communist violence was punished.

When the Communists called a general strike Mussolini announced that if the government did not crush it his men would. On 28 October 1922 columns of blackshirts began the **March on Rome**. They were not

Mussolini poses before a crowd as a 'son of the people'

really as warlike as they looked. Certainly the army could have dispersed them. But the King favoured fascism as an antidote to communism. As the blackshirt marchers neared Rome he invited Mussolini to be Prime Minister of a government of all parties. Sitting far away and safe in Milan, the leader of the Fascist Party could hardly believe his good luck. Few of his columns were within 60 kilometres of the Italian capital at the time. His office was ringed by police who could have arrested him easily. In spite of this the March on Rome had succeeded. Later Mussolini's propaganda writers exaggerated this bluff until those who took part in it were treated like soldiers who had won a battle.

Mussolini's Italy

Once in power Mussolini started to build up the idea of himself as a sort of 'superman'. Italians were invited to join him in a mighty effort to make Italy as great as she had been in Roman days. Photographs and films usually showed *Il Duce* (the Leader), as he was called, working furiously at his desk or outside cutting trees or digging ditches. Sometimes he appeared stripped to the waist, his great barrel chest glistening with sweat. On other occasions he wore a gorgeous uniform, and watched military parades with a grim look on his face. Each night his office light was left on to give the impression he was still working. He was portrayed as a 'son of the people' because his father had been a blacksmith. At the same time his cleverness and wisdom were emphasised. He was even photographed winning at chess, a game he could not play!

Not all of it was empty show. Mussolini's government was able to build bridges, railways, canals, hospitals and schools. Fine new roads, called *autostrada*, were laid between the main cities. Swamps were dried and forests planted. Many foreigners began to admire Mussolini. Catholics were particularly pleased when he signed the **Lateran Treaty and Concordat** with the Pope (1929). Ever since 1870 successive popes had refused to recognise the Kingdom of Italy because it had taken territory once ruled by them. Now the Pope was recognised as 'king' of the Vatican City, Rome (an area of about 40 hectares), and Roman Catholicism was declared to be the state religion.

The truth might have changed many people's minds. At first Mussolini was very popular. His constant demands for order, discipline, sacrifice and hard work pleased a people demoralised by the war. But after the savage murder by Fascists of a Socialist, **Giacomo Matteotti** (1924), he became less popular. Without violence and trickery Mussolini would not have won the 1924 election. It was arranged that the party which polled most votes would automatically receive two-thirds of the parliamentary seats. To get them his men beat up their political opponents. After such a 'victory' Mussolini gave up all pretence of democracy. The King remained as a figurehead but parliament lost the power to make laws. The Press was censored, so that it only printed what the Fascists wanted. The old *Squadristi* was turned into a Fascist militia which acted like a second police force. Workers were made to work longer hours and denied the right to strike. Children had to enrol in the Fascist Youth (*Ballila*). Opponents of the régime were sent away to concentration camps. Liberty was described by Mussolini as a 'more or less putrid [rotting] goddess'.

Day after day Italians were encouraged to be warlike; even the *Ballila* carried toy machine-guns. They were taught to despise free discussion and free choice. They were reminded of Roman greatness and urged to want a new Italian African Empire. Schoolchildren were made to chant 'Mussolini is always right'. So, indirectly, communism helped to produce a dictatorial system similar to its own but supported by the capitalists and middle class whom Marx had condemned. By 1930 foreign political groups, particularly the German Nazis, were copying Fascist methods, Fascist displays and badges, Fascist boasting and bullying (see Chapter 16). There were, of course, some differences. Hitler and his Nazis glorified the 'racially pure', German and Spanish Falangists (see Chapter 18) loved the Roman Catholic religion instead of worshipping Ancient Rome. Otherwise all were violently intolerant, all hated both democracy and communism, all worshipped a particular leader. Communism in action was violent, frightening and dictatorial. Fascism was to prove equally as bad.

Timeline

1867	Karl Marx publishes *Capital*.
1919	Comintern formed. Mussolini forms *Fascio di Combattimento*.
1920–2	Russian Civil War.
1922	Union of Soviet Socialist Republics (USSR) established. March on Rome brings Mussolini to power.
1924	Death of Lenin. Murder of Giacomo Matteotti.
1929	Trotsky forced to leave USSR. Lateran Treaty and Concordat.
1929–33	First Russian Five Year Plan.
1933–7	Second Russian Five Year Plan.
1936	Stalin begins purges.

Questions

1. a) What were the main obstacles which Lenin faced when he seized power in 1917?
   b) How did Lenin make sure that the Communists kept their grip on everyday life in the USSR after the Civil War? What was the NEP?

2. What was the main reason for Trotsky's quarrel with Stalin?

3. 'Lenin's methods lead to this, the party organisation at first substitutes itself for the party as a whole; then the central committee substitutes itself for the organisation; and finally a single dictator substitutes himself for the central committee.' (Leon Trotsky, 1904)

   Explain how Trotsky's prophecy about Communist Russia came true, bearing in mind the career of Joseph Stalin.

4. 'We are fifty or a hundred years behind the advanced countries. We must make good the lag in ten years. Either we do it or they crush us.' (Joseph Stalin, 1928)

   a) What do you think Joseph Stalin meant by the 'advanced countries'? Name two of them.
   b) In what ways did Stalin attempt to make up the 'lag'? How successful had he been by 1941?
   c) What do you think Stalin meant when he said 'Either we do it or they crush us'?

5. How did the situation in Italy after the First World War help Mussolini in his rise to power? What methods did he use to make that power more secure?

6. Write short paragraphs on each of the following:
   a) the March on Rome
   b) Karl Marx
   c) the Comintern
   d) Stalin's purges

14

Depression and New Deal
USA 1918–1939

After the First World War the USA enjoyed a period of great prosperity. To Americans Europe was a far away, unhappy place. They were prepared to lend European peoples money but not to take any part in their politics. Possibly because of this **isolationist** mood they chose as President in 1920 **Warren Harding**, an easy-going, pleasure-loving man who gave the best jobs to his friends. Harding's cronies, the 'Ohio Gang', were often inefficient and sometimes dishonest. Poker games and parties became as common at the White House as political conferences. The large industries, 'big business', were allowed absolute freedom; their bosses became economic dictators. Each American state governed itself with little help from the federal authorities. When Harding died suddenly, in August 1923, various scandals came to light. Two of his ministers had bought oil-fields reserved for the navy. The head of the ex-serviceman's bureau turned out to be a deserter posing as a colonel! It was a long way from the high standards of Woodrow Wilson (see Chapter 11).

Harding's successor was different. **Calvin Coolidge** was mean and respectable. But although he was a contrast as a man he was similar as a president. Like Harding he cut government activity to a minimum, leaving the states and big business alone. Indeed, Coolidge generally took a long nap every afternoon. Most Americans liked this situation. It seemed to leave them free to chase after more money. Even the poor were often proud of US prosperity. As one comedian joked: 'You can't lick this Prosperity thing. Even the fellow that hasn't got any is all excited over the idea'.

By the time 'Silent Cal' reluctantly gave up the presidency (1929) this rush after material things had become a mania. Slogans like 'Two chickens in every pot', were sure to attract votes, and the new President, **Herbert Hoover**, predicted that the USA was 'in sight of the day when poverty will be banished from the nation'. Certainly hard times were forgotten by many people. The USA became the most confident as well as the most powerful nation on earth. Other governments could not make ends meet. They had to borrow American money. Other governments could not keep a steady political system. They turned to communism or fascism. Only the USA seemed free from such troubles.

In fact the country was like a large ocean-liner heading for a shipwreck. On board the lights were blazing; the passengers were enjoying themselves. Outside, however, the sea was very cold and an iceberg was near. There were many reasons for this. Most important was the state of American agriculture. Year by year the demand for US wheat, cattle and cotton grew less. Before the First World War there had

The man who promised Americans 'Two chickens in every pot'. President Herbert Hoover

been more foreign money spent, or invested, in the USA than Americans had spent abroad. The difference between these two amounts had been made up by selling agricultural goods outside the USA. Afterwards this balance disappeared. Enormous sums of US money went to rebuild European cities or to feed the starving; Europeans spent little in the USA. Foreign businessmen and their governments could no longer afford to buy from American farmers, especially as Congress put high duties (tariffs) on foreign articles in order to protect US industries. Few wanted to increase their American debts so they imported from elsewhere. Britain, for example, bought wheat from Argentina and Canada.

Inside the USA other trends threatened the farmer. After the First World War the tradition that everybody was welcome in the USA stopped at last and the government's **Johnson Act, 1921**, limited immigration to an annual three per cent of foreign-born Americans. This slowed down the increase in population. Again, more motor cars decreased the demand for horse fodder. Rayon clothing became more popular than cotton. Even eating habits changed in a way which hurt the farmer. Americans ate more fruit, vegetables and milk and less bread and meat. Since the USA's chief products were wheat and cattle this had serious effects. By 1929 American farmers were producing more food than they could sell. Slowly their prices began to drop.

This was not the only problem. The new prosperity had been created in the wrong way. Far too many people had looked for easy ways of making money. Instead of investing in industry they had merely bought and sold Stock Exchange shares at a profit. People who were not rich, widows, factory workers, even bootblacks, risked their savings in new companies, hoping to make 'a fast buck'. Unfortunately, although there seemed to be a lot of companies, in fact, a relatively few rich men owned them all. Such trickery, called 'skulduggery', became commonplace, and it meant that only a slight change in the circumstances of these men would affect the whole country.

In addition, far too many Americans had borrowed to buy what they wanted. This created a huge amount of debt which could only be repaid if the debtors kept their jobs. The slightest increase in unemployment, the slightest drop in spending, would send shudders through the entire economy. Firms who sold less would sack some of their workers. This in turn would restrict buying and so cause more unemployment. In such a situation everything depended upon people remaining confident enough to go on spending. Providing they were prepared to run up debts on shares, cars, etc., all might be well. A small hole in the ship would not sink it if the passengers remained calm. Unfortunately, at the first bump the passengers on this particular 'ship' panicked and tried to jump overboard. A small accident was turned into disaster.

The Depression, 1929–32

This particular 'bump' resulted from a drop in prices caused by too many goods and too few buyers. In many parts of the world in 1929

Crowds gather in Wall Street, New York, on Black Thursday, 1929

there was over-production. Too much food, too much copper, rubber, silver and zinc were produced. Good harvests in the USA left even more food on the farmers' hands. At the same time share prices had been rising until they were at fantastic levels. Obviously firms would find it difficult to make the necessary profits. Cautious people lost confidence. Some began to sell their shares, thus causing price reductions. More and more people copied them. Soon large numbers were trying to get rid of their shares. The worst day for the Wall Street, New York, Stock Exchange was 24 October 1929, **Black Thursday**, when millions of shares were sold. Altogether, in three days, twelve million shares changed hands.

At first Americans thought this slump was temporary. Hoover believed it was and reassured people by saying 'prosperity is just around the corner'. Unfortunately, Americans now became as timid as they had once been reckless. Millions decided to save instead of spend. Workers in manufacturing industries were thrown out of work. Their unpaid hire purchase bills, in turn, made more unemployment. Confidence in banks failed and queues formed to withdraw money. As a result many smaller concerns went out of business. Farmers were particularly hard hit. When they failed to pay their mortgages they were evicted from their homes. Some refused to move and fired shot-guns at the landlords' men. Others paraded through the towns with banners saying, 'In Hoover we trusted, now we are busted.'

American unemployed queue for food during the Depression, 1930

Numbers of unemployed became desperate. Outside Washington crowds of ex-servicemen built a dilapidated camp called a 'Hooverville'. They had to be removed by soldiers. The Americans' love of freedom now proved a handicap. Coolidge and Hoover had both disliked old age pensions and sick pay. Americans in their opinion should learn to stand on their own feet. As a result the US unemployed were worse off than those of other countries. By 1932, twelve million men and women were out of work, and reduced to queueing for free meals given by charitable societies. Even to the visitor it was obvious that something was wrong. Towns and holiday resorts were almost deserted. In big cities there were long breadlines in the streets and beggars in the gutters. Often a train would go by without a single passenger. A young singer, Bing Crosby, made a hit with a song called, 'Brother, can you spare a dime?' Its lyric about an ex-soldier asking for bread made it the theme song of the **Depression**.

Hoover tried to solve the problem by traditional American methods. As far as possible, businessmen must be left to sort out their own difficulties. States should do as they thought best for their citizens. In the meantime he launched an appeal to feed the starving. It was no use. Businessmen did not feel charitable. They, too, had lost confidence and were not prepared to risk their money in new projects. Everywhere firms continued to close down. A state of near panic gripped the

'A commanding personality'. Franklin Roosevelt, President of the United States from 1933 to 1945

nation. One director summed up the situation when he remarked, 'I'm afraid. Every man is afraid'. Europeans wondered whether the USA would experience a revolution. Fortunately, the Americans remained democrats in spite of the disaster. Hopefully, they elected a new President, **Franklin Delano Roosevelt**, in 1932.

Roosevelt the man

Roosevelt came of a rich family which traced its ancestry back to the seventeenth century. He went to Groton School and Harvard University, the 'Eton' and 'Oxford' of America, and then qualified as a lawyer. Handsome, athletic and pleasure-loving, he could have lived an idle life. Instead he entered politics in 1910 as a Democrat. During the First World War he was Assistant Secretary of the Navy under Woodrow Wilson. Thanks to him the US fleet was able to fight the war efficiently.

In 1921 Roosevelt went swimming with his family at a holiday resort. It was warm so he did not bother to get dressed immediately. Suddenly he began to sneeze and ache all over. Next morning he was feverish and the following day he lost the use of his legs. The doctors diagnosed polio. Roosevelt had been struck down by a dreadful, and at that time almost unknown, disease.

Back in New York specialists expected him to die. He fought back and survived. Then they thought he would never walk again. Again Roosevelt screwed up his courage and refused to accept their verdict. A ring was fixed above his bed so that he could raise himself using his arms. By constantly practising he was able to sit up for short periods. Months of effort and pain produced better results. With metal tubing attached to his legs he managed to hobble about on crutches. In 1924 he found that the waters at Warm Springs, Georgia, definitely strengthened his legs. Between periods of treatment he lived as active a political life as possible.

In 1928 Roosevelt sought election to the important post of Governor of New York. A few people objected because he was a cripple. The majority of Americans felt differently. They admired him. Before his illness he had been a rich man who had always had it easy. Now he was a man who had suffered more than most, who had faced up to the most awful physical disaster and triumphed. He won the Governorship and four years later became President after a smashing victory.

Roosevelt had two advantages over Hoover. He was prepared to use the full resources of the Federal Government to end the Depression, and he possessed a commanding personality. Hoover had been a good and efficient President in normal times. In this crisis, however, he was handicapped by his own views about individual freedom, and failed to inspire people with confidence. On the other hand F.D.R., as Roosevelt was known, could inspire not only those he met but the entire nation. Using the radio, he spoke to them as a friend and neighbour. Americans grew to love his **fireside chats** because of their frankness. In the very first of them Roosevelt struck at the root of the problem, saying, 'The only thing we have to fear is fear itself'. He also

F.D.R. (Roosevelt) getting rid of out of date and unsuccessful policies. A newspaper cartoon of the thirties in the USA

showed a flair for the right slogan. Even before his election he had promised, 'I pledge you, I pledge myself, to a New Deal for the American people'. The words **New Deal** caught on immediately. Somehow they gave hope to millions who had lost faith. Today they are used to describe the period dominated by Roosevelt.

The New Deal

Although the New Deal laws to end the Depression were spread over many years, Roosevelt began with emergency action. For one hundred days, from 8 March to 16 June 1933, Congress allowed him to be a 'democratic dictator' by passing laws at breakneck speed. What followed astonished the world. Gone were the days when an American president could afford to take an afternoon nap. Now lights burned in Washington's government buildings far into the night as officials worked late with their new master.

Roosevelt ordered all the banks to be closed. This prevented depositors withdrawing all their money and so ruining a healthy business. He followed this with a radio speech beginning, 'I want to talk for a few minutes to the American people about banking'. Quietly he explained how no bank could stay in business if everybody demanded their money back on the same day. If his listeners stopped panicking in this way the government would guarantee that their money was safer in a bank than under a mattress. When banking houses reopened it was clear people had understood. Queues outside banks became a thing of the past. The American financial system was saved.

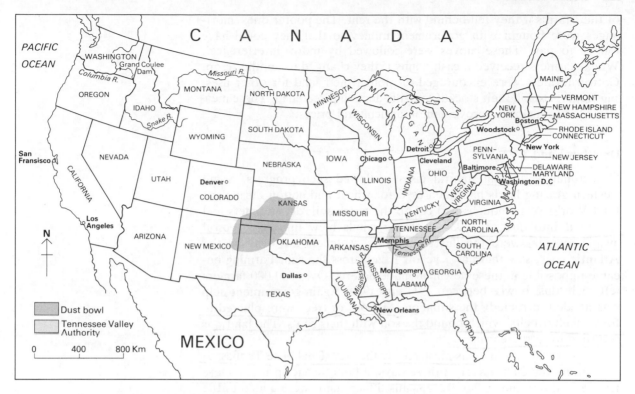

The United States of America showing the Dust bowl and the area of the Tennessee Valley Authority

The New Deal was based on three principles fairly new to American governments. First, it offered men jobs instead of charity. Second, it authorised old age pensions and sick pay where necessary. Finally, it helped American farmers with government action. All three involved federal 'interference' in state and local affairs. All three meant that private business would be regulated and controlled. To the rich these ideas seemed dangerously like socialism and they hated Roosevelt. The poor were too desperate to raise such objections. To them Roosevelt was simply a man who helped them.

A **Federal Emergency Relief Administration (FERA)** began to create useful jobs. Five hundred new airports, roads, schools, parks and playgrounds were built by the unemployed. A **Federal Theatre** gave work to 25,000 actors, writers and producers. Librarians were employed to catalogue books, artists to decorate public buildings. Boys were enrolled in the **Civilian Conservation Corps (CCC)** which cut trails, planted trees and dug reservoirs. Most of this work benefited the community. It created better amenities; it made life more beautiful; it brought entertainment to out-of-the-way places; it gave physical fitness to underfed youths. More important, it helped the out-of-work to regain their self-respect. They were paying their way and supporting their families. They were useful members of society again.

An **Agricultural Adjustment Act (AAA)** started similar schemes to change America's farming. With wheat prices as low as they had been three hundred years before, the need for this was urgent. A **Farm Credit Administration (FCA)** stopped farmers from being thrown out of their farms if they fell behind with the rent. The poorer ones' mortgages were bought with government money so that they could have longer to pay. These moves were followed by more 'interference'. Wheat farmers received a cash bonus if they changed to another crop. Cotton farmers were encouraged to plough their land for other uses; pig farmers to kill their stock if over-production threatened. These measures led to a slow improvement in agricultural prices.

Dust bowl and TVA

Unfortunately a great natural disaster slowed such progress. Some western grazing lands had been used for wheat and cotton during the First World War. Ploughs had cut up the tough soil; dry summers had turned it into dust. In 1934–5 strong winds blew this light topsoil away. So great were the dust clouds that watchers far away on the Atlantic coast saw them as a yellow haze across the sun. Farming became impossible in these new man-made deserts. Over 350,000 farmers left such 'dust bowls' between 1934 and 1939. Again government help was needed to remedy the situation. Millions of trees were planted to form 'shelter belts' which bound the soil with their roots. The land was returned to cattle rearing.

In other ways nature was mastered by the New Deal. The Tennessee was an unpredictable river in those days, a flood in the spring, a mere trickle in the summer. To prevent this fifteen dams were added to the one which had been built at Muscle Shoals in 1917. Since the river was over 1,000 kilometres long and ran through seven states (see map on page 125), Congress set up a **Tennessee Valley Authority (TVA)** with powers to work along it wherever necessary. Lovers of states' rights

An abandoned 'Dust bowl' farm in Texas

protested. But river traffic increased, flooding stopped and water power produced cheaper electricity. Another example of federal building was the Grand Coulee Dam on the Columbia River.

Not all the New Deal ideas were successful. The **National Recovery Act (NRA)** of 1933 insisted on fair dealing between workers and employers. It proposed sickness and unemployment insurance, shorter hours of work and better wages. Businessmen were ordered to put up a 'Blue Eagle' sign to show they obeyed its rules. It never worked properly. Rich industrialists like Henry Ford refused to join. The Supreme Court took advantage of its right to review government laws and declared that the NRA and other New Deal measures violated the US Constitution (rules of government). Roosevelt fought long battles with this Court throughout the 1930s. In 1935, however, he managed to set up a national system of unemployment and old age insurance with a **Social Security Act**.

In 1936 the American people re-elected Roosevelt as President. People who had heard only grumbling about him were surprised. The result showed that Americans trusted Roosevelt. As one wit put it, 'Everyone but the voters was against the New Deal'!

founder of ford (car).

Timeline

1920–3   Warren Harding President of USA.
1921   Johnson Act.
1923–9   Calvin Coolidge President of USA.
1929   Black Thursday on New York Stock Exchange. Depression begins.
1929–32   Herbert Hoover President of USA.
1933   Roosevelt begins first Presidency with 'Hundred Days'. Announces a number of New Deal laws which take effect during next five years.
1936   Roosevelt re-elected President.

Questions

1. What were (i) the causes and (ii) the results of the Depression in America between 1929 and 1932?

2. How did Roosevelt plan to overcome the effects of the Depression by the 'New Deal'?

3. Look at the cartoon on page 124.
   a) Who are the two men in the picture?
   b) Whose are the slogans referred to in the dustbin?
   c) Why is F.D.R. throwing these slogans away?
   d) What made Americans say 'In Hoover we trusted, now we are busted'?

4. Write short paragraphs on each of the following:
   a) Dust Bowls   b) Black Thursday, 1929
   c) the Johnson Act, 1921 d) 'Silent Cal'

15
From Empire to Commonwealth
The British Overseas 1900–1947

Dreams of empire

By the end of the nineteenth century Britain ruled a vast empire. It has been estimated that Britain's possessions covered one-quarter of the world's land surface and comprised one-fifth of the world's population. Not everybody in Britain was happy about this state of affairs but imperialists were filled with pride. They believed that, although the British might not be the best race in the world, they were the best at governing. Lord Curzon, for example, thought that the British Empire was '...the greatest instrument for good the world has seen'. Curzon, who ruled India as Viceroy in the early years of the twentieth century, saw the British Empire as a political power of the first order.

The British Empire in 1914

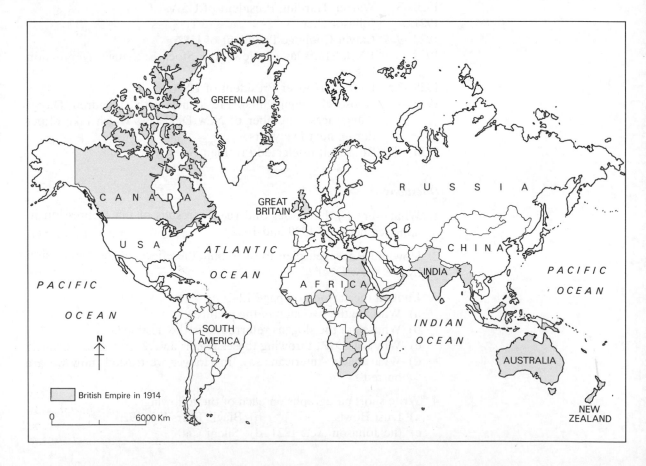

British Empire in 1914

0 _____ 6000 Km

Other imperialists thought the Empire could be made into an economic power, a vast free trade area similar to that of the United States. Joseph Chamberlain wrote in 1895, 'It is not enough to occupy certain great spaces of the world's surface, unless you can make the best of them, unless you are willing to develop them'. It was an attractive idea and in 1903 Chamberlain suggested that Empire goods should be allowed into Britain on more favourable terms than foreign products. Such '**imperial preference**' was rejected by the voters because Britain traded far more with foreigners than she did with her Empire. Steel, coal and cotton owners were doing far too well at that time to consider the idea.

Years later, in 1932, Joseph Chamberlain's son, Neville Chamberlain, actually began to do what his father had suggested; he put a ten per cent charge on all imports except Empire ones. The Dominions (Canada, Australia, New Zealand and South Africa) refused to do the same. At the **Ottawa Conference, 1932**, their representatives pointed out that if certain British goods were let in duty-free their own industries would suffer. The British were not happy either about giving Empire food priority when they could buy cheaper European food. The trouble was that Britain and her Dominions tended to produce much the same things. Economic co-operation would have been much easier if each had produced different goods to offer to each other.

Politically, also, the dreams of the imperialists came to nothing. Year by year the political ties between Britain and her Dominions grew less. The Dominions became self-governing states owing a vague loyalty to the King. At the Paris Peace Conference (see Chapter 11) each Dominion signed separately, whilst some refused to give up territories their troops had conquered during the war. Afterwards they sent their own ambassadors to foreign capitals. Although each Dominion had a Governor-General who was supposed to represent the King, he was usually treated as a monarch in his own right. George V himself never visited any Dominion after 1910.

It was not surprising, therefore, that in 1926 Mackenzie King, Prime Minister of Canada, suggested that this actual freedom should be made legal by Act of Parliament. After various conferences the **Statute of Westminster, 1931**, declared the Dominions to be free and independent states within a British Commonwealth of Nations. Yet this legal freedom did not prevent them fighting for Britain in two world wars. The ties that really mattered were friendship and a similar language and culture.

Australia

Possibly the strongest feelings of kinship and friendliness towards Britain were felt by Australians. This affection was highlighted dramatically in time of war. Nearly 15,000 Australians had volunteered to fight beside the British in the Boer War of 1899–1902 (see Chapter 4). In the First World War Australian units won fame, fighting bravely at Gallipoli and on the Western Front and suffering heavy losses (see Chapter 9). When Britain went to war with Germany again in 1939 the

Australian Prime Minister, Robert Menzies, broadcast within a few minutes of the British declaration of war. 'Great Britain has declared war upon her [Germany]', he stated, '. . . as a result, Australia is also at war'. To most Australians it was as simple as that.

The entry of Japan into the war in 1941 endangered Australia directly. When Japanese troops overran Britain's Asiatic possessions and captured the important base of Singapore (February 1942) Australians realised that they were no longer part of a powerful empire. For the first time Britain was unable to protect them. Whatever affection they might feel for the 'mother country', Australians had to look for help elsewhere. The only ally strong enough and willing to help was the USA. Soon after the fall of Singapore the Australian government appealed to the Americans who reacted by sending troops and ships to Australia. For a time the US Commander in the Pacific, General Douglas MacArthur, had his headquarters in Melbourne, Australia. Throughout the war the two countries fought side by side in many Pacific war zones.

The Dominions in war and peace

Australia and Canada faced very different problems. Australia is surrounded by vast, overpopulated Asian territories. Her answer in the early days of the twentieth century to the teeming millions around her was a strict 'White Australia' policy. Only Europeans were allowed to enter her huge open spaces. Asians were excluded in case they swamped her people and altered the Australians' Western way of life. New Zealand, which became a Dominion in 1907, did the same. Both countries developed government control of industry of a socialist type. In Australia big estates owned by one family were broken up, industrial disputes between workers and employers had to be settled by arbitration, voting was made compulsory and old age pensions were given at sixty-five. In New Zealand large-scale welfare schemes were adopted. Being 'young' countries, neither Australia nor New Zealand had an established upper class to fight such changes.

Canada's development was influenced by her giant neighbour, the USA. Like the USA, Canada welcomed European immigrants. Like her also she built trans-continental railways which linked the scattered provinces and towns. With plenty of gold, copper, iron and uranium and plenty of US money she was able to develop into an industrial nation. Her population rose steadily. When she became a Dominion in 1867 (see Chapter 4) she had a population of 4 million; by 1979 this had swollen to 23½ million. No similar increase occurred in Australia and New Zealand whose populations in 1979 were 14½ million and 3 million respectively.

Canada proved as loyal to Britain as Australia in time of war. In the First World War Canadian troops fought on the Western Front, winning a great victory when they drove the Germans off Vimy Ridge in April 1917. In the Second World War they declared war on Germany again. From the fall of France (1940) until the entry of the USA into the war (December 1941), Canada was Britain's chief ally, producing every sort of war material in factories which were safe from German air attack. Later, Canadian armies fought on many battlefields in North Africa and Europe.

Canada, of course, was never in danger in the same way as Australia. The Canadians were too near the USA to need to ask for American help; no US government could have tolerated an enemy occupation of Canada. Since the Second World War the American attitude that the whole of North America, including Canada, is part of the US defence zone against nuclear attack has caused Canadians to complain of US interference in their affairs.

Ireland

Ireland, unlike the Dominions, had never been treated as an equal partner by Britain. From 1170 English warriors claimed to have conquered the island, although their claim meant little in reality. Gradually, however, the English did increase their control. The Irish reply was to rebel, but they were too small and weak to win. After each rebellion they were usually treated more severely. In the North, for example, they were driven off their land, which was given to English and Scottish settlers.

Hatred between the English and Irish was aggravated by other developments. English merchants did not want Irish competition so they persuaded Parliament to restrict Ireland's trade and industry. The export of cattle, butter and cheese was forbidden. Only linen was imported because there was no English linen industry. Obviously, Ireland was to be kept poor so that the English could be rich. When England became Protestant Ireland remained devotedly Roman Catholic, thus creating another division between the peoples. Laws against English Catholics applied to Ireland as well. Irish peasants were forced to pay tithes (taxes) to the Protestant Irish Church established by the English. No Catholic was allowed to buy land owned by a Protestant, so an Irishman often found himself working for an English landlord.

In such circumstances Irish hatred of their conquerors became deeply rooted. The rebellions of 1594–1603, 1641, and 1798 were crushed with savage cruelty. Every detail, every hero was remembered by a romantic people. Fathers told their sons tales of what the English had done. After the Great Famine of 1845–7 millions fled to North America where they infected future generations with the same feelings. Only the Protestant settlers in the North, **Ulster**, (see map opposite) remained loyal to Britain. Surrounded by their enemies there was little else they could do.

During the nineteenth century many Irish grievances were removed. In 1829 greater freedom of religion was granted. In 1869 Gladstone stopped Irish Catholics paying tithes to Protestant clergymen. As the twentieth century dawned successive Conservative governments allowed the Irish to buy their land on easy terms. But this did not satisfy the Irish people. Most of them were prepared to stay under British rule, but they wanted an Irish parliament to look after local Irish affairs. They called this **Home Rule**. In Britain the Conservatives

The provinces of Ireland

An Ulster pledge to fight Home Rule

Ulster's
Solemn League and Covenant.

Being convinced in our consciences that Home Rule would be disastrous to the material well-being of Ulster as well as of the whole of Ireland, subversive of our civil and religious freedom, destructive of our citizenship and perilous to the unity of the Empire, we, whose names are underwritten, men of Ulster, loyal subjects of His Gracious Majesty King George V., humbly relying on the God whom our fathers in days of stress and trial confidently trusted, do hereby pledge ourselves in solemn Covenant throughout this our time of threatened calamity to stand by one another in defending for ourselves and our children our cherished position of equal citizenship in the United Kingdom and in using all means which may be found necessary to defeat the present conspiracy to set up a Home Rule Parliament in Ireland. ¶ And in the event of such a Parliament being forced upon us we further solemnly and mutually pledge ourselves to refuse to recognise its authority. ¶ In sure confidence that God will defend the right we hereto subscribe our names. ¶ And further, we individually declare that we have not already signed this Covenant.

The above was signed by me at_____
"Ulster Day," Saturday, 28th September, 1912.

God Save the King.

were against this, but after much argument a Liberal-controlled government gave Home Rule to the Irish in 1914. This was then postponed until after the First World War.

The idea of Home Rule had always been disliked by the Protestant North. Even before it was law Ulstermen had collected arms and ammunition to resist. Northern Irish officers serving in the British army at the Curragh military base near Dublin had said they would resign rather than force their country to have Home Rule (1914). Some English politicians agreed with this **Curragh Mutiny**. Years before, Lord Randolph Churchill had written about Home Rule, 'Ulster will fight and Ulster will be right'. This now became the Northern slogan. In the South, on the other hand, many Catholics regarded Ireland as one country. They, too, organised military units to fight any attempt by the North to avoid Home Rule. Matters had almost reached the stage of a civil war when the outbreak of a greater conflict in 1914 postponed the quarrel.

Whereas most Irish men and women would probably have been satisfied with a solution which avoided bloodshed, a few had always been violent. In the 1860s a society called the **Fenians**, financed by Irish

Roger Casement, hanged by the British for treason

Americans and reinforced by veterans of the American Civil War, carried out a series of killings and bombings in English towns. Many of its members died bravely on the scaffold for these actions. People influenced by the Fenians remained active in Ireland. In 1914 they formed the **Irish Volunteers** and began to buy weapons so as to take advantage of the civil war which seemed about to break out.

The Easter Rising

With Britain deeply involved in the war against Germany, a handful of Irish Volunteers decided to act. On Easter Monday, 24 April 1916, a poet and teacher, **Patrick Henry Pearse**, led a detachment of armed men into Dublin. They seized various large buildings, the General Post Office in O'Connell Street, the Law Courts and a biscuit factory, dug trenches in an open space called St Stephen's Green, and fired upon any soldiers who came near them. Over the Post Office they hoisted the green flag of the 'Irish Republic'. The **Easter Rising** had begun.

The British authorities were taken by surprise. There had been little violence in Ireland for some time. Now they were preparing for the great offensive on the Somme (see page 71), confident there would be no troubles in Ireland. Only a week before, a ship carrying German weapons had been intercepted on its way to Ireland, and one plotter, **Sir Roger Casement**, was easily arrested after he had landed from a German submarine. This seemed to have ended any immediate danger. The British authorities were justified in this view. None knew better than Pearse that the whole affair was hopeless. Even his superior officers in the Volunteers had forbidden him to rebel. What neither side expected was a suicidal act. They failed to understand a man like Pearse. Brought up with a deep respect for the Fenians, he was determined to give his life as an example to future generations of Irishmen.

Fighting grew fierce as the rebels defended their strongpoints against British rifles, guns and cavalry. Dublin's roads and squares became a battlefield. The Irish fired from the gutted shells of the larger buildings; the British replied from behind corners and overturned vehicles. Armoured cars prowled the streets pumping shells into houses. A British gun-boat steamed up the river Liffey and bombarded the General Post Office. At night flaming liquid from a burning warehouse was hurled into the sky, and the starving horses left from an unsuccessful British cavalry charge clattered over the cobbles in the empty ruined streets. Slowly the British casualties grew as they captured one 'fortress' after another. Pearse's Volunteers in the Post Office did not surrender until Saturday afternoon. As they were led away angry Dubliners gathered to curse them. Not only had the poet's rebellion failed. He had enraged his own countrymen by ruining large parts of Dublin and bringing business to a standstill.

The British now made a mistake. Their leaders were furious that Irishmen could rebel when thousands of other Irish soldiers were dying for Britain. Swiftly their military courts tried most of the rebels and sentenced the ringleaders to death. Pearse faced execution bravely; fourteen of his friends died with him. At once the mood of the Irish

Ruins of the General Post Office, Dublin, after the Easter Rising, 1916

changed from indifference to anger. The ruins of Dublin were forgotten; Irishmen were being shot as traitors by a foreign government. Soon the tales which were to make the Easter Rising another Irish legend were circulating. Orators read Pearse's last poem aloud. They told how the wounded James Connolly had been carried to his death on a stretcher. By the time Casement had been refused a trial 'in his own country' and hanged in Pentonville Prison, London, Pearse was no longer irritating or funny. Looking back, one can see that his death lit a flame which illuminated Ireland's path to independence.

'An expert at underground warfare'. The Irish leader Michael Collins

The war of independence

Two rebels who survived the Easter Rising were **Eamon de Valera** and **Michael Collins**. As far as they were concerned the Irish Republic existed from the moment the green flag was hoisted above the Post Office. Gradually the rest of the south came to agree with them. On the political front de Valera organised a party called **Sinn Féin**, Gaelic for 'Ourselves Alone'. In 1918 this party won 73 of the 105 Irish seats in a general election. Sinn Féin then set up an Irish parliament, the **Dáil Éireann**. Soon Ireland had two governments: the Dáil which most people obeyed, and the British administration which most people ignored. The Dáil raised taxes, held its own courts and was recognised by nearly all local authorities outside Dublin. Meanwhile, Collins turned the **Irish Republican Army (IRA)** into a deadly fighting force. Collins was no dreamer like Pearse. He was an expert at underground warfare, leading a few thousand in attacks of all sorts against the British. His men wore no uniform. They gathered for an ambush or bombing, carried it out ruthlessly and then melted away into civilian life. The British were at a disadvantage because there were no Irishmen they could trust. Again and again Collins himself escaped capture because he knew of British movements from spies inside their Headquarters.

At first the British answered violence with violence. To help the overworked police they organised a special force of ex-soldiers, nicknamed the '**Black and Tans**'. Their actions were generally brutal and often murderous. To this day they are hated in Ireland. The frequent ambushes, the fires and explosions, the vicious reprisals, turned Ireland into a land of terror. By 1921 both sides were exhausted, and ready for peace. Britain's Prime Minister, Lloyd George, realised that 100,000 troops would be needed to subdue Ireland. Rather than face such expense, he signed a truce with the Irish in July 1921. A Peace Treaty signed in December 1921 gave the twenty-six southern counties (the **Irish Free State**) complete control of their own government, finances and police. The six counties in the north (**Northern Ireland**) had already chosen to continue as part of the United Kingdom under the Government of Ireland Act, 1920 (see map opposite).

De Valera, as President of the Dáil, had told the Irish delegates who went to London for the negotiations not to agree to any treaty which left the Irish subjects of the British King. In fact, the Peace Treaty did contain a promise that the new Irish parliament would take an oath of loyalty to the British Crown. De Valera and his supporters in the Dáil at once denounced the Treaty. Even Collins, one of the delegates who signed it, had misgivings. He wrote, 'Will anyone be satisfied at the bargain? I tell you this – early this morning I signed my death warrant . . .'. The answer to his question was a civil war between those in favour of the Treaty and those against it. His prophecy came true. Collins was killed during the war. Nevertheless, it was the pro-Treaty forces who won. De Valera was arrested and spent a short time in jail. When released he formed a political party called **Fianna Fáil**. This is Gaelic and means 'warriors of Fáil' – Fáil being a poetic name for

A divided Ireland after 1921

Ireland. For some time members of his party refused to sit in the Dáil even when elected, because of the oath of loyalty. A country divided geographically was still deeply divided politically.

Eamon de Valera

Eamon de Valera, dominant figure in southern Irish politics for many years

Hopes that the division between the Irish Free State and the six counties of Ulster would be only temporary were soon dashed. The promised Boundary Commission was supposed to settle and, if necessary, adjust the border. However, when this Commission met, the Northern Ireland delegates refused to change the border. They were determined to have nothing to do with the Catholic-influenced government of the Irish Free State. Their refusal left a large number of Irish Catholics under British rule in Northern Ireland.

Eamon de Valera, leader of the Fianna Fáil Party, always regretted the loss of what he called 'our fairest province'. So did most southern Irishmen. De Valera could never understand why the northern Protestants were so against rule from Dublin and dismissed the idea that their Protestant religion would be threatened if they joined the Irish Free State. He also complained about the way Catholics in Northern Ireland were treated as 'second-class citizens'. In 1932 Fianna Fáil won a parliamentary majority. From 1932 until 1959, with a few breaks, de Valera was the dominant figure in southern Irish politics, first as Prime Minister and then as President of the Irish Free State. In 1937 a new constitution was introduced, and the country was renamed Eire. De Valera's long-term aim was for Eire to leave the British Commonwealth altogether. He was not interested in Dominion status. But, being a cautious man, he proceeded slowly and, in fact, did not negotiate personally the final break with the Commonwealth.

During the 1930s relations between Britain and the Irish Free State were not particularly friendly. De Valera stopped repayments of loans made by Britain in the past to help Irish tenants buy their land. He maintained that Britain had stolen the land in the first place. This led to a trade 'war' between Britain and the Irish Free State. It was ended in 1938 when de Valera negotiated a new treaty which, amongst other concessions, gave three Free State ports used by the British Navy (Lough Swilly, Cobh and Berehaven) back to the Irish government (see map on page 135). Quite soon these ports took on a new importance. In September 1939 Britain and Germany went to war and the seas around Ireland became a battleground.

Irish 'Emergency'

When the news of war reached Dublin de Valera decided that Eire should remain neutral. He knew that small countries rarely gain anything by taking part in a war between great powers. In any case most of his people wanted to stay out of the war, if only to show their independence of Britain. Many individual Irishmen did fight in the British forces but the de Valera government tried to remain friendly with both sides.

The problems caused by the Second World War are usually referred to as 'the Emergency' in southern Ireland. It was a time of hardship because the German naval blockade of the British Isles included southern Ireland. The most difficult question concerned the British desire to use the bases in Eire for warships needed to escort merchant ships and so protect them from attacks by German U-boats. Churchill, the British Prime Minister from 1940, even considered taking the ports by force. He felt that without them the life and death struggle with the German submarines might be lost.

Many British people felt bitter about the matter. To them it seemed that British sailors, sometimes taking food to southern Ireland, were being drowned because of de Valera's refusal to allow them to use the ports. De Valera, on the other hand, claimed that once the French ports were in German hands (June 1940) the northern sea route via the Ulster ports was the only possible one for Atlantic shipping. This was also the opinion of some British generals. De Valera knew also that to give Britain help of this kind would mean the end of Irish neutrality in the war. Nevertheless, the German invasion of Denmark, Holland, Belgium and Norway (see Chapter 20) showed the Irish leader just how little Hitler cared for the rights of small countries. Consequently de Valera gave the people of Britain and Northern Ireland what help he could. He sent the Dublin Fire Brigade to fight the fires caused by a German air raid on Belfast and he always sent home British airmen and sailors stranded in Ireland.

In a 'Victory Speech' at the end of the war Churchill attacked de Valera's attitude. Britain, he said, 'never laid a violent hand upon them [the southern Irish] though at times it would have been quite easy and natural, and we left the de Valera government to frolic with the German . . . representatives to their heart's content'. De Valera broadcast a reply, pointing out that had Britain invaded Eire she would have been committing the sort of aggression for which she condemned Germany. The Irish people liked the speech. They realised that neutrality during the Emergency, probably more than any other event since 1921, had shown the world that there was a truly independent Ireland.

India

Centuries after the English claimed to have conquered Ireland, the British and French went to India to trade. Wars between them followed, and after victories at Plassey (1757) and Wandewash (1759) the British East India Company found itself ruler of a large area called Bengal (see map on page 140). The Governor-Generals who administered it often had different aims. Some, like Charles Cornwallis, wished only to improve British rule. Others, like Richard Colley Wellesley, preferred to conquer more land from the Indian princes. After the Indian Mutiny (1857) British rule was supreme throughout the whole continent, either directly or through subject rulers. To most Englishmen India was the most exciting and romantic part of their Empire. Its varied races and religions, its strange ways, fascinated

them. To Disraeli it was 'the brightest jewel' in Victoria's crown and
he persuaded her to become Empress of India in 1877.

Yet, by 1900 India's 300 million inhabitants had ceased to be as
profitable to the British as in the mid-eighteenth century. Outwardly
the British ruling class seemed very grand. The Viceroy lived in luxury
like an Oriental Sultan. Behind such grandeur lay a different story.
Five thousand hard-working British District Officers tried to run a
desperately poor country where famines and plagues frequently killed
millions. Outwardly large irrigation schemes, long railway lines, imposing buildings and a good police force showed the traveller how India
had benefited from British rule. In fact, few Indians were treated as
anything but second-class Europeans: in 1915, for example, only five
per cent of the higher civil servants were Indians. No educated Indian
could doubt that he belonged to a conquered race.

Until the twentieth century such a minority could do little because
they believed the British to be unbeatable. Then movements and wars
in the outside world began to suggest otherwise. Japan's defeat of
Russia (see Chapter 5) and the Young Turk rebellion (see Chapter 7)
showed that non-European races could copy and defeat Western nations. Encouraged by English Liberal politicians, these few started to
demand a greater say in the government of their country. Slowly Britain shed bits of her power. In 1909 the **Morley-Minto Reforms** increased the duties of Indian provincial councils, although supreme authority still rested with the Viceroy and his Governors. Then came the
First World War and afterwards Wilson's idea of self-determination
(see Chapter 11). This, and Britain's obvious weakness, caused the two

*Indian princes pose for a
photograph with Britain's
Viceroy, 1919*

Mahatma Gandhi comes to London in his quest for Indian independence, 1931

most powerful Indian organisations, the Hindu Congress and the Muslim League, to demand self-government. Had not India contributed £200 million and 800,000 soldiers to the war effort? Was she not entitled to some reward for this sacrifice? A new leader, **Mohandas Karamchand Gandhi**, who had lived his early life in South Africa, started to organise *hartals* (strikes) against the British. His simple way of life deeply impressed the peasants and soon he was called Mahatma or 'great Soul'.

Gandhi was a pacifist (against war) who hated violence and preferred to fast nearly to death to get his way. Unfortunately, many of Gandhi's followers disobeyed their beloved leader when he was not actually present. During 1919 riots and disorder spread throughout India, partly because of Britain's treatment of Muslim Turkey and partly because certain wartime regulations restricting freedom had not been cancelled. The worst incident occurred at **Amritsar** in the Punjab (see map on page 140) where British troops opened fire on a mob, killing 379 and wounding 1,000 people. The man responsible, General Dyer, was afterwards censured and retired from the army. Nevertheless, such a massacre was used by Indian propagandists to stir up ill-feeling against British rule.

The drift towards partition

From Amritsar onwards British concessions never quite caught up with Indian demands. In 1919 the **Montagu-Chelmsford Reforms** gave far more self-government to Indians. Health, education and agriculture were to be run by Indian provincial councils. Police and finance remained in British hands. This system of shared government was called a dyarchy. India was also promised Dominion status in the future. In 1935 the **Government of India Act** went further. Indians were given entire control of the provincial councils; her people were allowed to vote if they owned property of a certain value. These reforms were not enough for Indians like Gandhi or **Jawaharlal Nehru**. They complained that the Viceroy was still supreme ruler and all Indian parliaments subject to the British House of Commons. Only 'immediate independence' would satisfy them.

In the meantime India drifted towards partition. About a quarter of India's population were Muslim. In the past Muslim warriors had conquered Hindu India, ruling it until the arrival of the British and French. Although they consisted of various races, they felt that the bond of a common religion made them a distinct people. Their leader, **Mohammed Ali Jinnah**, feared that if India gained independence the Muslims would be swamped by the superior numbers of Hindus. In 1934 he suggested that Muslims should become independent, not only of the British but of the Hindus as well. Most Muslims agreed with him. They demanded a separate state which they called **Pakistan**. The word, which means 'land of the pure', also possessed letters representing some of the Muslim peoples and territories, P for Punjab, A for Afghan, K for Kashmir and S for Sind (see map on page 140). Although the Hindu Congress was horrified it soon became clear that,

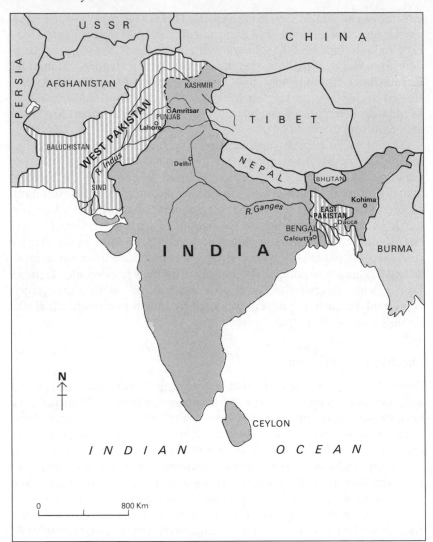

India after 1947, showing East and West Pakistan

as with northern and southern Ireland, any attempt to unite the peoples of India and Pakistan would lead to civil war.

The Second World War involved India more deeply than the First World War because of the Japanese attack on nearby Burma (see page 197). As in 1914–18 Indian troops fought all over the world, but their main effort was against the Japanese whom they helped to defeat at **Kohima**. At home, the pacifist Gandhi ran a 'Quit India' campaign against the British, whilst Nehru and the Hindu Congress refused to co-operate in the war effort because they were not given independence straight away. Soon after victory in the war the new British Labour Government decided to give India her freedom.

Immediately, Jinnah began to press his claim more strongly. 'A Muslim League', he announced, 'will not yield an inch in its demand for Pakistan'. Bloody riots between Hindus and Muslims convinced the

Partition in India was violent and bloody. Bodies after a riot between Hindus and Muslims, Delhi 1947

British that these demands could not be refused. In Britain the government resigned itself to a divided India and fixed 1948 as independence year. In India the last Viceroy, Lord Louis Mountbatten, regarded the matter as more urgent. He named 15 August 1947 as the date for freedom. In nine weeks British officials performed their last, and in some ways their most difficult, task. They divided the police, government and army of a continent into three parts. On that day three countries, East Pakistan, West Pakistan and India, gained their freedom.

The surgery proved to be violent and bloody. Four and a half million Hindus fled to India; six million Muslims to Pakistan. In the Punjab the Hindus were furious that their own claims for a separate state had been passed over. They rioted and massacred large numbers of Muslims. Further west, Muslim **Kashmir** was invaded by Pakistani troops to prevent its Hindu ruler giving it to India. Indian troops entered the country to stop this and the unhappy land has been divided ever since. Few Indians have ever accepted that Pakistan was necessary. Few Muslims have ever doubted that it was. As in Ireland, so in India, the British left a country divided by religion.

Timeline

1857	Indian Mutiny.
1907	New Zealand becomes a Dominion.
1909	Morley-Minto Reforms.
1914	Curragh Mutiny. Irish Volunteers formed.
1916	Irish Easter Rising.
1919	Sinn Féiners form Irish Parliament in Dublin (Dáil Éireann).
	Amritsar riots in India. Montagu-Chelmsford Reforms.

1919–21   Sinn Féiners wage war against Britain.
1920   Government of Ireland Act. Northern Ireland accepts Home Rule. Irish Free State formed.
1926   Fianna Fáil formed.
1931   Statute of Westminster.
1932   Ottawa Conference.
    Fianna Fáil party wins Irish election. De Valera becomes Prime Minister.
1935   Government of India Act.
1939–45   Southern Ireland stays neutral during the Second World War.
1947   Pakistan and India become independent.

Questions

1. Look at the reproduction of 'Ulster's Solemn League and Covenant' on page 132.
   a) Explain what you understand by the term 'Home Rule' in relation to Ireland.
   b) Why did some Ulstermen object to the idea?
   c) What did the Ulstermen promise to do if Home Rule was set up in Ireland?
   d) Why was the quarrel about Home Rule 'postponed' for two years after this Covenant was published?

2. 'Possibly the strongest feelings of kinship and friendliness towards Britain were felt by Australians.'
   How did Australians show these feelings during the First and Second World Wars?

3. Describe the events which took place in Ireland between 1920–1 and explain the part played by the British government. What were the results?

4. Draw a simple sketchmap of India, Pakistan and Kashmir in 1947. Explain (i) why India was divided in this way and (ii) the part played by Mahatma Gandhi, Jawaharlal Nehru and Mohammed Jinnah in the events which led to independence.

5. Write short paragraphs on each of the following:
   a) the Statute of Westminster, 1931
   b) the Easter Rising, 1916
   c) Eamon de Valera
   d) the Government of India Act, 1935

16
The World of Adolf Hitler
Germany 1918–1933

Adolf Hitler was born in April 1889 at Braunau, Austria-Hungary (see map on page 144). His father was a customs official employed on the German border. He did not do well at school and in 1908 went to Vienna because he wanted to be an artist. When the Art Academy rejected him he tried to earn a living painting and selling postcards. This produced little profit so he did any odd job, even beating carpets and shovelling snow. At times he was very poor. He lived in doss-houses, his clothes were ragged and full of lice. Probably because of these miserable experiences, Hitler grew to hate Vienna. Its mixture of races, Jews, Croats and Czechs, irritated him. Like most Austrians he despised these subject peoples and loved everything German. In particular, he was infected with the Viennese dislike of Jews, and this terrible prejudice remained with him all his life.

Hitler was pleased when his country went to war in 1914. On the day war was declared he joined a dense, excited crowd in the Odeon Platz. This historic scene was photographed. Years later, when Hitler was world famous, someone noticed him in the picture. The long face with its unmistakable moustache looks delighted. Soon afterwards he crossed into Germany and joined a Bavarian regiment. In spite of what his enemies said later, he seems to have been a brave soldier. He took part in the fighting at the First Battle of Ypres, the Somme and in the

Hitler in an excited crowd greeting the news of war, 1914

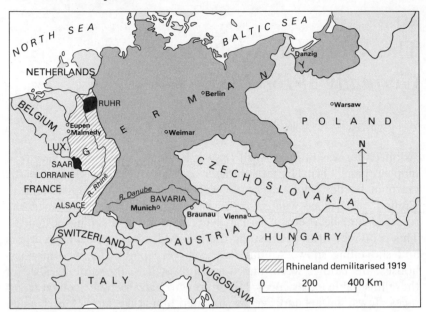

final 1918 offensives (see Chapters 9 and 10). Mostly he served as a runner, carrying messages to and fro. It was a dangerous job. Once he was gassed and he was awarded the Iron Cross, First Class, for bravery. Hitler enjoyed warfare, probably because it was more exciting than civilian life. He left the army in 1918 with the rank of corporal, convinced, as he said, that war was 'the greatest of all experiences'.

He returned to a defeated and divided Germany. The new **Weimar Republic**, named after the small town where its first parliament met, was far different from the proud, imperial country founded by Bismarck. Few Germans admired a government which had been born out of defeat; whose representatives had signed the hated Versailles Peace Treaty. From the start it was plagued by revolutions, riots and disobedience of every kind, especially as its constitution allowed the German provinces a great deal of freedom. In Berlin a rising of revolutionary socialists called **Spartakists** had to be crushed by the army; a similar rebellion was put down in Munich. Unfortunately, as in Italy, the German army did little about disorder organised by parties of which its leaders approved. Ex-servicemen were able to join together in units called **Free Corps** and allowed to murder and beat up their opponents. Unofficial 'courts' sentenced and executed their enemies.

In four years 376 political murders took place in Germany. If the killers were Communists they were caught and put to death. If not they were given light sentences or allowed to escape. Nowhere was this lawlessness more widespread than in Munich, capital of Bavaria (see map above). Here the authorities made no secret of their contempt for the Weimar Republic. Some even wanted Bavaria to become independent again under its old royal family. When Munich's police chief was told that there were murder gangs operating in the city he replied, 'Yes, but not enough of them'.

Political troubles were only part of the story. In 1923, when the **French army occupied the Ruhr** coal-fields because Germany had failed to make certain payments of reparations (see Chapter 11), German workers began a new war with their old enemy. All over the Ruhr there were strikes and acts of sabotage. Before long factory and mining work stopped altogether. Since the area produced eighty per cent of Germany's coal, iron and steel, the economic effects were felt throughout Germany. Production slowed down, causing widespread unemployment. Worse still, German money, which had been losing value steadily since 1918, now collapsed. In January 1923, 72,000 marks equalled £1. Ten months later it took 16,000 million marks to equal £1. Germans found their savings wiped away overnight; their wages almost useless pieces of paper.

Corporal Hitler, photographed in the trenches during the First World War

Hitler's political apprenticeship

Hitler began his political career in Munich where he was employed by the army to turn soldiers against pacifist and democratic ideas. From the start he appealed to the feelings, not the reason, of those around him. Standing on chairs and tables in smoke-filled beer-halls he was forced to scream and yell to be heard. Once he had an audience's attention he would work himself into a frenzy, spitting and shouting. The effect of such displays was strange. To some he seemed a madman. To others he was more like a hypnotist. Men as well as women were known to burst into tears as they listened. Before long Hitler had a following which he called the German Workers' Party. In 1920 this organisation was joined by the **National Socialist German Workers' Party (Nazis)**. Their badge was the swastika.

Hitler knew that the people around him were looking for someone to blame for their troubles so he gave them plenty of 'enemies'. Usually some section or class of Germans agreed with him. He claimed, for example, that the German army had never been defeated but had been let down by Jews and communists at home. This 'stab in the back' theory about the so-called **'November criminals'** who had signed the truce in November 1918 was untrue. It was General Ludendorff who had told the civilians that they must sign a peace treaty because the army could no longer defend the Fatherland. Yet it suited many Germans, particularly army officers, to believe Hitler's story. Again, Hitler blamed the Peace Settlement for most of Germany's troubles. Here was an unfair, dictated peace, he claimed, which had taken much land from Germany (see page 94). To a certain extent this was true, although Hitler never mentioned the sort of treaty which his country had imposed upon Russia at Brest-Litovsk (see page 83). Hitler's promise that he would ignore the Peace Settlement if he came to power impressed young officers who saw no future in an army restricted to 100,000 men and iron and steel manufacturers who had few tanks, warships or guns to build for a disarmed Germany.

In other matters Hitler struck just the right note. His demand for a union (*Anschluss*) between the new Austria and Germany was supported by many Germans. His denunciation of democracy as a weak and ineffective form of government pleased many more. Few Germans knew what democratic government was like. They had been brought up in a country where real power rested with the Kaiser, the Chancellor and the Generals. Furthermore the actual system of voting in the Weimar Republic had led to many small political parties who were forced to form coalitions in order to govern at all. Finally, his promise of a few socialist measures, such as nationalisation of department stores, gained him some working-class votes, though he was careful to condemn communism in order to please German capitalists.

Above all, Hitler always offered a simple solution. Everything would be all right if the Jews were deprived of all money and power, or the communists crushed, or the 'November criminals' hanged. Germany had only to stand up and fight or ignore the terms of the Versailles Treaty to become great again. In desperate times many people believed in such desperate remedies. Had not Bismarck united Germany with two quick wars after centuries of argument?

None of these ideas was particularly novel. But Hitler's way of constantly repeating them, as well as his violent actions, was different. Hardly had his Nazi Party been founded than it established a 'Gymnastics and Sports' division. These **Stormtroopers** turned out to be young thugs who broke up other party meetings and injured political opponents. More surprising still, Hitler never tried to hide what his Nazis were doing. Indeed, he boasted of their exploits. Here were sincere, angry men ready to do something for the Fatherland, he seemed to be saying. Such brutality appalled some decent Germans but it also fascinated and attracted many young men who might otherwise have turned communist. Hitler's party never debated a matter, or formed committees, or voted. Instead, they held mass rallies to show their strength, marched for hours past their leader, or listened spellbound to his speeches. In 1930 they even made a marching song out of the story of a young Nazi, **Horst Wessel**, killed in a street fight with communists.

Typical Nazi Rally, 1932

Hermann Goering, photographed when he commanded the German 'Luftwaffe' (Airforce)

The Beer-Hall Putsch (revolution), 1923

A strong government would have put Hitler in prison. The Bavarian leaders encouraged him because he was against the Republic and against communism. On 8 November 1923, after only four years in politics, Hitler went too far. No doubt encouraged by the Italian Fascists' successful March on Rome the previous year (see page 116), he rushed into a Munich beer-hall, jumped upon a chair, and announced a 'National Revolution'. The next morning 3,000 of his armed Storm-troopers assembled with swastika banners and began to parade through the streets led by Hitler, Hermann Goering, a famous fighter ace, and General Ludendorff. It looked as though the Nazis' own 'March on Berlin' had begun. Unlike Mussolini, however, Hitler had made two mistakes. First, he had not made sure of the active support of the army. Apart from Ludendorff and a few detachments led by Major Ernst Röhm, it was against him. Second, he was unknown outside Bavaria whereas Mussolini had been a national figure before his 'March'.

When police barred the way with rifles at the ready. Hitler shouted 'Surrender! Surrender!' and the procession surged forward. Who fired first will probably never be known; afterwards each side blamed the other. Within minutes the street was littered with dead, wounded or those who had thrown themselves to the ground. Goering was badly wounded. Hitler either fell or was dragged down by a dying friend. Only Ludendorff behaved like a true Prussian. Upright as if on parade he marched towards the flying bullets and pushed his way contemptuously through the police cordon. Altogether sixteen Nazis and three policemen were killed in this unsuccessful *putsch*. Hitler was arrested and his party was banned.

In a peaceful and well-organised country this would have been the end of his career. In Bavaria at that time Hitler was safe. Many government officials had been in sympathy with him. Some had even promised to join the *putsch* and had only deserted him when they had realised where the army stood. At his trial Hitler was allowed to make long speeches, to interrupt and to cross-examine witnesses. These exploits received much publicity, helping him to become well-known for the first time outside Bavaria. In the end he was sentenced to five years in prison, a ridiculous punishment for armed rebellion, and in fact served only nine months. Whilst living in a pleasant room at Landsberg Prison he wrote *Mein Kampf* (My Struggle), a book in which he tried to demonstrate that he was an intellectual. In fact Hitler's writing was not as effective as his speaking. He never had a good command of his own language and *Mein Kampf* was dismissed by one literary man as '164,000 offences committed against German grammar...'.

Nevertheless, Hitler came out of Prison determined never to try violent revolution again. He found a more stable Germany. **Gustav Stresemann**, Chancellor at the time, had set himself the task of making Germany great by peaceful means. To do this it was first necessary to restore the value of the German mark (see page 145). Under the **Dawes**

Plan (1924) arrangements were made for Germany to pay reparations by annual instalments. At the same time large amounts of US money became available to help economic recovery. Old, useless money was withdrawn from circulation and a new currency – the *rentenmark* – was issued whose value was guaranteed by a mortgage raised on all German land and property. When people knew this their confidence returned. Soon more real money meant more jobs and so more food. Industries were revived, new factories built. All over the country this borrowed money was used to construct theatres, airfields, swimming-pools and sports' stadiums. By 1928 only 650,000 men were unemployed, the lowest figure for ten years. Germany entered upon a period of prosperity which made the post-war troubles seem a nightmare which had passed forever.

Foreign affairs showed a similar improvement. Under Stresemann, Germany began to be accepted as a great power once more, instead of as the beaten 'naughty boy' of the world. In 1925 Britain and France joined her in signing the **Locarno Pact**. By its terms Germany promised never to change her frontiers with France or Belgium, and only to attempt an alteration of her eastern boundaries by peaceful means. Next year she was made a member of the League of Nations (see Chapter 11), and two years after that she signed the **Kellogg Pact** by which most European nations agreed to outlaw war. Even the bitter feelings over war reparations died down a little when the **Young Plan (1929)** allowed for payments to be spaced over fifty-nine years.

None of this was any use to Hitler. The hatred and revenge he preached needed discontent and misery to make it effective. Although he discovered a brilliant propaganda chief in **Joseph Goebbels**, a crippled journalist who was an expert liar, he still could not make any real headway. His party remained a noisy, brutal and well-organised minority, giving Hitler a comfortable living but not the power he wanted. In May 1928 the Nazis polled only 810,000 votes out of 31 million cast. In 1930 they held a mere 12 seats out of over 600 available in the German Reichstag (parliament). The Nazi leader was laughed at as the crank who had failed in the 'Beer-Hall *Putsch*'. Throughout this period some sure instinct seemed to tell Hitler that one day things would change for the worse. Week after week he raged and roared about the Versailles Treaty, about the danger of Jews and communists. Week after week he tried to get money and support from industrialists. Week after week he built up the intricate Nazi organisation which later terrorised all Europe. Gradually his party became known throughout Germany, especially when, in 1929, he joined two rich men, Alfred Hugenberg and Emil Kirdorf, in a nationwide campaign against reparations and the 'War Guilt' clause of the Versailles Treaty (see page 94). Within months this apparently small gain opened the door to real power.

Joseph Goebbels, chief of Nazi propaganda

Hitler becomes Chancellor

~~chacellor of germany~~

In 1929 Stresemann died. Soon afterwards the world depression, starting in the USA (see Chapter 14), hit Germany with awful force. Every European country was affected by the American collapse but none so

German unemployed queue for work during the Depression, 1931

severely as Germany. Her new prosperity had been built upon loans of 7 billion US dollars. Now these loans stopped. The result was a fall in wages and a closing of factories and businesses which made the 1923 troubles seem trivial. In 1929 there were 1,320,000 unemployed in Germany, by 1932 this figure had increased to 5,102,000. Here was Hitler's chance. For years he had prophesied disaster. Now his warnings had come true. Once more he had the national misery he needed. No longer was he dismissed as a crackpot. Packed audiences applauded his wild speeches. Unemployed men flocked to become Stormtroopers.

Some of these people wanted another *putsch*. Hitler, however, had learned his lesson. Although he hated democracy, he was determined to gain power by democratic means. For two years he fought election campaigns, both for Nazi membership of the Reichstag and also for the position of President for himself. Goebbels used every trick he knew to ensure success. Films of Hitler, records of his speeches, millions of swastika posters, were sent all over the country. During the election for President, Goebbels hit upon the idea of sending Hitler from meeting to meeting by aeroplane in a 'Hitler over Germany' campaign. His arrival at a meeting was memorable. Hour after hour, the waiting crowd would listen for the sound of a plane. Its steady drone drawing near, the sudden silence, and then the appearance in a spotlight of Hitler himself, would send them wild with joy.

Perhaps as a result of all this effort, there was a remarkable increase in the Nazi vote. In 1930 their seats in the Reichstag rose from 12 to 107. Two years later Hitler polled 13 million votes in a personal contest with Field-Marshal Hindenburg for the Presidency, quite an achievement for an ex-corporal! Altogether, the Nazis gained 37 per cent of the total votes cast in the 1932 elections, thus becoming the largest German party. Unfortunately for them, Hitler did not win the Presidency and the Nazis had still to gain the clear majority necessary for power.

It was now that the German Constitution came to Hitler's aid. Under **proportional representation** a political party was given seats in the Reichstag according to the number of votes cast for it throughout the country, not as the result of an individual contest in each constituency. This system can lead to many small political parties. For example, at no time between 1919 and 1933 did any one German party enjoy an overall majority in the Weimar Republic. This would not have mattered if two or three of the five largest parties electorally – the Social Democrats, the Catholic Centre Party, the Communists, the German National People's Party and the Nazis – had agreed to work together in a coalition government. But in the Germany of the time, a Germany defeated in war, a Germany full of unemployed people, where street fights were a commonplace, the parties merely quarrelled amongst themselves. The only way out of the crisis was to allow President Hindenburg to rule by emergency decrees.

Consequently, from 1929 onwards Germany was not ruled by an elected Reichstag government but by the few advisers of an eighty-four-year-old Field-Marshal. This situation proved Hitler's opportunity. He decided to persuade these men to let him become Chancellor. For this delicate game he had three trump cards to play. First, he had the mass support for the Nazis built up by successive elections. Second, he could suggest that only he and his Nazis could ward off the danger of a communist revolution. Finally, he could allow the violence of his Stormtroopers to suggest that if he did not get power legally there would be civil war. The way Hitler alternated between blackmail and persuasion showed him to be a master of ruthless politics. His three main rivals, two generals, Heinrich Brüning and Kurt von Schleicher, and a politician, Franz von Papen, were slowly but surely outwitted. At the very moment when votes for the Nazis were beginning to drop, von Papen, Hindenburg and the army chiefs decided that the way to deal with Hitler was to make him Chancellor of a Cabinet composed of his political opponents. Von Papen, in particular, was sure he could handle the Nazi leader.

On 30 January 1933 Hitler became Chancellor of Germany. What followed was similar to the fate of the lady in the limerick:

> There was a young lady of Riga
> Who smiled as she rode on a tiger
> They returned from the ride
> With the lady inside
> And a smile on the face of the tiger

Field-Marshal Hindenburg who appointed Hitler Chancellor of Germany in 1933

In 1924 the Bavarian Prime Minister had lifted the ban on the Nazi Party with the remark: 'The wild beast is checked. We can afford to loosen the chain'. Now Germany's leaders made the same mistake. They were about to go for a ride on a tiger named Adolf Hitler.

Timeline

1889 Hitler born.
1919 Weimar Republic formed.
1920 Nazi Party formed.
1923 French army occupies Ruhr. Inflation in Germany.
      Hitler stages unsuccessful Beer-Hall Putsch.
1924 Dawes Plan
1925 Locarno Pact.
1928 Kellogg Pact.
1929 Young Plan.
1929 Depression hits Germany.
1933 Hitler appointed Chancellor.

Questions

1. 'The great mass of working-men want only bread and circuses. They have no understanding for ideals of any sort whatsoever, and we can never hope to win the workers to any large extent by an appeal to ideals. We want to make a revolution for the new dominating caste which is quite clear in its own mind that it has the right to dominate others because it represents a better race...' (Adolf Hitler, arguing with a Socialist, Otto Strasser, in 1930).

   a) What do you think Hitler meant by 'bread and circuses'?
   b) Who were the 'new dominating caste' in Hitler's opinion?
   c) Do you think Hitler would have been offered the Chancellorship of Germany had his political opponents realised that he believed he had 'the right to dominate others'?

2. In what ways did conditions in Germany between 1918 and 1933 help Hitler to gain political power?

3. What arguments and methods did Hitler use to build up the Nazi Party?

4. Write short paragraphs on each of the following:
   a) 'the November Criminals'
   b) the Weimar Republic
   c) the Beer-Hall Putsch, 1923
   d) the Locarno Pact, 1925

17
Swastikas over Europe
Causes of the Second World War

Hitler's first action as Chancellor was to demand an election. In public he asked for four years of power. In private Goering promised a rich supporter that if the Nazis won it would be the last election for a hundred years. A week before polling day part of the Reichstag (parliament) building caught fire. People who rushed to the scene found Goering standing outside shouting, 'This is a communist crime against the new government'. Sure enough, a Dutch Communist, Marianus van der Lubbe, was captured inside. Next morning newspapers displayed headlines like, 'Arson Signals Red Revolution'. Hindenburg accepted this explanation and agreed to Hitler's demand that all political freedom should be cancelled. Ordinary Germans were also deceived. The truth was a little different. No official German communist organisation had known anything about van der Lubbe. Later the

The burnt Reichstag, 1933

Communists forged documents to prove that the Nazis were responsible. The Nazis always maintained that there had been a Communist plot. Actually van der Lubbe had acted alone, hoping that the burning would encourage a workers' rising against Hitler.

The headquarters of German democracy had been ruined. German democracy itself soon followed it. Although the Nazis received only forty-two per cent of the votes cast, their allies, the Nationalists, polled eight per cent. Added together, this just gave them the half share they needed to rule Germany. Not surprisingly, this new Reichstag decided to abolish parliamentary government. From that moment until 1945 Germany was ruled by the **Enabling Law** which gave Hitler law-making powers independent of the Reichstag. Before long other political parties were banned and genuine opposition became unknown. Arrest, imprisonment, torture and death without trial became commonplace. Jews, of course, were particularly ill-treated. From 1935 the **Nuremberg Laws** deprived them of all rights as citizens. They could not marry non-Jews, could not get jobs, could not, in some cases, buy food. Soon thousands were leaving Germany.

Hitler was a very good organiser. Even before he came to power he had created a political party which was really a miniature government, complete with departments to control all sides of life. It was this political octopus whose tentacles now gripped Germany. Trade unions were abolished. Workers were forced to join the **Nazi Labour Front** and strikes became illegal. Children were enrolled in the **Hitler Youth**, an organisation which issued daggers instead of proficiency badges and taught racial hatred. Women were dissuaded from working outside the home and encouraged to raise large families. The Protestant churches either joined the Nazi-controlled German Christians or found their leaders persecuted and imprisoned. A Concordat (treaty of friendship) which Hitler signed with the Pope promised Catholics religious freedom but it meant little in practice.

Heinrich Himmler, much feared chief of the Nazi police

To enforce such rigid controls the Stormtroopers were soon replaced by the black-uniformed SS (*Schutzstaffel*, meaning 'Protective Squad') led by **Heinrich Himmler**, who gained control of Germany's police forces, especially the Secret State Police (or **Gestapo**). Terror ceased to be a matter of occasional beatings-up and murders. It became a system, using large concentration camps, behind whose electrified fences, watch towers, searchlights and machine-guns, prisoners disappeared for good. Even so most Germans accepted Hitler's rule. His persecution of the Jews did not worry the average man in the street. Hitler's theory of the racial superiority of the German flattered the people. Slum clearance and more work gave hope to men and women fresh from the sufferings of the post-war depression, whilst his defiance of foreigners roused all the old German pride, laid low by the 1918 defeat. To many Germans Hitler was the new Bismarck sent to save their country.

The only threat to Hitler's power was quickly eliminated. **Ernst Röhm**, the Stormtroopers' chief, hated the army and its Prussian generals and wanted his men to become the core of a new people's army. Hitler knew that the army was strongly supported by rich businessmen and the middle classes. He also needed help from certain leading generals if he was to succeed Hindenburg as President. For these reasons Röhm was not made Minister of Defence as he had hoped, nor were Stormtroopers formed into an army. Gradually his discontent became dangerous. At first Hitler tried to soothe his old friend with promises. Röhm refused to be pacified. Since he was tough and brutal his challenge could not be ignored. On 30 June 1934 a conference between the two was arranged at Wiessee, Bavaria.

The result showed just what a tiger had been allowed to rule Germany. No conference took place. Instead, SS men dragged Röhm's attendants out of their hotel beds and murdered them. Röhm was taken to Stadelheim Prison where Hitler offered him a pistol to kill himself. When he refused he was shot. All over Germany bewildered Stormtroopers suffered a similar fate. Very few knew why they died. One remarked, 'Gentlemen, I don't know what this is all about but shoot straight!' Old scores were also settled, Gustav von Kahr, who had helped ruin Hitler's Beer-Hall *Putsch* (see page 147), was hacked to death with pick-axes. General von Schleicher was riddled with bullets as he opened his front door. Von Papen escaped only because he was a personal friend of Hindenburg. His two secretaries were killed. Afterwards, Hitler admitted sixty-one deaths and gave his usual explanation. Röhm and his men had planned revolution. The country had been saved by Hitler's swift action. So ended the purge known as the **'Night of the Long Knives'**.

Ernst Röhm, leader of the Stormtroopers. He was murdered on Hitler's orders in 1934

Germany rearms

Hitler showed a similar ruthlessness with his foreign enemies. Since his earliest days his two political aims had been to improve on Bismarck's work by including all Germans inside the Reich and to conquer living space (*lebensraum*) for Germany in the East by subduing the Poles and Russians. The first was against the terms of the Versailles Treaty. It conflicted with the French policy of keeping Germany small and surrounded by countries friendly to France. Nevertheless, it seemed to many only fair because Austria was almost entirely German and Czechoslovakia had a large German population. After all, the Peace Settlement had been founded on Wilson's idea of self-determination (see Chapter 11). The second aim was clearly a threat to peace so Hitler at first hid it by signing a friendship treaty with **Poland** (1934). It was to be five years before he felt strong enough to reveal the full extent of his deadly plans.

From the start Hitler showed contempt for all peace-keeping organisations. In 1933 he took Germany out of both the League of Nations and the disarmament talks at Geneva. Then in 1934 Austrian Nazis murdered their Chancellor, **Engelbert Dolfuss**, and tried to join their country to Germany. This *Anschluss*, or union, failed because Dolfuss's successor, Kurt Schuschnigg, quickly restored order, and Mussolini moved his troops to the Austrian frontier. Obviously Italy was against the German occupation of a country which included territories she claimed as Italian. Nevertheless, Hitler continued to attack the

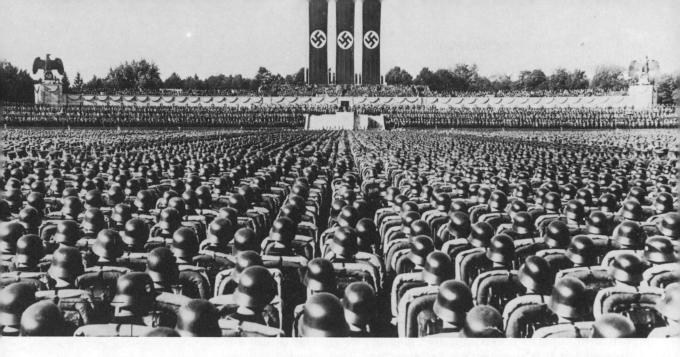

Nazi rally at Nuremburg, 1936

Versailles Treaty in his speeches and to disobey its terms. By 1935 for example it was clear he was rebuilding the German air force and army.

European politicians were puzzled and worried. France, in particular, felt insecure. Internally she was split between communists and socialists on one side and anti-communist, fascist groups on the other. Her terrible war losses had not been replaced by a rising birth rate as in many other countries and she was very short of young men. She feared another war above all things. Consequently her governments acted cautiously and defensively. In the 1920s they had signed treaties with Poland and Czechoslovakia hoping that they would assist France in a war with Germany. At home her Generals relied on massive concrete and steel defences along the border behind which they hoped France would be safe. Unfortunately the **Maginot Line**, as it was called, was a gate without a fence; it ended at the Belgian frontier (see map on page 158). A few military experts thought that a future war would be won by swift-moving tank armies. The idea was ridiculed. The French, once famous for their attacking spirit, were paralysed into inactivity by the memory of Verdun (see page 70).

Britain was in two minds about Hitler. By this time many Britons believed that the Versailles Treaty had been unfair to Germany. Hitler's demands for the return of the Rhineland and for the incorporation of Austria into a greater Germany; his claim that Germany was a great power which needed armed forces of at least the size of her neighbours, seemed reasonable. Moreover, his anti-communism appealed to politicians who feared the spread of Bolshevism. The development of the bombing aeroplane had also convinced many people in Britain that in the next war there would be no sure defence for their island. They, too, felt insecure. Like the French they wished to avoid war at almost any cost. Far from condemning Hitler, Britain was at first almost friendly towards the Nazis. In 1935, for example, she signed an agreement allowing the German navy to be increased.

Abyssinia and the Rhineland

Mussolini was far from friendly with Nazi Germany in its early days. He resented the Nazis' imitations of Fascism; thought Hitler's 'master race' theory 'nonsense'; and dismissed the Nazi leader himself as a 'mad little clown'. His dislike was not purely personal. German moves against Austria threatened territories which Italians had always claimed as their own; territories for which they had fought during the First World War but which had been denied them at Versailles (see page 94). The Anglo-German naval agreement was a further grievance, for it allowed the very rearmament which had been forbidden in the Peace Settlement. It came at a time when Mussolini was trying, by holding talks at **Stresa**, to interest Britain and France in an alliance against Germany.

However, Mussolini's own invasion of **Abyssinia** (Ethiopia) in October 1935 caused uproar in Britain, where this new attempt to gain an African empire was condemned, not only as aggression, but as a threat to British colonial possessions (see map opposite). The British government felt that some action was necessary. They decided to try to limit the amount of land taken by the Italians and secret talks between the British Foreign Secretary, Samuel Hoare, and the French Prime Minister, Pierre Laval, were commenced with this idea in mind. News of a possible **Hoare-Laval Pact** leaked out, causing anger amongst some sections of the British public to whom it seemed like a surrender to aggression. Consequently, the British plan was dropped. In the meantime, while Italian troops conquered Abyssinia quite quickly, Britain had adopted a tough policy which infuriated Mussolini and drove him into the arms of Hitler. The League of Nations was persuaded to deny Italy vital supplies. When oil sanctions were suggested, Hitler sent coal from Germany. This proved the first move in a process which drew the two dictators together. In 1936 they formed a sort of unofficial alliance called the **Rome-Berlin Axis**. Their co-operation in helping General Franco during the Spanish Civil War (1936–9) increased their friendship (see Chapter 18), and in 1939 they signed the **Pact of Steel**.

Just before Franco's rebellion Hitler took his first decisive step in Europe. On 7 March 1936 his troops marched into the **Rhineland** (see map on page 158). This action, which broke the Versailles Treaty and the Locarno Pact (see page 148), was a gamble. The German army was not strong enough for war; its officers had orders to retreat at once if the French began to fight. Afterwards Hitler admitted, 'The forty-eight hours after the march into the Rhineland were the most nerve-racking of my life.' He need not have worried. Some French generals were secretly fascist. Others were only prepared to defend French territory. They assured their government that the French army was not fit to launch an attack.

Britain sent a protest but did little else. Many Britons believed that the Germans had a right to walk into what was described as 'their own backyard'. They suggested that now was the time to remedy the mistakes of Versailles and negotiate a fairer settlement of Europe with

European colonies in Africa in the 1930s

Hitler and Mussolini reviewing troops, 1937

Hitler. A minority, including Winston Churchill, objected to the way force had been used to solve a European problem. Militarily, the re-occupation of the Rhineland was disastrous for France. Germany now had a more defensible frontier and she built a line of fortifications, the **Siegfried Line** (see map on page 158). The French were cut off completely from their Eastern allies. To some people 7 March 1936 is the date when the Second World War became unavoidable.

Appeasement and Anschluss

Next year (1937) **Neville Chamberlain** became Britain's Prime Minister. So far his country had done little about the European situation. Chamberlain had a more definite policy. In his opinion most of Europe's troubles were due to the Paris Peace Settlement, and he believed Hitler when he said that he wished merely to remedy the mistakes of 1919. All that was necessary was to find out the limits of the Nazi leader's demands and negotiate a final settlement. This policy, **appeasement** as it was called, bypassed certain difficulties. Hitler was a fanatic. His idea of negotiation was to bully and threaten until he got his own way. Röhm, after all, had been willing to negotiate with Hitler when he had been murdered. Although most Nazi aggression lay in the future, *Mein Kampf* was full of statements which showed that Hitler's aims were unlimited. Furthermore, on 5 November 1937, Hitler secretly told his generals that he intended to create Germany's 'living space', starting with invasions of Austria and Czechoslovakia. Appeasement was doomed from the start.

Austrian Nazis celebrate the 'Anschluss', 1938

To gain his objectives Hitler used 'Trojan horse' tactics. Troy had been captured because its defenders had foolishly dragged a hollow wooden horse inside the walls. Later the Greek soldiers hidden inside it came out and let the rest of their army into the city. Both Austria and Czechoslovakia possessed such 'horses'. In Austria large numbers of Germans wished to join Germany now that they were no longer part of the Habsburg Empire. In Czechoslovakia over three million Germans lived in the **Sudetenland**. If these people could be stirred up by Nazi propaganda, if they could be made to riot and demand *Anschluss* (union) with Germany, Hitler would have an excuse to occupy both countries.

Austria came first. Week after week Austrian Nazis called for the *Anschluss*. Week after week they organised riots and violence. To counter such pressure the Austrian government tried to form defensive alliances with Czechoslovakia and Yugoslavia (March 1938). Hitler objected and instead forced them to accept a Nazi, **Arthur Seyss-Inquart**, as Minister of the Interior. The rest was easy. Seyss-Inquart, although supposed to be in charge of law and order, allowed wholesale rioting. Then he arranged with Goering to ask the German army to enter the country to prevent bloodshed. This time Mussolini did nothing against the more powerful Germans. Within days Hitler was in Vienna, master of the city where he had once lived in poverty (see page 139). Tears filled his eyes as he visited his birthplace and laid flowers on his parents' graves. It was a proud moment for the German dictator.

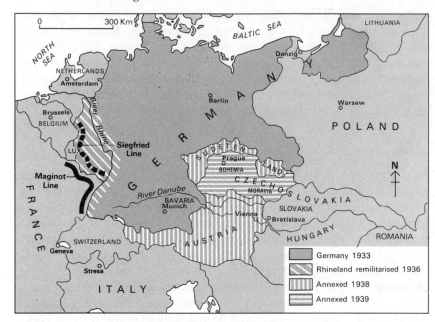

The road to war. Hitler's occupation of the Rhineland, Austria and Czechoslovakia

The Czechs were appalled. Germany now almost encircled them (see map above), controlling all road, rail and river communications in the Danube Valley. They were not reassured when Hitler promised, 'I give you my word of honour that Czechoslovakia has nothing to fear from the Reich'. Chamberlain was not so worried. After all, Austria was really German. He felt that the Versailles peacemakers should have united the two states anyway. Only a month after the *Anschluss* Chamberlain negotiated an agreement with Mussolini (April 1938). By this Britain recognised Italy's claim to Abyssinia and in return Mussolini agreed to the gradual withdrawal of his troops from Spain. Possibly Chamberlain hoped this would pull Italy away from Germany. If so he was mistaken. Italy was becoming more dependent upon her powerful ally with every day that passed. Mussolini himself, after a visit to Germany in September 1937, came away so deeply impressed by Nazi discipline and power that he introduced goose-stepping (German light-stepping march) to his troops and started a campaign against the Jews.

Meeting at Munich

Hitler now turned upon Czechoslovakia. Local Nazis were soon persuading the Sudeten Germans to complain about their ill-treatment by the Czech government. This time, however, Hitler encountered more resistance. The Czechs had a good army and good defences. They had an alliance with France which promised help if they were attacked. One month after the Austrian occupation, alarmed at the disorder in the Sudetenland, they mobilised their army. Stirred by this, the Soviet Union and France guaranteed aid if Germany attacked. Hitler was taken aback, particularly as he had not planned to move at that moment. Publicly he assured everybody that his intentions were peaceful.

Neville Chamberlain, the British Prime Minister who thought he had saved Europe from war by the Munich agreement

Privately he never forgave the Czech leader, **Dr Edward Beneš**, for standing up to him. 'It is my unalterable decision to smash Czechoslovakia by military action in the near future', he promised.

Chamberlain meanwhile decided that the demand for the return of the Sudetenland to Germany was reasonable. Here was another Versailles mistake which needed rectifying. Consequently, Britain and France joined with Hitler in urging the Czech government to surrender part of their country. The Czechs refused because they stood to lose their best defences and most of their railway system. As the crisis grew, Chamberlain decided to go and see Hitler. Three times he met the Nazi leader, listening to his ravings, enduring his rudeness, sometimes experiencing the charm which Hitler could display if he wished. Finally, at **Munich**, in September 1938, Hitler was persuaded to accept the Sudetenland. The Czechs knew they had been betrayed but there was little they could do if Britain and France would not help. Hitler, too, was furious, although he hid his anger. He had wanted the Czechs to defy him so that he had an excuse to overrun their entire country. 'That fellow Chamberlain has spoiled my entry into Prague', he grumbled. Poor Chamberlain returned to England convinced that his appeasement policy had given, in his own words, 'Peace in our time'.

He was soon disillusioned. Hitler had no more German 'Trojan horses' left so he began to complain about the ill-treatment of the Slovaks by the Czechs. He warned that Germany might have to take Slovakia under its protection. Dr Beneš had left the country after Munich. His successor, President **Emil Hacha**, was not so brave or determined. When he looked like defying Germany he was invited to Berlin where Goering threatened to destroy Prague if he resisted. This so frightened Hacha that he fainted. On 15 March 1939 German troops

'The moment of truth'. Nazi troops enter Prague, Czechoslovakia and so for the first time occupy a non-German state

crossed the Czech border and the country ceased to exist just twenty years after its creation. This was the moment of truth for Chamberlain and the whole world. All the concessions, all the reasonableness, had been in vain. Hitler's aims were seen to extend far beyond even an enlarged Germany. Sadly Chamberlain introduced conscription in a Britain officially at peace. Grimly he pledged British support for Poland if she were attacked.

It was now that Hitler made a mistake. He understood the worst motives of men but not their better feelings. So far as he was concerned the British and French politicians were 'little worms'. After Munich Hitler saw Chamberlain not as a decent man struggling to preserve peace, but as a coward. The settlement that September convinced him that Britain and France would never fight, however much they protested. His generals were not so sure and some even considered kidnapping a leader who was likely to lead the country to disaster. Hitler ignored them. Throughout the summer of 1939 he demanded the return of Danzig and the Polish Corridor (see page 92). A few years earlier this might have been considered justifiable, although it amazed the Poles who looked upon Hitler as their ally against the Soviet Union. This time, however, Britain and France responded by warning Germany that they would defend Poland if she were invaded. Hitler never really believed this. Success had gone to his head in a way it never did with Bismarck.

The Nazi-Soviet Pact

By late summer 1939, the Nazi leader had completed his plans for the march into Poland. The main obstacle was the Soviet Union. The old Tsarist Empire had included large parts of Poland. It was unlikely that Stalin would allow the country to be snatched from under his nose by Hitler. The Soviet ruler had little love for the German dictator and was quite prepared to fight Germany if he could be sure Britain and France would join him. During 1939 Stalin tried to get a comprehensive agreement with the West, offering to defend every state between the Baltic and the Black Sea if Britain and France would do the same. Unfortunately, many leading people in Britain and France still feared any contact with communism. More important, the countries which the USSR offered to protect, particularly Poland, were more frightened of the USSR than of Germany. Consequently the negotiations failed.

This was Hitler's chance. Although he had spent his entire political career denouncing communism he now offered to sign a pact of friendship and non-aggression with the Soviet Union. On 24 August 1939 the outside world was amazed to learn that these two enemies had signed such an agreement. Hitler regarded this as his masterstroke because it ensured that if war did come he would be fighting on only one front. And, although he had promised the Russians eastern Poland, Finland, Estonia and Latvia (see map on page 93), he never intended to allow them to keep these territories. 'After Stalin's death (he is seriously ill) we shall crush the Soviet Union', he told his generals.

*British cartoon about the
Nazi-Soviet Pact, 1939*

Stalin did not expect Hitler to keep his word either; at the signing
ceremony he reminded the German representatives of the 'buckets of
filth' Hitler had poured upon him in the past. However, the communist
dictator was sure he could only gain from a long war in which Britain,
France and Germany exhausted themselves. Seldom have two countries entered an alliance so dishonestly.

The **Nazi-Soviet Pact** made the invasion of Poland certain. A week
later the German propaganda machine announced that one of the German frontier posts had been fired on by Poles. German soldiers had
been killed, it claimed. In fact, drugged concentration camp prisoners,
dressed in German uniforms, had been brought to the spot and shot.
On 1 September 1939 German tanks rolled across the Polish border.
On this occasion matters did not go in the usual way. For the first time
the Germans met desperate resistance. For the first time there were no
empty protests, or requests for interviews. At 11 a.m. on 3 September
Britain declared war on Germany; France followed six hours later.
Chamberlain was heartbroken. 'Everything that I have worked for,
everything I have believed in during my public life, has crashed to ruins',
he told the House of Commons. Hitler was surprised. When told the
news he remained silent for some time and then said, 'What are we
going to do now?' Nobody answered this question but Goering probably spoke what the others felt when he said, 'If we lose this war, God
help us.' The 'worms' of Munich had turned.

Timeline

1933   Reichstag fire. Enabling Law. Germany leaves League of Nations and disarmament talks in Geneva.
1934   Night of the Long Knives. Friendship treaty with Poland.
1935   Nuremberg Laws. Stresa Talks. Anglo-German naval agreement. Italy's invasion of Abyssinia (Ethiopia).
1936   Hoare-Laval Pact made public. German occupation of the Rhineland. Rome-Berlin Axis.
1938   Germany occupies Austria and, after Munich meeting, occupies Sudetenland in Czechoslovakia.
1939   Germany overruns most of Czechoslovakia. Pact of Steel between Germany and Italy. Britain and France guarantee Poland's frontiers. Nazi-Soviet Pact. Germany invades Poland. Britain and France declare war on Germany.

Questions

1. Look at the cartoon on page 161.
   a) Who are the two European leaders shown bowing to each other?
   b) What is the body lying between them meant to represent?
   c) Why did the Nazi-Soviet Pact come as a great surprise to many people?
   d) What did the two leaders hope to gain from this Pact?

2. 'When years ago I went forth from this town I bore with me precisely the same profession of faith which today fills my heart... If Providence once called me forth from this town to be leader of the Reich [Germany], it must, in so doing, have charged me with a mission [aim] and that mission could only be to restore my dear homeland to the German Reich.' (Adolf Hitler, speaking in Linz, Austria, after the German occupation, 12 March 1938)

   a) From your reading of this book so far would you say that Hitler's 'dear homeland', Austria, had ever been part of Germany, as Hitler was suggesting?
   b) What other steps did Hitler take to bring all German-speaking people under German rule between his occupation of Austria and the outbreak of the Second World War in 1939?

3. Explain the events which turned Mussolini, the Italian dictator, from an enemy of Hitler into an ally.

4. Write short paragraphs on each of the following:
   a) *lebensraum*
   b) the Night of the Long Knives, 1934
   c) the Nuremberg Laws
   d) the burning of the Reichstag, 1933

18
Rehearsal in Spain
The Spanish Civil War

Persons, countries and economic systems have all been blamed for the war which broke out in 1939. Marxists think it was the inevitable result of competitive capitalism; in other words, that trade rivalry between nations leads to more warlike competition. Churchill believed that it resulted from being too easy with Hitler. The Second World War, in his opinion, 'could have been prevented without the firing of a single shot'. Some put the responsibility on the Versailles peace-makers. Their decisions, they claimed, made it certain that the First World War would be continued. Others see the USA's isolationism and refusal to guarantee French frontiers against German attack as a major cause (see page 95). Most historians regard Hitler as the chief villain. Here was an evil man whose actions made war certain. Since the Second World War was the most terrible in history these opinions are worth discussing. Perhaps if the true causes can be found a similar disaster can be avoided in the future.

People at the time were also divided about the matter. If you were a Fascist you blamed the Jews, the Communists or Western democracies. If you were a Communist you blamed Hitler, Mussolini and their followers. If you were less extreme politically you probably regarded fascism as slightly worse than communism. Certainly some young people felt so disgusted by Nazi and fascist methods that they favoured communist ideas. They also thought that the First World War had been caused by the rivalries of the capitalist system. Their dislike for this 'dragon' made them see communism as some sort of 'St George'. They would have been appalled had they known the truth about Stalin's Soviet Union.

Strangely enough, all this hatred, all these clashes of opinion and principle, came to a head, not over Austria, or Czechoslovakia or Poland. They came to the boil on 17 July 1936 when Spanish generals, led by **Francisco Franco**, rebelled against their Republican government. A backward, almost forgotten country suddenly became the focus of a world problem. Few could have foreseen that this would happen. In fact, the causes of Franco's rebellion had little to do with fascism or communism. Spain's mountain ranges have often proved a barrier to a united country (see map on page 164). In the days before modern communications they helped divide the country into small areas, whose people developed different ways, customs, and even, in some cases, languages. To outsiders they are all Spaniards. To themselves they are Castilians, Aragonese, Andalusians, Catalans or Basques, just as the British are English, Welsh or Scots.

This divided country was also a poor one. Whilst other countries

General Francisco Franco, rebel against the Spanish Republican government and later Fascist dictator of Spain

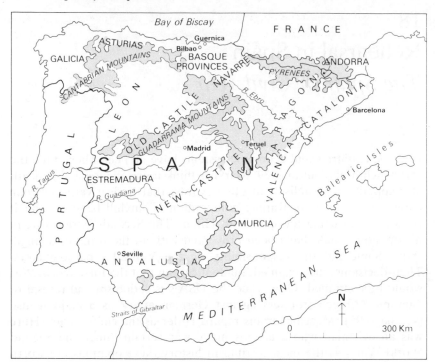

Spain – a country divided by mountain ranges

became rich by developing mines, building iron-works and mass-producing goods in factories, Spain remained largely agricultural. Only two regions, the iron-foundries of Bilbao and the Barcelona textile-mills, were developed industrially. In earlier times Spain's main wealth had come from sheep-rearing. The high plateaux of medieval Castile had been dotted with wandering flocks which trampled upon the peasants' fields and crops. By the 1750s good cornland was often overgrown with weeds, and, because few men are needed to look after sheep, it was possible to ride for days without seeing a house. In the nineteenth century there was a change. Landowners once again became interested in growing crops. So flocks were discouraged by constant ploughing; communally-owned land was sold by government order; and two products, wheat and olives, were given priority.

If such land had been shared out among a fair proportion of the people all might have been well. Unfortunately, in some areas trouble arose because of what are called *latifundia*, that is, farms which are very large. Enormous estates were created, owned by wealthy families who hired labourers to work the fields but often left large parts uncultivated. In nineteenth-century Seville, for example, five per cent of the inhabitants owned seventy-two per cent of the farming land. Deprived of the meadows upon which they might have kept a pig or some poultry; unable to afford to buy land themselves, the mass of the people became landless. Spain's countryside became infested with poor labourers who earned a living by working by the day, month or season. Such *braceros*, as they are called, had no rights, no guarantee of a job and no interest in the soil they worked. Since there were usually about

2,500,000 of them they constituted an army of bitter, hungry and discontented people. Only the rifles of the army and the Civil Guard, a sort of armed police force, kept them in order.

Despite their sufferings, many Spaniards remained devoted to the old ways. They loved their priests, and hated the liberals who wished to improve conditions for them because this involved attacks upon the Church. Others, however, turned to the most revolutionary belief of our time, **anarchism**. An anarchist dislikes all government. In his ideal world nobody would give orders and the country would be an association of independent districts or societies. The founder of the movement, a Russian, **Michael Bakunin**, wanted to destroy all governments. He also hated anyone who owned anything. Another anarchist, **Pierre Proudhon**, detested Christianity and, besides announcing 'property is theft', coined another favourite anarchist slogan, 'God is evil'.

Such beliefs were first introduced into Spain by an Italian, **Guiseppi Fanelli**, in 1868. They spread quickly amongst the badly treated workers of Barcelona and the *braceros* of Andalusia. Bakunin never visited Spain but his love of destruction infected a passionate people in a terrible way. Violence and killing became usual in anarchist areas and it was almost impossible to rule these parts of Spain at all. Consequently, by the twentieth century Spain was a deeply divided country. Her liberals wished to found a modern democracy. Her monarchists and army men supported the Church and the old ways. Her separatists demanded independence for their regions. Her anarchists wanted no government at all. She was also a very poor and underdeveloped country, experiencing only one short period of prosperity during the First World War when there was a great demand for her mineral products.

Michael Bakunin who wanted to destroy all governments

Drift to war

In 1931 Spain's King, Alfonso XIII, left the country, because he feared that if he remained ruler there would be a civil war between his followers and their opponents. In his place a liberal Republican government began to introduce reforms. Elections became more democratic, Church property was confiscated and schools taken from their control. *Braceros* were assured that the *latifundia* would be split into smaller lots which they could buy. Basques and Catalans were promised their own governments. Lovers of the old ways, particularly army officers, began to fear that Spain would disintegrate into tiny republics of the Balkan type. Sincere Catholics worried in case the Church they served would be destroyed.

Anarchists and communists, however, were not satisfied and wanted more changes. Their quarrels and hatred split the Republican side itself into those who wanted a middle-class revolution of the old French type; those who wanted a workers' revolution similar to the Bolshevik one; and those who wished all government control to cease. Such pressures led to a new, even more revolutionary government, composed of liberals, socialists and communists – the **Popular Front**. Their victory in the 1936 elections was too much for the army chiefs and they decided to rebel. On 17 July 1936 leading generals seized power in

Spanish North Africa, where they were joined by Franco, who had been flown from the Canary Islands. Next day the revolt spread to the Spanish mainland and rebellious troops, mainly members of the Foreign Legion, were transported into Spain.

If Franco thought this was going to be a quick and easy seizure of power he was mistaken. This time large numbers of ordinary Spaniards decided to fight the army. In Barcelona the anarchist trade unions armed themselves, defeated the rebels and executed them. In Madrid the Republican government issued rifles to socialist workers who proceeded to capture the Montana Barracks after a savage battle. Elsewhere victory went one way or the other according to luck or special circumstances. Before July ended a line could be drawn across Spain, running north-east to the Guadarrama Mountains, down to Teruel and north to the Pyrenees (see map opposite). To the north and west, except for a coastal strip held by the Basques, the Franco rebels (Nationalists) were in control. To the south and east the country was held by Republicans. Franco and his legions were faced with the task of conquering their own country.

So far the whole affair had been typically Spanish. Time and again such revolts had changed the government. But this time something new happened. Franco had a few fascist supporters; the Republic had some communist supporters. Neither extremist group had anything like the following enjoyed by the socialists and liberals; in 1936, for example, there were no Fascist and only sixteen Communist members in the

Franco is proclaimed ruler of Nationalist Spain, 1936

Spain: division between Nationalists and Republicans in 1936

Nationalists

Republicans

Spanish Cortes (parliament). The people's revolt worried Franco and he appealed for help to Hitler and Mussolini, claiming that he was fighting to prevent a communist take-over. Probably he saw no difference between communists and socialists (although the latter usually believe in democratic methods, not one-party dictatorship). Neither Hitler nor Mussolini really cared about Spain, but both saw the value of a hostile state on France's southern border. As a result German Junkers aircraft flew Franco and his staff to Spain and Italian fighters escorted his troops when they sailed across the Straits of Gibraltar in merchant ships.

World involvement

This step had far-reaching effects. All over the democratic world, particularly in the USA, Britain and France, men and women decided that Franco's rebellion was just another fascist conspiracy breaking surface like an underground fire. People who were tired of the bullying dictators, who were worried by Mussolini's brutal invasion of Abyssinia and Hitler's occupation of the Rhineland (see Chapter 17), decided that this was a chance 'to do something' about fascism. They started to form army units and medical groups to go to Spain. The Spanish Republicans meanwhile asked for British and French aid. France had a socialist Popular Front government similar to the Spanish one (see page 114). Although prepared to help she was discouraged by Britain and anxious not to become involved in a war in case Germany attacked. Britain for her part proposed that no foreign country should interfere. She set up a **Non-Intervention Committee** which was supposed to see that no foreign aid entered Spain.

Germany and Italy joined the Committee at first but took little notice of its recommendations. Mussolini, in particular, poured 'volunteers' into Spain until he had large armies fighting for Franco. Unhappily and reluctantly the Republicans turned to the only country which was prepared to help, the Soviet Union. In October 1935 most of Spain's gold reserves, amounting to £63,256,684, were shipped to the USSR to pay for weapons and supplies. Franco, in turn, persuaded Mussolini to send troops and Hitler to send his well-equipped mechanical Condor Legion. By Christmas 1936 the war had ceased to be a private Spanish quarrel. It had become part of the international contest between communism, fascism and democracy. Hitherto the rival forces had fought in the streets of European cities with sticks and stones. In Spain, organised as armies, they were about to close in a death grip.

The story of Soviet interference in the war is a strange one. Stalin believed that Germany and possibly Italy were likely to attack him. For this reason he had tried not to offend Britain, France and the USA in case he needed their help. Communists all over Europe were told to be democrats. Revolutionary talk was discouraged and Popular Front alliances with socialists and liberals were formed. The policy met with a certain amount of success. By 1936 neither France nor Spain was anti-Soviet Union, but in neither was there an openly communist régime.

When it became clear that Hitler and Mussolini were working to establish a fascist Spain, Stalin adapted this peacetime policy to fit the situation. If possible Franco must lose, but communism must not win either, because Stalin knew that Britain and the USA would never tolerate a communist Spain. So began a cold-blooded process of prolonging Spain's agony by sending just enough aid to keep the Republicans fighting. Hitler, too, had the same idea because he wanted Mussolini to be too busy to interfere in Austria. German equipment and men went to Franco but German firms were allowed to sell arms to the Republicans.

The brave men who rushed to fight knew nothing of such wickedness. Inside Spain, communists organised an expert army called the **Fifth Regiment**. Each battalion was strengthened by a carefully chosen 'Steel Company' who learned rules like, 'Never leave a comrade, dead or wounded, in the hands of the enemy', and 'If my comrade advances or retreats without orders, I have the right to shoot him.' These rules were not ignored: of the first 400 men who went into action only 80 seriously wounded men survived. Such discipline was desperately needed on the Republican side. Most of Franco's men were well-trained professional soldiers. The Republicans were armed workers and anarchist gunmen with no idea of obeying military orders. Often they would stand and argue with their commander. Sometimes they left the front line to go home for the weekend. The anarchists, of course, were particularly undisciplined soldiers. They refused to salute or line up, ignored all training and refused to obey any order they disliked.

By November 1936 Franco's men had fought their way from the Mediterranean coast to the outskirts of Madrid (see map on page 166). Everywhere they had defeated desperate, disorganised resistance. Only the Spanish capital stood between them and the mastery of Spain. The Nationalist generals felt confident that their assault would be successful. Unfortunately for them two new factors now spoilt their plans. First, the entire population of the capital prepared to resist them. Communist leaders like Dolores Ibarruri, known as **La Pasionara** (Passion Flower) broadcast radio appeals to the people of Madrid telling them to die fighting. Monotonously other announcers repeated the French slogan at Verdun, 'They shall not pass'. Even regiments of women were enlisted, trained and marched off to the trenches. As a result the Nationalists' first offensive met suicidal resistance which slowed it down and inflicted severe losses. And no sooner had they begun to make some headway than the **First International Brigade** entered Madrid.

The international war

The International Brigades were communist-organised armies of foreign volunteers. They were assembled via Paris by **Josip Broz**, later Marshal Tito of Yugoslavia. From late August 1936 their recruits began to flow into Spain, by sea from Marseilles or by secret paths across the Pyrenees (see map on page 164). They were a varied mixture of

Dolores Ibarruri. Called 'La Pasionara', she urged the Republicans to defend Madrid against Franco

*Madrid under heavy
bombardment, 1936*

nationalities, British, French, Italian, German, Polish, Russian and American. Some came because they hated fascism. Some came for adventure. All were determined to stop the Nationalists. Republican Spaniards gave them a tremendous welcome, offering wine and grapes, cheering and singing the communist anthem, *International*. On a November evening their commander launched them into their first battle in Madrid with the cry, 'For the revolution and liberty – forward!' They fought all night in beautiful parkland dotted with gum trees, grappling with Spanish Legionaries. In the morning one-third of them were dead but the enemy had been driven back. For three weeks these men gave the defenders of Madrid the necessary skilled backing to resist a professional enemy. When the battle died down the city was divided between the two sides. This situation lasted for the rest of the war; in some cases the opposing sides held houses in the same street. Franco could bomb Madrid but he could not take it.

From this time onwards the war became a slow, terrible struggle between equally matched sides. In some ways it resembled the First World War. Long lines of trenches were assaulted, lines of men were machine-gunned to death, heavy artillery pounded day and night. But in the mountains men fought as they had done a hundred years before, creeping over rough ground, or charging on horseback to the sound of bugles. And there was a foretaste of the Second World War in the heavy bombing of Madrid and Barcelona and the almost complete destruction of the Basque town of **Guernica** by a mixture of fire and explosive bombs. Behind the Nationalist lines life became steadily more fascist. Behind the Republicans communists established a Stalinist system of terror. In such conditions the men who had dreamed of a democratic Spain were ignored or eliminated.

After Munich (September 1938) Stalin decided that the French and British would never help him against Germany. As we have seen he signed a treaty of friendship with Hitler, the Nazi-Soviet Pact (see Chapter 17). Even before this he had slowed the flow of aid to the Republicans. Starved of supplies and ammunition the Republican armies began to be pushed towards the sea. At **Teruel** they started with a victory and ended with a shattering defeat. On the **Ebro** they fought for six months against a hail of shell-fire, which systematically obliterated their positions. Nevertheless their fierce resistance had forced Franco to meet Hitler's demand for a forty per cent share in Spanish iron-mines. During Christmas 1938 he was at last given enough supplies, weapons and ammunition to destroy the Republic. In January 1939 **Barcelona**, a stronghold of anarchism, fell to Franco's troops. About 500,000 people began to flee towards the French frontier, trudging along mountain passes or choking the narrow streets of towns and villages. In February the Republican government held its last parliament meeting before crossing into France. In March the Republican troops in **Madrid** mutinied and the war was over.

By that time a Spanish army revolt had been expanded into a major war, costing 600,000 lives and ruining large parts of Spain. The world which helped to do this almost immediately turned to its own fearful war. The excitement died away. Even before the end of the war, it was no longer necessary to go to Spain 'to do something' about fascism. Yet Spain had acted like a mirror. It had shown Europe the reflection of things to come.

A Madrid mother looks anxiously for bombers as she hurries to a shelter

Timeline

1931   Flight of Alfonso XIII.
1936   Popular Front government elected. Franco's revolt begins Spanish Civil War. British Non-Intervention Committee formed. First International Brigades. Battle for Madrid. Foreign intervention.
1937   Destruction of Guernica.
1938   Battles of Teruel and Ebro.
1939   Barcelona and Madrid captured. Spanish Civil War ends.

Questions

1. a) Explain why both Hitler and Mussolini gave help to Franco's forces during the Spanish Civil War.
   b) How did Franco come to power in Spain?

2. 'The story of Russian interference in the war is a strange one.' Explain what part Russia played in the Spanish Civil War.

3. Write short paragraphs on each of the following:
   a) the International Brigades
   b) the Non-Intervention Committee
   c) Guernica
   d) Anarchism

19

The Road to Pearl Harbour
The Far East 1917–1941

The USA managed to isolate herself from all this European turmoil. Having rejected the Versailles Treaty, it was 1920 before she concluded a peace with Germany. Of the League of Nations, President Harding remarked that he would not enter it, 'by the side door, back door or cellar door'. Instead of being horrified at this attitude, most Americans felt pleased. In their opinion they had been fools to enter the First World War at all. It was not their quarrel, they had suffered heavy losses and gained no territory. Afterwards the USA was left with large debts which most of her allies could not, or would not, pay. Many Americans felt disillusioned and were determined not to be caught again.

If this policy was short-sighted where Europe was concerned, it was disastrous when applied to the Far East. Since the start of modernisation the Japanese population had increased steadily. In 1852 it had been 27 million. By 1910 it was 49 million and 30 years later it was 72 million. Japan is smaller than the American state of California, with plenty of infertile mountain ranges. Her leaders felt that their people must move into the relatively empty areas of Asia nearby (see map on page 172). It was this urge which lay behind the conquests of the Chinese and Russian wars (see Chapter 5). It was helped by lack of European competition during the First World War. Japan was able to increase her merchant shipping tonnage from 21 to 31 million tonnes and flood the world with cheap goods, particularly textiles. She was also able to bully China into accepting the **Twenty-One Demands** which virtually made her a satellite of Japan.

Successive US governments attempted to check Japanese power and influence in two ways. First, they insisted that China ignore the Twenty-One Demands and that all friendly nations be allowed an **Open Door** into that country. The Japanese were annoyed but since the USA had a powerful navy and China was supposed to be an ally they gave way. Second, the USA tried to limit the alarming growth of the Japanese fleet. At the **Washington Naval Conference, 1921**, Japan was persuaded to reduce her battleship strength. In future any building was to be in the ratio of five battleships for Britain and the USA to three for Japan. Britain, on her side, felt embarrassed by her 1902 alliance with Japan (see page 47) now that the reason for it, namely the German naval rivalry, had gone. She was glad to exchange it for a **Four Power Treaty** between herself, the USA, Japan and France, by which each promised to respect the others' rights in the Pacific and Far East. A later **Nine Power Treaty**, involving smaller nations with interests in the area, like the Netherlands, guaranteed China against invasion.

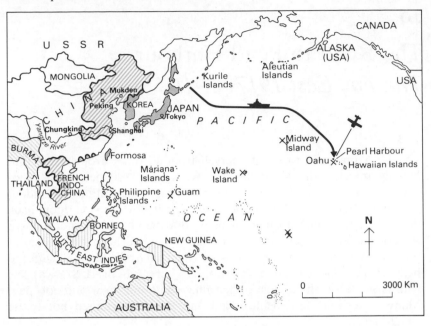

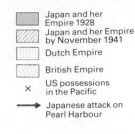

The Pacific zone, scene of Japanese plans for a new empire

None of this was popular with the Japanese man in the street. Like the Italians after the war (see page 93), he felt that his wartime allies had cheated him of his just reward. As far as the USA was concerned, this ill-feeling deepened when the **Johnson Act, 1921** (see page 120) stopped Japanese immigration into America. It widened into a more general anti-Western feeling when some European countries placed import duties on Japanese goods. As ill-feeling towards Western nations developed, Japan's military and naval leaders slowly undermined the infant democracy within the country. The influence of various officer groups and secret societies was used to make the people more aggressive. To such men, China's weakness seemed an opportunity which might not last forever. Better to strike now, they argued, before China became more able to defend herself.

Nowhere were these opinions more strongly held than amongst the generals in Manchuria. Here Japanese soldiers and businessmen worked hand in hand developing mines and laying railways. To them the riches of other parts of Manchuria, and of China itself, seemed very tempting. Being far away from their homeland they took little notice of the Japanese government. In 1928, for example, their agents murdered a Chinese chieftain, hoping to provoke a general war. The Tokyo government refused to back them and the plan failed. Then, in 1931, while China was distracted by floods, and Europe and the USA by economic difficulties, the Japanese army in Kwangtung province arranged for a railway line near **Mukden** to be damaged (see map above). This incident was blamed on the Chinese, and used as an excuse to move troops deeper into Manchuria. Before long the Chinese city of Shanghai was under bombardment from Japanese troops. A home government order to stop was disregarded.

The Japanese invasion of China; Japanese and Chinese fight in the streets of Tientsin, 1937

The Manchurian invasion provided the first real test for the League of Nations because both Japan and China were member states. Clearly it was a case of Japanese aggression. Unfortunately, the League did little more than condemn Japan's action and send a commission to 'investigate' the fighting. With the USA and the USSR not members of the League and Britain unwilling to act alone, the fate of China was sealed. Obviously the Nine Power Treaty was a worthless piece of paper as far as the Kwangtung army was concerned. Its troops pushed on and by 1932 a puppet state called **Manchukuo** had been set up in Manchuria. In Japan its supporters overthrew the Cabinet and murdered the Prime Minister. It was obvious that the Japanese warlords (military commanders), encouraged by their success in Manchuria, were aiming at military dictatorship.

During the 1930s Japanese aggression grew steadily. Japan had wanted China as a partner in a crusade against the Western nations. Her refusal to join Japan eventually made the Japanese launch a full-scale invasion of China. On 7 July 1937 a skirmish took place between Japanese and Chinese soldiers at the **Marco Polo Bridge** near Peking. Although the Chinese apologised for the incident, and although the Japanese army had no right to be there anyway, the affair was used as an excuse to deliver an outright attack. In Japan itself some military leaders were worried. What if the Soviet Union moved against Manchuria whilst they were heavily committed in China? Even so the local army chiefs had their way. China fought back fiercely without success. Within a year most of her well-populated areas had been seized and the Nationalist Chinese government was forced to retire to Chungking (see map on page 172). There, surrounded by mountains and protected by the Yangtze river, they were able to defy the Japanese.

The American awakening

Roosevelt was worried by these developments because he was a peace-loving man. As with 'New Deal' for his home policy (see page 124) he coined another phrase for foreign affairs. The USA, he proclaimed, wished to be a '**Good Neighbour**' to all (1933). This applied especially to the Latin American states (see Chapter 29). Gone were the days of American bullying and interference. Panama was given more freedom. US marines were brought home from Haiti. The Platt Amendment (see Chapter 5), which allowed the USA to intervene in Cuban affairs, was repealed by Congress. In diplomatic matters US officials treated the Latin Americans with more courtesy: one of Roosevelt's ministers learnt Spanish so that he could negotiate without an interpreter. In 1933 the President even went in person to a conference of Latin American states in Buenos Aires.

Such moves had a certain amount of success. Unfortunately no amount of courtesy could alter the growing tension in Europe and the Far East. When Germany and Japan signed the **Anti-Comintern Pact** against the Soviet Union (November 1936), Roosevelt was fearful of friendship between two such aggressive governments, and he tried to alert the American people to the danger. In 1937, speaking of the wars raging in Spain and China, he said, 'If these things come to pass in other parts of the world, let no one imagine that America will escape, that America may expect mercy, that the Western Hemisphere will not be attacked...'. The reaction to this warning was hostile; even members of his own Democratic Party called him a warmonger. The outbreak of the Second World War two years later still found Americans in an isolationist mood. The ordinary man showed little interest, whilst American generals were convinced France and Britain could win without help. As late as July 1940 Roosevelt was having to reassure his people, 'We will not use our arms in a war of aggression; we will not send our troops to take part in European wars.'

The fall of France in 1940 (see Chapter 20) started the awakening. Amazed at the power of the German army, Congress for the first time introduced compulsory military service as well as laying plans to enlarge the US navy. In the Atlantic, German U-boats began sinking American merchant ships so Roosevelt ordered his naval commanders to 'shoot at sight' at German or Italian submarines. Meanwhile every available piece of war equipment was shipped to Britain to help her repel any invasion. Most important, fifty old US destroyers were given to the Royal Navy in exchange for British Caribbean bases.

A year earlier such aid would have been impossible. At last the grim realities of the situation dawned upon Americans. Late in 1940 they elected Roosevelt President for a third term, something which had never happened before. Strengthened by this vote of confidence, Roosevelt now proposed his famous **Lend-Lease Scheme**. By this, goods were to be sent to Britain on the understanding that they would be returned after the war. If destroyed, they would be regarded as having been used for the benefit of the USA. At a press conference he explained it with typical simplicity.

Roosevelt and Churchill on board a British warship off Newfoundland, 1941. They promised freedom for all peoples in an Atlantic Charter

Suppose my neighbour's house catches fire and I have a length of garden hose four or five hundred feet away. If he can take my garden hose and connect it up with his hydrant, I may help him to put out the fire. Now what do I do? I don't say to him before that operation, 'Neighbour, my garden hose cost me fifteen dollars; you have to pay me fifteen dollars for it.' What is the transaction that goes on? I don't want fifteen dollars – I want my garden hose back after the fire is over . . .

In this neat way the old grievance over money loaned during the First World War was avoided. From March 1941 onwards Britain and her allies were given US supplies to help them carry on fighting.

Five months later Churchill and Roosevelt met off the Newfoundland coast and signed their famous **Atlantic Charter**, promising freedom for all peoples and a new world peace organisation after 'the final destruction of the Nazi tyranny'. The USA was as near to fighting Germany as possible without actually declaring war.

Pearl Harbour

In the meantime the Japanese leaders debated what to do. The conflict in Europe seemed to offer them the same freedom they had enjoyed in the First World War (see page 67). Tempting possibilities surrounded them. Their soldiers favoured further movement into China and Manchuria. Their sailors wished to move south and seize the oil of the Dutch East Indies (Indonesia). The main problem was the USSR. In 1940 Russian tanks had defeated the Japanese on the Manchurian border. Clearly the USSR was no longer as weak as in earlier days. On the other hand, Japan's chiefs felt certain Germany would win the war. This being so they were anxious that they, and not the Germans, should seize the Dutch, British and French possessions in the Far East. If only they could be sure that the Soviet Union would not attack, Japanese armies and navies could drive south against Indo-China, Siam (Thailand), Burma, Malaya and the Dutch East Indies (see map on page 172); Japanese industries could obtain oil, tin and rubber.

General Hideki Tojo, leader of Japan during the Second World War

The question was answered in June 1941 when German troops invaded the USSR. This was the green light as far as Japan was concerned, for the Soviet Union would now be fully committed on her western frontiers. By December 1941 all was ready. Prince Konoye, the peace-loving Japanese Prime Minister, was forced to resign and was replaced by **General Hideki Tojo**, a ruthless man nicknamed 'Razor'. With a military dictatorship established, it was merely a matter of suitable weather and sufficient supplies before Japan challenged the USA for control of the Pacific. French Indo-China had already been occupied when France fell (June 1940). Out in the Pacific, warships, planes and men stood ready. Older men probably remembered the sudden attack on Port Arthur (1904) when Japan first engaged a European power (see Chapter 5). Now she was about to challenge a far greater opponent.

When French Indo-China fell Roosevelt stopped all supplies of scrap iron to Japan and froze her assets in the USA so that trade between them stopped. Even so, the American President was convinced that Hitler's Germany was a greater menace than Japan. The Japanese, on their side, tried to hide their warlike intentions. They desired only peace, they said. If only the USA would persuade China to stop fighting all would be well. However, Roosevelt's experts had cracked the Japanese code and intercepted vital messages. By this time the President knew Japan's leaders intended to start a war of conquest. He demanded that Japan respect other people's territory. Negotiations continued until 26 November 1941 when the USA again demanded that the Japanese cease warlike preparations. Thereupon Tojo broke off diplomatic relations as a prelude to war. The Japanese message stating this arrived in Washington but there was a delay in decoding it. Consequently its exact contents were known only six hours before Japanese planes bombed the US base at **Pearl Harbour** (Hawaiian Islands) on Sunday 7 December 1941.

Just over a month before, six Japanese aircraft carriers, two battleships, two cruisers and nearly fifty smaller craft left Tankan Bay

(Hitokappu) in Iturup in the Kurile Islands (see map on page 172). On board were 423 planes, many equipped to fire British-made torpedoes specially adapted for shallow water. Their orders were to cross the North Pacific, pass between the Aleutian and Midway Islands and launch their attack. Success depended upon absolute secrecy; somehow this large force must reach its objective without being seen.

The man behind the plan was **Admiral Isoroku Yamamoto**. For years he had argued that since the USA was potentially much more powerful than Japan her only chance of success in a war was to destroy the existing US fleet before it began, rather as Russia's fleet had been destroyed in 1905 (see page 42). To achieve such a knockout blow he had developed a fleet of aircraft carriers. With these the short-range bombers of the day could be placed near enough to US bases to make effective raids. 'The presence of the US fleet is a dagger pointed at our throats', he wrote. The Japanese fleet which ploughed across the empty North Pacific that November carried not only the hopes of a proud nation but the life dream of Admiral Yamamoto.

As the ships pitched and rolled in heavy seas, the plan for bombing Pearl Harbour was explained to the pilots. It seemed impossibly dangerous. One man admitted afterwards that he felt 'a cold chill' as he listened. The chances of getting all the way to the Hawaiian Islands without detection seemed slim indeed. In fact luck was with them, because for most of the voyage bad weather cut down visibility. Nothing delayed their progress. Speed was maintained even in fog and if a man fell overboard he was not rescued. The larger ships, like *Kaga* (Increased Joy) and *Kasumi* (Mist of Flowers) were never seen by scouting aircraft. Since that time critics have blamed the Americans for being so careless. The truth was that the US commanders knew an attack was coming but they did not know where. Units of their fleet, south-west of Oahu (see map on page 172), were actually patrolling in the wrong direction.

The Japanese assault had been planned most carefully. Everything about Pearl Harbour, its beach gradients, its tides, the flow of its shipping, the position of its battleships, was known to Japan's spies. Even Sunday had been chosen deliberately because extra warships would be in port for the weekend. Whatever may have been known in Washington or in the Pacific fleet, the Americans in Pearl Harbour seem to have been completely unaware of any danger. Few men were even awake when Commander **Mitsuo Fuchida** arrived over the base just before 8 a.m. leading the first wave of 183 aircraft. Here and there sailors were cleaning dirty brass or wiping the dew from gun-barrels. On Waikiki beach neon-lights still flickered; radios were playing dance music. In the harbour American warships were anchored in pairs, so close that Fuchida could hardly believe his luck. Shortly before, the Japanese planes had been detected by a US radar operator but his superior officer had decided they must be friendly.

Within minutes the airfield and the ships were under bombardment. Surprise was complete. Only four American aircraft managed to go into the air at all and they were quickly shot down. Another 117 were destroyed on the ground. Fuchida's men dived until almost level with

the warships' superstructures, then released their torpedoes. Huge
boiling water-spouts and black smoke marked the explosions. A giant
cloud of steam and smoke arose from the USS *Arizona* as her boilers
and forward magazine blew up. Astonished Americans reacted with a
pathetic bravery which increased their losses. Some rushed on deck
and fired revolvers at the red-and-yellow-striped planes. One man took
cover behind a dustbin-lid and fired a machine-gun.

By the time the second wave of 170 Japanese aircraft appeared over
Pearl Harbour at 9 a.m. it was difficult to see the crippled US ships
through the flames and smoke. Four were sunk and the *Arizona* was
going down in a mass of burning oil taking 1,000 men with her. This
time the Americans put up a terrific curtain of fire. One Japanese pilot
described how 'shells bursting like flowers' were all round him. When
the Japanese finally flew away at 1.30 p.m. 8 battleships were disabled
and 2,403 Americans dead. That evening a Japanese submarine commander reported, 'Pearl Harbour shone red in the sky like a thing of
fire'.

*Flames envelop a sinking US
warship at Pearl Harbour,
Hawaiian Islands, 7 December
1941*

It has shone red in the history of the United States ever since. As an attack it was in many ways a failure. Enormous stores of oil were left intact to supply the US fleet in the battles ahead. Three big US aircraft carriers were away at sea. It was not the devastating blow the Japanese needed. Politically, however, it wiped away twenty years of isolationism in a few hours. Never again were Americans to believe that what happened elsewhere in the world did not concern them. Never again were they to be caught unprepared as they were that Sunday morning. Fuchida's planes attacked in 1941. What they did then influences US policy to the present day.

Timeline

1917   The Twenty-One Demands. USA's 'Open Door' policy.

1921   Washington Naval Conference. Four and Nine Power Treaties. Johnson Act.

1931   Japanese occupation of Manchuria.

1936   Anti-Comintern Pact.

1937   Marco Polo Bridge incident. Japan invades China.

1940   US Congress approves conscription. Destroyers sold to Britain. The Lend-Lease Scheme.

1941   Atlantic Charter. Roosevelt freezes Japan's assets in USA. Japanese planes attack Pearl Harbour, Hawaiian Islands. USA enters Second World War.

Questions

1. Describe the Mukden incident and explain why it was a real test for the League of Nations and why the League failed to act.

2. In what ways did the USA try to check Japanese power and influence in the Far East between the two world wars? How far were these measures successful?

3. 'Particularly in the middle and western parts of the United States, where Europe seemed very far away, most people believed that the best thing for the United States to do this time was to keep out of it and to let the Europeans sort out their problems amongst themselves.'

   What events caused the American 'man in the street' to change this attitude towards the Second World War in Europe?

4. Write short paragraphs on each of the following:
   a) Roosevelt's 'Good Neighbour' Policy
   b) the Anti-Comintern Pact
   c) the Lend-Lease Scheme
   d) Admiral Yamamoto

20
Blitzkrieg
The Second World War in Europe

There was little cheering in Paris, London or Berlin when the Second World War started on 3 September 1939. Nobody talked of peace by Christmas as they had in 1914. Nevertheless, Hitler still hoped for a quick victory. It was obvious that the long First World War stalemate in the West had favoured Germany's enemies, allowing time for Britain and the USA to mobilise greater resources. Consequently the Gemans sought ways of returning to a war of movement. Two writers: **Charles de Gaulle**, and a German, **Heinz Guderian**, had suggested that a tank army used like a giant battering-ram could destroy a fixed front. The French General Staff rejected de Gaulle's theories. The German High Command decided to re-model their army on such lines.

The fate of Poland in 1939 proved who was right. Her army was a large one of the First World War type, equipped for trench warfare. The German army had as its spearhead six Panzer (armoured) tank divisions supported by dive-bombers. Behind were forty-four motorised divisions. Over dry ground and in good weather this force demonstrated the new 'lightning war' (**Blitzkrieg**). Years before, Hitler had said, 'If I were going to attack an opponent . . . I should suddenly, like a flash of lightning in the night, hurl myself upon the enemy.' Now his troops did just that. Within ten days Poland's army was finished as an effective force. By 17 September the Russians began hurriedly invading those Polish provinces promised them in the August Pact (see page 160). Before the end of the month there was no independent Poland.

This stunning conquest should have caused the British and French to organise tank armies. In fact a quiet period, nicknamed the 'phoney' war, followed for nearly six months. Although a British Expeditionary Force (BEF) went to France, as in 1914 it did not march into any battles. During the winter British entertainers sang, 'Run Rabbit, Run' – which meant Hitler – or 'We're gonna hang out our washing on the Siegfried Line' – a reference to the German frontier defences (see page 157) – to happy audiences. Air Raid Precautions (ARP) squads waited for bombers which did not come. The only exciting news concerned the desperate **Winter War** being fought by the Finns after Stalin had demanded bases in their country. This ended in March 1940 with the defeat of Finland.

Hitler, meanwhile, was completing his war plans and listening to his admirals. In their opinion the Imperial Navy's failure during the 1914–18 war had been partly because Germany had such a small, easily-blockaded coastline. If the army occupied Denmark and Norway their U-boats could operate from long, sheltered coasts. On 8 April 1940

German and Soviet attacks and conquests, 1939–40

Winston Churchill. In 1940 he promised the British victory after 'blood, toil, tears and sweat'

Hitler did what they asked. With complete air superiority this second *Blitzkrieg* easily overwhelmed two such weak countries. The British seemed helpless. When the Royal Navy intervened it lost two destroyers and the aircraft carrier *Glorious*. An expedition sent to help the Norwegians captured and held Narvik for a time (see map above) but eventually had to leave in June. Only the destruction of most of Germany's navy balanced these defeats.

The German conquest of Norway finished Neville Chamberlain's career. From the start he had miscalculated. He thought the German invasion of Norway and Denmark a mistake and had talked of Hitler having 'missed the bus'. In a noisy, two-day debate the House of Commons made it clear that they thought their Prime Minister had missed the bus! Some Members of Parliament demanded that he resign and after an historic debate Chamberlain did so. On 10 May **Winston Churchill** became Prime Minister of a Coalition government of all three parties (Conservative, Liberal and Labour).

Churchill's life up till then had not been a complete success story. It was true that at first fortune had smiled on him. He had charged with the 21st Lancers at Omdurman (1898), reported the American war in Cuba (1898) and made a daring escape from the Boers (1900). As a minister of the Liberal government of 1906–14 he had helped lay the foundations of the Welfare State. When war broke out in 1914 it was

his swift action as First Sea Lord which ensured that the British fleet
was ready. Then things started to go wrong for him. He was blamed
for the unsuccessful attack on Antwerp (1914), the disaster at Gallipoli
(1915) and the ill-fated expedition to Archangel against the Bolsheviks
(1919). Such failures made people regard him as a bad war leader. In
1925 an American remarked, 'It is doubtful if even Great Britain could
survive another world war and another Churchill'. After 1933 his constant warnings about Hitler caused many to think of him as a warmonger. No one doubted his great talent. Quite a few feared his headstrong and extreme ways.

   Now the situation was far different. Britain was no longer seeking
peace and appeasement. She was fighting for her life. In this crisis the
British turned instinctively to Churchill. Chamberlain had never
seemed warlike, no matter what he said. Churchill was always firm
and decisive. Three days after his appointment he told the House of
Commons, 'I have nothing to offer but blood, toil, tears and sweat',
but he promised 'Victory at all costs'. There could be no doubt he
meant it. Britain had a leader to match Hitler in determination.

   Even as Churchill took charge the real war began in Western
Europe. On 10 May 1940 Hitler launched **Operation Yellow**, an invasion of the Netherlands, Belgium and France. Paratroopers descended from the skies, causing confusion and destruction behind the
front. Dive-bombers blasted supply roads or left cities like Rotterdam
in ruins. Tank armies crashed into the Maginot Line at the point
where it ended on the Luxembourg border (see map on page 158).
After three days of confused battle the Panzers broke through at Sedan.
As they raced down the Somme Valley to the sea at Abbeville, British and French forces which had advanced into Belgium to stop a
Schlieffen-like swing on Paris were cut off. For several weeks they
tried to fight their way out, although short of ammunition and fuel.
Then, as the French fell back across France, the British commander,
Lord Gort, sensed that they were past help. Disobeying the French
High Command, he retreated to **Dunkirk** so that his troops could
escape home.

*British troops line up on the
beach at Dunkirk, May 1940*

The Fall of France, 1940.
German troops march through
the Arc de Triomphe in Paris

The Fall of France, 1940.
German troops march through
the Arc de Triomphe in Paris

Once the plight of the British Expeditionary Force was known in England, an armada of pleasure boats, yachts and dinghies, set out from the south coast of England to rescue them. The result was startling. Long lines of weary troops waded into the sea and scrambled on to anything that floated. While they waited to be rescued they lay in the sand and tried to dodge enemy bombs and bullets. In six days over 300,000 British and French soldiers were brought to safety by sailors and civilians who never rested. Churchill called it 'a miracle of deliverance'.

For the French there was no miracle; her enemies were gathering for the kill. Mussolini, surprised as everybody else by the swiftness of the German success, was anxious to share the spoils of victory. 'I only need a few thousand dead so that I can sit at the peace conference as a man who has fought', he remarked. On 10 June 1940 Italy declared war on France and Britain.

Certainly there seemed little danger of a long war. Three days after Italy's declaration, Paris was abandoned to the Germans. Elsewhere lines of defence planned by the French generals existed only on paper, because the French army was no longer an efficient fighting force. Nine days later, in the forest of **Compiègne**, in the same railway carriage used by Foch to receive the German Generals in 1918 (see page 87), the French were forced to sign a humiliating armistice. Northern France was occupied by the Germans. Only a puppet French government based at **Vichy**, remained to rule the south. One soldier, Charles de Gaulle, spoke with the old French spirit. Arriving in London, he announced, 'France has lost a battle but not the war.' He began to organise a **Free French** force even as the British crippled the French fleet at **Mers el-Kebir** in North Africa, in case it fell into enemy hands. Hitler thought the war in the West was over and offered Britain peace. To his surprise Churchill refused. The Nazi leader was forced to plan an invasion of Britain.

Britain's 'finest hour'

Years before, a critic had written sarcastically of Churchill: 'He is always unconsciously playing a part – an heroic part. He sees himself moving through the smoke of battle – triumphant, terrible, his brow clothed with thunder'. This may have seemed funny in peacetime. Now there really was smoke and Churchill moved through it in a manner which was truly heroic. 'I felt', he wrote, 'as if I were walking with destiny and that all my past life had been but a preparation for this hour.' In his speeches he expressed, as no-one else could, the defiant spirit of the British. The response was immediate. People flocked to work in the armaments factories. They joined a new force, the **Local Defence Volunteers (LDV)**, later known as the **Home Guard**, and prepared to fight the Panzers with every sort of weapon, including pitchforks, pikes and shotguns. It was a desperate moment. Yet it proved to be, as Churchill predicted, Britain's 'finest hour'.

Fighter planes were the first need, Spitfires and Hurricanes. Encouraged by Goering, who promised an easy victory, Hitler loosed his *Luftwaffe* (air force) on Britain (13 August) intending to gain control of the air as a preparation for a sea assault. **The Battle of Britain** which followed was a crisis for civilisation. Day after day the sky above southern England was the scene of confused dog-fights between British and German planes. People below saw only silvery specks wheeling and twisting high above in the sky. Usually they heard the steady drone of engines; sometimes the chatter of machine-guns. For those who took part it was a mixture of boredom, excitement and fear. Hours of waiting would be followed by a few dizzy minutes cartwheeling about the sky, their earphones buzzing with shouts, warnings, oaths and commands. Some returned safely. Others had to clamber from a burning plane or float patiently in the Channel. Death was very near all the time. 'By the end of the Battle of Britain', recalled a survivor, 'I had lost almost every friend I had. I was twenty-three...'. A few were professional, peacetime pilots like Douglas Bader. Most had been civilians a few months before. Such men had to learn to fight and live with fear. 'When I was in a fight I was so scared that my left foot used to twitch and quiver. I couldn't stop it', wrote 'Ginger' Lacey, the top scorer for Fighter Command during the battle.

Neither German nor British pilots realised the battle's importance, or even who was winning. The British were helped by radar, which allowed them to rest on the airfields until the enemy approached instead of tiring themselves with constant patrols. They had a fine commander in Air Marshal Hugh Dowding. The Germans might have won if they had kept up their attacks on airfields and radar stations

A German bomber dives to destruction during the Battle of Britain, 1940

instead of switching to bomb London (7 September). Hurricanes and Spitfires were probably more manoeuvrable than German Messerschmitt 109s, although they were not as fast. One fact is certain. Day by day the RAF inflicted heavier casualties than it received. On 17 September 1940 Hitler postponed indefinitely his plan of invasion. Britain had been saved, not by a large army, but by several thousand pilots. In Parliament Churchill summed it up in a memorable sentence. 'Never in the field of human conflict was so much owed by so many to so few.'

Britain now settled down to siege conditions. Night after night German bombers bombed and burned London and other large cities. The British replied by building long-range bombers which later raided Germany by the hundred. The seas around Britain witnessed once more those grim battles with U-boats common in the First World War. Coasts and beaches were mined, covered with barbed wire and fortified by gun emplacements. Windows disappeared behind sandbags, people slept in metal shelters in the garden. Rationing, bombing and the blackout (the covering up of most street and house lighting) made Britain into a dark and dismal land as the second Christmas of the war approached.

Hitler invades the Soviet Union

The only land operations were far from Britain. Mussolini's forces were poorly equipped. His navy had no fighter cover and many of its ships were crippled by British aerial attacks at **Taranto** (Italy). His army had few suitable tanks or motorised vehicles. They invaded Greece and Egypt but in both cases met with defeat. When the Greeks drove the Italians back into Albania (see map on page 188) Germany was forced to invade Yugoslavia to help. A British force which went to aid Greece was driven out, both from the mainland and from **Crete** (1941). In Egypt, however, the British mustered every available tank and smashed the Italian armies. Hundreds of thousands of men surrendered. The Italian African Empire fell like a pack of cards. Again the Germans had to help. Their specially trained **Afrika Korps**, led by General Erwin Rommel, landed and drove the British back into Egypt. The war seemed to be developing into a stalemate.

At this moment Hitler made a fatal mistake. France, Poland, Yugoslavia and Greece had been overrun. Bulgaria, Italy, Hungary and Romania were on his side. Europe lay at his feet. It seemed time to make the old German dream of *lebensraum* in the East (see page 154) come true. On 22 June 1941 his armies broke the 1939 Pact (see page 160) and invaded the Soviet Union in **Operation Barbarossa**. The Soviet army's display against Finland had not been impressive. The Nazi generals expected it to collapse as quickly as the French army. At first they seemed to have calculated correctly. The Soviet army was ill-prepared and badly equipped. Many of its officers were poorly trained; its aircraft were out of date, its guns drawn by horses or tractors. In a few months the Germans carved their way towards Kiev,

Operation Barbarossa. The main German attacks on the Soviet Union, June 1941

Leningrad and Moscow with dreadful efficiency (see map above). Millions of Russian soldiers were killed or captured by encircling movements. By October the Germans were besieging Leningrad and approaching **Moscow**. Large numbers of people began to leave the capital. Government offices were evacuated. Only Stalin and his advisers stayed on in the Kremlin, the government buildings in Moscow.

Then the Russian winter set in. German troops shivered without adequate clothing. Their vehicles froze or sank in the mud. This slowed their advance, allowing time for the Soviet Union to awake like a sleeping giant. Stalin's régime was more efficient and ruthless than the old Tsarist government. Swiftly the situation began to change. Vast armies of peasants were recruited to replace those lost. Complete factories were dismantled and moved to safety behind the Ural Mountains. The USA decided to include the USSR in her Lend-Lease Scheme (see page 174). Whilst the inhabitants of Leningrad heroically defended their city, the Soviet army was able to launch a mighty counter-attack near Moscow, on 6 December 1941.

Led by General Zhukov this counter-attack almost broke the German front for good. Only a frantic order from Hitler, telling his troops to stand and die, temporarily halted the Russian advance. Such suicidal tactics could not go on forever. On 15 January 1942 the

German and Russian troops fight a desperate battle in the streets of Stalingrad, 1942

Nazi leader allowed his troops to retreat to heavily defended positions, called 'Hedgehogs'. Here they lived like starving wolves in a frozen countryside, holding off an army and a people infuriated by their cruelty. Hatred of Stalin's government was forgotten. Now it was a Russian war against the foreign invader, as in the days of Napoleon.

With the spring Hitler tried again. In Egypt Rommel pushed towards the Suez Canal until he was only 80 kilometres from Alexandria (see map on page 188). In Russia the German Sixth Army swung south towards the Crimea and the Caucasian oil-fields. But now Pearl Harbour had been attacked (1941) and the USA was in the war (see Chapter 19). With her large industries safe from bombing, the USA was able to send massive supplies which helped to swing the balance against Germany. A re-equipped and strengthened British Eighth Army, led by a new commander, General Bernard Montgomery, attacked Rommel at **El Alamein** (October 1942). His Afrika Korps was smashed and driven back into Tunisia.

The German Sixth Army conquered the Crimea but was halted at **Stalingrad**, where an awful battle raged for five months. Inch by inch the Germans fought their way into the pile of rubble which had once been a city. New Soviet armies then counter-attacked, and threatened the Germans with encirclement. The German commander, General von Paulus, wished to retreat before it was too late. Hitler refused to let him. As a result 300,000 Nazi soldiers were trapped in the ruins, living like savages, gnawing at horse meat and wrapped in rags

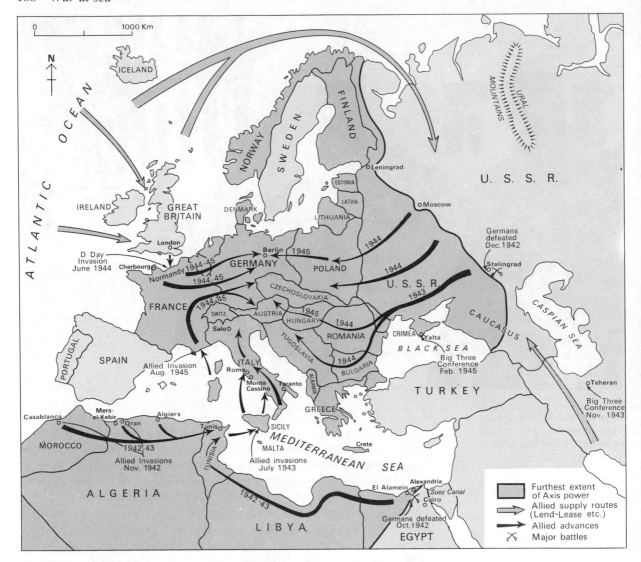

Main rows of map labels and annotations:

0 1000 Km

N

ICELAND

ATLANTIC OCEAN

IRELAND

GREAT BRITAIN

London

D Day Invasion June 1944

Cherbourg

Normandy 1944-45

1944-45

FRANCE

1944-45

DENMARK

NORWAY

SWEDEN

FINLAND

Leningrad

ESTONIA

LATVIA

LITHUANIA

Moscow

U. S. S. R.

Germans defeated Dec.1942

Stalingrad

Berlin 1945

GERMANY

POLAND

1944

1944

CZECHOSLOVAKIA

SWITZ

Salo

AUSTRIA

1945

HUNGARY

1944

ROMANIA

1943

CRIMEA Yalta

CAUCASUS

CASPIAN SEA

BLACK SEA

Big Three Conference Feb. 1945

PORTUGAL

SPAIN

Allied Invasion Aug. 1945

Rome

ITALY

Monte Cassino

Taranto

ALBANIA

YUGOSLAVIA

1944

BULGARIA

GREECE

TURKEY

Teheran

Big Three Conference Nov. 1943

Casablanca

Mers-el-Kebir

Oran

Algiers

Tunis

MOROCCO

1942-43

Allied Invasions Nov. 1942

ALGERIA

TUNISIA

1942-43

LIBYA

SICILY

MALTA

Allied invasions July 1943

Crete

MEDITERRANEAN SEA

El Alamein

Alexandria

Suez Canal

Cairo

Germans defeated Oct. 1942

EGYPT

URAL MOUNTAINS

Legend:

Furthest extent of Axis power

Allied supply routes (Lend-Lease etc.)

Allied advances

Major battles

Main Second World War battle areas. Europe and North Africa

against the cold. When the Russians at last moved in, their awful bombardment turned the snowy countryside black with soot, smoke and burnt corpses. German troops fought savagely because they feared falling into Russian hands. A mere 97,000 were left alive when von Paulus surrendered in January 1943.

These two defeats – El Alamein and Stalingrad – proved to be the turning-points of the war. Goering's *Luftwaffe* had suffered so severely that it had lost control of the air. In the Battle of the Atlantic, as the struggle to get food and supplies into Britain was called, Germany's few battleships, the *Graf von Spee*, *Bismarck*, *Gneisenau* and *Scharnhost*, had been sunk or destroyed in harbour. German U-boats were being tracked down efficiently by aircraft or by new scientific devices like radar and asdic (a system of underwater detection). In any case swiftly built US merchant ships were replacing the losses. German towns and factories were being bombed night and day. Her allies were either weak, like Italy, Romania, Bulgaria and Finland, or too far away, like Japan. Against the Nazi war machine were ranged the combined industrial resources of the USA, the British Empire and the Soviet Union. Like Imperial Germany before her, Nazi Germany had challenged too many countries to a fight. Defeat was inevitable, unless the Allies offered peace, and Churchill, Roosevelt and Stalin were not likely to do that.

In November 1942 an Anglo-American army commanded by **General Dwight Eisenhower** landed in Algiers and Morocco (see map on page 188), forcing the remains of Rommel's Afrika Korps to surrender. The following July these forces, aided by Montgomery's Eighth Army, invaded Sicily. A new government appointed by the Italian King immediately imprisoned Mussolini and decided to fight for the Allies. Unfortunately, most of the country was controlled by German troops, and some Italians stood by their old leader. A daring Nazi parachute raid rescued Mussolini and took him to the north where he formed a puppet state, the Salo Republic. While Italians fought on both sides, the Germans were able to delay the Allied advance in a country ideal for defence. A succession of mountains and rivers barred the way. Each was defended with great skill and courage. At **Monte Cassino** (see map opposite) it took four months to capture the ancient monastery from the Germans. Rome did not fall until June 1944.

D Day in Normandy

By that time Western Europe was near to liberation. For some time Stalin had demanded that the British and Americans open a second front to relieve pressure on the USSR. Such an invasion against Hitler's 'Atlantic Wall' defences was complicated and dangerous. Months of planning were necessary before the mighty army, under the command of Eisenhower and Montgomery, was fully prepared. On 6 June 1944, after days of rain and wind, 5,000 vessels approached the Normandy coast and started a series of landings.

Allied troops scramble ashore in Normandy. 'D Day', 1944

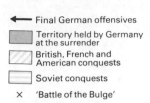

Final German offensives
Territory held by Germany at the surrender
British, French and American conquests
Soviet conquests
× 'Battle of the Bulge'

Final stages of the Second World War in Europe

D Day (D for deliverance) took the Germans by surprise. They had expected an assault on the Channel coast at a later date. Their commander, Rommel, was away visiting his wife in Berlin. Nevertheless they fought back bravely. On some beaches progress was easy. On others a fearful slaughter took place. At the end of the first day 130,000 men were ashore. Six days later the number had risen to 326,000. Every possible device was used to make success certain. Gliders dropped parachutists far inland to hamper German communications. A temporary harbour called Mulberry was towed across to France to provide shelter for the shipping. A pipeline, **Pluto** (pipeline under the ocean), was laid on the sea-bed, so that oil could be pumped direct from Britain to feed the mechanised armies. Yet the Germans fought so fiercely that it was August before the Allies broke out of their bridgehead and occupied Cherbourg (see map on page 188).

Germany was now faced with a two-front war. In desperation Hitler ordered the bombardment of London, first with jet-driven flying bombs (V1s) and then supersonic rocket bombs (V2s). These new weapons did great damage and killed many people but they could not alter the result of the war. Some of Hitler's officers lost all hope and tried to kill him. In July 1944 they placed a bomb in a briefcase near his chair during a conference at Headquarters. It exploded but he escaped with singed hair and torn trousers. The plotters were caught,

One of the last photographs of Hitler

tortured and hanged. The German army had left its defiance of Hitler far too late.

The war's last nine months saw an almost steady advance on Germany from east, west and south. Against overwhelming numbers of fresh troops the German High Command frequently had little more than boys and old men to offer resistance. From the east the Soviet army overran Romania, Bulgaria and Hungary. From the south Allied troops completed the conquest of Italy and poured into the Po Valley. In the west Eisenhower's armies continued to stream forward on a wide front. Their last remaining natural obstacle was the River Rhine. In September 1944 an attempt was made to cross the Rhine in the Netherlands so that the Allies could drive down behind the German front defences. Paratroops were dropped at Eindhoven, Nymegen and Arnhem (see map opposite). All these attacks failed. At **Arnhem** the attackers landed in the middle of two Panzer divisions. Nevertheless the Rhine was crossed and, in October, the Allies captured their first German town, **Aachen**.

Hitler, meanwhile, decided on a gamble. Massing twenty-eight divisions and scraping up equipment from all over Germany, he ordered a last, desperate offensive. On 15 December 1944, helped by thick mist, fanatical young Nazis smashed into the American line in the Ardennes. Within two days they were through and only 13 kilometres from the US First Army Headquarters. As the Americans recovered from their surprise, the weather cleared enough to allow heavy bombing of German supply columns. A fierce defence of Bastogne settled the matter. Before long US troops were driving into the salient (corner) formed in their lines. When the **Battle of the Bulge** ended in January 1945 the Germans were back where they had started.

On 13 April the Russians took Vienna. Eight days later they were in the suburbs of Berlin. By the end of the month Russian and American troops met at Torgau. Germany was cut in two. Hitler spent his last days 15 metres below the ruins of the Chancellery building in Berlin. Since the attempt on his life the previous year he had been a sick man. More and more he had lost touch with reality. Armies which no longer existed were told to stand and die. Orders were given to destroy entire towns rather than let them be captured. Finally, the news that Mussolini had been shot by Italian resistance fighters made him decide to commit suicide. On 29 April 1945 he married Eva Braun, a woman who had loved him for years. Afterwards, at a wedding breakfast, he drank champagne and talked continuously. Later, in the early hours of Monday 30 April, he shot himself. Eva Braun had been given a revolver but she chose poison. With Russian shells exploding near the Chancellery garden, a servant carried the two bodies upstairs and placed them in a shell-hole. Here they were soaked in petrol and set alight. As the flames roared up Goebbels gave the Nazi salute. Then he, too, died by his own hand.

Although **Admiral Doenitz** was made leader in Hitler's place, the Third Reich survived for only another week. On 7 May 1945 Germany surrendered unconditionally, defeated militarily for the second time in under thirty years.

Eva Braun, who married Hitler the day before he killed himself

Timeline

1939   Poland overrun. Second World War begins.
1940   Winter War, Finland defeated. Norway, Denmark conquered. Fall of France. Dunkirk evacuation. Italy declares war on France and Britain. Battle of Britain.
1941   Pearl Harbour. USA declares war on Germany. Germany invades USSR·
1942   Battles of Stalingrad and El Alamein.
1943   Defeat of German Africa Korps. Allied invasion of Italy. Fall of Mussolini.
1944   Russians invade Eastern Europe. D Day Allied invasion of France. Rome and Paris captured. Allies cross the Rhine. Battle of the Bulge.
1945   Americans and Russians meet at Torgau. Mussolini murdered. Hitler commits suicide. Berlin captured. End of war.

Questions

1. 'The defence of Southern England will last four days and the Royal Air Force four weeks. We can guarantee invasion for the Führer [Hitler] within a month.' (Hermann Goering, July 1940)

   'The gratitude of every home in our Island...goes out to the British airmen... Never in the field of human conflict was so much owed by so many to so few.' (Winston Churchill, August 1940)

   a) What great event caused Goering to be proved wrong and Churchill to be grateful? Give details.
   b) In what way was this great event 'a crisis for civilisation'?

2. 'We have only to kick in the front door and the whole rotten Russian edifice [building] will come tumbling down' (Hitler at the time of the invasion of the USSR, 1941)

   Explain why Hitler failed to conquer the USSR quickly.

3. 'From two miles out the assault troops began to see the living and the dead in the water. The dead floated gently, moving with the tide toward the beach as though determined to join their fellow fighting men. The living bobbed up and down in the swells savagely pleading for help the assault boats could not tender...' (R.W. Thompson, writing on D Day)

   a) Why were the Germans taken by surprise when the Allied troops landed in Normandy?
   b) What special inventions helped to make this large-scale landing a success?
   c) What desperate measures did Hitler take after he learned that the Allied troops were firmly based in Normandy?

4. Write short paragraphs on each of the following:
   a) the 'phoney' war   b) Dunkirk
   c) Stalingrad   d) the Hitler Bomb Plot

21

From Midway to Hiroshima
The Second World War in the Far East

American economic restrictions placed on Japan in 1941 (see page 176) left only two alternatives. She could either give up her warlike plans or seize the whole of South East Asia and develop it as an industrial supply area. The first alternative was out of the question as far as her aggressive leaders were concerned. The second seemed to offer a good chance of success. The Philippines, Borneo, the Moluccas, Celebes, Timor, Java, Sumatra, Malaya, Thailand and Burma were poorly defended. Of the European countries interested in the region, the Netherlands was already occupied by German troops, the USA was clearly unprepared, whilst the Soviet Union, which might have challenged the Japanese in Manchuria, was fully engaged fighting Germany. Against Japan's experienced army there were only badly equipped troops, spread over thousands of kilometres and split into scattered units. Against Japan's navy of 200 warships, the British and Americans could only muster 90, against 7,500 planes only 1,000. Japan was free to concentrate her forces and strike where she wished.

The only real threat to such a plan, the American fleet, seemed to have been crippled at Pearl Harbour (see page 178). Following this, Japanese sea-borne task forces struck south at the Philippines, Malaya, Thailand, Borneo and the islands of Wake, Guam and Hong Kong (see map below). Everywhere they were successful. Wake, Guam

Pacific battle zones, 1941–5

Japan and her empire by May 1942
Furthest extent of Japanese conquest
Allied attacks
Major battles

Scene on deck of the sinking British battleship, 'Prince of Wales'

and Hong Kong fell during December 1941. Malaya and Thailand were overrun and **Singapore**, the largest British base in the Far East, was captured (February 1942). The Dutch surrendered their East Indian Empire (now Indonesia) on 9 March. In the **Philippines** American troops led by General Douglas MacArthur put up a tougher resistance. At **Bataan** and **Corregidor** they held out for some months, inflicting heavy losses on the Japanese. Then shortages of food and medical supplies led to widespread disease. Bataan surrendered in April and Corregidor a month later. By 20 May 1942 the British were driven back to Burma, Australia was threatened and South East Asia belonged to Japan.

With these lands conquered, fighting shifted to the sea. Here a revolution in naval warfare was about to take place. The attack on Pearl Harbour and the sinking of two British battleships, the *Prince of Wales* and *Repulse*, by Japanese bombers proved what sailors, particularly

Yamamoto, had been arguing for years. Gun-firing warships were out of date. Modern battleships were aircraft carriers which fired aeroplanes, not shells. A new type of sea fight in which the opposing fleets never saw each other was now possible. No longer would dreadnoughts swing into line of battle. Instead, their successors could gather in large circles so that cruisers and destroyers could form a protective screen around them. Dive-bombers and torpedo planes would replace shells; ranges increase to 80 kilometres or more. Victory would go to the side which sank the most carriers.

Japan's easy victories made her leaders even more ambitious. In May 1942 a strong force was sent through the **Coral Sea** to capture the Solomon Islands and attack Port Moresby, New Guinea (see map on page 193). Unknown to the Japanese, US experts had discovered the key to their wireless code. Consequently the Americans knew of the Japanese move and gathered their fleet to intercept in the Coral Sea. There followed, in May 1942, the first carrier to carrier battle in history. It resulted in the sinking of two Japanese carriers and the loss of the USS *Lexington*. More Japanese planes were destroyed than American. For the first time a Japanese invading force turned back.

Turning point at Midway

The Battle of the Coral Sea was only a setback for Japan, but it was followed by disaster. Earlier in the year American long-range bombers, led by **General James Doolittle**, had set off from the carrier *Hornet* and bombed Tokyo. Although the damage was not severe the proud Japanese leaders felt deeply insulted. They decided that the attack must have come from **Midway Island**, an American base which barred the way to the Hawaiian Islands (see map on page 193). Yamamoto insisted on sending a strong fleet to assault the island. Some Japanese leaders had misgivings but nothing could be denied the Admiral after Pearl Harbour. A force of 5 aircraft carriers, 11 warships and 5,000 men was sent across the Pacific (May 1942).

Fame or no fame, Yamamoto had made several mistakes. First, he believed that two, not one, American aircraft carriers had been destroyed at the Battle of the Coral Sea. Second, he thought that two other US carriers were far away. In fact, three carriers were moving against his task force, guided by intercepted messages. The Japanese had already started attacking Midway when US torpedo aircraft appeared overhead. Their first attack was beaten off. Then, before the victorious Japanese fighters could regain height, and whilst their bombers were being rearmed with special bombs for use against ships, wave after wave of American planes roared down. In five terrible minutes most of Yamamoto's dreams were shattered. Three Japanese carriers, *Akagi, Kaga* and *Soryu*, became blazing wrecks as burning petrol, exploding bombs and torpedoes tore them apart. By next morning all three had disappeared. A fourth, the badly damaged *Hiryu*, managed to sink the USS *Yorktown* before being destroyed.

This battle proved to be a turning point. Never again was the Japanese Imperial Navy so powerful or so dangerous. Each month afterwards US submarines and planes were able to destroy increasing numbers of Japanese merchant ships. Every one sunk represented a deadly blow at Japan's weakest point. Without a large merchant marine her industries were gradually starved of supplies; her far-flung conquests could not be developed properly. Without a powerful war fleet to retain command of the seas, all other Japanese efforts were doomed. Midway for the Japanese, like Stalingrad for the Germans, was the beginning of the end.

Roosevelt and his advisers always regarded the European war as the more important of the two. Far more men and equipment were sent across the Atlantic than to the Pacific; one Far Eastern campaign was even called, appropriately, 'Operation Shoestring'. Nevertheless, the US admirals and generals in the Far East carried out a clever policy in this most difficult of wars, with its enormous distances, awful jungle, and fanatical enemy. Japan's new empire resembled in shape gigantic flowers sprawled across the Pacific. Its blossoms were the islands, large and small, its stems the shipping routes between them. Cut these 'stems' and many of the smaller 'flowers' would wither away. So the Americans began to 'leap-frog' or 'island-hop' across the Pacific, seizing vital bases and air strips, blocking sea lanes and leaving the islands in between to run out of supplies.

The American Marine Corps was well-equipped for such an operation. Between the wars their generals had studied and learnt from the lessons of Gallipoli (see page 73). Special types of landing craft were developed, capable of moving into shallow water and discharging their cargoes with the minimum of risk. Amphibious lorries and jeeps were also employed to sail in and crawl up the beach. Even so, the conquests were hard. The Japanese despised a man who surrendered. They fought to the last, regarding all defeats as dishonour. **Guadalcanal** in the Solomon Islands (see map on page 193) was taken quickly, but the Japanese returned and fought seven battles to recapture it. At first they inflicted heavy defeats on the US naval forces. Then the Americans called up reinforcements and hit back. When the Japanese finally gave up, 'Iron-bottom Sound', as the Americans named the narrow strip of water between Guadalcanal and Florida Islands, was littered with wrecks and bodies.

Leyte Gulf and Burma

Only gradually did the contests become easier as the Japanese ran short of supplies. With the Australians holding the jungles of New Guinea, the Americans proceeded in grass-hopper fashion towards Japan. In November 1943 the **Gilbert Islands** were cleared. Two months later the **Marshalls** were captured by massive forces amounting to over 100,000 men. By June 1944 the chief islands forming Japan's inner defence line, the **Marianas**, **Tinian** and **Guam**, had fallen (see map on page 193). As the Japanese Empire withered so the danger to the Japanese homeland increased.

From the Japanese point of view the crisis came in October 1944 when General MacArthur led his troops ashore in the **Philippines**. It

American 'island-hopping'. General MacArthur going ashore after a troop landing

US troops landing at Okinawa (see page 198)

was unthinkable that they should lose the islands. From them they controlled the sea routes to the Dutch East Indies. Once lost the Japanese fleet would be cut off from the oil which was its life-blood. It was better to risk the entire Imperial Fleet because, as their commander said, 'there would be no sense in saving the fleet at the expense of the loss of the Philippines'. The result was the largest sea fight of the war in **Leyte Gulf**. Here the dive-bombers screamed, the torpedoes sped towards their targets, the mighty ships vanished in smoke and steam, as the Americans took a terrible revenge for Pearl Harbour. When the fighting died down the Japanese navy had lost 4 aircraft carriers and 2 battleships. On shore, meanwhile, their suicidal soldiers suffered appalling casualties trying to halt the American advance. When Manila, the Philippine capital, at last fell, their losses totalled 170,000.

Far away in Burma (see map on page 193), British and Indian troops were fighting a less rewarding battle, with no short-cuts to victory. Every inch of jungle, every mountain and hill, had to be taken from a clever and ruthless enemy. In this difficult terrain the British 14th Army under General William Slim fought a series of campaigns intended to open up the Burma Road and so get supplies through to China. To help such operations General Orde Wingate led bands of guerrilla fighters, called **Chindits**, into the jungles behind Japanese lines. Such men lived in a strange green world, surrounded by enemies and supplied by air. Many died of disease as well as wounds.

The Japanese concentrated their efforts against the British. Their attacks on China were little more than annual sweeps to destroy the rice crop. In March 1944 they invaded Assam but after three months of fierce fighting they were defeated at **Imphal** and the British were able to invade Burma. From that victory onwards the Imperial Army was on the defensive. Step by step it was driven back. In fifteen months of warfare three Japanese armies, amounting to 347,000 men, were destroyed. By January 1945 the Burma Road was opened once more and Singapore and Rangoon were being bombed by the Allied air forces. That summer the men under Lord Louis Mountbatten's command stood ready to reconquer Malaya.

Such preparations proved unnecessary. Both Franklin D. Roosevelt and, after his death in April 1945, **President Harry Truman** had been worried by the thought of invading Japan. Each looked round for some less costly way of defeating a fanatical enemy who would fight to the death. Aerial bombardment was one possibility. From November 1944 Japan suffered the most terrible bombing in history. On 9 March 1945, for example, 41 square kilometres of Tokyo were burned in a fire which killed 78,000 people. To help such raids two islands, **Iwo Jima** and **Okinawa** (see map on page 193), were assaulted so that American planes could operate nearer the Japanese mainland. The enemy's reply was a ferocious resistance. Few of their soldiers gave in. At sea suicidal *Kamikaze* (meaning divine wind) pilots dived to their deaths on US ships. As a result 15,000 Americans died capturing these two bases. Such losses increased the US High Command's fears. If this was how islands hundreds of kilometres from Japan were defended what would happen when the homeland itself was invaded? It was true that the Japanese government had asked Russia on 13 July 1945 to help it negotiate a peace. But many Japanese were known to be against unconditional surrender in case it meant losing their Emperor, whilst some army chiefs favoured a last stand.

Horror at Hiroshima

Three days after the Japanese peace-feeler came news which changed the situation. For some years scientists had known that if an atom could be split by bombardment from other atoms the energy released would be a million times as powerful as the equivalent amount of high explosive. In 1939 three physicists, **Albert Einstein**, **Leo Szeland** and **Enrico Fermi**, had fled from Europe to the USA to escape fascist persecution. They warned President Roosevelt of the danger to the world if the Nazis produced such a bomb. At first Roosevelt did little about the matter but once the USA was at war he set up a special establishment for nuclear research. Within a short time Fermi created the self-sustaining nuclear reaction which is the half-way stage to making an atomic bomb. As the work expanded from laboratory to factory proportions, a new town was built at Oak Ridge, Tennessee, to house the necessary workers and equipment. Finally, a disused school near **Los Alamos** in New Mexico was chosen to complete tests. In this lonely

The first atomic bomb explodes on Hiroshima, 6 August 1945

The Super Fortress, nicknamed 'Enola Gay' after the pilot's mother, which dropped the first atomic bomb

spot, on 16 July 1945, a flash seen 400 kilometres away quickly turned into a purple and orange fireball. The tall tower holding the device was vaporised. A new age had begun in man's history.

President Truman saw in this terrible demonstration a way to end the war swiftly. On 6 August 1945 a B29 bomber, nicknamed *Enola Gay* and commanded by Colonel Paul Tibbetts, arrived over the Japanese city of **Hiroshima** with a nuclear bomb. It was 8.15 a.m. on a beautiful summer morning. The city lay in the sloping rays of the dawn sun, like a quilt of sparkling light and deep shadow, the River Ota dividing it with silvery lines. Tibbett's bomb aimer lined his instruments up on a bridge crossing the river at one of its widest points. Bomb doors were opened and the long device, weighing 4,500 kilograms, fell away. The big plane jerked violently upwards after losing such a load. Forty-three seconds later an atomic bomb exploded on human beings for the first time.

Survivors have different stories to tell of what they experienced in that awful moment. At first there seemed to be no sound, just blinding light. *Enola Gay's* tail gunner saw the world go purple as a ball of fire with a temperature of 100,000,000 °C at its centre spread across the landscape. Some Japanese spoke of a blackness, some of a rainbow-coloured object, others of a blue and gold blossom shape. To many it was like an enormous photographic flash-bulb exploding. Its effect was to turn the centre of Hiroshima into an oven in which thousands were burned to nothing. Only permanent shadows, like blurred photographs, indicated where human beings had once been. Further away people died more slowly and horribly, from radiation and fire. Even those living many kilometres from the city found that it burned everything black. People's faces, their bodies, even the print in books was affected.

The first fearful heat was followed by a wind with a speed of 800 kilometres per hour. It uprooted trees, flattened buildings and caused a 'rain' of flying glass which tore people to shreds. Clothes were ripped off, pillars under the explosion were driven straight into the ground,

'My God what have we done?'
Hiroshima after the explosion

blades of grass turned into dangerous objects which pierced people's bodies. In the harbour this hurricane produced tidal waves which drowned many who had hurled themselves into the water to escape. Simultaneously the thousands of charcoal stoves being used to make breakfast started scores of fires to add to the gigantic blaze ignited by the bomb. Flimsy wood and paper houses burned fiercely; larger buildings collapsed in flames. Half-mad people ran wildly through the streets, their faces black, their skin trailing in strips, their eyes hanging out. One man remembered years afterwards: 'I climbed on top of a pile of corpses. Layer upon layer of them. Some were still moving, still alive. I had to get over them. I can still hear the cracking of their bones.' For hours afterwards people continued to die. Thirteen square kilometres of Hiroshima were turned into what an American observer described as a 'huge, dirty, grey and rusty brown stain'. High up and far away another US airman gazed at the mushroom cloud over 6 kilometres high and exclaimed, 'My God, what have we done?'

Ordinary air raids had already killed more than the 80,000 who died at Hiroshima. But this time it was different. For weeks afterwards victims began to suffer from a mysterious illness. Their skin became disfigured with tiny bleedings. Their hair fell out. Then they died. Ever since, this radiation disease, called by the Japanese the 'sickness of the original-child bomb', has continued to kill. Today people who were not

Stunned survivors of the attack at Nagasaki waiting for help

even born in August 1945 die and suffer from the poison let loose that day, or in later atomic tests. Radio-active materials, such as Strontium 90, are released by atomic explosions and fall to earth thousands of kilometres away. There they are absorbed by the soil and so into plants. The animals who feed on these plants transmit the poison through their meat and milk to human beings. In the human body these radio-active materials can cause disease and suffering, particularly cancer. So the bomb dropped on Hiroshima, and the one dropped three days later on Nagasaki, because the Japanese Government had still not surrendered, continue to punish the innocent.

The one good result of this nightmare was the end of the war. Some of the Japanese military men wished to go on. The Emperor Hirohito wisely ordered his people to surrender and there was no resistance when the US soldiers arrived. On 2 September 1945 a Japanese delegation surrendered to General MacArthur on board the USS *Missouri* in Tokyo Bay. Afterwards the General said this in a broadcast to the American people,

Men since the beginning of time have sought peace . . . Military alliances, balances of power, leagues of nations, all in turn failed, leaving the only path to be . . . war. The utter destructiveness of war now blots out this alternative. We have had our last chance . . .

Timeline

1941–2	Japanese overrun South East Asia. Singapore captured. Battles of Coral Sea and Midway.
1943	Americans begin 'island-hopping' strategy.
1944	Philippines recaptured. Battle of Leyte Gulf. British defeat Japanese in Burma.
1945	Battles of Okinawa and Iwo Jima. First nuclear bomb exploded in New Mexico, USA. Hiroshima and Nagasaki destroyed by atomic bombing. Japanese surrender.

Questions

1. 'We had been caught flat-footed in the most vulnerable condition possible, decks covered with planes armed and loaded for an attack.' (A Japanese officer, speaking of the situation on the aircraft carrier *Akagi* during the Battle of Midway, 1942)

   a) What mistakes had Admiral Yamamoto made which led to the Japanese defeat at Midway?
   b) Why had the Japanese leaders decided to attack Midway Island in the first place?
   c) In what way were the Pacific battles between the Japanese and United States ships during the Second World War a new kind of sea-warfare?

2. Describe the American strategy of 'island-hopping' as used in the Pacific war against Japan. Mention the main battles which were fought as a result.

3. Write short paragraphs on each of the following:
   a) the Battle of the Coral Sea, 1942
   b) Chindits
   c) Hiroshima
   d) Strontium 90

22

The Troubled Peace
The United Nations and the Cold War

The Second World War was worse than the First. At least 10 million soldiers died in action. Germany (3.25 million), the Soviet Union (3 million), and Japan (1·5 million) probably lost most. Britain (400,000) and France (167,000) emerged with far fewer killed than in 1918. The USA, in spite of its worldwide efforts, lost only 325,000. Material destruction was tremendous. The centre of Europe and much of Japan lay in ruins. The damage has been valued at £120 billion, but this figure does not include the cost of eight years war in China. Worse than all this were the 12 million civilian casualties. Such a high figure was partly the result of heavy bombing and widespread food shortages. Mainly it was due to systematic extermination of the Jews by the Nazis in concentration camps. By October 1946 the full story of this slaughter had been revealed at the **Nuremberg Trials** where British, French, Russian and American judges tried the leading Nazi survivors.

Hitler had, of course, always hated Jews. Even before 1939 their life in Germany had been unbearable. During the war his armies captured territories inhabited by large numbers of them. In 1942 he decided on what he called 'the **final solution** of the Jewish problem'. By this he

Victims of a German concentration camp, 1945

meant their mass murder. The first rough and ready massacres took place in the USSR and Poland. Young, fit Jews were forced to work as slaves before being made to dig their own graves. Then they were shot. Later this method was replaced by carefully planned extermination which saved ammunition. Death factories were established at **Treblinka** and **Auschwitz**. At these places death was mass-produced in the same way that other factories made cars or machinery. The victims arrived in cattle-trucks and within half an hour they had been destroyed in gas chambers which could accommodate 2,000 at a time. Children were allowed to play until the last moment and then told they were going to have a shower. One Nazi remarked of this method, 'We knew when the people were dead because their screaming stopped'. Afterwards the bodies were used to help the war effort. Gold teeth were removed and sent to the German National Bank. Hair was shaved off and made into mattresses. Flesh was melted down for fat. What remained was burned. At Auschwitz such work took place over an area of 39 square kilometres containing gas chambers and synthetic petrol and rubber works. In this savage way 6 million Jews were killed. The appalled Nuremberg judges sentenced 12 Nazi leaders to death and others to long terms of imprisonment.

The United Nations

Even as the tale of the death camps was shocking the civilised world, the Allies set about trying to stop a future war. Before the defeat of Japan the representatives of fifty nations met in the San Francisco

Opera House and signed a **United Nations (UN) Charter** to replace the old covenant (constitution) of the League of Nations. They agreed to keep the peace, encourage co-operation between nations and defend human rights. Wilson's League had failed because some of the largest nations had not joined and because it had no armed force at its disposal. Now all the winning or neutral countries were members. Furthermore, **Article 43** of the Charter stated that the UN could call on its members to provide troops to deal with aggression. A large headquarters building, thirty-nine storeys high, was built in Manhattan, New York, overlooking the East River. Here the new parliament of the world, the **General Assembly**, met to solve the world's problems. Long before this glass and marble skyscraper was completed in 1952 the UN itself had caused both hope and disappointment.

The General Assembly meets annually and consists of five representatives from each member state. Here general discussion and debate can take place. A **Security Council** of eleven representatives meets regularly to deal with crises. Six of the seats in this Council are given to states in rotation; five are permanently held by Britain, the USA, the USSR, France and China. Any decision has to be passed by a majority of seven which must include these 'Big Five'. Consequently the five victors in the Second World War still have an extra power to veto (cancel) UN decisions. At the time this seemed a good idea. But within a few years it was obvious that France and Britain were no longer world powers, whilst China had been taken over by a Communist government (see Chapter 23) which was not represented on the Security Council. Indeed, for many years the ex-government of **Chiang Kai-shek**, based on the island of Formosa (now Taiwan), was recognised as 'China'. Worse still, the two super-powers, the USSR and the USA, upon whom the peace of the world clearly depended, soon became bitter enemies. The Soviet Union, in particular, used the veto constantly in the early years to keep out states which she thought would be unfriendly towards her. For example, Russian representatives on the Security Council vetoed Italy's application for membership six times and that of Japan four!

For some years the USA was able to count on majority support in the General Assembly. At least forty states out of a total membership of sixty could be relied upon to vote for any American proposal. Later, as more newly-independent states were admitted to the UN, this was no longer the case. The so-called 'Third World' of underdeveloped African, Asian and Latin American states found both the super-powers wanted their votes. Small nations came to the UN to preserve their liberties and to get what they considered their rights. Unfortunately, some also came to state their grievances, whilst refusing to listen to any other point of view. The quarrels between Jew and Arab and between Indian and Pakistani have continued despite UN resolutions and good intentions. However, it is only fair to point out that problems only come to the UN when the states involved have failed to solve them. A former Secretary General (the UN's chief official), the Burmese **U Thant**, once described the United Nations Organisation as 'a last ditch, last resort affair'. Long standing quarrels, such as that between the Arab world and Israel, cannot be solved by the placing of a military peace-keeping force in the war zones. The most that can be achieved is a lessening of tension. In a direct confrontation between the Soviet Union and the USA, like the one over Cuba (see Chapter 26), the UN can do little.

Steaks, chocolates and rice

If the UN's peace-keeping powers have been handicapped by the division between East and West, its **Specialised Agencies** have brought health and happiness to millions. When it was formed the UN took over some older international organisations, such as the **International Telecommunications Union (ITU)** (founded 1865), which co-ordinates telegraph and telephone links between countries, and the **Universal Postal Union (UPU)** (1874) which performs a similar service for mail. It also inherited departments of the League of Nations, such as the **International Labour Organisation (ILO)** and the **International Court** at the Hague in Holland. The ILO employs experts to make studies of the work conditions in various industries throughout the world. They give advice and training and, from time to time, issue codes (or laws) as guidelines for member nations. The ILO has two training centres, one at Geneva in Switzerland and the other at Turin in Italy. The International Court deals with disputes between nations.

Since the end of the Second World War the gap between the rich and poor areas of the world has widened. In the industrialised zones, Europe, Japan and the USA in particular, the standard of living has reached very high levels. People who eat steaks, chocolates, salads and

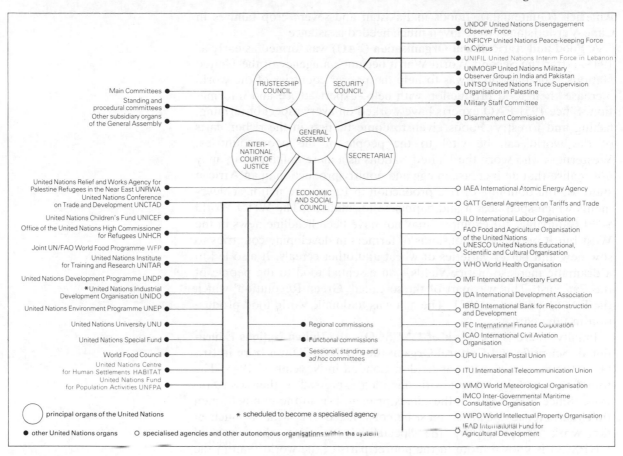

UNDOF United Nations Disengagement Observer Force
UNFICYP United Nations Peace-keeping Force in Cyprus
UNIFIL United Nations Interim Force in Lebanon
UNMOGIP United Nations Military Observer Group in India and Pakistan
UNTSO United Nations Truce Supervision Organisation in Palestine
Military Staff Committee
Disarmament Commission

TRUSTEESHIP COUNCIL
SECURITY COUNCIL
GENERAL ASSEMBLY
INTER-NATIONAL COURT OF JUSTICE
SECRETARIAT
ECONOMIC AND SOCIAL COUNCIL

Main Committees
Standing and procedural committees
Other subsidiary organs of the General Assembly

United Nations Relief and Works Agency for Palestine Refugees in the Near East UNRWA
United Nations Conference on Trade and Development UNCTAD
United Nations Children's Fund UNICEF
Office of the United Nations High Commissioner for Refugees UNHCR
Joint UN/FAO World Food Programme WFP
United Nations Institute for Training and Research UNITAR
United Nations Development Programme UNDP
*United Nations Industrial Development Organisation UNIDO
United Nations Environment Programme UNEP
United Nations University UNU
United Nations Special Fund
World Food Council
United Nations Centre for Human Settlements HABITAT
United Nations Fund for Population Activities UNFPA

Regional commissions
Functional commissions
Sessional, standing and *ad hoc* committees

IAEA International Atomic Energy Agency
GATT General Agreement on Tariffs and Trade
ILO International Labour Organisation
FAO Food and Agriculture Organisation of the United Nations
UNESCO United Nations Educational, Scientific and Cultural Organisation
WHO World Health Organisation
IMF International Monetary Fund
IDA International Development Association
IBRD International Bank for Reconstruction and Development
IFC International Finance Corporation
ICAO International Civil Aviation Organisation
UPU Universal Postal Union
ITU International Telecommunication Union
WMO World Meteorological Organisation
IMCO Inter-Governmental Maritime Consultative Organisation
WIPO World Intellectual Property Organisation
IFAD International Fund for Agricultural Development

○ principal organs of the United Nations   * scheduled to become a specialised agency

● other United Nations organs   O specialised agencies and other autonomous organisations within the system

The United Nations Organisation

fruit, who own fine houses and, perhaps, two cars, have a life-style which highlights the plight of millions of starving poor in Asia, Africa and Latin America. This rich–poor division tends to run across the middle of the globe, making a north–south contrast which one day may become more dangerous to world peace than any East–West division. As U Thant wrote of his years in charge of the United Nations,

> 'I became increasingly convinced that the division of the world into rich and poor ... is much more important ... and in the long run much more explosive, than division of the world based on differing ideologies [beliefs]'.

It is this gap which the Specialised Agencies attempt to close.

A **World Health Organisation (WHO)**, helped by richer member countries, has achieved some remarkable successes. Many diseases like typhus, cholera, smallpox and malaria, have been curbed by WHO doctors and nurses. By 1976 the WHO services had helped wipe out smallpox in fifteen West African states. Malaria, a worldwide scourge for centuries, was eliminated from large areas of the globe. The WHO also helps the victims of both natural and man-made disasters. Thousands of refugees from the civil war in the Lebanon (1976–9) were helped by WHO. In 1976 the survivors of earthquakes in Latin

America (Guatemala), floods in Pakistan and severe crop failures in Cape Verde Islands were given much needed assistance.

A **Food and Agricultural Organisation (FAO)** was formed as early as 1943. After the Second World War it became an agency of the United Nations. The basic idea was to help the poorer countries of the world increase their food production with help, expert advice and information. Since 1951 FAO experts have worked on every aspect of farming, fishing and forestry. Foods given to domestic pets in the richer parts of the world can be vital to the people of the poor countries. Westerners who scorn the United Nations as a mere 'talking shop' may not realise that an increase in egg and poultry production in an African state, or the doubling of rice production in Egypt, are major achievements which spell health and happiness for millions. The WHO World Seed Campaign, for example, may not have been headline news in the West but it persuaded thousands of farmers in developing countries to sow new and better varieties of wheat and other cereals. It also led to a dramatic increase in rice yields – an essential food to the people of the Far East. This was part of the so-called 'Green Revolution' which the FAO launched in 1971. The aim was to double world food production in ten years.

Finally, there is the work of UNESCO – the **United Nations Educational, Scientific and Cultural Organisation**. UNESCO was born in Britain; its first conference was held in London in November, 1945. The founding members set out with this idea expressed in their constitution: 'Since wars begin in the minds of men, it is in the minds of men that the defences of peace must be constructed.' As with so much of the work performed by the Specialised Agencies, the work of UNESCO is known more in the poorer parts of the world than in the industrialised nations. Its schools, universities and training colleges, its battle against illiteracy, are important aspects of the life of these regions. Sometimes its work is quiet and undramatic. It may encourage a people to study their own way of life, art and music. Sometimes its work hits the headlines, as when it sent experts to save the ancient temples at Abu Simnel in Egypt from being submerged by water during the construction of dams for an irrigation project. Like the United Nations itself, UNESCO is based on the belief that increased knowledge and education may one day defeat hatred and conflict between peoples. With all its faults and failures, the United Nations represents the ideal of one world rather than a world divided by ignorance, hatred and inequality.

The Iron Curtain

Men's dreams of peace after 1918 were dashed by the rise of Hitler. Since 1945 similar hopes have wilted under the stress of the Cold War between Communist and Western countries. Although disappointing, it is not surprising. Only a common war purpose made the USA and Soviet Union allies. Whilst Germany remained to be defeated Stalin and Roosevelt met at conferences and managed to reach agreement. In fact the differences between the two countries and the two men were

Harry S. Truman, successor to Roosevelt and US President until 1952

deep. Ever since 1917 Russia had developed a Communist system which is the natural enemy of the free enterprise capitalist economy of the USA. Ever since 1917 Western leaders had looked upon the Soviet Union as a menace to freedom. At first they had tried to overthrow the Bolsheviks by force (see page 109). When this failed they refused to recognise the Soviet government for many years, and despised and condemned its leaders. They feared and hated the undemocratic ways, the purges and terrors of Stalin's régime (see Chapter 13).

A weak Soviet Union might have been dependent on the USA for help. Despite her terrible losses, however, the USSR emerged from the war more powerful than before. The huge Soviet army poured into Eastern Europe like a human sea, engulfing country after country. By the time the war ended Russia had swallowed 51,800 square kilometres of land and 22 million people. Her border was 480 kilometres to the west of its 1939 position; her troops were on the south side of the Carpathian mountains; her hold had strengthened on the lands bordering the River Danube. Czechoslovakia and Poland, as well as the German province of Prussia, were forced to yield her land (see map on page 190).

Before such power Europe lay ruined and helpless. Hungary, Romania, Bulgaria, Czechoslovakia and Poland had been liberated by Soviet troops during their advance on Germany. Germany, France and Italy had been defeated. Britain was exhausted. Only the US army and US atomic weapons could have stopped further Soviet advances. In the 1830s a Frenchman had predicted that the USSR and the USA would be the two great powers of the future. 'Each of these seems to be marked out by the will of heaven to sway the destinies of half the globe', he wrote. Now this had almost happened.

Roosevelt had realised that a country as powerful as the Soviet Union would influence its smaller neighbours after the war. What neither he nor his successor, President Truman, seem to have fully understood is that such states would not be allowed to choose their own governments. Yet, as early as 1941, Stalin had made it clear that the Soviet Union would only permit friendly countries on its borders. He remarked, for example, that twice in thirty years the USSR had been invaded through an unfriendly Poland. He had also admitted that in such countries, 'any freely elected government would be anti-Soviet and that we cannot permit'. In other words the Soviet Union would have to interfere if she wanted Communist states around her.

At first Stalin moved cautiously. Russian officials in Eastern Europe rounded up many anti-communists and, using the excuse that they were Nazis, sent them to Siberia. Then Soviet-trained leaders built up Communist parties, usually in alliance with non-communists. In some countries this was easier than in others. Bulgaria, for instance, had a long tradition of friendship with Russia whereas Poland had one of bitter hatred. Gradually, however, the watchful Soviet army encouraged Communist parties to take sole charge. Many opponents were shot: one Hungarian ruler described later how he had dealt with his enemies, 'one by one, cutting them off like slices of salami'. By 1948 Hungary, Bulgaria, Romania, Poland and Czechoslovakia all had

Communist governments. The right of freedom to choose a government, which had been promised in the Atlantic Charter (see page 175), was disregarded. In March 1946 Winston Churchill, speaking at **Fulton, Missouri** in the USA, had stated, 'From Stettin in the Baltic to Trieste in the Adriatic, an iron curtain has descended across the continent.' Some people had thought he was exaggerating. Within two years Czechoslovakia had gone Communist and most of the Western world realised he was right. A vastly enlarged Soviet Union was surrounded by **'iron curtain'** countries whose rulers took their orders from Moscow (see map opposite).

The only states which succeeded in defying the USSR did so partly because they had never been occupied by Soviet troops, partly because of outside help or their dislike of the Soviet Union. Turkey defiantly mobilised her army when she felt Soviet pressure and, helped by Allied money, managed to hold out. Greece was the scene of a fierce civil war between communists and anti-communists which ended with victory for the latter in 1949. Yugoslavia had a distinctive Communist régime headed by **Josip Broz (Marshal Tito)**. Of all the small countries attacked by Hitler, only Yugoslavia had defeated the Nazi armies almost single-handed. She resented taking orders from outsiders and when Stalin suggested a joint Russian-Yugoslavian bank with a director appointed by him she refused. Many non-communist Yugoslavs supported Tito for patriotic reasons.

Winston Churchill making his 'Iron Curtain' speech at Fulton, Missouri, 1946

The growing hostility between East and West, caused by the Soviet Union's desire for power, was made worse by Russia being Communist. Because Communist parties existed in most Western countries, governments began to fear them as 'Trojan horses' standing ready to open the gates to the enemy. The menace of the USSR was seen not just as that of armies and weapons, but of dangerous ideas which would turn men's minds against their rulers. To many people Communists were crusaders who would betray their country for a cause. A similar fear worked in reverse. To Communists, capitalism is an inefficient and unjust system which can only avoid slumps and unemployment by putting men on armament work. Free enterprise countries, so the argument goes, need occasional wars to keep their system running properly. This theory was explained in a broadcast to the Soviet people by Stalin in February 1946. He warned that the USA was likely to attack and announced a large-scale rearmament programme. Probably the USA's refusal to share her atomic secrets with the Soviet Union had roused his always suspicious nature. So mutual fear and distrust caused both sides to quarrel almost before the Second World War was over.

Western Europe's reaction to all this was to form defensive alliances. In 1947 Britain and France signed a fifty-year treaty of co-operation. Later the **Benelux** countries (Belgium, Luxembourg and the Netherlands) joined them (1948). None of this would have helped much had the Soviet Union attacked. Only the USA could really curb or master such a mighty power. Fortunately there were few isolationists left on the other side of the Atlantic. The lessons of Pearl Harbour and the Second World War had been well learned. President Truman

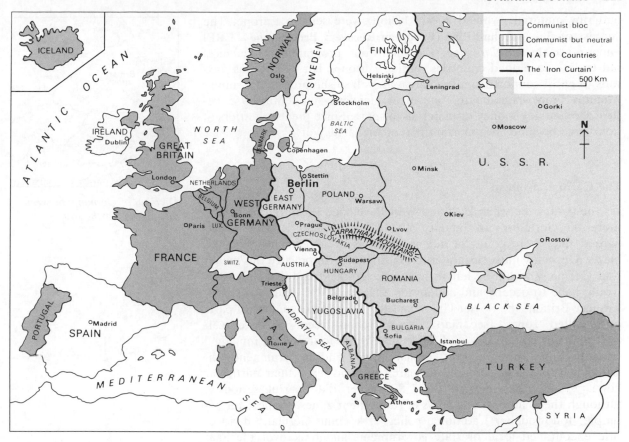

'Cold War Europe'. Warsaw Pact versus NATO countries

made it clear that his country would defend the existing frontiers of Europe with armed and nuclear force if necessary. He invited European states to join in a vast Western alliance for defence.

In April 1949 the **North Atlantic Treaty Organisation (NATO)** was formed, consisting of the USA, Britain, France, Belgium, Luxembourg, the Netherlands, Canada, Denmark, Iceland, Norway, Italy and Portugal (see map above). Greece and Turkey joined in 1951 and West Germany (see page 214) in 1954. Spain would have been welcomed by the USA but some European governments still hated Franco. Eventually the USA signed a separate treaty with the General in 1953 which allowed her bases in Spain. American policy was to restrict the Soviet Union to her existing position in Europe. On no account was she to move any further westward. This idea of **containment** was disliked by some anti-communists because it did nothing for the millions under Soviet domination. But only another world war involving atomic weapons could free these people. The Americans would risk war only if the Russians crossed more frontiers.

Fortunately for Europe, the USA gave more than military aid. Turkey and Greece were able to defy Russia with American money and materials supplied under a plan called the **Truman Doctrine**. Then General George Marshall announced a scheme to fight 'hunger, poverty, desperation and chaos' in Europe. Supplies of food, fuel, machinery and raw materials, valued at $13 billion, were sent to Europe. The success of this **Marshall Plan (European Recovery Programme – ERP)** encouraged the USA to suggest a 'Point Four' programme of technical aid to less-developed countries outside Europe. The USSR was anxious to enlist support from such areas as well so she proposed a similar **Molotov Plan**, named after one of her leaders, but it was 1955 before she had any money or materials to spare. Since then such offers of help have become an important part of the Cold War.

Division of Germany between the Allies after the war

The German problem

As the contest between East and West developed it centred more and more on Germany. In January 1943 Churchill and Roosevelt had agreed that there could be no negotiations or agreements with the Nazis. Germany must surrender unconditionally. In practice this meant that Germany would be left without a government and that the Allies would have to occupy and administer it. Four of the victorious states, France, Britain, the Soviet Union and the USA, were to control parts of it called 'zones' (see map above). Nobody seems to have realised that this could only work effectively if the four powers remained friendly. Should they quarrel Germany might end up permanently divided, with no side prepared to march out and leave their particular zone. France, Britain and the USA never did quarrel seriously, although they had different ways of ruling their zones. France, for example, followed her traditional policy of keeping Germany divided. She encouraged local or state governments and took over the Saar coal-fields. The Soviet Union and the USA, however, did disagree. Each set up their own type of administration. The result was a Germany divided into a Communist-dominated east and a democratic west.

The worst effects of these divisions were felt in Berlin. The old German capital was in the Russian zone, but it too was partitioned between the four powers into sectors. Again, such an arrangement was only workable if no-one quarrelled. Indeed the four-power occupation of Berlin was meant to symbolise the fact that Germany would one day be reunited. Unfortunately, with each side acting independently, Berlin became the centre of a political tug-of-war. Stalin had demanded that Germany must repay his country for the damage her armies had caused inside the Soviet Union. The Western Allies (Britain, France, the USA) had agreed, only to find that Stalin's idea of compensation was to strip his zone of most of its factory equipment. By contrast, they began to build up German industries in their zones. When the Western Allies allowed free elections in their zones in 1948 the Russians were angry. They accused them of putting Nazi supporters back into power. Soon a revived West Germany faced a partially-ruined East Germany.

The crisis came over money. The old German mark had become a worthless piece of paper which was ignored by investors abroad. Unless the Germans were given a currency in which foreigners had confidence they would never be able to help their country pay her way. Such a situation suited the Russians. Indeed the Allies had agreed at

Division of Berlin between the Allies. Berlin was in the Russian zone (now East Germany). The Berlin Wall was built in 1961 (see page 214)

Berliners watch an airlift plane arriving with supplies, 1948

the **Potsdam Conference, 1945**, to limit German production of money permanently. Now this was felt to be unbearable by the Western Allies who saw that their plans for a healthy German economy would fail if a new currency was not issued. For a time they tried to persuade the Russians to agree to the new money so that the whole of Germany could benefit. When it became obvious that the Soviet authorities would never do so they introduced it in the Western zones. Such a decision made the division of Germany even more permanent. Now it was no longer just frontier posts and guards which divided it but two entirely different economies.

This angered the Russians. They reacted by striking at what they thought was their enemy's weakest point. The British, French and US sectors in Berlin were 161 kilometres inside the Soviet zone. The two million Berliners they ruled were surrounded by powerful Russian forces. From the moment the new currency began to be distributed fake 'incidents' started to make contact with West Berlin difficult. In March 1948 the Russians turned back four trains from the Western zones. Later they forbade freight trains to leave West Berlin without their permission. In June an important bridge over the River Elbe was closed because it was said to be in need of repair. When the Western Allies decided to introduce the currency into their sectors of Berlin as well as West Germany a smouldering situation burst into flames. On 23 June 1948 all road, rail and canal links between Berlin and the border with the West were closed. Electricity which came from the Soviet sector was cut off. It was clear that Berlin was to be strangled until the Allies were forced to leave.

Berlin Airlift

This blockade was a clear challenge. In effect, the Soviet Union was announcing that she did not want the Western Allies in Berlin. Some Americans feared even more than that. As US General Lucius Clay remarked, 'When Berlin falls, Western Germany will be next'. Whether this was an exaggerated view or not, Stalin was certainly prepared to test his opponents by the toughest action short of war. At first the worried statesmen in Washington, Paris and London considered withdrawing the new currency. But Clay insisted that if Russia really wanted a war no question of money would make any difference. 'If Soviets want war it will not be because of Berlin currency issue but because they believe this is the right time', he wired his government. Like the Sarajevo murder it would merely be an excuse. Accordingly the British, French and US governments decided to hold firm and supply Berlin by air.

Day by day the colossal job of supplying food and fuel for two million people was carried out by fleets of transport planes. At first only 100 were available. Then the whole operation was intensified until it resembled an aerial invasion. The French built a new airfield at Tegel in Berlin; the British enlarged theirs at Gatow (see map opposite). Soon aircraft were landing at the rate of one every five minutes at the US Tempelhof Aerodrome. The flow of silver planes, 'like a string of pearls in the sky', as one woman remarked, gave the Berliners hope. They accepted severe rationing, they shared fires, they worked by candlelight. Despite being tempted to buy food in the Soviet sector, few did so. Nearly all seemed inspired to defy the hated Russians. By October it was obvious it would be possible to supply the city throughout the winter. As the weather grew worse, flying became dangerous. Pilots had to 'feel' their way along the narrow air corridor allowed by the Russians. Over fifty were killed in crashes in fog or on icy runways. In spite of this the airlift went on night and day, helped by the highspeed unloading.

The Russians gave way in May 1949, when all lines of communication were opened again. Long before that, however, Stalin had given up hope of winning. Unfortunately the **Berlin Airlift**, which cost £100 million, finished all hope of a united Germany. The Western Allies amalgamated their zones, forming the **Federal Republic of Germany (West Germany)**. Stalin replied by organising the **German Democratic Republic (East Germany)**. The two have glared at each other ever since, symbol of an even greater division between the communist and non-communist world.

Across Europe, from the Baltic to the Black Sea (see map on page 211) the Communist authorities have fortified a border 2,900 kilometres long. At intervals high wooden watch towers are manned by soldiers equipped with revolvers, machine-guns, binoculars and signal rockets. In front is a strip of freshly ploughed earth which will

Workmen building the Berlin Wall, 1961

show footmarks and a barbed wire fence set in concrete. For many kilometres on each side the country is silent and deserted. Human beings have left it. Its cottages are empty, its roads lead nowhere. It is inhabited by birds and animals who live and multiply without fear. It seals off Eastern Europe and divides Germany. In Berlin it is marked by a wall, the **Berlin Wall**, where many people have been killed trying to cross to the West.

Winston Churchill's 'iron curtain' has become a reality.

Timeline

1945	United Nations Charter signed. Potsdam Conference.
1946	Nuremberg Trials. Churchill's 'iron curtain' speech.
1947	Truman Doctrine. Greek Civil War until 1949. Communists take over Eastern European countries.
1948	Marshall Plan.
1948–9	Berlin Airlift.
1949	North Atlantic Treaty Organisation (NATO) formed. Germany divided into Federal Republic of Germany and German Democratic Republic.
1961	Construction of Berlin Wall.

Questions

1. 'Whether nations live in prosperity or starve to death interests me only in so far as we need them as slaves... otherwise it is of no importance. Whether 10,000 Russian females fall down from exhaustion while digging an anti-tank ditch for Germany, interests me only in so far as the anti-tank ditch for Germany is dug... Our concern, our duty, is to our own people and our blood... We can be indifferent to everything else...'
   (Heinrich Himmler, speaking to SS men, October 1943)

   a) Explain how this Nazi attitude led to 'the final solution of the Jewish Problem'.
   b) After the war what did the Allies do to the leaders who carried out such policies?

2. a) Explain why it was thought the United Nations would be more successful than the League of Nations.
   b) Explain why the Security Council is important. Who were the original members and why? Under what circumstances can the Security Council's decision be cancelled? Why was this allowed?
   c) Write a short paragraph on the 'Specialised Agencies' of the United Nations.

3. Explain the events and policies which led to the so-called 'Cold War' between East and West.

4. Write short paragraphs on each of the following:
   a) Marshal Tito   b) NATO (see also Chapter 31)
   c) the Marshall Plan   d) the Berlin Airlift, 1948–9.

23
Sun, Chiang and Mao
China until 1953

The Chinese are the largest group of similar people in the world. In 1900, for example, their population was twice that of the varied races making up the Russian Empire. They have also been civilised for longer than most nations. Two centuries before Christ's birth they enjoyed a well-developed social life, controlled by a monarchy and an efficient civil service. For this reason they have frequently regarded themselves as superior.

Their history has two distinct sides. On one hand their lives have been guided by the philosophies of **Confucius** and by **Taoism**. Confucius believed that men were naturally virtuous. Consequently he thought examples of good behaviour would bring out the best in them. Great emphasis was placed on love of family and worship of ancestors. The result was a leisurely, peaceful way of living, enriched by politeness and elaborate ceremonies. The Taoist was just as peace-loving but he wanted a simpler life. He preferred villages to towns and discouraged any co-operation which might lead to large organisations.

By contrast, Chinese history has been as violent as that of any other country. To Confucius the soldier was the lowest, the scholar the highest type of man. Nevertheless China was ruled by a succession of dynasties (royal families) founded by soldiers (warlords). Each emperor reigned as long as he was strong. If the family began to produce weak, ineffective rulers it was overthrown by another warlord who in turn became emperor. There were also foreign invasions. In the Middle Ages Mongols from Asia conquered China and gave it a dynasty which ruled until it was replaced by the Ming family in the fourteenth century. From 1644 until 1912 conquerors from Manchuria, called **Manchus**, supplied China with a line of emperors and a ruling class.

Fortunately the peace-loving aspects of Chinese life usually proved the stronger. Foreign rulers adopted Chinese ways and Chinese customs. Indeed they frequently regarded themselves as the guardians of Confucianism who would set the perfect example for their people. They were usually infected by the Chinese dislike of foreigners. No court was ever sent a Chinese ambassador and the Great Wall of China was built to keep out intruders (see map opposite). Although it failed in its military purpose it remained as a visible sign that the Chinese wanted nothing to do with the outside world.

Confucius, Chinese philosopher

Western interference

The increasing industrial and military power of the West during the nineteenth century first threatened and then destroyed this ancient

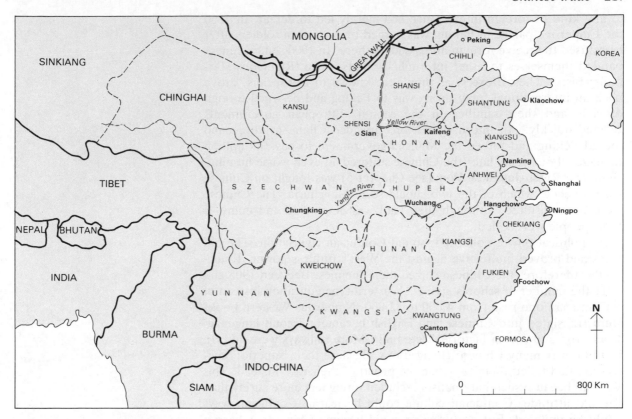

China – showing the provinces and the Great Wall of China which was built to keep out intruders

civilisation. The Chinese had a highly organised economy. They were successful merchants. Their inventors had developed paper, printing, gunpowder and the compass. Their handworkers were very skilful. Unfortunately they did not devise an engine driven by cheap fuel, nor did they mechanise their factories. Consequently China's industries became out of date.

This might not have mattered if outsiders had not been interested in the rich prize of Chinese trade. To Western merchants, however, China's unwillingness to do business seemed stupid and obstinate. As with Japan (see page 38), they reacted by forcing their way in. First Britain, and then other countries, compelled the Chinese to open ports for trade and to lease land for development. They built railways and established factories. They claimed and got extra privileges so that their citizens did not have to obey Chinese laws. They turned Shanghai, Canton, Foochow and Ningpo (see map above) into international cities where Europeans behaved almost as conquerors. Areas traditionally under Chinese influence, Indo-China and Sinkiang for example, were taken over by French and Russians. Shantung, with its port of Kiaochow, was seized by Germany. The Japanese forced a war on China in 1895 and occupied Korea soon afterwards (see page 39). On all sides a proud people found their rights ignored and their country invaded.

By 1900 Manchu power was clearly collapsing under the strain. Rebellions had ruined large parts of the country whilst their resistance to any kind of foreign interference had merely led to defeat. In 1860 the Emperor's palace in Peking was burned by European soldiers after he refused to receive foreign ambassadors there. In 1900 some Chinese banded themselves together into military units called 'Righteous Harmony Fists'. These **Boxers**, as they were known to Europeans, drove back an international force on its way to Peking and besieged foreign officials and their families in the capital. European governments reacted quickly. An international force invaded China, captured and looted Peking and forced the Manchu government to pay £67 million damages. Four years later the Chinese suffered an even worse humiliation. The **Russo-Japanese War** (see Chapter 5) was fought on Chinese soil to decide which of the two should seize Manchuria. The Chinese were not consulted, although their land was devastated and many of their people were killed.

As political power collapsed, so did Confucian civilisation. The old ways had proved ineffective against the West's ruthless power. Reluctantly, therefore, the Chinese copied their enemies. Between 1905 and 1911 the number of schools giving a Western-type education instead of a Confucian one rose from 4,000 to 52,000. Numerous Western books were translated into Chinese and English became a second language. Coal, iron and cotton factories were built. More railways were laid. In a subtle way many Chinese changed too. Because their 'superior' civilisation had failed them they became proud of their race instead. This was sad because such nationalism excluded foreigners more surely than the old attitude. Confucian culture could be learnt; Confucian ways could be imitated. But no foreigner could become Chinese! A barrier more effective than the Great Wall now existed in the minds of the people.

Double Tenth

The last strong Manchu ruler, the Empress Tzu-hsi, died in 1908. Her successor was only three years old so his father ruled as Regent. Revolutionaries who were tired of such family rule saw their chance. One, **Sun Yat-sen**, had written books suggesting that the Manchus should be overthrown and a republic established. Although the government drove such men abroad, their ideas could not be kept out. Educated Chinese were interested in Sun's republicanism and his socialist ideas for organising industry. In 1911, therefore, reformers staged risings throughout the country. Some were crushed, but others, particularly the one at Wuchang on 10 October 1911, were successful. When a people's army supporting Sun Yat-sen marched against the government forces, civil war seemed likely until both sides signed an armistice (December 1911). Two months later, with the abdication of the young Emperor, China became a republic. The revolution on the tenth day of the tenth month, the **Double Tenth**, had ended a monarchy which stretched back 2,300 years.

The new republic soon ran into trouble. First, President Sun Yat-sen's Kuomintang (Nationalist) government had to fight soldiers led by Yuan Shih-kai, a warlord who wanted to be emperor. No sooner had

Sun Yat-sen, founder of the first Republic of China

Chiang Kai-shek, ruler of Kuomintang (Nationalist) China

this threat faded with Yuan's death than the Japanese used the First World War as an excuse to bully China. Having captured Kiaochow from the Germans, they issued their notorious **Twenty-One Demands** (1917). These proposed to let them build railways in China, take over an iron-works and impose advisers on the Kuomintang. If put into force, China would have ceased to be an independent country. The USA was especially annoyed. She believed in an 'open door' policy; with all nations having equal rights of trade in China. Under US pressure Japan gave way (see Chapter 19). Even so her government forced China to declare war on Germany so that she would have to buy Japanese supplies and weapons. Sun never wanted this to happen. Unfortunately, by 1918 large parts of the country had stopped obeying him. Entire provinces were ruled by warlords like Chang Tso-lin of Manchuria.

In the 1920s the feeling in favour of Western ways but against Western control continued. China's simple peasant speech, Pai Hua, gradually replaced the complicated classical language favoured by Confucians. Many more Chinese went abroad as students. The sexes mingled freely in public places. Bolshevism itself was adopted by a small group led by **Mao Tse-tung**. This sturdy peasant had grown up in the real inland China, far from the glossy shops and neon-lit waterfronts of the big cities. He knew what it was to work hard. He had seen the sorrow and misery of the peasant at close quarters. To such a man communism seemed the answer to his country's problems. Soon he was using his gifts as an organiser and writer to build a strong political party. At the same time, the very people who copied Western ways often organised strikes against European employers or refused to buy British goods. China was perched dangerously between two worlds.

Sun Yat-sen died in 1925. Outwardly his memory was treasured by the government. Large portraits decorated most public buildings. His Will was read in schools each day. On Purple Mountain overlooking Peking his body was enclosed in an imposing tomb. In spite of this reverence China did not develop as he would have wished because his successor was a far different man. Sun had been a revolutionary dreamer, not a man of action. He could inspire much better than he could lead. His successor and friend, **Chiang Kai-shek**, was a landowner's son who had trained as a soldier in Japan. His friends were American businessmen, not socialists. In his opinion order was more important than ideas, though he favoured the old Confucian morality. In place of the disorder of Sun's time, Chiang tried to impose his rule by a successful march through the country with a large army (1926). All classes of the community: peasants, merchants, shopkeepers, even communists, at first supported him because they were sick of disorder. By 1927 Chiang was in control of Shanghai and all of China south of the Yangtze River (see map on page 217). By 1930 China enjoyed a peace created by dictatorship not democracy.

It is difficult to know what Chiang's Kuomintang government might have done for China. Perhaps Chiang would have been a great leader. Perhaps he would have developed a truly democratic system. We shall never know because two rival forces, the Communists and the

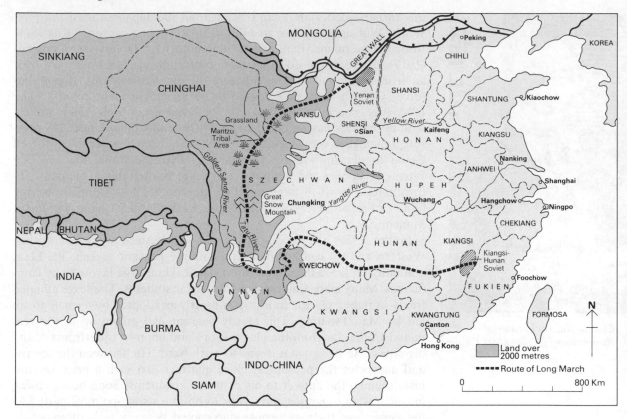

Communist epic. The Long March, 1934

Japanese, destroyed his work. The initial threat came from the Communists. From 1927 onwards Chiang quarrelled with them, crushed several Communist rebellions, and led expeditions against their strongholds. At first he succeeded in overrunning the Communist state formed in 1931, the Kiangsi-Hunan Soviet. Then Mao, the Communist leader, decided to retreat to an even more inaccessible area, Shensi province in the bend of the Yellow River (see map above). In October 1934, 100,000 Communists left Hunan on what became a 9,000-kilometre march. Before the 20,000 survivors reached Shensi over a year later they had crossed twenty-five rivers, toiled over eighteen mountain ranges and fought more than a dozen pitched battles with Chiang's troops. They had seen their comrades die of exhaustion, starvation and frost-bite, they had shot those who would not go on. They had crossed the Yangtze River under shelling and bombing and dodged the poison arrows and rocks hurled by Tibetan tribesmen. Today a veteran of this **Long March** is honoured in China. His survival helped to ensure that Chinese communism would live on too.

China's vast distances saved the Communists. Three years later the Kuomintang forces were retreating into the interior, pursued by the Japanese (see Chapter 19). In the past China's conquerors had come from the north; that is why the Great Wall had been built. The new threat against her long coastline could only have been stopped by a large navy. Without one, Chiang's government stood little chance. His aircraft and weapons could not be replaced once his few factories were

Communist victory, Mao Tse-tung announces the founding of the People's Republic of China, 1 October 1949 (see page 222)

captured. By January 1940 the Japanese held most of the railways, all the large ports and the lower reaches of the rivers. Chiang retreated to Chungking and the Japanese felt confident enough of victory to sign a peace treaty with a Chinese puppet régime led by Wang Ching-wei. China now had three separate governments – Chiang's Kuomintang, the Japanese based in the north-east and Mao's Communists in the new Yenan Soviet based in Shensi province.

The entry of the USA into the war ensured that Japan would be beaten. It did not mean, however, that the Kuomintang would return because year by year the Communists grew stronger. Their policy was a clever one. They used guerrilla tactics against the Japanese and rarely risked a big battle. Their organisation was efficiently run by fanatical followers. By contrast, the Kuomintang grew weaker, although its armies did little to fight the invader. Cut off from the more freedom-loving merchants and traders of the coast, Chiang's government was forced to rely upon rich landowners. This turned the peasants against the Kuomintang. At the same time dishonesty spread amongst Kuomintang officials and money began to lose its value. After the war the USA sent **General Marshall** to try to patch up the quarrel between Chiang and Mao. It was no use. In 1946 Mao's armies began to move south and the war against Japan was followed by a civil war.

To everyone's surprise it was all over quickly. The Kuomintang was now too corrupt and demoralised to put up a fight. Although given ample supplies by the Americans, Chiang's men retreated without offering genuine battle. Whole divisions surrendered to the Communists. American equipment was traded to the enemy. In most villages the peasants welcomed the disciplined Communist soldiers, just as they had accepted Chiang in 1926 because he brought peace and order. The Kuomintang government retreated to Formosa (Taiwan), an island off the Chinese mainland (see map on page 220). On 1 October 1949 Mao Tse-tung became Chairman of the new **People's Republic of China**. China had a new 'emperor' and a new communist philosophy to replace Confucianism.

Korean quarrel

Mao's men had spent their lives fighting a determined enemy. Against discouraging odds and with incredible suffering they had gained control of the world's largest nation. They faced the future with more than the usual Chinese confidence. Possibly because of this they found themselves at war with the USA within a year.

The dispute concerned Korea, an area under Chinese influence for centuries but ruled by Japan since 1910. With the defeat of Japan in 1945 (see Chapter 21) American troops moved in from the south and Russians from the north. In order to round up the enemy the two authorities decided that Japanese in Korea below the 38th parallel of latitude (see map opposite) should surrender to the Americans, those above to the Russians. The line itself made no sense for any other purpose. It crossed rivers and mountains. It divided the agricultural South from the more industrialised North. There had been, and was, only one Korea.

As the Cold War grew worse a situation developed in Korea similar to that in Germany (see page 212). Stalin encouraged the Communist régime in the North which fortified the border with the South. The Americans demanded free elections to form a government for the whole country. The Soviet Union refused to allow this so the USA referred the question to the United Nations. In the South an old revolutionary, **Syngman Rhee**, headed a government favoured by the USA; in the North **Kim Il-sung** led the Communist one. Neither government was democratic. Each claimed to represent the whole of Korea and each demanded that Korea be united under his control.

This was the position on 25 June 1950 when South Korean troops patrolling the 38th parallel thought they heard thunder. To their horror the noise was the sound of gun-fire as the North Korean army crossed the border and invaded South Korea. This attack was almost certainly encouraged by the Soviet Union. Mao's government had little influence in North Korea at the time; there was not even a Chinese ambassador at Pyongyang, the capital. It is unlikely that Kim Il-Sung would have dared to attack an American-supported regime without Soviet backing. Certainly most of the North Korean army's equipment was Russian. Contained militarily in Europe by NATO, it seemed that Stalin was testing the Americans elsewhere.

President Truman acted promptly. In his mind were the lessons of pre-war days. When Manchuria, Abyssinia, Austria, Czechoslovakia and Poland had been attacked, the League of Nations had done little except protest. The banding together of countries to keep the peace (**Collective Security**) had failed then. It must not fail now. The Soviet representatives at the United Nations had walked out a few months before as a protest because Communist China was not admitted to

First moves in the Korean War

South Koreans and US troops retreat before the North Korean offensive

The tables are turned. UN forces drive the North Korean armies back to the Yalu River

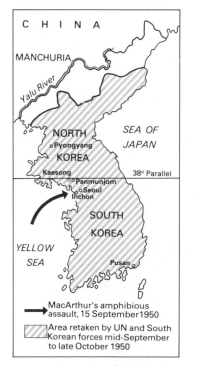

MacArthur's amphibious assault, 15 September 1950

Area retaken by UN and South Korean forces mid-September to late October 1950

membership. As a result there was no Soviet veto to stop military aid being sent to South Korea. American troops were already on their way from Japan. Other nations, including Britain, sent small contingents. The United Nations was at war five years after its foundation.

The war with North Korea lasted ninety days. At first the Communists swept all before them and pinned the UN forces in a narrow coastal area around Pusan. Then General MacArthur organised an amphibious assault behind their lines at **Inchon** (see map opposite). It was as dangerous as any sea-borne attack during the Second World War. Inchon's tide rose and fell over 9 metres. At low water nearly 5,500 metres of mud-flats stretched out to sea, making it almost impossible to bring in landing craft. On some days, however, a particularly high tide covered them. One was 15 September 1950. On that evening US battleships and aircraft smashed the defences and US 'Yellow Legs', as the Marines were called because of their gaiters, swarmed ashore. Inchon was captured quickly and within days the Americans were in **Seoul**, South Korea's capital. Taken by surprise, thousands of civilians were trapped between the two armies. As the killing continued and the town burned, a press reporter noted: 'A tiny figure wrapped in a Marine's wool jersey stumbled down the street. Her face, arms and legs were almost eaten away by fragments of an American white phosphorous shell. She was blind but somehow alive.' Such horrors were multiplied many times before the town fell.

China enters the war

UN forces were now astride the enemy's main road from the north. Starved of essential supplies and attacked on two sides, the North Korean army ceased to exist. Over 140,000 men were killed or captured and the advance north became almost a triumphal procession. As the tanks rolled on and the bombers roared overhead, one American pilot reported, 'We've run out of targets'. In their excitement, the US and British leaders decided to cross the 38th parallel and unite Korea. China's reaction was to warn them to stop. Mao had no reason to like the USA. American arms had aided Chiang. American fleets stopped him from attacking Formosa. America's veto kept China out of the UN. Now he feared that the UN armies would not halt in Korea but would cross the Yalu River and enter Manchuria (see map opposite). His warnings were ignored. On 15 October 1950 MacArthur was asked if there was any danger of China entering the war. He replied 'Very little'. Next day 300,000 soldiers of the Chinese 4th Field Army crossed the Yalu River into Korea.

The Chinese were experienced and very tough. They were experts at camouflage and night marching. Their commander, Lin Piao, had no intention of just defending land. He wanted to destroy utterly the hated Americans. At first the UN troops had no idea that such a powerful force was in the country. They ran into one ambush after another and suffered terrible losses. Soon they were reeling back before mass attacks staged by waves of Chinese who added to the usual din of battle by using whistles, cymbals and bugles as signals. The Chinese casualties were severe but they drove all before them. By April 1951 they had reached the 38th parallel and seemed set to push the UN armies into the sea.

MacArthur knew that every kilometre the Chinese covered lengthened their supply lines. He proposed to wait and then attack their bases, roads and railways inside China. President Truman refused to let him. China was not officially at war with the USA; the Chinese army was supposed to be a 'volunteer' one. Such 'aggression' might lead to a third world war. In the uproar following the Chinese intervention Truman realised that the crossing of the 38th parallel had been a mistake. Now the only hope was to hold that line but avoid further advances. Basically, Truman saw the real danger from communism as being in Europe. MacArthur believed it to be in the Far East. These differences grew into a quarrel and in April 1951 MacArthur was dismissed.

As the career of one of America's greatest soldiers ended abruptly, the war swung in the UN's favour. After desperate trench battles the Chinese were held and then defeated. The Soviet Union, meanwhile, began to lose interest in a war dominated by **China**. Consequently peace talks were started at Kaesong (July 1951). Later these were continued at **Panmunjom**. There was much argument. Syngman Rhee still wanted to control all Korea so he was against peace. The Communists often used the negotiations as opportunities to get worldwide publicity for their propaganda. It was two years before an armistice was signed in a special 'peace pagoda'. On 27 July 1953 a war which had cost 1,820,000 lives ended. The UN had its first victory and the Communists their first post-war military defeat.

The Korean War changed the West's attitude to China. For nearly 100 years she had been a victim of aggression. Many people had felt sorry for her. The Korean War showed her to be a fierce, aggressive giant who was modernising at an alarming speed. Nations who had wronged her in the past began to fear for the future.

⟹ Chinese attacks late October 1950 to April 1951

The Chinese enter the Korean War

Timeline

1900	Boxer Rebellion crushed.
1908	Death of Empress Tzu-hsi.
1911	Revolution of the Double Tenth.
1917	Japan's Twenty-One Demands.
1925	Death of Sun Yat-sen.
1926	Chiang Kai-shek takes control.
1934	Communists' Long March.
1937	Japanese invasion of China.
1949	Communists seize control of China. Mao Tse-tung Chairman of People's Republic of China.
1950–3	Korean War.

Questions

1. 'The increasing industrial and military power of the West during the nineteenth century first threatened and then destroyed this ancient civilisation.'

   a) Write a short paragraph describing this 'ancient civilisation' which was 'threatened and then destroyed'.
   b) Why did European countries want to trade with China during the nineteenth century? How successful were they?
   c) Give an example of the way the Chinese tried to stop European interference in their internal affairs.

2. 'The UN had its first victory and the Communists their first post-war military defeat.' How far is this an accurate verdict on the Korean War?

3. Describe the events which led to the setting up of the People's Republic of China in 1949. How were the Communists helped in their struggle?

4. Write short paragraphs on each of the following:
   a) the Twenty-One Demands
   b) Sun Yat-sen
   c) Chiang Kai-shek
   d) the Long March, 1934

24

War and Peace

North Africa and the Middle East since 1945

When the Second World War ended in 1945 the situation in North Africa and the Middle East did not seem to have changed much. France still administered Algeria, Morocco, Tunisia, Syria and the Lebanon. Britain controlled Palestine (now Israel) and Transjordan (now Jordan) and strongly influenced the governments of Iraq and Egypt. But the desire for self-government (**nationalism**) was an ever present threat to these two powers. After all, the Arabs are united by a common religion, Islam, and a common language, Arabic. Furthermore, the Islamic religion actually forbids an Arab to be ruled by an unbeliever. However, Arabs had been divided for centuries by geography, by differing interests, histories and cultures, even, in some cases, by fierce feuds. A united 'Arab Front' against colonial rule seemed a long way off. Yet within a few years a different balance of power in the world, plus hatred of the Jews, led many of these Arab colonies to get rid of their British and French masters.

The Middle East after 1945

The first **Arab League**, consisting of Egypt, Iraq, Syria, the Lebanon, Transjordan, Saudi Arabia and Yemen (see map on page 226), was formed in 1945. The British liked it because they imagined it would be under their influence. They soon found that it was not. The Second World War had changed the world situation in a way which suited the nationalists. France had fallen in 1940. Britain was weak after a desperate struggle. Neither country could compare in power with the Soviet Union or the USA and these two giants claimed to be against colonial rule. The Arab politicians who began to organise riots and strikes knew that their masters were weak. They felt sure they could count on sympathetic support from Soviet and American governments. Sure enough, when the French crushed some Syrian riots, the UN was encouraged by the USSR and the USA to demand that they leave. France evacuated Syria and the Lebanon and the British left Transjordan.

Ben Bella, fighter against French rule in Algeria

War in Algeria

It is fairly easy to give a colony independence when there are only soldiers and a few civilians to evacuate. The British and French, after all, were hardly more than visitors in some areas. The colonial problem becomes dangerous where there are large numbers of settlers from the home country. Are they to be abandoned to the local nationalists? Or must they leave the country in which they now have lived since birth? Since such colonists are often a privileged minority who despise the natives the answer to these questions is difficult. In Algeria in 1954 there were over 3 million French settlers (*Colons*). Many knew no other home. Some had never visited France. For this reason French governments looked upon Algeria as different from other North African possessions. It had been French since 1830. It was classified as part of France itself and was ruled directly from Paris. Earlier *Colons* had built roads and towns. They had established thriving industries. Their descendants occupied the richest land and held the best jobs in Algeria. They wished to remain on top and they were supported by army officers who thought the French army could not afford another defeat. Algeria, they proclaimed, must be held.

Against them was a small group of desperate Arab nationalists who resented all foreign governments. Woodrow Wilson's idea of self-determination and the promises about self-government made in the Atlantic Charter (see page 175) encouraged the nationalists. In May 1945 riots, beginning at Setif, near Constantine (see map opposite), gradually expanded into full-scale war. The *Organisation Secrète*, run by **Ben Bella** and others, grew from a few conspirators to an army, the **Front de la Libération Nationale (FLN)**. It declared war in 1954, copying the tactics used by the French during the German occupation.

For seven years sabotage and murder occurred all over Algeria. As in Ireland, so here, a few determined fanatics needed vast numbers to hold them in check; altogether 20,000 Algerians occupied the attention of 500,000 French troops. Many thousands died as a result. Great cruelty, including torture of prisoners, was shown by both sides. Many

Algeria and the western Mediterranean area

Frenchmen turned against the war, some because they thought the Algerians had a right to rule themselves, others because they knew that such military operations were ruinously expensive. Unfortunately every effort to make peace was opposed by the *Colons*.

In 1958, when the *Colons* heard that the Paris government might negotiate with the FLN, their military friends organised a revolt in France. The rebels supported General Charles de Gaulle who had led the Free French forces against Germany during the Second World War (see page 184). With their support, de Gaulle assumed power as President of a new Fifth Republic. To their surprise, however, the General decided to end the war. Again the *Colons* tried to interfere and the **Organisation de l'Armée Secrète (OAS)** was formed to overthrow the Fifth Republic. Bomb outrages occurred in France and Algeria. Attempts were made to kill de Gaulle. The General's reaction was typical. He called upon the home army to support him and most of it did. Four important generals connected with the OAS were imprisoned and the Algerian War was ended in March 1962. Sadly, the defeated *Colons* left Algeria which was thus deprived of their skills and money. Morocco and Tunisia had been granted self-government in 1956, so now all of French North Africa was independent.

General Charles de Gaulle. He gave Algeria her independence

The new Israel

The Algerian struggle had been simply an Arab versus French contest. Further east the battle was more complex. A great deal of the world's oil lies under the Middle East. This means that industrialised countries are certain to be affected by what happens there. Western politicians may have lost interest in empires. They are vitally concerned about oil because their economies depend upon it.

By the end of the Second World War another kind of nationalism, Zionism, had established itself in the heart of the Arab lands. The birth of this Jewish movement has already been described in detail (see Chapter 12). Palestine was the original home of the Jew. Persecuted and driven from Europe, many Jews became even more dedicated to the idea of a new Israel in the Middle East. Those already in Palestine were surrounded by hostile strangers with whom they shared neither language nor religion. They reacted by banding together under fiercely determined leaders. **David Ben Gurion**, first Prime Minister of the new Israel, has written of his early days in Poland: 'There I followed the plough, and as the black clods of earth turned and crumbled, and the oxen trod with the slow and heedless dignity of their kind, I saw visions and dreamed dreams.' Such dreams of a Jewish homeland in Palestine were a nightmare as far as the Arabs were concerned.

David Ben Gurion, first Prime Minister of Israel

Before the war the Arab leaders had refused to consider a new Israel. They had also resented the arrival of Jews from Europe. Afterwards more Jews came, even though the British authorities forbade immigrant ships to enter port. Many ships got through and some of their passengers helped to swell the Jewish underground forces. Groups like **Haganah**, the **Stern Gang** and **Irgun Zwei Leumi** had helped the British during the war because they hated the Germans.

Israeli terrorists destroy the King David Hotel in Jerusalem, 1946

Now they felt angry at the ban on refugees. The sabotage and killing of pre-war days started again. Ambushes and bomb outrages became everyday occurrences. In July 1946 the **King David Hotel** in Jerusalem, headquarters of the British, was blown up with heavy loss of life.

Britain was tired by a long war. She had a new Labour government which was not imperialist and willing to grant India independence (see page 141). Her people and many others in the world felt sorry for the Jews after the full story of the concentration camps became known. Surely, they argued, the Arabs could spare a small part of their land for them? In America rich, influential Jews persuaded their government to suggest that 100,000 more refugees should be allowed into Palestine. The British knew what effect this would have upon the Arabs. Angrily they countered by proposing that the Americans send troops to help keep the peace. When the USA refused Britain handed the problem over to the United Nations and announced that she would evacuate Palestine on 14 May 1948.

A United Nations committee visited the country in 1947 and proposed it should be divided between Jew and Arab. Such a suggestion stood little chance of being accepted. Partition had been rejected as a solution by the Arabs before. Realising this, the Jews took matters into their own hands. On the day the British troops left they proclaimed the independent state of **Israel**. The enraged Arabs invaded at once, confident of an easy victory. To their surprise, Haganah turned

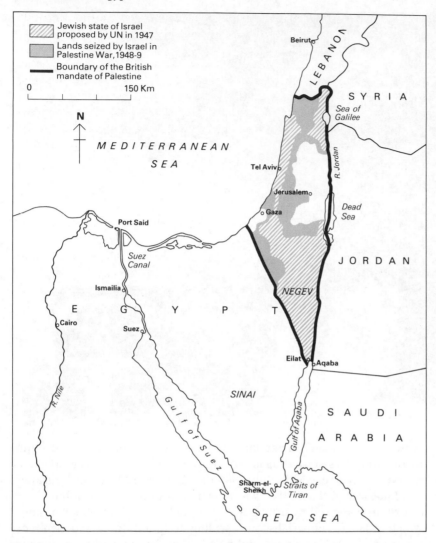

Map legend:
- Jewish state of Israel proposed by UN in 1947
- Lands seized by Israel in Palestine War, 1948-9
- Boundary of the British mandate of Palestine

0   150 Km

N

MEDITERRANEAN SEA

LEBANON
Beirut
SYRIA
Sea of Galilee
R. Jordan
Tel Aviv
Jerusalem
Gaza
Dead Sea
JORDAN
Port Said
Suez Canal
Ismailia
NEGEV
Cairo
Suez
EGYPT
R. Nile
Eilat Aqaba
SINAI
SAUDI ARABIA
Gulf of Suez
Gulf of Aqaba
Sharm-el-Sheikh
Straits of Tiran
RED SEA

itself into a highly efficient force which defeated them. Only Jordan's British-trained Arab Legion managed to hold Jewish troops back round the Old City of Jerusalem. Elsewhere the Israelis seized more land than they had been allotted in the UN plan (see map above).

For the Arabs the **Palestine War**, as it was called, had been a disaster. Over 600,000 Palestinian Arabs either fled or were expelled from land their ancestors had tilled for a thousand years. Their miserable camps on the Israeli border gave the Arabs even more cause to hate the Jews. Every Arab government promised its people that one day they would destroy Israel.

Nasser's Egypt

No state hated Israel more than Egypt at this time. After 1948 she took an active part in raiding Jewish settlements and joined enthusiastically in the Arab refusal to buy Israeli goods. More important, she

General Gamal Abdel Nasser, creator of a new Egypt

would not let Israeli ships use the Suez Canal. This hostile attitude increased after Nationalist officers led by **Colonel Gamal Abdel Nasser** and General Mohammed Neguib seized power (July 1952). Nasser, a professional soldier, was disgusted during the 1948 war against Israel to find that Egyptian supplies and weapons were poor. He returned home with a feeling that the army had been let down by the government. He and some friends formed a Free Officers' Committee which later overthrew King Farouk's dishonest and inefficient régime. At first Neguib led the government but he was little more than a figurehead. Quite soon, Nasser took over and became President, forcing Neguib to retire.

Nasser did a great deal for Egypt. Large estates belonging to rich landowners were broken up and given to the peasants. Some factories were nationalised. Various new industries were developed so that Egypt need not depend so much on cotton for a living. A big new irrigation project, the **Aswan High Dam**, was started to provide water in desert areas and so reduce Egypt's poverty. At the same time, Nasser stirred up Arab nationalism with speeches and radio propaganda. He gave aid to the Algerian rebels, built up the Egyptian army and tried to form an Arab League with Egypt as the leading partner.

Three events turned this dangerous situation into a world crisis. In February 1955 the Israelis decided to punish Nasser's raiders. They crossed into Egyptian territory near Gaza (see map opposite), blew up an army post and killed thirty-seven Egyptian soldiers. The **Gaza Raid** turned border skirmishing into a small war. Seven months later Nasser bought weapons and aircraft from an "Iron Curtain' country, Czechoslovakia. This alarmed both the Israelis and the Western powers. Israel knew that Nasser's Ilyushin jet bombers could raid her cities easily whilst his MIG15 fighters were better than her own Meteors. She began to think of disabling Egypt before she herself was attacked.

The USA, worried in case Egypt went Communist, hurriedly offered to finance the building of the Aswan Dam. Nasser accepted the offer but, perhaps in the hope of getting more US aid, he continued to be very friendly with the Soviet Union. The American reaction to what they regarded as blackmail was to withdraw all offers of aid (July 1956). This led to the third and most important event. On 26 July 1956 Nasser nationalised the **Suez Canal** so that he could use its revenues to finance the dam construction.

The Canal ran through Egyptian territory, although Egypt was supposed to keep it open for all shipping. However, it was administered by a private company whose shareholders were mainly British and French. Consequently the nationalisation move outraged the British and French governments. France, for her part, had long disliked Nasser because he had helped the Algerian rebels. To **Sir Anthony Eden**, the British Prime Minister, Nasser was another Hitler-type dictator whose actions would probably lead to a Middle Eastern war. Soon after the nationalisation of the Canal, Eden said of Nasser, 'I want him destroyed . . . I want him removed'. As early as August 1956 British and French generals were holding meetings to discuss a possible seizure of the Suez Canal by force.

'How do we start this war?'

Israel had already decided to invade the Sinai Desert region of Egypt because of the murderous raids launched on her from there. She also wished to reach the Gulf of Aqaba so that her ships could break the Egyptian blockade by sailing into the Red Sea (see map on page 230). In September the French, angry at Nasser's seizure of the Canal, began to consider the possibility of co-operating with such an Israeli attack. At first they did not tell the British of their plans because Britain had a treaty obligation to defend Jordan, an Arab country which might be involved in any war with Israel. But at a meeting held at Sèvres in France in October 1956 the British were told that Israel would not attack Jordan in any future war. At this meeting the three countries decided on a plan. Israel would attack Egypt and Britain and France would send troops into the Canal Zone under the excuse of keeping the two sides apart and the Canal open for shipping.

Not long before a British politician had been shown the plans for a British seizure of the Canal and had remarked, 'Very interesting, but how do we actually start this war?'. Eden saw the Israeli attack as the excuse he needed to seize the Canal and overthrow Nasser. For years after the attack, both British and French politicians denied that there was such a plan. The Israelis never denied it. Following the meeting they altered their plans in a way which showed that they expected British bombers based on Cyprus to destroy the Egyptian air force and so prevent the bombing of Israeli cities. The Israeli general, **Moshe Dayan**, had no intention of going near the Canal anyway. His troops were ordered to open the Gulf of Aqaba.

On 29 October 1956 the Israeli army invaded Sinai, the only Asiatic part of Egypt. In six days their soldiers defeated and scattered the Egyptian army, destroyed its bases and reached the Gulf of Aqaba. Two days later the British and French governments ordered the Egyptians and Israelis not to fight within 16 kilometres of the Canal. This ultimatum was accepted by Israel and rejected by Egypt. Next day British bombers attacked Egyptian airfields and soon afterwards British and French troops landed at Port Said (see map on page 230). The Egyptians put up a fierce defence of Ismailia. Otherwise they were easily defeated.

On BBC radio Sir Anthony Eden explained that this action was meant to place 'a protective shield' between the two armies. He claimed that he wished to save the Canal from damage. In fact, this 'shield' was roughly 150 kilometres behind the fighting, the Israelis were attacking other objectives and the Egyptians had already blocked the Canal by sinking ships.

Empire sunset

In Britain the Labour Party opposition staged an all-out attack upon Eden's Conservative government. Even some of the Prime Minister's own Cabinet resigned in disgust at what had been done and the way in which it had been done. In many ways the Suez attack was the last

Sunken ships block the Suez Canal, 1956

action of the old-style British imperialism. This aggressive interference in the affairs of a smaller country was condemned by both Russian and American delegates at the United Nations. The US President, Dwight D. Eisenhower, was particularly angry. Although a staunch ally of Britain in wartime, he shared the American dislike of imperialism. He had been against the British–French plan from the start. Now he was furious that it had occurred without his permission. US Treasury officials were ordered to stop all financial help to Britain if she did not withdraw her troops from Egypt.

The British were in the middle of a money crisis. With many of his own people against the invasion, there was little Eden could do except stop the landings in Egypt. Soon afterwards he resigned. It was a sad end to a distinguished career as a soldier, politician and statesman. He had miscalculated the mood of the people and the attitude of the Americans. He had expected the Arabs to overthrow Nasser as soon as British troops landed. Instead, he found the whole Arab world rejoicing that two imperialist powers had been made to look foolish.

Nasser had managed to turn a military defeat into a major political victory. His hold on his people was stronger than ever. The Israelis, too, were pleased with the outcome of the war. They had broken the Egyptian blockade, stopped the border raids and taught the Egyptian army a severe lesson. For the first time the world looked in admiration at the military skill of the Israeli army.

For a short time the French considered carrying on alone. Then they also evacuated the Canal Zone and UN officials and soldiers moved in to stop the fighting. But the French did not forgive the Americans. Later they withdrew from NATO and made their own nuclear weapons. For Britain things could never be the same again. Once British poets had boasted that the sun never set on their Empire. Now the older dominions and India were independent; the Middle East was free of British control; Africa was splitting into separate states. Clouded by two world wars, overshadowed by the power of the Soviet Union and the USA, Britain's imperial sun had set.

The Six Days War

Nasser remained the leading figure in the Middle East for twelve years after Suez. He used his power and prestige to try to unite the various Arab countries. But his plans could only succeed if he posed as a bitter enemy of Israel. It was this hatred of the Jew, not any liking for each other, which brought Arab states together. Time and again, therefore, Nasser was forced to sound more warlike than he really was to win Arab support. In 1967 this attitude led Egypt and much of the Arab world into a disastrous war.

For some time raids in the 'no-man's-land' between Syria and Israel had been getting worse. Armed bands recruited from the bitter Palestinian refugees were encouraged to cross into Israel. Israeli troops and aircraft replied with counter-attacks against Syria. In 1967 Nasser decided to make a sensational move. In May he ordered the UN forces which had manned the Egypt–Israel border since the Suez War to leave. In their place he massed the large Egyptian tank army in Sinai. At the same time the **Straits of Tiran** leading into the Gulf of Aqaba (see map on page 236) were closed to Israeli shipping by the seizure of Sharm-el-Sheikh, a fortified post commanding its entrance. The Israelis had always said that the closing of these Straits by the Egyptians would be regarded as an act of war. But Nasser felt confident that the Soviet Union would block all UN attempts to get the Straits reopened. And, if war did come, Nasser had the whole Arab world, including Jordan, on his side. Israel would be attacked on all her land frontiers.

Then the Israelis struck back as they had done in 1948 and 1956. On 5 June 1967 they used the excuse of a probing movement by Egyptian tanks to launch a full-scale attack on their enemies. Their well-trained air force struck at Egypt's airfields so fiercely that two-thirds of Nasser's air force was destroyed on the ground. Those Egyptian planes which took off were shot down. Left without air cover, the Egyptian army in Sinai was wiped out within two days. Meanwhile, Israeli para-

*End of an army. Wrecked
Egyptian vehicles in Sinai. Six
Days War, 1967*

troopers captured Sharm-el-Sheikh and the Jordanian army was driven
out of **Old Jerusalem**. Within six days Egypt had lost all her territory
in Sinai and about half of Jordan was occupied by the Israelis. Nasser's
life's work was ruined.

Soldiers with suitcases

Ever since this devastating war the Arab world has demanded that
Israel abandon its conquests. In November 1967 the United Nations
passed Resolution 242, stating that Israel should have 'secure and recognised' frontiers. Unfortunately, Arabs and Israelis had different
ideas of what these should be. Fighting between the two sides continued. Russian armaments and technical experts poured into Egypt;
the Soviet Mediterranean Fleet made 'goodwill' visits. In 1970 the Russians supplied SAM3 anti-aircraft missiles and MIG21 fighters. They
were flown by Soviet crews. The fighting along the Suez front became
so fierce that both the USSR and the USA persuaded the two sides to
accept a ceasefire under the Rogers Plan (named after William Rogers,
the US Secretary of State). In Jordan, King Hussein was forced to
drive the Palestinian guerrillas out of his country because of their constant raids upon Israel. This bloody fighting in September 1970 led the

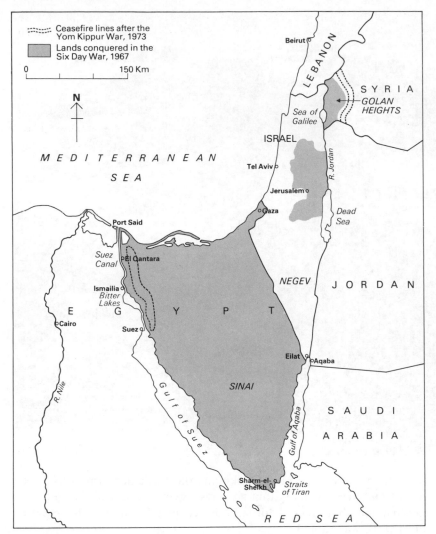

Palestinians to form the 'Black September' terrorist gang. It was this gang which murdered some Israeli athletes at the Munich Olympic Games in 1972.

In 1970 Nasser died. His successor, **Anwar Sadat**, repeatedly threatened outright war if Israel did not withdraw from Sinai. The Israelis wondered whether to strike first. They decided this would make them even more unpopular with the UN and world opinion. Their inactivity brought them to the brink of disaster. On 6 October 1973 the Jews were celebrating Yom Kippur – the Day of Atonement – when all Jews ask God for forgiveness of their sins. On that day 200 Egyptian planes and 2,000 Egyptian guns attacked the Israeli defensive lines on the Suez Canal. Egyptian troops crossed the Canal and cut the hoses which were meant to spray flaming oil on to the water if there was an attack. Other commandos used high-pressure jets of water to move the large sand hills put up to stop attacking tanks. Within hours Egyptian flags were flying over the Israeli line at El Qantara, Ismailia and north of the Bitter Lakes (see map opposite). Egyptian troops were eating the breakfasts cooked by their enemies. Israeli tanks which raced into action were met by soldiers who seemed to be carrying suitcases. These 'suitcases' were one-man missile launchers. Fired from the shoulder, these projectiles could knock the turret off a large tank.

In the north, Syria attacked along the Golan Heights. A vital observation post on top of Mount Hermon was captured by Syrians who landed in helicopters. Its loss meant that the Israelis could not see the 1,000 Syrian tanks rolling forward to attack them. All over Israel radios blared the alarm code word 'Stewpot! Stewpot!'. Israel stood near to total defeat.

The war we all lost

The fact that it was a holy day gave the Israelis one advantage. The roads were empty and free for lorries, tanks and guns to move to the fronts. The Israelis decided to hold the Egyptians whilst they pushed back the Syrians who were near Israel's borders. For days the fate of Israel depended upon small groups of men who fought to the last against huge odds. Their sacrifice saved the state of Israel.

Then it was the turn of the Egyptians to be surprised. There was a gap between the Egyptian Second and Third Armies at the head of the Bitter Lakes. The Egyptians were planning their next moves and unaware of any danger. But Israeli General Ariel Sharon had left weak spots in the old sand walls when he was planning a raid into Egypt several years before. The spots were marked by red bricks. Sharon's men moved through these gaps, crossed the Canal and won a fierce battle. By doing so they cut the Egyptian army in two. Within days the Israelis were deep into Egypt, fighting amongst date plantations and maize fields instead of desert. Even as Sadat was telling the Egyptian people that they had won a great victory the Egyptian Third Army was cut off and trapped. It was the Russians who saw the danger first. Their leader, Alexei Kosygin, flew to Cairo to tell Sadat the dramatic news. Unless they called for a truce, both Egypt and Syria would lose the war.

Fighting ended on 25 October, just as the Israelis reoccupied Mount Hermon. The war had cost 12,000 Arab and 2,000 Israeli lives. But a small country like Israel could not afford such losses. Both sides had nearly lost the war. The Arabs could no longer be despised as fighters by the arrogant Israelis. Now other Arab states, like Saudi Arabia, began to use their control of oil to make the West persuade Israel to give up what she had won. They increased the price of oil, causing industrial depressions in many European countries. The USA managed to persuade the Israelis to give up some of their conquests in 1975. Israeli troops withdrew from parts of the Sinai Desert. But Syria remained Israel's bitter enemy.

So the **'Yom Kippur' War** led to an oil war. Every home in the Western world was affected in some way by these price increases. As one Western journalist remarked, 'The conflict in the Holy Land was the beginning of the war we all lost.'

'Peace Jimmyana'

In March 1979 President Sadat of Egypt and the Prime Minister of Israel, Menachem Begin, signed a peace treaty ending a state of war between their countries which had lasted for thirty years. This peace had been hastily organised, after many last minute delays, by President Jimmy Carter of the United States. Arguments over the control of Jerusalem, the rights and wrongs of the Palestinian people and how soon the Israelis would withdraw from occupied territory remained unresolved. Egypt's old allies, Jordan, Saudi Arabia and Syria, denounced the treaty as meaningless and a betrayal of everything for which the Arabs had fought. Sadat himself was described as a 'traitor' by the Arab world. Nevertheless, it was now clear that there was an alliance in the Eastern Mediterranean between the United States and the two strongest military powers in the region, Egypt and Israel. Another general war, like that of Yom Kippur, seemed unlikely.

What was the real significance of this treaty, which pressmen laughingly called the 'Pax [peace] Jimmyana' after the famous 'Pax Romana' (Roman Peace) imposed by the Romans on the Ancient World? Basically, both Egypt and Israel desired peace. In 1977 President Sadat had even gone to Israel and stated Egypt's terms for a peace settlement to the Israeli *Knesset* (Parliament). The Americans wanted peace too. They also wanted to safeguard vital supplies of oil from the Middle East. These had been threatened by Soviet influence in the Gulf States, for instance in the Marxist-governed South Yemen, and by the overthrow in Iran of the Shah's government. Iran, one of the chief suppliers of oil in the region, had been taken over earlier in 1979 by an anti-Western, Islamic group. During the confusion caused by this **Iranian Revolution**, supplies of oil to the West had been interrupted and then rationed. The energy crisis, first highlighted in 1973, had now become a major source of worry to the industrialised nations of the West. The United States, an especially greedy user of oil, saw its own position threatened by even more expensive Arab oil.

Of course, the 'Peace Jimmyana' was not just about oil. It was about solving the explosive situation in the Middle East. Years of war and hatred cannot be wiped away by a peace treaty; genuine and deeply felt grievances remain. But perhaps a treaty in which an Arab state actually recognises Israel's right to exist will be a first step towards a general settlement. The Israelis will have to give up a great deal of their conquests. The Palestinians will have to be given some sort of self-government. The 'war we all lost' may lead gradually to a peace which will benefit the entire world.

Timeline

1945	Arab League formed.
1947	UN plan for partition of Palestine.
1948	British withdrawal from Palestine. Jewish state of Israel proclaimed.
1948–9	Palestine War.

1952	King Farouk overthrown. Colonel Nasser President of Egypt.
1954	Algerian War begins.
1955	Gaza Raid.
1956	Nasser nationalises Suez Canal. British and French attack on Suez. Suez War.
1958	Fifth Republic formed in France with de Gaulle as President.
1962	Algerian War ends.
1967	Six Days War.
1973	'Yom Kippur' War. Beginning of 'energy crisis'.
1975	USA persuades Israel to withdraw from some occupied territory.
1979	Peace Treaty signed between Egypt and Israel. Iranian Revolution.

Questions

1. 'To deny the loan for the Aswan Dam to Nasser is a very dangerous action; it can affect the Suez Canal. I know Nasser... I was Ambassador for my Government in Cairo, for several years. Beware how you handle the situation with the loan, because a most likely consequence of a refusal is the seizure of the Suez Canal.' (Couve de Murville, French Ambassador, speaking to American officials, 1956)

    a) How far was Couve de Murville's prediction proved correct?
    b) What steps did the French and British governments take to deal with the 1956 Suez crisis?
    c) What part did the Israelis play in these events?
    d) What part did the United States government play in the crisis?

2. 'We have decided to drench this land with our blood, to oust you, aggressors, and throw you into the sea for good.' (Broadcast by Syrian government radio to Israel, 1966)

    How successful were the Arabs in 'throwing the Jews into the sea' during the Six Days War, 1967?

3. Why was the 'Yom Kippur' War between the Arab world and Israel in 1973 described as the 'war we all lost'?

4. Write short paragraphs on each of the following:
    a) Arab nationalism
    b) FLN
    c) General de Gaulle
    d) Palestinian refugees

25
The Impossible Dream
Africa since 1900

The first contact between Europeans and Africans was unhappy. White traders came to West Africa to seize slaves and take them to the West Indian and North American plantations. They brought manufactured goods, cloth and tin kettles, which the African chiefs wanted. At first they received in return criminals and prisoners of war. Later the chiefs seized people of other tribes. From November until April, when the winds and seas were favourable, the African natives lived in terror of armed raiding parties. Lucky ones fled inland and escaped. Between the sixteenth and nineteenth centuries about twenty million did not. They were sold for saucepans and bits of material, shipped to the New World (North America) and in many cases worked to death. The slavers only visited the African continent for a few weeks each year. They neither knew nor cared about the country or its people.

As Europeans turned from slave trading to exploration and conquest, ignorance was joined by prejudice. The Dutch and German settlers who colonised the south, for example, despised the African because of what they regarded as his primitive way of life. They acted, to quote one colonial governor, 'As much as possible to rule the country as if there were no inhabitants'. But there were inhabitants – and they had been there a very long time. When the great stone ruins of Zimbabwe, north of the Limpopo River (see map on page 251), were examined by Europeans, it seemed clear to them that such structures could not have been built by local people. Some 'experts' suggested that the Phoenicians had done the work! We now know that Africans built Zimbabwe in the Middle Ages. In Africa a settled way of life, developed over many centuries, was usually based on the idea of kinship: that is, a number of families who shared the same language and interests were grouped in communities, which Europeans called tribes. These communities usually had a common ancestor whose 'spirit' was thought to link them together. Most Africans were farmers, although in West Africa there were a number of traders and a few manufacturers. Nowhere were there the wild savages imagined by the colonists.

Acting as though there were no inhabitants, the colonial rulers who came during the 'Scramble for Africa' (see Chapter 3) drew lines across the continent to suit themselves (see map on page 22), rather as if a conquering power were to create a European 'country' consisting of half of France, part of Switzerland and a section of Germany. As one educated African remarked about the largest British colony, 'God did not create Nigeria, the British did'. During this period, despite the work of a few devoted missionaries, many old established civilisations were disrupted, as natives were taken from their farms and used as

Ruins of ancient Zimbabwe, once part of the Kingdom of Monomatapa

cheap labour in the new mines and factories built by the colonists. Such work had to be done by Africans because, as one British official explained in 1905, 'Europeans will not do manual work in a country inhabited by black races'. This was a policy which led to crowded shanty towns where the black natives lived and which deprived the old style communities of many men who were needed for farming.

Fortunately, not all Europeans thought of Africans as savages of the wrong colour. The slave trade and, later, slavery itself, were abolished by white men who proclaimed that all human beings, of whatever colour, were created equal by God. By 1900 many educated Western people were worried by the way the African continent was being exploited. And the ordinary 'man in the street' often showed little interest in 'his' empire. As one British imperialist complained, 'Why bother to keep an empire for people who are dead set on chucking it away?' After the First World War President Woodrow Wilson gave a few educated Africans hope. Although his self-determination principle was intended mainly for Eastern Europe, it could obviously apply to colonial territories as well.

From the earliest colonising days some white men had claimed that they had a mission to educate the African so that he could enjoy the benefits of civilisation. This idea was embodied in the League of Nations **mandate** scheme set up to deal with the colonies taken from Germany after the First World War. The countries, mainly Britain and

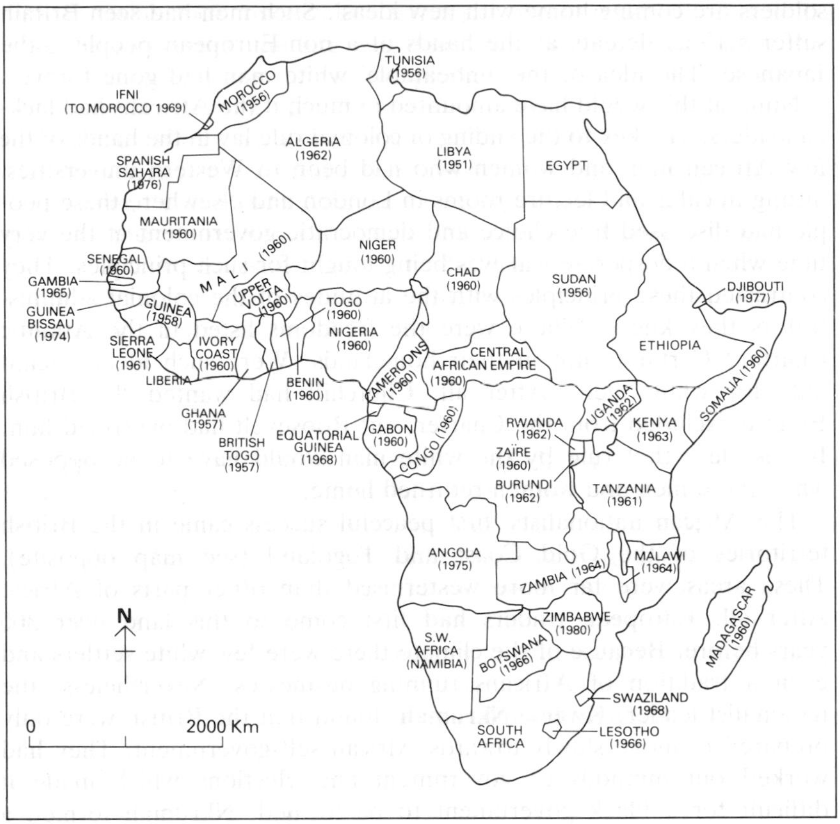

TUNISIA (1956)
IFNI (TO MOROCCO 1969)
MOROCCO (1956)
ALGERIA (1962)
LIBYA (1951)
EGYPT
SPANISH SAHARA (1976)
MAURITANIA (1960)
NIGER (1960)
MALI (1960)
CHAD (1960)
SUDAN (1956)
DJIBOUTI (1977)
SENEGAL (1960)
GAMBIA (1965)
GUINEA BISSAU (1974)
GUINEA (1958)
UPPER VOLTA (1960)
TOGO (1960)
NIGERIA (1960)
CENTRAL AFRICAN EMPIRE (1960)
ETHIOPIA
SIERRA LEONE (1961)
IVORY COAST (1960)
LIBERIA
BENIN (1960)
CAMEROONS (1960)
GHANA (1957)
BRITISH TOGO (1957)
EQUATORIAL GUINEA (1968)
GABON (1960)
CONGO (1960)
RWANDA (1962)
ZAÏRE (1960)
UGANDA (1962)
KENYA (1963)
SOMALIA (1960)
BURUNDI (1962)
TANZANIA (1961)
N
0   2000 Km
ANGOLA (1975)
ZAMBIA (1964)
MALAWI (1964)
ZIMBABWE (1980)
MADAGASCAR (1960)
S.W. AFRICA (NAMIBIA)
BOTSWANA (1966)
SWAZILAND (1968)
SOUTH AFRICA
LESOTHO (1966)

some cases this has been bad, leading to a vicious dictatorship like that of Idi Amin in Uganda. In other cases it has produced a system far more suited to the old, African way of life.

Above all, the change of government from white European to black African was rarely a revolution which would help the ordinary African in any way. The new rulers behaved very much as their old colonial masters had done when they took over the existing system. The Africans who were freed from colonial control in the 1950s and 1960s were promised great improvements. Before he gained independence for Ghana, Nkrumah promised, 'If we get self-government we'll transform the Gold Coast [Ghana] into a paradise in ten years'. Less than ten years later a discontented army overthrew Nkrumah; six years on, in 1972, they deposed his successor, Kofi Busia. And in 1976 the military masters of Ghana declared that they had tried 'the Westminster (British) pattern' and it had failed. They were now, they said, looking for another pattern. 'The search', said a spokesman, 'would take a long time and in the end it would be based on local realities and local experience'. Few members of the black ruling groups who took over their countries in the 1950s and 1960s ever tried any such thing.

From Congo to Zaïre

Three immediate problems usually faced the new states: lack of experts to run industry and government; ethnic (or tribal) divisions between

Zaïre (Belgian Congo), showing the breakaway province of Katanga

different parts of the country; and, in certain cases, trouble with white settlers who were unwilling to give up their privileges and power. Lack of experts was certainly the trouble with the Belgian Congo (now Zaïre) which was given a hurried independence in 1960 (see map on page 244). This huge tropical area started its colonial life in the 1880s as almost the personal property of **King Leopold of Belgium**. The King, who never visited the area, ordered a form of slave labour to be used to mine its rich copper deposits. From 1908 the Belgian government took over and tried to improve conditions for the Africans there. At times the Congo was regarded as a 'model colony', although in fact little was done to teach blacks the higher skills and crafts or to educate their leaders for self-government.

Then the wave of anti-colonialism sweeping Africa, what the British Prime Minister, Harold Macmillan, called 'the wind of change', reached the Congo. There were riots in **Leopoldville** (now Kinshasa) and the police opened fire, killing forty-nine and wounding many others. Belgians were worried by such disturbances in their model colony. Their government knew that most of the neighbouring French territories had been granted independence. They probably feared more riots and bloodshed if they did not do the same. Whatever the exact reason, surprised Congolese leaders who were invited to Ostend in Belgium in January 1960 were offered self-government within six months. They accepted, and a vast area of central Africa, split into different regions with different interests and leaders, was left totally unprepared for independence. On the day the new Prime Minister, **Patrice Lumumba**, took over the whole area it had a civil service of 9,000 Belgians and 11,000 Africans. Many of the Belgians went home soon afterwards and most of the Africans could barely read!

Lumumba, at least, dreamed of creating a united country out of the chaos. His **National Congress Movement (MNC)** managed to gain a clear majority at elections held just before independence. But other leaders decided to break away from the Congo, in particular **Moise Tshombe**, ruler of the rich copper-mining province of **Katanga** (see map above). Lumumba knew that the Congo would be a poor country without its copper so he refused to accept the withdrawal of Katanga and appealed to the United Nations for help. The Secretary General of the United Nations at the time, **Dag Hammarskjöld**, sent various forces into the Congo to try to keep the peace. These units, including soldiers from Ghana, Nigeria and Ethiopia, did very little and certainly made no effort to bring Katanga under the rule of the central government in the Congo. Lumumba then asked the Soviet Union to help.

Moise Tshombe. He failed to make Katanga independent of Zaïre

The Soviet-backed drive on Katanga failed because Tshombe's army was well-trained and well-equipped. This failure, and the fact that he was now labelled a communist because of his appeal to the Russians, led to Lumumba's overthrow by **General Sese Seko Mobutu**, Chief of Staff of the Congolese army. Mobutu's troops drove out the Russians and handed Lumumba over to his arch-enemy, Tshombe. Later it was announced that he had been killed whilst trying to escape. Hammarskjöld continued to seek peace but was killed when his plane crashed on its way to a meeting with Tshombe. Katanga was finally beaten in

1964. Tshombe fled abroad but returned later to be a minister in Mobutu's Cabinet. When he was again expelled he went to live in Spain but was kidnapped whilst travelling in his private plane by Algerians who looked upon him as a traitor to African nationalism. He died mysteriously in Algeria in 1969.

Lumumba as a prisoner (see page 245)

General Mobutu has ruled Zaire ever since. Various attempts to overthrow him have failed. During a civil war in Angola in 1975 he backed one of the losing groups. This caused the victorious Soviet-backed government to close a railway link vital for the export of Zaïre's copper. However, this quarrel was patched up. Meanwhile Zaïre found a new source of wealth in oil. By 1976 she was self-sufficient, that is, was supplying her own oil needs, and had started to export oil as well.

Oil-field in Africa

Nigeria: African giant

Nigeria is not really one country but an artificial grouping of 80 million people who speak 248 different languages or dialects. Within its borders large tribes like the Hausa, the Yoruba and the Ibo have their own cultures and are separate nations by European standards. Also, the British had ruled parts of Nigeria in different ways. The whole northern area had been treated to Indirect Rule and, in fact, had not been amalgamated with the south until 1914. This meant that the northern peoples, like the Hausa, had been cut off from Western political ideas much more than those of the south, like the Yoruba. Consequently, nationalist ideas first arose in the south.

Nigeria, showing tribal divisions and Biafra

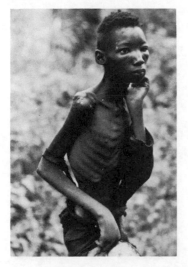

The Biafran War brought starvation to this Nigerian teenager and thousands of others

Britain had 'made' Nigeria and Britain was faced with the problem of what to do with such a large, diverse area (see map opposite). The British government would have preferred a strong central authority because it believed that each of the three main regions needed the other economically. On the other hand the great differences, religious, political and tribal, between the regions made Britain decide to set up a **federation** of Nigerian states (1954), rather on the American or Australian model. Indeed, several of the more developed regions were given self-government before the whole country achieved independence in 1960.

This federation was workable only on paper. During some of the first elections it became clear that there was a struggle between north and south and that the north, with more people, always won. Southerners began to fear that they would be dominated by the powerful and warlike Hausa tribe of the north. The division was made worse by the fact that the north tended to be Muslim and the south largely Christian. During 1966 large numbers of Hausa and Ibo were massacred by enemy tribes. In the same year Hausa army officers, led by **General Yakubu Gowon**, took over the government. Gowon announced a plan to reorganise the country politically and this led the ruler of the Eastern Region, **Colonel Chukwerneka Ojukwu**, to declare that his area had withdrawn from Nigeria (1967). The new country, he said, would be called **Biafra** (see map above).

A long and bloody civil war followed. Gowon was against the division of Nigeria, particularly as it would involve the loss of Biafra's rich oil-fields. Ojukwu represented the Ibo, and his people, fearing mass murder, fought on against great odds. The Soviet Union and Britain supported Gowon whilst the French gave aid to the Biafrans led by Ojukwu. By 1968 starvation was causing 25,000 deaths a day in Biafra. This was because the rebel area was surrounded and cut off from most supply routes. In 1970 the Biafran army gave up. Ojukwu fled to the Ivory Coast and his successor, Colonel Philip Effiong, surrendered. Biafra was then divided into three of the nineteen regions which make up Nigeria today.

Gowon tried to rule fairly but he was a soldier holding the country together by military means. Oil revenues were making the ruling group of Nigeria rich but they were not solving the main problem, which was how to return to civilian government without causing another break-up of the country. Gowon was overthrown in 1975 but his successor was another soldier, **Brigadier Murtala Mohammed**. Mohammed was murdered in 1976 by officers determined to overthrow his government. They failed and Mohammed's friend, **General Olusegun Obasanjo**, took over. He promised civilian government by 1979 and held talks with leaders of the different regions. The election took place and **Alhaji Shehu Shagari** took office as President on 1 October 1979. The new constitution is modelled on that of the USA, which is better suited to Nigeria's federal system than a British-style system of government.

The stories of both Zaïre and Nigeria showed African leaders the danger of divisions within their borders and the difficulty of creating in a few years nation states of the type which took centuries to develop in

Europe. In many ways Biafra was a separate state but very few African countries would recognise it because they knew there were similar situations within their own lands. The President of Togo put their point of view when he said, 'Recognition of Biafra would mean disorder for all Africa'. Colonialism may have ended but the problems it had created would not go away.

The rule of 'Fancy Belt'

Most of the states which won their freedom without much fighting had only a few white settlers. Kenya and Southern Rhodesia (see map on page 242) were exceptions. In the late nineteenth century white settlers went to the region north of Nairobi known then as the White Highlands, and began to grow crops like coffee and tea. In 1920 the British named this area **Kenya Colony and Protectorate**. Kenya was ruled by a Legislative (law-making) Council which had only white members until 1944, this in spite of the fact that there were 6,000,000 Africans compared with 170,000 Indians and 60,000 Europeans living in Kenya at the time. After the Second World War there was a strong feeling among the blacks, particularly the powerful **Kikuyu** tribe, that the settlers had taken too much land during the 'White Highlands' period. This led, between 1952 and 1956, to the growth of a terrorist movement called '**Mau Mau**'. The Mau Mau were very violent. At secret ceremonies in the forests of Kenya they swore to kill Europeans and any Africans who co-operated with them.

The leading Kikuyu politician was **Jomo Kenyatta**. He gave himself this name, which means 'fancy belt', because he always wore a fancy belt. Although Kenyatta spent long periods in England, as early as 1928 he joined the Kikuyu Central Association to protest about land rights. After the Second World War he returned to Kenya where he was much disliked by the white settlers. They felt that he had too much influence with the Africans and, during the Mau Mau troubles, he was tried and convicted of being one of their leaders – a charge he always denied. British troops fought hard and eventually suppressed the Mau Mau in 1956. Kenyatta remained in prison until 1959 and, upon his release, was sent away to a remote village.

From the British point of view Mau Mau was an evil which had to be destroyed. Nevertheless, its activities made the end of white rule in Kenya certain. The British government realised that behind Mau Mau lay discontent about genuine grievances. In an effort to give Africans more say in the running of Kenya, two political parties were allowed to be formed in the late 1950s. These were the **Kenya African National Union (KANU)** and the **Kenya African Democratic Union (KADU)**. KANU, representing the powerful Kikuyu and Luo tribes, demanded black African rule and the release of Kenyatta. The smaller KADU party represented those blacks who were afraid of domination by the Kikuyu. In 1960 the British gave way over multi-racial rule and the black Africans won a majority on the Kenya Council by democratic means. As a result Kenyatta returned and he took part in conferences in London to decide Kenya's future.

Jomo Kenyatta

African suspects being rounded up during Mau Mau unrest, 1952

In December 1963 Kenyatta became Prime Minister of an independent Kenya and, a year later, President of the Republic of Kenya. He held this position until his death in 1978. In many ways Kenyatta, the one time Mau Mau suspect, proved a moderate leader who preferred the West to the Communist states. However, by 1970, the Kenyan parliament had no real power and was expected to agree to the decisions of the ruling group. Even the government party, KANU, had little say in the running of Kenya. In 1975 Joseph Kariuki, a leading businessman, complained that, 'Kenya has become like a tree growing very tall very quickly, but it is going to fall because it does not have deep roots, is not firmly rooted in the people and in society'. Kariuki was referring to the few wealthy men, including Kenyatta, who now controlled Kenya. In the same year Kariuki was found murdered. A parliamentary committee which investigated the murder found evidence to suggest that the government special police were involved. But those who criticised the government were arrested in the Nairobi Parliament Building by plain clothes police!

Meanwhile Kenya's business boomed, although most was foreign-owned and controlled. This illustrated a fact obvious in other African states. Although foreigners no longer controlled the countries politically they often controlled them economically. As European and American businesses did their deals with African politicians, it became clear that

Britain gave way. In 1964 Northern Rhodesia achieved independence as **Zambia** and Nyasaland as **Malawi** (see map on page 251).

Southern Rhodesia's white government now demanded a similar independence. Britain wanted to know when black Africans would be given voting rights in Southern Rhodesia, since she could not allow minority rule permanently. White Rhodesians argued that few blacks were fit for self-government. Successive British governments agreed but asked when the settlers were going to educate the blacks for such responsibilities. The answer came when an ex-Fighter pilot, **Ian Smith**, won the 1965 election in Rhodesia with a party called the **Rhodesian Front**. Smith represented the people who were not prepared to hand over the country to black Africans. Many of them talked of 'defending white civilisation'. Smith said that he could not foresee black majority rule 'in a thousand years'. On 11 November 1965 he issued a **Unilateral (one-sided) Declaration of Independence (UDI)**. This meant that his white minority government had rebelled against British rule.

Ian Smith, Prime Minister of a white-dominated Rhodesia from 1965 until 1979

The British government, led at that time by Harold Wilson, refused to recognise UDI. They put a ban on all trade with Rhodesia and the United Nations encouraged other countries to do the same. Such **sanctions**, as they are called, did not work very well because Rhodesia could get supplies through South Africa and Mozambique, then controlled by Portugal. Since a British invasion of Rhodesia was practically impossible, there were various attempts to change the white Rhodesians' minds by negotiation. In December 1966 Harold Wilson and Ian Smith met on a British warship, HMS *Tiger*. They seemed to have agreed on some form of black participation in government but, back in Salisbury, Smith's ministers objected.

In 1970 Rhodesia declared herself a republic. Britain refused to recognise Rhodesia's republican status which, like UDI, she regarded as illegal. Next year, however, negotiations were reopened with the British government. By November 1971 an agreement had been signed between the new British Prime Minister, Edward Heath, and Ian Smith. A new constitution (form of government) would gradually give black Africans more seats in the Assembly (parliament) and so more power. Ever since the early 1960s the British had said that any legal independence for Rhodesia must satisfy the so-called **Six Principles**, the most important of which was 'unimpeded progress towards majority rule' – in other words black African rule. It is doubtful whether the white settlers of Rhodesia intended to do this of their own free will. However, another of the principles was that any new constitution must be 'tested by public opinion'. This meant that there must be some sort of opinion poll before the 1971 agreement could be enforced. In May 1972 a Commission led by Lord Pearce went to Rhodesia and carried out such a poll. The Commission's report showed that whilst the agreement was favoured by Europeans and Asians, the black Africans were solidly against it. So this settlement was never put into force.

From sanctions to war

Sanctions on Rhodesia were a failure. At the time of UDI Rhodesia imported about eighty per cent of her merchandise. Above all, she was over-dependent on exporting her tobacco crops. Ten years later the country had developed thriving new industries, particularly after many tobacco farms switched to growing cotton. Rhodesian-made clothes were certainly 'smuggled' out of the country and it was said that they were sold in London stores without tabs showing where they had been made! A great deal of this trade went by rail through Mozambique to the ports of Beira and Maputo (see map on page 251). Despite the world boycott, international oil companies supplied Rhodesia's needs. And even when there were shortages of goods Rhodesians either made their own or imported them secretly from European countries.

Until 1974 Smith had every reason to feel pleased with himself. His government had defied Britain and the world. His industry was far from crippled. His opponents, men like **Ndabaningi Sithole**, leader of the **Zimbabwe African National Union (ZANU)**, and **Joshua Nkomo**, leader of the **Zimbabwe African People's Union (ZAPU)**, were in prison. Above all, the country was ruled by white men. Then came an event far away from Rhodesia which changed the situation. Portugal was still a colonial power with vast African territories, including Mozambique and Angola. Her troops had been fighting a ruthless war with African nationalist guerrillas who belonged to such organisations as **Frelimo** (Mozambique Liberation Front) and **UNITA** (the National Union for Complete Independence) in Angola. Such a government could be relied upon to help Ian Smith's régime in every way. Then, in 1974, came a revolution in Portugal which overthrew one of the oldest

UNITA guerrillas continue their fight for independence against the Soviet-backed régime in Angola (see page 254)

twentieth-century dictatorships and put a new government in power. The new Portuguese government promptly gave its African territories their independence.

White Rhodesia's chief weakness was now exposed. It is a landlocked country, dependent on neighbouring states for an outlet to the sea. Mozambique's long border with Rhodesia now became a refuge and training ground for black Africans determined to overthrow the Smith government by force. Soon these nationalists were fighting a full-scale guerrilla war against the Rhodesian government. Smith hastily completed the rail link with South Africa, and for a time managed to keep the railways through Mozambique open. At the same time he released Nkomo and Sithole and tried in vain to negotiate some sort of deal with them. Meanwhile the Africans stepped up the guerrilla war with attacks on white farms in Rhodesia and the villages of blacks who 'co-operated' with white men. When Rhodesian troops and planes began to attack African nationalist fighters in their Mozambique bases the new President of Mozambique closed the Rhodesian border (1976).

Other countries suffered by this blockade. Mozambique herself lost an annual £17,000,000 in customs and port dues alone. Zambia could not get her supplies of copper out. But the chief sufferer was Smith's Rhodesia. 1976 was the year when most of Rhodesia was declared 'an operational area' (war zone) and most roads could only be used safely by day. It was the year when Angola (see map on page 251) was conquered by a Soviet-backed army. It was also the year when the United States, startled by what had happened in Angola, sent her Secretary of State, Henry Kissinger, to talk with the so-called **'Front Line Presidents'**. These were the leaders of African states close to Rhodesia, men such as Kenneth Kaunda of Zambia and Julius Nyerere of Tanzania. The same year South Africa, fearful of African attacks on her own borders if the guerrilla war in Rhodesia continued, tried to persuade Smith to make a settlement with the **Patriotic Front**. The Front was an alliance of various nationalist guerrilla organisations, the most powerful of which were ZAPU, led by Joshua Nkomo, and the section of ZANU which was led by Robert Mugabe.

Kenneth Kaunda, ruler of Zambia

The result of all this pressure was seen in September 1976. In an historic broadcast, Ian Smith accepted the principle of black majority rule, although he made it plain that he did not consider it 'the best solution for Rhodesia's problems'. He managed to make an agreement with two moderate African leaders, **Abel Muzorewa** and Ndabaningi Sithole. As a result the first 'one man, one vote' elections in Rhodesia's history were held in April 1979. Muzorewa emerged as victor and became Prime Minister, but the Patriotic Front claimed the elections were a fraud and the guerrilla war continued. This election was also denounced by Britain, the United States and the Front Line Presidents. Consequently, Muzorewa failed to stop either the war or the economic sanctions against Rhodesia which had been imposed at the time of UDI in 1965.

At the **Commonwealth Conference at Lusaka** (Zambia) in August 1979 the representatives of Britain and other Commonwealth countries persuaded all parties, including the Patriotic Front, to come to a

Mugabe's supporters celebrate his election victory, 1980

Robert Mugabe, first Prime Minister of an independent Zimbabwe

conference at **Lancaster House**, London, next month. The aim of the Conference was to end the war and to give Rhodesia a government all Rhodesians would accept. This so-called Constitutional Conference lasted for two months and during that time the Patriotic Front continued the guerrilla war in Rhodesia. The Conference ended with agreement on terms for a new constitution (form of government) for Rhodesia, now called **Zimbabwe**, the ancient name for the country. Arrangements were made for the country to be governed temporarily by British officials, led by Lord Soames, and policed by British soldiers during the election period.

During the months leading to the election guerrilla troops came out of the bush and lived in special camps supervised by the British. However, they were not disarmed. When the elections were held in February 1980 the result was an overwhelming victory for **Robert Mugabe** and his wing of the Patriotic Front. In April 1980 he became Prime Minister of a government which included Joshua Nkomo and members of his party as well as white ministers. Abel Muzorewa obtained few votes, as Mugabe had predicted. The war was now over, together with white minority rule. 'Illegal' white Rhodesia had ceased to exist. In its place was the independent black state of Zimbabwe.

South Africa

Rhodesia and Kenya had settler problems. In South Africa the 4½ million whites who dominate 20 million blacks and other non-whites are in a different position. The first colonists reached the Cape in 1652 (see Chapter 4). Just as the British in North America provided the basis for a nation of Americans, so these Dutch, French and German settlers became **Afrikaners** (Boers). They cannot be sent home like the Algerian colonists or the Kenyan whites. To them Africa is home, and because they have no other country they are determined to stay.

If it were merely a matter of keeping black Africans out, there might be a solution. An Afrikaner state could be formed with the blacks and so-called coloureds (people of mixed blood) excluded. But the Afrikaner has always wanted the black to work for him. In the old days his farms needed slaves. Now the diamond and gold mines employ thousands of blacks; the factories have black and coloured workers. The social life which has developed in South Africa, therefore, is affected by three things. First, most Afrikaners believe that black Africans are so different from whites that they must never be given European education or privileges. Second, the whole economy would collapse without black and coloured workers. Third, most Afrikaners know that if they treat blacks and coloureds as political equals their minority government will be overwhelmed.

When attacked by enemies, the Afrikaners' tough ancestors turned their wagons into a circle (*laager*). With such protection they fought bravely and usually won. The modern Afrikaner has devised a political system which he thinks will protect him from black domination as surely as the *laager* saved his forefathers. He still possesses the best weapons, the tanks, aircraft and rifles, necessary to win a pitched battle. In addition, he has passed laws which separate him as far as possible from the blacks and coloureds. It is true that not all white South Africans are Afrikaners. Some are descendants of the British men and women who came to the Cape after it became British in 1815. But the Afrikaner has never liked British rule and British customs, as the successive treks and the two Boer Wars of the nineteenth century show (see Chapter 4). Since 1948 he has become increasingly dominant in politics, finance and industry in South Africa. His **Nationalist Party**, which won the election in 1948, has made it impossible for any other party to win an election.

Apartheid

The Nationalists have tried to reduce contact between the different races of South Africa to a minimum. Intermarriage between black and white is illegal because it would produce more coloureds and dilute the white race. Separate townships, schools and universities have been built for the non-white peoples of South Africa. Public buildings, beaches, trams and buses are arranged so that black and white mix as little as possible. These measures are all part of the system of **apartheid**, or forcible separation of the races. For many they have caused great unhappiness. In 1954 some mission schools for black Africans were closed in case they gave higher education to their black pupils. Most blacks from that time on, with a few exceptions, were taught only basic skills. Only in the 1970s did an increasingly complex industry find that it needed more skilled black labour.

Entire suburbs, like **Sophiatown** near Johannesburg (see map on page 251), were destroyed because mixed races lived there, and the

Apartheid notice in South Africa

black inhabitants were moved forcibly to a new town. Coloureds are in a particularly unfortunate position because some are classified as European and some as African. The so-called 'pass laws' help to enforce apartheid. They state that all South Africans have to carry identity cards to indicate their status – European, Black African, Coloured, Indian or Asiatic. Non-white people have to show these passes to get in or out of white communities. Those not carrying them are punished. The **Suppression of Communism Act (1950)** made it illegal to oppose apartheid in South Africa and stated that communism was anything which caused hostility between whites and non-whites! This Act, and much later ones, such as the **Affected Organisations Act (1974)** and the **Riotous Assemblies Act (1974)** allowed the government to ban newspapers without giving a reason and to imprison people without trial.

In 1960, at **Sharpeville**, a large crowd demonstrated against the pass laws. They were fired on by the police who killed sixty-seven. Horror

After the Sharpeville shootings, 1960. The South African government says this photograph is a fake

at this massacre led to disputes at a conference of Commonwealth countries in London and as a result South Africa left the Commonwealth in 1961. More recently, in 1976, unrest at the compulsory use of Afrikaans (the Afrikaner language) in schools led to demonstrations and riots. They began at **Soweto**, a black housing complex south-west of Johannesburg (see map on page 251), but later spread to many parts of the country. The riots were soon against apartheid, rather than any particular grievance. This time large numbers of coloureds as well as blacks joined in the fighting. The police used automatic rifles, shot-guns and teargas. An estimated 500 demonstrators were killed.

The South African government has tried again and again to defend its policies. In 1959 a South African politician, **Dr Hendrik Verwoerd**, tried to show that apartheid is not just a way of keeping the whites on top. He proposed to set up a number of self-governing states, called **Bantustans**, within South Africa's borders. Inside these 'states', the blacks would be allowed to rule themselves and develop in any way they wished. Quite a few Bantustans have been set up but over eighty per cent of the land in South Africa still belongs to the whites. In 1976 the black government of the Transkei Bantustan claimed that they

*Homes in the Transkei
Bantustan*

would build a 'non-racial society'. But such 'states' are more like reservations than independent countries. The inhabitants are made to live in them whether they like it or not. They have no say in South Africa's foreign policy and nearly all their fit men work away from home in the industrial and mining areas of South Africa.

South Africa against the world

In September 1966 Verwoerd was stabbed to death in the South African parliament by a parliamentary messenger named Demitrio Tsafendas. Later it was announced that Tsafendas was mad and he was put in an asylum. Verwoerd's successor was **Johannes Vorster**, an experienced politician with a reputation for toughness where security was concerned. However, Vorster did not behave quite as expected. He realised that, however strong and rich South Africa might be, because of gold and thriving industries, she could not afford to ignore the hostility of virtually the whole world.

Vorster did not intend to abandon apartheid, although he did ease some of its more strict rules. What he tried to do was to establish friendly, trading links with black African states to the north. He offered to help them with their industrial development and in several cases his offer was accepted. Malawi's President, Dr Hastings Banda, for example, agreed to accept financial help to build a new capital city. Small successes of this type were soon dwarfed by larger failures. The end of Portuguese rule in Angola and Mozambique (1974–5) and the Russian-backed Cuban invasion of Angola brought the tide of black nationalism much nearer to South Africa's borders. Vorster sent South African troops into Angola but he had to withdraw them in the face of international hostility, especially from the United States. At home he was faced by increasing terrorism and rioting by discontented blacks on the one hand, and the opposition of extreme Afrikaners who feared he was abandoning apartheid on the other. The latter broke away from Vorster's United Party and formed the Purified National Party, the HNP.

Vorster or no Vorster, the opposition to apartheid and white rule in South Africa remained a major factor in world politics. All over the world liberal-minded people demanded that the South African government give up its racist policies. They organised bans on South African goods, tried to limit the trade between South Africa and the West and boycotted South African sport because it was organised on racialist lines. A lot of this opposition was channelled through the United Nations which frequently condemned apartheid. In particular, the United Nations called upon South Africa to withdraw from **Namibia**, formerly South West Africa.

South West Africa was colonised by Germany towards the end of the nineteenth century. After the First World War, when Germany was deprived of all her colonies, the South African government was asked by Britain to administer the country. This was looked upon as a temporary measure to be abandoned as soon as the Namibian people were able to govern themselves. The South Africans never regarded the occupation as temporary. From the start they treated Namibia as a fifth province of South Africa, allowing white settlers to buy the best land cheaply. After 1948 apartheid was also introduced to the territory.

Nowhere is 'South Africa against the world' more clear than in Namibia. The United Nations demands that the South African government allow free elections. The South Africans produce constitutions which appear to give Namibia independence. But her enemies claim that at the most Namibia is just another Bantustan. Young blacks join **SWAPO**, the **South West African People's Organisation**, which wages an active guerrilla war against the South African army. Meanwhile, the Afrikaner still believes that God gave him the land he rules so firmly. As one white farmer said in a BBC interview in 1979, 'We developed the country. We worked for it ... It was our expertise. South Africa, the country we got, was a bare piece of ground...'. There is no doubt that the ruling whites will fight very hard to keep their wealth and privileges. They are inside their *laager*, watching the 'enemy' come closer and closer.

Timeline

1919	Woodrow Wilson proclaims self-determination.
1941	Atlantic Charter.
1952–6	Mau Mau rebellion in Kenya.
1953	Central African Federation formed.
1954	Nigerian Federation formed.

1957 Ghana gains independence.

1960 Nigeria gains independence. Belgian Congo (Zaïre) given independence.

1960–4 Civil War in the Congo.

1961 Tanzania (Tanganyika) gains independence. South Africa leaves the Commonwealth.

1963 Kenya gains independence.

1964 Zambia and Malawi gain independence.

1965 Rhodesia's Unilateral Declaration of Independence (UDI).

1967 Eastern Region (Biafra) leaves Nigerian Federation. Arusha Declaration (Tanzania).

1967–70 Biafran War.

1975 Angola and Mozambique gain independence from Portugal.

1976 Mozambique closes border with Rhodesia.

1976 Communist forces, assisted by the Soviet Union and Cuba, take control of Angola.

1980 Zimbabwe (formerly Rhodesia) gains independence.

Questions

1. Look at the photograph on page 257.
    a) Why is this notice in two languages?
    b) What is the other language besides English?
    c) Who are the 'non-whites' in South Africa?
    d) This notice forbids whites and non-whites to mix at a picnic site. What other places in South Africa are divided so that the two do not mix?
    e) What is the name of the South African government policy which prevents integration between whites and non-whites?
    f) What is the purpose of this policy?

2. 'We could not possibly have held by force our territories in Africa . . . General de Gaulle could not contain Algeria . . . The march of men towards their freedom can be guided but not halted. Of course there were risks in moving quickly. But the risks of moving slowly were far greater.' (Iain Macleod, British Colonial Secretary, 1959)

    a) Do you think Iain Macleod was right in saying that Britain could not have held its African territories by force?
    b) Which African countries were 'guided' to freedom successfully?
    c) Which newly independent African states experienced difficulties? Describe in some detail the history of at least one such African state since it attained independence.

3. Write short paragraphs on each of the following:
    a) Rhodesian UDI, 1965
    b) the Slave Trade
    c) the Mau Mau
    d) Kwame Nkrumah

26

From Stalin to Détente
Russia since 1945

In post-war Poland men used to tell of a strange Russian animal produced by mating a cow with a giraffe. It grazed in Poland but was milked in the Soviet Union. Poles who heard the joke knew what it meant. After the war Poland had been forced to sell her goods to the USSR at well below world prices. As a result her workers laboured long hours for low wages. Polish industries seized by the Germans were not returned to their original owners. Instead their output, and sometimes even their equipment, was sent to the USSR as part of 'German' repayments. Poland's Communist government was not independent. Its army was commanded by a Russian, Marshal Konstantin Rokossovsky. It was administered at every turn by Soviet 'experts'. The slightest disagreement with Soviet policy led to dismissal, imprisonment or possibly execution. The same situation existed in other 'Iron Curtain' countries (see Chapter 22): Hungary, Bulgaria, Romania or Czechoslovakia. Eastern Europe was a colony of Stalin's new empire.

In the Soviet Union itself life was as hard as ever. Recovery from the immediate effects of the Second World War was swift. Smashed houses often had good foundations; they could be rebuilt by slave labour. Equipment poured in from East Germany and Eastern Europe to restock the factories. The new industries east of the Ural mountains were working well. But Stalin's determination to make the USSR a great industrial power meant that heavy industries like iron, steel and coal, were given priority. Working hours were long, wages low, housing very short. On the farms men, and sometimes women, pulled the ploughs because horses and tractors were scarce. Another **Five Year Plan** (see Chapter 13) drove the Russians to still greater efforts to modernise the Soviet Union. Meanwhile, the **MVD (Secret Police)** spied on people and terrorised them. Informers were encouraged to denounce any critics of the system. Any who did criticise were imprisoned in labour camps.

At the top of this pyramid of misery sat Stalin. His power was now greater than ever. The Communist Party had lost its grip on affairs; its Congress (Parliament) did not meet between 1939 and 1952. Stalin ruled directly through a few favourites and an efficient police force. Sitting late over his evening meal he would fire orders at his ministers whilst government clerks remained on duty to carry them out. As remote from his people as any of the old tsars, he had little idea of what living conditions were like in the Soviet Union. For the last twenty-five years of his life he never saw a village or a collective farm. His knowledge of the world came from watching films made by his own propagandists.

Nikita Khrushchev, ruler of the Soviet Union after Stalin

All over the USSR Stalin was treated as a god. Giant statues of him disfigured cities; huge portraits covered walls. He was said to be an expert on every subject. His writings about Marxism were treated with the reverence Christians give to the Bible. Books and films portrayed him as the only possible successor to Lenin, as the world's greatest revolutionary hero and the winner of the war. Numerous towns were given his name: travellers could visit Stalinsk, Stalinabad, or Stalingrad. On his seventieth birthday he received so many presents that a special museum had to be built to hold them. By that time he was a far more powerful Russian ruler than any of the tsars. During this century only Hitler and Mao Tse-tung have ever been treated in a similar way.

From Stalin to Khrushchev

One or two people influenced this lonely man. Just after the war, Andrey Zhdanov, the defender of Leningrad, was his closest adviser. This friendship lasted until Zhdanov's policy of toughness towards the USA led to the failure of the Berlin Blockade (see page 213). He died just in time to avoid execution, but several of his friends disappeared mysteriously. Gradually a new favourite, **Nikita Khrushchev**, fought his way to the top. This child of a peasant owed his success to hard work and continuous flattery of Stalin. Before the war he had supervised the digging of the Moscow Metro (underground railway). This project had little practical value. Houses, hospitals and schools were needed far more urgently. But the Metro was big enough for the Soviet Union's propagandists to write about. It could be portrayed as an example of communism in action. It was meant to show that Marxism worked. Khrushchev proved to be the perfect choice as a foreman. Week after week he bullied the workers into desperate, dangerous attempts to keep to Stalin's rigid timetable of construction. During the war, he drove the front line soldiers in the same way. He saw the appalling misery of the people and knew better than most the price the Soviet Union paid for her victory. When peace came he took charge of the Ukraine until 1952. His reputation as a manager and agricultural expert was high by the time he became Stalin's right-hand man.

Stalin died in an atmosphere of suspicion and fear. In January 1953 he received a letter accusing certain doctors of having poisoned Zhdanov. His Minister of State Security was promptly threatened with execution if he did not obtain confessions. As the unfortunate medical men were tortured and interrogated, people wondered whether this was the start of another fearful purge. They need not have worried. The last foreigner to see the old dictator alive was the Indian ambassador on 17 February 1953. Stalin seemed as distrustful as ever and remarked grimly that there were wolves who needed to be exterminated. Soon afterwards Moscow radio announced that he had suffered a stroke and died (5 March). Amidst officially organised national mourning, his body was laid beside that of Lenin in the Kremlin.

It was as though a cloud had been lifted from Soviet life. Stalin had turned the Soviet Union into the second most powerful state on earth,

Mourners queuing to see Stalin's body, March 1953

despite his failures. Unfortunately, most of his achievements had been at a huge cost in human lives and happiness. The easing of tension and bettering of living conditions which followed his death can be exaggerated. At first a government headed by two men, **Georgi Malenkov** and **Nikolai Bulganin**, tried to make life in the USSR more pleasant. They wanted to produce the small luxuries which improve the ordinary man's comfort. Even so, they could not completely change a way of life and a system of government built up over forty years. They released hundreds of thousands of prisoners from forced labour but did not close the camps, which remained open to receive 'anti-social elements'. They reduced the power of the MVD but it remained an offence to collect information about the USSR or to criticise her leaders. There was still no democracy such as exists in most Western countries.

Attempts to give people more things to buy were not altogether successful. Only a few television sets, a few more shoes and other goods, drifted into the shops. This was partly because the concentration on heavy industry was replaced by expensive space research. Only in one important way did life become better. Sudden deaths, tortures and confessions grew less common. The sinister head of police, **Lavrenti Beria**, disappeared. Surprised owners of the 'Great Soviet Encyclopaedia' were told to cut out the pages dealing with him and to insert a new set about the Bering Sea! Later it was announced that he had been shot. Beria's execution meant less terror because, with their chief gone, police power was reduced. By 1955 Khrushchev had become the chief power in Russia. But he did not shoot Malenkov or Bulganin and the slight 'thaw' in Soviet life continued.

De-Stalinisation

In 1956 exciting news filtered out of the Soviet Union. Speaking privately to the **Twentieth Congress** of the Soviet Communist Party, Khrushchev listed many of Stalin's mistakes. Stalin, it appeared, had misunderstood the true spirit of communism. He had failed to prepare properly for Hitler's invasion. His decision to dismiss Trotsky and the other Bolsheviks had been right. His execution or murder of them had been wrong. Very few of the dead dictator's crimes were ignored. Khrushchev even read a letter which indicated how prisoners had been made to confess. One unfortunate man had explained how his interrogators had 'taken advantage of the knowledge that my broken ribs have not properly mended and have caused me great pain. I have been forced to accuse myself and others.'

Khrushchev's speech had far-reaching effects. Although never published inside the Soviet Union its main points were soon common knowledge. All over the Communist world the statues came down and the towns were renamed. News of Stalin's death had led to a rising in East Germany in 1953. Now the Twentieth Congress encouraged criticism, riots and revolts in several countries. The Poles promptly dismissed all their Stalinist leaders. A similar movement in Hungary developed into open rebellion against everything Russian (October 1956). Khrushchev was taken by surprise at this reaction to his more liberal policy. When the Hungarian Communist leader, **Imre Nagy**, threatened to withdraw from the Warsaw Pact (see page 267) and demanded the withdrawal of all Russian troops he decided to act. If one country broke away, the entire Soviet security system built up since the war would be threatened. Russian tanks smashed the rebels in the streets of Budapest. A Russian firing squad shot Nagy.

The **Hungarian Revolt** showed that Khrushchev's policy of easing the Soviet hold on her satellite countries could lead to difficulties. In less spectacular ways things went wrong. Khrushchev was fond of showy speeches and slang expressions which hit the headlines. Promises and threats were uttered recklessly, usually on world or countrywide tours where they received maximum publicity. Nobody knew where Khrushchev would be next, or which set of experts would be lectured on how to do their job. The Soviet Union and the whole world were treated like his workmen on the Metro. One minute he smiled and joked; the next he lost his temper and predicted that the USSR would 'bury' the capitalists of the West. Once he excitedly took off his shoe at a UN General Assembly and banged it on the table! Such a way of governing had its disadvantages. Foreigners wondered whether to take him seriously. Russians remembered his noisy promises and noted that the good times he predicted did not come.

In spite of his reputation as an agricultural expert it was in farming that Khrushchev failed most. Ever since Stalin's day collective farms had been unpopular because most peasants preferred to work their own land. Not surprisingly, therefore, private farms often produced more than collective farms. In 1958 for example, Khrushchev complained that private cows multiplied whereas socialist cows did not. He tried giving cash bonuses to peasants who worked in collectives but it made little difference. In 1963 a very bad harvest caused a famine which reminded older people of earlier days. Khrushchev was compelled to buy 12 million tonnes of foreign grain. Communists were shaken by this evidence of inefficiency in their system.

Yuri Gagarin – first human to go into orbit, 1961

Such failures were due partly to an expensive space research programme. When the Second World War ended the Soviet army seized many German rocket scientists and their equipment. In the USSR these men developed larger and more powerful rockets. Reckless expense and great secrecy led to sensational results. In 1957 a Soviet rocket sent an artificial satellite, the '**Sputnik**', round the earth. Four years later a Russian, **Yuri Gagarin**, became the first man to go into orbit. Westerners who still regarded Russians, in Khrushchev's words, as 'peasants who drink cabbage soup out of leaky straw boots' were astonished. Americans in particular realised that such rockets could easily drop atomic warheads on US cities. The old containment policy (see page 211), which involved ringing Soviet territory with bombers, was obviously out of date if Soviet missiles could leap-frog over them. America began to spend far more money on space research.

At first, ordinary Russians were delighted. In less than forty years their country had passed from almost medieval backwardness to leadership in an important branch of science. By 1963 some were tiring of such achievements. Although still proud, they wondered why a government which could launch a rocket could not provide fresh milk in the winter or install an efficient telephone system. Similar complaints are often heard in Western countries.

Peaceful co-existence

The drive to improve the Soviet Union's standard of living meant a more peaceful foreign policy because the armies and modern weapons needed to confront the West were very expensive. Quite early in his career as Soviet leader, therefore, Khrushchev mentioned the possibility that the two rival worlds might live together without war. As a good Communist he still believed that capitalism was doomed to destruction. As a realist, he also knew how different were communism and capitalism. The two systems, he remarked, would only agree when 'shrimps learnt to whistle'. Nevertheless, he admitted that the old notion of constant revolutionary struggle needed to be modified now that atomic weapons had made war mean world disaster. In its place he suggested **peaceful co-existence**. Wherever he went his speeches seemed to suggest, 'Let us see which system is best but let us do it without fighting!'

Khrushchev's co-existence policy might have been more successful had not John Foster Dulles been American Secretary of State. So far as he was concerned Truman's containment policy was wrong because

John Foster Dulles, architect of US foreign policy in the 1950s

it meant leaving millions of people under Soviet domination. Possibly Dulles realised that any attempt to change this situation would mean war but he encouraged 'Voice of America' broadcasts to the peoples of Eastern Europe, and talked of 'liberating' the area and of 'rolling back the Iron Curtain'. His enemies called this attitude **brinkmanship** because they thought he was leading the world to the brink of war. His friends saw him as a champion against Soviet aggression in Eastern Europe.

In 1954, after much argument, Dulles persuaded the West Germans to contribute an army of 500,000 for NATO defences. The French, and even some Germans, were worried by such rearmament even though it strengthened Western defences. Eastern European nations invaded by Germany during the Second World War were alarmed. Khrushchev had just signed a peace treaty with Austria and withdrawn the Soviet army from her territory. Dulles's move, although sensible from a Western point of view, made it easier for the Soviet leader to organise a **Warsaw Pact** consisting of the USSR, Poland, Czechoslovakia, East Germany, Hungary, Bulgaria, Romania and Albania (1955). This gave the Communist bloc an alliance similar to NATO (see page 211), and only Albania later left this defence system.

The worst case of brinkmanship came from Khrushchev himself. In 1959 **Fidel Castro** had led a successful revolt against the Cuban dictator, **Fulgencio Batista**. Americans owned large sections of Cuban industry and their government had been friendly with the defeated leader. Castro's success upset these arrangements because he nationalised

'Nuclear war threatened mankind'. The Cuban Missile Crisis, 1962 (see page 268)

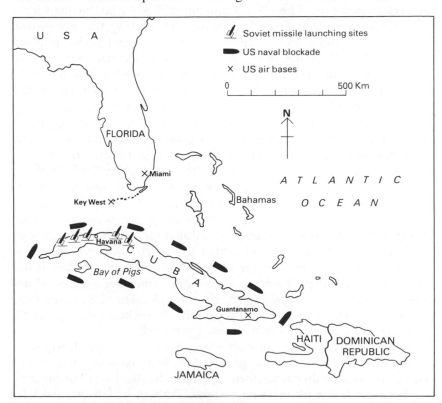

CHERRY PICKER

LAUNCH PAD WITH ERECTOR

LAUNCH PAD WITH ERECTOR

MISSILE READY BLDGS

OXIDIZER VEHICLES

FUELING VEHICLES

the land, set up communist-type co-operative farms and seized some American property. The US government replied by not buying Cuba's main crop, sugar. The serious situation created by this refusal was Khrushchev's opportunity. Seeing a chance to extend Soviet influence to within 150 kilometres of the American coast (see map on page 267), he offered Cuba $100 million in aid and promised to buy her sugar crop. The USA reacted by helping some of Batista's men who wished to overthrow Castro. These Cuban rebels landed in the Bay of Pigs (1961), but few Cubans supported them and most were captured. While Castro angrily seized more US property as a reprisal, Khrushchev feared the Cubans would be overthrown by the Americans.

Soviet missile sites in Cuba – an American photograph

The situation was already tense when in October 1962 President Kennedy announced that there were Soviet missile launching sites in **Cuba**. Strong counter-measures were started. The American fleet was ordered to ring the island and stop any Soviet ships carrying rocket equipment. The Soviet Union was told that the sites must be dismantled and warned that any rocket fired from Cuba would be treated as an attack by the USSR on the USA. Khrushchev at first denied that there were any sites. Later he denounced 'American aggression' and promised that his ships would go through. The US government ordered troops to Florida and prepared 156 rockets for firing at the Soviet Union. Nuclear war threatened mankind.

At this critical stage both sides began to draw back. Khrushchev realised that he had been too provocative. Secretly he ordered his missile ships to slow down. Kennedy appeared to stand firm but privately he began to talk with the Soviet leader. Perhaps he felt that the USA had interfered too much in Cuban affairs. After days of agony for both men the ships turned back and the missile sites were destroyed. Behind the scenes, the Soviet Union and the USA had agreed that Kennedy would not encourage Cuban rebels nor would Khrushchev put rockets on her soil. In private, also, both were deeply affected by the fact that for a few days millions of lives had rested on one word from them. They decided to install a special telephone link between the Kremlin and the White House. Over this '**hot-line**' the two could talk at a moment's notice and possibly avoid an accidental war. Next year (1963) they signed a **Test Ban Treaty** which stopped all Soviet, British and American nuclear tests in the atmosphere. This Treaty helped to limit the spread of such weapons, although neither France nor China would agree to it.

China and Czechoslovakia

The Cuban Crisis showed that the Soviet Union was not yet a match for the USA. One country only continued to despise US power. To China, America was a 'paper tiger' fit only to frighten cowards. Mao Tse-tung, her leader, did not heed Khrushchev's warning that the 'paper tiger has nuclear teeth'. In his view the Soviet leader was a traitor who had tried to alter communist belief. 'Peaceful co-existence' was revisionism because it revised or contradicted Lenin's theories. The true Marxist must ignore such opinions and policies. Throughout the 1950s trouble smouldered between the two Communist giants, aggravated by the personal dislike felt by Mao and Khrushchev for each other. Peking newspapers attacked the Soviet Union repeatedly in an indirect way. Their writers referred to 'revisionists' or 'bourgeois elements' (middle-class people) instead of the Soviet leaders. By 1960 matters were bad enough to come into the open. Soviet aid to China was cut off, Russian experts returned home, and China was left with an immense debt to repay. Finally, in 1963, the two governments exchanged 'letters' which denounced each other's brand of communism.

In fact this was far more than a dispute between Marxists. For hundreds of years Russia and China have confronted each other along a frontier over 9,000 kilometres long, which runs through some of the most desolate terrain in the world. Where exactly the border should be has never been clear. Certainly during the previous 150 years Russian settlers had driven deep into territory claimed by the Chinese. In 1964 Mao stated that the disputed areas amounted to 1,800,000 square kilometres, adding grimly that China 'had not yet presented her account' for it. The Soviet Union has refused to consider such claims and fighting has taken place along the borders for years. Since there are three Chinese for every one Russian and the USSR is twice the size of China it seems likely that China may eventually want more land whether she has any right to it or not. An increasing Chinese population might prove a stronger reason to attack the Soviet Union than all the arguments about Marxism.

Khrushchev's eleven-year record was not good. Too often his promises had remained mere words, too often he had failed. The Hungarian

Revolt, the Cuban Crisis, and the shortage of wheat had shown him to be both reckless and inefficient. In October 1964 he was forced to retire and was replaced by **Leonid Brezhnev** and **Alexei Kosygin**. Although less spectacular, the rule of these two men proved little different from that of the man they had replaced. In 1968 they faced a problem similar to one faced by Khrushchev and they solved it in the same way.

For some time it had been clear that the Czechoslovak régime of **Alexander Dubček** was becoming too liberal for the Russians. In particular, the freedom allowed the Czech press often led to outspoken attacks upon other Communist countries. At first the Soviet leaders merely grumbled. They summoned a meeting of their Warsaw Pact allies – Poland, East Germany, Hungary, Romania and Bulgaria – and issued a 'Warsaw Letter' calling upon Dubček to 'suppress anti-socialist forces' and other Western influences in his country. But when this was ignored, they moved with devastating suddenness. On 20–21 August 1968, 200,000 Soviet and Warsaw Pact troops, aided by 400 planes, invaded Czechoslovakia to 'save' it.

Leonid Brezhnev, photographed in 1977

Russian tanks in the streets of Prague during the Soviet invasion of Czechoslovakia in 1968

Alexander Dubček. He tried, unsuccessfully, to liberalise communist Czechoslovakia

The astonished Czechs put up no military resistance. Here and there bewildered and angry crowds attacked tanks; some rioters were shot dead. But other kinds of protest were widespread. Shouts of 'Your fathers came as liberators – you come as oppressors,' greeted Soviet troops who seemed to have expected a joyous welcome. In the streets of Prague and Bratislava (see map on page 158) wreaths quickly covered the pools of blood left by murdered Czechs. Secret radios broadcasted attacks on the Russians; illegal leaflets, some of them in Russian, appeared on street corners. Walls were daubed with 'Russians go home' and 'Dubček. Freedom'.

Western countries condemned the Soviet invasion but no military action was taken. Czechoslovakia had been part of the communist world for twenty years. Nobody felt like risking a world war to change the situation. Before he was arrested Dubček managed to scribble on a piece of paper, 'Keep firm. The sun will rise again'. In fact, an anti-communist dawn in Eastern Europe seemed unlikely for many years.

SALT and détente

The 'thaw' in East-West relations which was started by Khrushchev led to two important developments, although both happened after his fall. By 1969 the spread of nuclear weapons and new, sophisticated launching systems caused the Soviet Union and the USA to try to limit and balance their war-making powers. A start had been made with the Test Ban Treaty in 1963. Now, **Strategic Arms Limitation Talks (SALT)** began between the two super-powers. These talks were long and complicated because almost each year new weapons systems posed new and different threats. However, both the Soviet Union and the United States showed that whilst they wanted to be equally strong where nuclear weapons were concerned, neither wanted to start a nuclear war.

SALT talks and agreements continued throughout the 1970s. Meanwhile, as Brezhnev gained more control over the Soviet Union he began to look for international acceptance of the Soviet 'spheres of influence' created by the Second World War and the Cold War (see Chapter 22). Long negotiations followed and eventually, in August 1975, a **Final Act** was signed at Helsinki, Finland, between statesmen from the East and West. In return for accepting the existing boundaries in Europe, the Western powers were promised more trade with Eastern (Communist) bloc countries and more concern for basic human rights behind the Iron Curtain. This agreement, which was neither an alliance nor a sign of friendship, led to '**détente**', or a gradual relaxation of the tension between East and West. Critics of such a relaxation of tension saw little to praise in the Final Act. The West, they claimed, had agreed to Stalin's conquests and received nothing in return. They could see little hope of a change in the Communist way of life. Had not Brezhnev said at the time, 'No-one should try to dictate to other people . . . the manner in which they ought to manage their internal affairs'? Those in favour of the Helsinki agreement in the West argued that only war, and possible total destruction, could loosen the Soviet grip on Eastern Europe. They hoped that by agreeing to what could not be changed anyway they might soften the harshness of Communist rule in the Soviet Union.

Russia since détente

How far did *détente* change the life of the Russian people? Brezhnev was a harder master than Khrushchev but much easier than Stalin. He tightened the grip of a police state which allowed neither freedom of speech nor any real political life as it is understood in the West. Those who criticised the Communist system from within the Soviet Union, the so-called **dissidents**, were harassed and persecuted. Famous dissidents well-known in the West, like **Aleksandr Solzhenitsyn**, a writer, **Andrei Sakharov**, the 'father' of the Russian hydrogen bomb, and **Roy Aleksandrovich Medvedev**, an historian, were all ill-treated in one way or another. They were not shot, as they would have been in Stalin's time, but they were sacked from their jobs and, in the case of Solzhenitsyn, forced to go abroad. The most common government reaction to criticism was economic: a professional man who even signed a protest petition about Communist policy would lose his job and might never work again. All the apparatus of the police state – petty restrictions, spying, telephone bugging and labour camps – remained.

Aleksandr Solzhenitsyn, writer and leading Russian dissident

However, the Communist Party did not invent the police state in Russia. The old time rulers of the country, the tsars, were often as fond of such terror as Stalin himself. Ivan the Terrible (1530–84) and Peter the Great (1672–1725) both used a secret police and killed or imprisoned thousands of people who dared to disagree with them. Peter censored all books and journals and made Russians carry passports if they wished to move about in their own country. Like Stalin, he tried to modernise Russia without thought for human life or suffering. In 1785 another powerful Russian ruler, Catherine the Great, forbade anybody to travel abroad without permission. This tradition has been carried on by the Communist Party. Today foreign travel is a privilege, granted only to favoured groups like high Party officials, ballerinas or famous sports personalities. Even the habit of putting a critic of the government in an asylum was used before the Soviet Union existed. Pyotr Chaadayev, a nineteenth-century Russian scientist, was declared to be insane because he described Russia as 'backward'.

The Jews were the only badly treated racial group allowed to leave the Soviet Union in large numbers during the 1970s. The sight of Jews marching through Moscow carrying banners proclaiming 'Let my people go' showed the world that the Soviet Union was still a police state. But it also indicated that Brezhnev was no Stalin. He was just as determined to control Soviet life, but his methods were different. Jews found it difficult to leave the Soviet Union. They were harassed by government officials, sacked from their jobs, confined to their homes, and sometimes put on trial and imprisoned. But they were not executed, and, during the 1970s, nearly 100,000 Jews left the USSR with official permission. *Détente* had made the rulers of the Soviet Union take some notice of public opinion abroad.

'Hunger such as you have never known . . .'

Economically, the Soviet Union under Brezhnev was better off than ever before. The 1971–5 Five Year Plan was the first to set as its target the making of more consumer goods like cars, televisions and refrigerators. But it was inefficient and led to shortages of a kind that Western Europeans experienced only during the Second World War. There was also much shoddy workmanship and old-fashioned design. Russian refrigerators had about a third of the capacity of Western ones. Russian washing machines were rarely automatic. Quality goods of all kinds were in short supply and nearly every Russian had a funny story about the planners. One city built round a new car-making complex had few shops, cinemas or other amenities. The thoughtful idea of supplying the workers with locally made beer was rather spoilt because in the plan the brewery was to be built long after the car factory, not at the same time!

Perhaps one can only judge Russian standards of living in terms of Russian history. Even a dissident realised how life had improved for the ordinary man when he said,

> 'I know people who have lived through the Revolution, the Civil War, the time of Stalin – industrialisation, collectivisation, and the Terror – and then the war. They have lived through hunger such as you have never known . . . Think of it, in one lifetime, to have lost a father under Stalin, then a brother in the war, not ever to have seen your grandparents alive . . .'

It is against this grim background that one should view the USSR's economic progress, although there is no doubt that conditions for the ordinary person would have been far better if successive governments had not concentrated on building an immensely powerful army, navy and air force. The USSR's leaders claimed that this war machine was necessary to make the Soviet Union safe after two fearful wars.

Modern Russian car assembly line

Perhaps some Russian people would agree with them. What is certain is that *détente* has not made much difference to human freedom inside the USSR. In the whole of Russian history there has been only one free election – in November 1917. There is unlikely to be another in the twentieth century.

Timeline

1953   Death of Stalin
1956   Khrushchev denounces Stalin at Twentieth Party Congress. Hungarian Revolt.
1957   'Sputnik' launched.
1959   Fidel Castro leads Cuban revolt against Batista.
1960   USSR ends aid to China.
1961   Yuri Gagarin orbits earth.
1962   USSR and USA quarrel over Cuba (Cuban Crisis).
1963   USSR breaks with China. Test Ban Treaty between USSR and USA.
1964   Khrushchev forced to retire and replaced by Brezhnev and Kosygin.
1968   Soviet invasion of Czechoslovakia.
1969   Strategic Arms Limitation Talks (SALT) begin between USSR and USA.
1975   Final Act of Helsinki talks. Era of *détente*.

Questions

1. How did Stalin carry out his plan to make the USSR a great industrial power, after 1945?

2. 'The fate of Cuba and the maintenance of Soviet prestige [influence] in that part of the world occupied me even when I was busy conducting the affairs of state in Moscow . . . one thought kept hammering away at my brain: what will happen if we lose Cuba?' (Nikita Khrushchev, *Memoirs*, 1970)

   a) What steps had the USSR taken to help maintain Soviet influence in Cuba?
   b) What happened to make Khrushchev fear that the USSR might 'lose Cuba'?
   c) What was the final outcome of the Cuban Crisis of 1962?

3. Describe the development of '*détente*' between the USSR and the Western world. How far do you think it has helped to keep the world at peace?

4. Write short paragraphs on each of the following:
   a) Russo-Chinese relations in the 1950s and '60s
   b) the Twentieth Congress of the Soviet Communist Party
   c) the Hungarian Revolt, 1956
   d) the Czech Crisis, 1968

27

Revolutions Lost and Won
The Far East since 1945

In South East Asia anti-colonial feeling was increased by Japanese conquests during the Second World War (see Chapter 19). Guerrillas who took to the jungles and fought the Japanese Emperor's men later used such tactics against their original European masters. The Indonesians did not want the Dutch back; the Vietnamese did not want the French. Apart from this, their motives for fighting varied. Rebel leaders often thought of themselves as communists or liberals. Their peasant soldiers knew little of such ideas. They fought against the landlord who made them poor, the government which treated them badly. They suffered and died because they loved their land and hated the foreigner.

Japan

Defeated Japan was effectively ruled by the Americans for some years. Under their direction, her war machine was quickly dismantled. Tojo and other military leaders were tried and executed as war criminals and the warlike Shinto (see page 39) was abolished as a state religion. Emperor Hirohito ceased to be treated as a god; instead his position became similar to that of a British monarch. Different political parties were allowed to develop so that democracy could be re-established. Old pre-war textbooks were so biased and nationalistic, particularly in history, that they had to be destroyed. For several years most Japanese teachers and pupils had no printed history books at all.

In many ways US rule was beneficial. For example, a land reform system imposed on the Japanese gave much land to hard-working farmers who modernised and re-equipped agriculture. Efficient food production helped feed a population which had reached 112 million by 1976. Indirectly, Japan's geographical position (see map on page 193) meant that when the Americans went to war in Korea (1950–3) and Vietnam (1961–72) the country became a centre supplying all kinds of war equipment to the US forces. The Korean War (see Chapter 23) gave Japanese industry a flying start from which it benefited enormously. By the mid-1970s Japanese steel production was third in the world, behind that of the two super-powers, the Soviet Union and the USA. The pre-war image of Japan as the home of cheap but shoddy goods was replaced by one of an extremely modern country turning out high quality products.

By 1974 Japan possessed the largest and most modern shipbuilding industry in the world. She produced more commercial vehicles than any other nation, she had developed atomic reactors and a fast and

*Making portable radios.
Workers in a modern
Japanese factory*

very efficient railway system. Besides her textile industries, the
Japanese began to make some of the best cameras, motor-cycles, cars,
televisions, optical equipment and all kinds of precision machinery.
And this 'economic miracle' had been achieved with few raw materials: Japan has no oil and is the world's largest importer of crude oil,
nearly all of it from the Arab countries of the Middle East. However,
the Japanese policy of selling far more than they bought caused anger
amongst her economic rivals. In 1976, for example, the European
countries in the European Economic Community (see Chapter 31)
demanded that the Japanese import more of their goods. They knew
that Japan's success was threatening them in the very areas where they
earned a good part of their living – steel, shipbuilding, cars, electrical
and electronic goods.

The Yom Kippur War between the Arab countries and Israel in
1973 and the Arab policy of increasing the price of crude oil (see
Chapter 24) caused Japanese economic growth to slow for the first
time since 1945. The four-fold increase in oil prices could be paid by
Japan. Furthermore, the Arab countries had no quarrel with the
Japanese. However, Japan's absolute dependence on outside supplies
of oil did hit the economy and there were bankruptcies and unemployment. During the war years there had been a saying in Japan – 'a drop
of oil is worth a drop of blood'. Now there was no question of fighting
to get oil. The Japanese just had to pay more to keep the life-blood of
their economy going.

Meanwhile, not every Japanese is happy with the way their country
has developed. Just as before the war the country became militaristic
(see Chapter 19), now only material things seemed to matter to a government run nearly all the time by businessmen. The great efforts
needed to develop Japanese industry caused pollution in the cities on a
scale known only in parts of the USA. As Japan moved into the 1980s,
there were not only questions about the future of Japanese industry
but protests at the destruction of her traditional culture.

Red power

Since 1949 Red (Communist) China's shadow has lengthened until it extends into territories far from her borders. Although not as yet a super-power like the Soviet Union and the USA, China's sheer size of population and the revolutionary beliefs of her leaders have made her a disturbing force in the world. Everything about China, whether a failure or a success, is big. Everything she does is news. There can be little doubt that her government is among the strongest and most successful in the country's long history. Above all, it appears that China's four 'plagues' – flood, drought, disease and famine – are on the way to being conquered, or at least controlled.

Mao Tse-tung inherited a ruined country (see Chapter 23). In 1949 most roads, railways and bridges were damaged through fighting or neglect. Industrial production was at half its pre-war level. There were shortages of almost every commodity. Prices were high and money so inflated that a small suitcase of bank notes was needed to buy a coat. Such difficulties were as great as those facing Russia in 1917 (see Chapter 13), and they were tackled with a similar ruthless thoroughness. To please the peasants, who had after all given the Communists their victory, large estates were broken up and given to the farmers. All trading companies, heavy industries and banks were nationalised. Prices and wages were fixed. Newspapers and radio stations became government property and were used to explain Communist policy. Those who refused to help, or criticised state actions, were executed

Mass display in Communist Peking

or made, in Mao's words, to 'remould themselves through labour into new people'. Becoming a 'new' person could be a grim experience. Long hours of hard work were followed by equally long periods of political study.

Because Mao wanted to turn China into an industrialised state, he announced in 1952 his first **Five Year Plan**. Country people were persuaded to pool their resources and to share tools and equipment. Their 'collective' farms were run by committees of peasants for the benefit of all. At first these schemes were popular because they produced better crops. Later the Communists experienced difficulties similar to those experienced by the Soviet leaders in the 1920s (see page 113). Farmers love to own their land and usually work harder growing food for themselves and their own families than for the state.

In spite of some peasant discontent this first Plan was a success. Although communications were still poor, industry did increase production and many individuals performed record amounts of work. Encouraged by this, Mao decided on a further speed-up of development. By this time he had quarrelled with the Russians and he gave up Soviet-style 'Plans' in favour of what he called a **Great Leap Forward** (1958). The central idea behind the Great Leap Forward was 'walking on two legs', that is, relying on two things, industrial and scientific activity and the muscles of China's enormous manpower. The countryside was to be reorganised into 26,000 large collective farms called **communes**. Each commune was big enough to be almost self-sufficient, with its own schools, hospitals, roadbuilding squads and even its own small army unit. The Great Leap Forward set very high targets for industry. Everybody worked very hard. Even peasants produced materials like pig-iron in their gardens.

The Great Leap Forward proved too great. The peasant dislike of collectivised farming was as strong as ever. A succession of droughts and floods between 1959 and 1961 reduced food production to its 1956 level and caused near-starvation amongst China's fast-increasing population. The quarrel with the USSR ended all Soviet aid in 1960 (see Chapter 26). Finally, Mao's desire to make China powerful led to enormous expenditure on weapons and armies, and to invasions of Tibet, India and Korea. It also involved large-scale aid to Communist resistance groups, especially in Vietnam.

The Cultural Revolution

By 1966 Mao had decided that the old revolutionary spirit was failing. The Soviet Union, in his opinion, set a bad example. Its communism had ceased to be that preached by Marx and Lenin. Private businesses were allowed to restart; private farms flourished. There was inequality and unfairness in Soviet life once more. Soviet leaders were far more friendly with the capitalist world than in Stalin's day. They talked of 'peaceful co-existence' instead of war (see page 266). Mao himself was seventy-two years old. He seemed anxious that Red China should follow the true communist path after his death. For these reasons he launched his so-called '**Cultural Revolution**'.

Red Guards preparing for a parade during the Cultural Revolution display a picture of Mao on the back of their lorry

Significantly Mao ordered the young to carry out this work. Large numbers of teenagers, called **Red Guards**, marched into Chinese cities and began to demonstrate against anything Western. Men with long hair, or those wearing pointed shoes or narrow trousers, were lectured and sometimes attacked. Even traffic lights annoyed the Guards because red was used to indicate stop! At the same time the young were told to become 'pilgrims of Mao'. Many took this literally and tramped over the route of the Long March (see page 220). Most carried copies of Mao's poems because the thoughts in them were regarded as inspiring. Whilst Mao set a personal example of fitness by swimming 14·5 kilometres down the Yangtze River, his devoted followers proclaimed that nothing was too difficult for those who followed his wise advice.

Whilst foreigners might laugh at the extreme antics of some of the Red Guards, the idea behind the Cultural Revolution was a great one, involving the re-education of a complete nation. There was much of the old Chinese morality as well as the new revolutionary spirit in all this. Mao told his people to live simply, work hard, help the poor and share their possessions. He particularly disliked the idea of experts, however important and necessary, growing apart from the people. In a speech he said,

> From entering primary school to leaving college is altogether six-teen or seventeen years. I fear that for over twenty years people will not see rice, mustard, wheat or millet growing; nor will they see how workers work, or how peasants till the fields.

Here was the voice of the peasant's son who had risen to power by winning the hearts and minds of the country people.

The immediate result of Mao's 'Revolution' was that schools and colleges remained shut for two years whilst teachers and students went to help with farming and industrial projects. At the same time the activities of the Red Guards led to complaints, riots and even deaths. Some politically-minded Chinese doubted whether Mao was really worried about the future of Marxism. They interpreted Red Guard activity either as an attempt to defeat high-ranking political opponents or as an indirect attack on Soviet ideas. Agricultural experts thought that more work and less demonstrating would produce better crops. Industrialists complained that work had often been brought to a stand-still by Red Guard attacks. By the time of Mao's death in September 1976 many Chinese were wanting and waiting to turn China in a new direction.

'Learn from Taching'

Years of confusion were made more confusing to people outside China by lack of news. Few foreign journalists were allowed into the country so they had to rely on second-hand information. Their stories varied a great deal. Western people tended to be both amused and frightened by what they read. Was a great nation going mad, or was it really building a better life? Was Mao a true revolutionary, or was this just another power struggle between cliques wishing to rule after his death? Certainly there was a quarrel between Mao and a leading comrade and general, **Lin Piao**, which ended with Lin's flight and death in an air crash in 1971. It has been claimed since that Lin had plotted to over-throw Mao and had fled in an aeroplane when his plans failed. There was even a suggestion that his plane was shot down by Chinese fighters as it headed for the Russian frontier.

Economically, the turning point for China was its break with the Soviet Union. After 1960 the Chinese began to develop their own in-dustries far more. They also began to trade with non-communist coun-tries: by 1974 eighty per cent of their trade was with such countries, particularly Japan. China now had important heavy industries. In 1973 she was the world's fifth largest producer of steel and the third largest of coal. And perhaps because Mao, the peasant's son, was in charge, there was an emphasis on keeping down the size of towns. The Chinese were told to 'learn from Taching', a new oil-field where wheat fields ran right up to oil-drills. The ideal was, as Prime Minister **Chou En-lai** said in 1962, that 'the city looks like the countryside and the

Lin Piao – he plotted unsuccessfully against Mao

Taching oil-field, China, 1978

Ho Chi Minh

countryside looks like the city'. This was the idea behind the industrial work done in the communes.

Both before and after Mao's death there has been a move towards links with the West, possibly because of China's ever worsening quarrel with the USSR. In 1971 Communist China became a member of the UN. US President Richard Nixon visited China during Mao's lifetime (1972), and in 1978 leading Chinese went on official visits to the United States. Such trips would have been unthinkable in the Cold War days of the 1940s and the 1950s. Since Mao's death some opponents of the Cultural Revolution have come to power. There has been more emphasis on modernisation and trade, and less on keeping the Revolution 'pure'. Some of Mao's ideas have been condemned, although the blame has been laid on the '**Gang of Four**', which included Mao's wife, who were said to have influenced him.

Vietnam: the lost revolution

Before the Japanese attack in 1941 (see page 176) modern Vietnam, plus Cambodia and Laos, was ruled by France and known as French Indo-China (see map on page 172). By the time the French returned to Indo-China after the war, hardly anybody wanted them back. Most people had become used to constant fighting against the Japanese. The North had even gained its independence under the leadership of **Ho Chi Minh**. This man symbolised his people's fight against invaders like the Japanese and colonial rulers like the French. As a youth he had seen the Western world from the bottom as a labourer and dishwasher in a London hotel. Later he had studied communism in Moscow where he met Lenin, Trotsky and Stalin. Back home this frail-looking but very determined man organised guerrilla resistance with the help of a fellow communist, **Vo Nguyen Giap**. Their habit of fighting by night and hiding by day was very successful in a country of rice fields, intricate canal systems, rugged mountains and thick jungle.

One of Mao Tse-tung's generals once said of such 'underground' warfare:

> There are those who cannot imagine how guerrillas could survive for long in the rear of the enemy. But they do not understand the relationship between the people and the army. The people are like water and the army is like fish. How can it be difficult for the fish to survive where there is water?

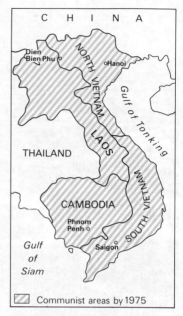

Vietnam, scene of a long and bitter struggle, 1946–75

Since Ho Chi Minh believed in giving the land to the peasants, it was not surprising that the 'water' often welcomed the 'fish' in Vietnam. In 1945 his victorious **Vietminh** fighters had defeated the Japanese in the North and were about to spread southwards. Ho's dream of an independent Vietnam seemed about to come true.

Defeat in Europe in 1940 had made the French military men touchy about their power and influence. They were in no mood to give away France's 'possessions' in the area. At first their government did recognise North Vietnam as a separate territory (see map above). Soon, however, they picked a quarrel with the North and set about its reconquest. Even with lavish American money and equipment, this proved beyond their means. A town captured by day was lost by night unless troops stayed and fortified it. Villages and roads had to be guarded ceaselessly. No French officer could be sure that any Vietnamese was really his friend. Although thousands of concrete defence posts were built to guard vital roads, canals and bridges, a sea of enemies flowed all around the French. It was like trying to sweep back water with a broom. After eight years of slaughter the French longed for a pitched battle. 'If only the enemy would stand and fight', grumbled their officers.

In 1954 French troops retired behind strong defences at **Dien Bien Phu** (see map above) and invited attack. This move was based on two calculations. First, they were confident that once Giap's scattered groups concentrated for battle they would be unable to obtain sufficient food and supplies. Second, they felt certain that the Vietminh had no heavy artillery. Both assumptions were proved wrong. As Giap's men gathered before the fortress, an army of 80,000 peasants trundled bicycles loaded with food, weapons and ammunition through the jungle. Simultaneously other men dragged heavy Chinese guns into position. Day by day, hour by hour, the net closed in on Dien Bien Phu. Battered by artillery fire, attacked by large numbers, it was forced to surrender. The French were driven out of Indo-China for good.

Once again Ho Chi Minh seemed about to unite his country. Once again he was disappointed. At the **Geneva Conference**, where an armistice was signed with the French in July 1954, it was suggested that

French troops at Dien Bien Phu, 1954

North and South Vietnam remain separate until the people could elect a single government for both states. Nobody, including the rulers of North and South Vietnam, really liked this. The USA had just seen all the money she had given to the French wasted. She refused to sign such an agreement. With nothing definite decided, Indo-China remained divided between the North Vietnam of Ho Chi Minh and a South Vietnam ruled by President **Ngo Dinh Diem**.

President Diem did not want to hold free elections because he feared the Vietnamese might vote for a mainly communist opposition party called the **National Liberation Front (NLF)**. He also felt certain that many voters would prefer Ho Chi Minh to himself. His excuse for not holding elections was that Vietcong guerrillas, supporting the NLF, were still operating in the South, although the Geneva settlement had stated they must cease their activities. John Foster Dulles, US Secretary of State, agreed with Diem because he was anxious to limit the spread of communism in Asia. Dulles had just organised some Far Eastern countries, together with the USA, France and Britain, into a **South East Asia Treaty Organisation (SEATO)** for this purpose. Soon American aid was flowing into South Vietnam and American experts were landing to give advice on the new guerrilla war which was growing worse every day.

The 'Last Crusade'

Following these moves Vietnam became a quicksand which sucked the

South Vietnamese villagers being helped on to a US helicopter, 1966

USA into an unwanted war. South Vietnam was always a weak state, threatened from without by North Vietnam and undermined from within by guerrilla forces called the **Vietcong**. President Diem was a Catholic who favoured Christians and so annoyed the large Buddhist population. His government was also dishonest and corrupt. As many ordinary Vietnamese turned to the NLF, the USA gradually became more involved in South Vietnam. 'Military advisers', sent in to give the South Vietnamese army expert help, were followed by troops who were supposed to defend certain large bases containing US equipment (1955). By 1962 the new US President, **John Kennedy**, had committed the USA even more deeply. In that year 10,000 American troops were operating in South Vietnam. In 1963 the prospect of civil war between government and opposition led certain generals to overthrow Diem's régime. During this rebellion President Diem was shot.

The murder of President Kennedy in the United States (see page 295) did not alter US policy towards Vietnam. His successor, **Lyndon Johnson**, reacted strongly when the US fleet patrolling the Gulf of Tonking (see map on page 282) was fired on by North Vietnamese gun-boats in

US marines open fire on the enemy, Vietnam 1968

August 1964. Johnson asked the US Congress for authority to take whatever action he thought necessary in the interests of US security in South East Asia. As a result the US air force began to bomb targets in North Vietnam, whilst US troops were ordered to enter the fighting against the Vietcong. Meanwhile South Vietnam's political system grew weaker with a succession of generals and an air-marshal ruling as dictators. The USA continued to prop up this shaky structure with more and more soldiers. By the beginning of 1968 there were 550,000 US troops fighting an undeclared war between the Vietcong and the United States.

Many people, in the USA and elsewhere, were against American intervention in Vietnam. Not all of them were communists, and in the USA itself a great number were students who did not wish to take part in the war. Such protesters claimed that the NLF was a genuine liberation movement inspired by Ho Chi Minh, not a Communist conquest of the country from outside. They particularly condemned the ferocious and often indiscriminate bombing raids on the North by the US air force. The seeming hopelessness of the US task added to this discontent. To find the Vietcong enemy was 'like trying to identify tears in a bucket of water', in the words of one American soldier. Certainly it was a war for which few of the USA's Second World War-trained generals had any experience. And although the Americans gave South Vietnam new schools, houses, clinics, seeds and fertilisers, many of her people still seemed to prefer the Vietcong. President Johnson denied this. In his opinion the so-called 'support' of the Vietcong was produced by terrorist methods. Meanwhile men and women in many countries rioted and demonstrated to show their fear, anger and pity at what was happening in Vietnam.

By 1967 it was clear that neither side could win an outright victory. **Richard Nixon**, who succeeded Johnson as President of the USA in 1968, decided to strive for outright peace in the Far East. In this he

Richard Nixon, controversial President of the USA

was helped by his leading foreign affairs adviser, **Henry Kissinger**, who travelled the world trying to seek solutions to dangerous problems like the Middle East and Vietnam. During Nixon's Presidency US troops were withdrawn steadily from Vietnam, leaving a large, American-supplied Southern army of Vietnamese to fight the Communists of the North. Long peace negotiations between representatives of the USA, North and South Vietnam, and the Vietcong, took place in Paris. Kissinger was opposed by the North Vietnamese negotiator, **Le Duc Tho**. After years of hard bargaining all parties agreed in January 1973 on what they called an 'ending of the war and restoring of the peace in Vietnam'. The Paris settlement suggested that one day Vietnam must become one country but that in the meantime an international commission was to see that the ceasefire was kept by both sides. Nobody took sufficient account of the presence of North Vietnamese troops in the South, although even Kissinger estimated that there were at least 145,000 – a very sizeable army.

The war in Cambodia – a wounded soldier is helped from a helicopter by a nurse

The US government admitted that 45,933 American soldiers had been killed in Vietnam since the USA first intervened in February 1955. President Nixon announced in a broadcast to the nation that 'the day we have all worked and prayed for' had come. He complained that the war had led to 'criticism from a small and vocal minority' – a strange way to describe international protests and fierce rioting all over the United States. One journalist called America's involvement in Vietnam 'the Last Crusade'. Its defeat was the worst military setback in US history since Pearl Harbour.

Proof that it was a defeat and not a peace settlement came quite quickly. Fighting between North and South Vietnam never stopped and, whilst the Communists in the North continued to receive supplies of Soviet weapons, ammunition and equipment, the US Congress gradually cut supplies to the South. The disgrace and resignation of President Nixon over the Watergate scandal (see Chapter 28) led to the election of a Congress whose members had little interest in South Vietnam. In January 1975 the North Vietnamese army launched a well-prepared offensive. For the first time the US air force was not ordered to retaliate with massive bombing. The Communists used this as a signal for an all-out invasion of the South which brought their troops to **Saigon**, the Southern capital, by April. Ho Chi Minh's dream of one Vietnam was a reality.

The Paris peace settlement of 1973 had also stated that Vietnam's neighbours, **Laos** and **Cambodia** (see map on page 282), should remain neutral and untouched. This however seemed unlikely. By May 1975 the Communists in Laos, the **Pathet Lao**, had taken over most of the country. Meanwhile, a particularly brutal Communist movement called the **Khmer Rouge** took over Cambodia. When the capital city, **Phnom Penh**, was taken (April 1975), the entire population of about two million inhabitants was driven out into the countryside. It was estimated that about half these people were formed into labour corps and moved about the country to work on various agricultural projects. The idea seemed to be to re-populate the towns eventually with reliable Communist Party members. But by now Vietnam had the best equipped and most experienced army in South East Asia. In early 1979 it was announced that 'rebels' helped by the Vietnamese army had invaded Cambodia. The Khmer Rouge régime was overthrown. China complained bitterly about this invasion, calling the new government 'puppets' of both the Soviet Union and Vietnam.

The rulers of Vietnam disliked the Khmer Rouge because it looked to China, not the Soviet Union, for inspiration and help. China replied with a short but massive invasion of Vietnam in 1979. The idea, said the Chinese, was to 'punish' the Vietnamese for their takeover of Cambodia. More significantly, it was probably a warning to the Soviet Union not to 'interfere' so openly in South East Asian affairs. Clearly the whole area had become the scene of a power struggle between the USSR and China.

Timeline

1952   First Chinese Five Year Plan.
1954   French defeated at Dien Bien Phu. Geneva Conference. SEATO formed.
1955   Beginning of US involvement in Vietnam.
1958   Great Leap Forward. Chinese Communes organised.
1959–61 Failure of Great Leap Forward.
1966   Mao's Cultural Revolution.
1968   Beginning of US withdrawal from Vietnam.
1971   Communist China admitted to UN.
1972   President Nixon visits China.
1973   Ceasefire agreement to end war in Vietnam.
1975   South Vietnam overrun by North. Saigon falls. Laos and Cambodia taken over by Communists.
1976   Death of Mao Tse-tung.
1979   Vietnamese invasion of Cambodia.

Questions

1. 'By 1966 Mao had decided that the old revolutionary spirit was failing.'
   a) What steps did Mao take to revive the 'old revolutionary spirit'?
   b) What results, good and bad, came from these steps?

2. 'The Japanese amazed the world by their adaptability.' What factors helped the post-war Japanese 'economic miracle'?

3. a) Why was the US government worried about what happened to Vietnam? Describe the stages by which the USA became involved in the war.
   b) Why did the USA suffer 'the worst military setback in US history since Pearl Harbour' in Vietnam?

4. Write short paragraphs on each of the following:
   a) The Great Leap Forward, 1958   b) Dien Bien Phu
   c) Ho Chi Minh   d) Henry Kissinger

28
The Search for Justice
USA since 1945

The USA suffered less than most nations which fought in the Second
World War. Although she lost three times as many men as in the First
World War, her death-roll was small beside that of Germany, the
Soviet Union and Japan. There had been no invasion of her shores, no
bombing, epidemics or famine. Since she supplied much of the equipment and arms for the Allies, her industrial output had doubled in six
years. Mass-production techniques developed during the war made
goods so fast that by 1945 an American worker could produce three
times as much per hour as his British counterpart.

In spite of some poor areas, the USA was the world's richest country. Her people comprised six per cent of the earth's population yet
they received forty per cent of its income and owned fifty per cent of
its industries. And this affluence continued, particularly in agriculture
where it was helped by better farming methods, improved weedkiller
and chemicals. The US farmer, who on average had grown food for
ten people in 1940, was growing food for twenty-five in 1960. At that
time American industrial workers owned half the world's telephones,
radios and televisions. Their standard of living was far higher than that
of workers in similar industrialised nations in the West. The USA in
many ways had become the 'promised land' which the Pilgrim Fathers
had set sail for in 1620.

Although 'big business' grew bigger still as firms amalgamated
(joined together), its leaders were never as free as they had been in
the 1920s. Roosevelt's New Deal (see Chapter 14) had established controls which were not removed by later administrations. Oil production,
for example, was regulated by the government from 1935. Military
aeroplanes were made by private companies but these manufacturers
had to accept a lot of federal government control. Rivalry between
corporations was stopped or limited if it looked like leading to ruinous
competition. Most firms preferred to amalgamate rather than to fight
each other. Slowly but surely, the USA moved into the era of the
multi-national corporations – international companies with trading interests all over the world.

Such 'bigness' was copied by American trade unions. The two
largest, **The Congress of Industrial Organisations (CIO)**, and the **American Federation of Labour (AFE)** united into a single union claiming to
represent seventeen million workers. American trade union leaders,
unlike European leaders, tended to agree to stay out of politics in
return for high pay and good working conditions. In the USA there is
no political party which represents, or is financed by, the trade unions,
as the Labour Party is in Britain. Consequently, there was an emphasis

The wealthiest country in the world, Manhattan Island, New York

on direct action to get better pay and hours as well as welfare and pension schemes. US governments, for their part, have tended to take a strong line against militant union action. In the past strikes sometimes led to riots in which workers were killed by armed police. In 1946 a threat that steel workers might go on strike caused President Truman to announce that all strikers would be called-up into the army!

Such 'strike-breaking' was condemned by many US politicians. Nevertheless, the **Taft-Hartley Act, 1947**, made 'closed shops' illegal. In other words, workers did not need to belong to a particular union to get a job. This Act made unions liable to pay damages if they broke contracts with their employers, forbade payments of their funds to political parties and would not allow Communists to hold responsible positions within union organisations.

McCarthy's 'witch hunt'

Fear of communism is very strong in the USA and was especially so during the ten years following the Second World War. It was bad enough to see victory turned into a grim Cold War with the Soviet Union (see Chapter 22) and a hot war with China in Korea (see Chapter 23). On top of this it was disheartening for Americans to realise that communism was triumphant in China and that only one kind of European dictatorship had been defeated in 1945. Worse still were disturbing signs of communist activity nearer home. A British atom scientist, Klaus Fuchs, was imprisoned for giving nuclear secrets to the Soviet Union. In Canada the police uncovered a large Soviet spy ring. In the USA itself a State Department official was found to have once been a Communist, and a man and wife team, Julius and Ethel Rosenberg, were executed for spying. To some Americans it seemed that the government was riddled with spies. When the USSR exploded her first atomic bomb, in September 1949, they felt certain that Soviet scientific progress was the result of information sent by spies and traitors in America.

In such circumstances it was not difficult for some Americans to imagine that there was a Red conspiracy to undermine the country. So when **Senator Joseph McCarthy** from Wisconsin told the American people there was such a plot the nationwide uproar which followed caused Congress to allow him to 'investigate'. McCarthy, who became Chairman of the Senate Permanent Subcommittee on Investigation, was thoroughly dishonest. Whilst he posed as a patriotic American he was in fact hoping to make sure that he would be re-elected Senator for his State through his activities. McCarthy began his investigation with a phone call to a friend. This friend told him that there had been two genuine investigations of people who worked for the government. Both had suggested that a certain number of government employees might be unsuitable for their jobs. McCarthy immediately asserted that 205 in one report and 57 in the other – later called the 'Heinz Varieties figure' – were Communist. In fact, when he began his 'witch hunt' McCarthy had not got a single name.

Joseph McCarthy. He claimed there was a 'Red conspiracy' in the USA

McCarthy's first appearance before the Senate was memorable. It was clear that he knew very little about the so-called Communists on his list. He even described one as 'a high type of man . . . who opposed communism'. As one Senator remarked, 'Could anything but sheer lunacy lead a man discussing communists to say that one of the communists was an important example because he was not a communist?' But if the Senate was not fooled, large numbers of Americans were. Just as seventeenth-century people had been ready to suspect any old lady with a cat of being a witch, so McCarthy found people ready to see every civil servant, university lecturer or even film star as a possible traitor. During the next few years innocent men and women were accused of being Communists without any evidence and bullied until their reputations were in shreds. The Committee meetings became tragic farces, with McCarthy waving sheets of blank paper supposed to contain the names of dozens of Communists. These papers were never shown to anybody.

Eventually McCarthy made the mistake of attacking the US forces. Most Americans were proud of the army, navy and air force which had helped defeat Germany and Japan. They might believe that a certain civil servant was a Communist but when the Senator denounced General George Marshall, one of the most popular and respected soldiers in the USA, they began to have doubts. Soon afterwards, television cameras were allowed to record McCarthy in action. For the first time large audiences saw this evil man shouting and bullying witnesses. Some Americans realised that they had been deceived. McCarthy was censured by the Senate in 1954 and so lost much of his influence and power. Not one of the hundreds of 'subversives' accused by McCarthy was ever found guilty.

Truman and Eisenhower

When Roosevelt died in 1945 he was succeeded by his Vice-President, **Harry S. Truman** of Missouri. Truman won the next presidential election in 1948 and continued in power until 1952. Roosevelt's death was the end of an age. He had remained in office longer than any other US President. He had created the New Deal and fought the Second World War almost to the end. His achievements made Truman feel very ordinary. On the morning after he became President, Truman confided to a friend, 'Did you ever have a bull or a load of hay fall on you? If you ever did, you know how I felt last night'. The problems he inherited were enormous. American soldiers were fighting in many parts of the world. Japan was far from beaten. His first major decision was probably the most awful in history – whether to drop the atomic bomb on Japan or not. His order to destroy Hiroshima and Nagasaki (see Chapter 21) will probably be argued about for centuries. In the later years of his presidency Truman faced the problems of the Berlin Blockade (see Chapter 22) and the Korean War (see Chapter 23).

Truman was a 'New Dealer' who had supported Roosevelt. As President, he followed his old chief's example, launching a new **Fair Deal** policy promising better pensions and a higher standard of living. But the US political system often allows the opposition party to have a majority of members in Congress. This happened in Truman's time and he found many of his schemes blocked by a Republican-controlled Senate and House of Representatives. Truman was particularly frustrated when his **Civil Rights Bill** was rejected. The blacks of the USA were not always treated as equals by white Americans. This was especially true in the South where their ancestors had once been slaves. In particular, it was difficult for them to exercise their voting rights. Truman's Civil Rights Bill would have allowed all adult Southern blacks to vote. Truman's only success in the difficult matter of black and white relations was to end segregation (separation) in the US armed forces. But in the South, black and white children continued to go to different schools and many hotels, restaurants and buses barred blacks.

As the 1952 Presidential Election drew near the Republican Party looked for a new candidate. No Republican had been President since 1933. Saddled with the blame for the Depression (see Chapter 14), their men had been defeated at successive elections. Hopefully, they decided to choose probably the most popular man in the USA, **General Dwight D. Eisenhower** of Kansas. Eisenhower was a long-serving soldier who had won fame in the war as the commander of the Allied invasions of North Africa and France. Afterwards he had directed the NATO forces in Europe. No American was more liked by his troops, or more tactful in dealing with his allies. Appropriately, the Republicans chose for their campaign slogan, 'I like Ike'. And enough people liked Eisenhower to give him the Presidency.

President Dwight D. Eisenhower, 1952

Eisenhower had no political experience at all. It is doubtful whether he had ever bothered to vote in an election. Even as a soldier he was used to leaving detailed planning to his senior officers. Only the grand strategy was his concern. As President he allowed Secretary of State Sherman Adams to control most aspects of home affairs. Similarly, on foreign policy he let John Foster Dulles virtually run US relations with the rest of the world. Dulles was a 'Cold War warrior' who regarded communism as a moral evil and tried to restrict or destroy its influence.

Eisenhower disliked too much federal government power. He preferred to let state governments or private enterprise run things. Consequently 'big business' was freed from some of its shackles. Its influence also increased: Eisenhower's first Cabinet consisted of eight millionaires and an ex-plumber! The days of ambitious, federal-controlled projects like the Tennessee Valley Authority (see page 126) were over. Atomic energy plants and a dam on Snake River, Idaho, built for the government, were handed over to private companies.

On one important matter Eisenhower found himself following Truman's example. He, too, disliked discrimination against blacks. 'There must be no second-class citizens', he proclaimed – and appointed the liberal-minded **Earl Warren** as Chief Justice of the Supreme Court. In the USA any arguments about the exact meaning of the Constitution (the written rules and laws of the country) are settled by the Supreme Court. Under Warren, the Court decided that separate black and white schools were illegal. It ordered them to reorganise as schools for both white and black children. This mixing is called desegregation. Some Southern states defied this ruling. Others shut down all their official schools and opened private ones which were still segregated.

President Eisenhower was in two minds. Although against discrimination he was conservative enough to feel that Warren was going too fast. Privately, he called his appointment of Warren 'the biggest damfool mistake I ever made'. But as a soldier he believed in orders being obeyed. The crisis came in September 1957 when 9 black pupils were due to be enrolled with 2,000 whites at **Little Rock Central High School, Arkansas**. Governor Faubus of Arkansas called out the local National Guardsmen (part-time soldiers) to stop the black children entering the school because he said it would lead to riots and disorder. His opponents claimed that the only mob violence was caused by white supporters of the Governor. Eisenhower sent in troops of the 101st Airborne Division to escort the blacks into the school. The pupils were enrolled, guarded by soldiers with rifles and bayonets. Southern whites were outraged. 'Eisenhower has lit the fires of hate', raged one Southern politician. Governor Faubus became a hero to the whites and was re-elected continually until he chose to retire in 1967.

Whilst such ugly incidents kept the 'Colour Problem' in the news, a black Baptist minister, the **Reverend Martin Luther King,** organised a **Civil Rights Movement** which used peaceful methods to combat racism. First in Montgomery, Alabama (1955), and then in other towns his supporters began sit-ins in stores and restaurants reserved for 'whites only'. At the same time they refused to travel on streetcars which had

Martin Luther King, campaigner for black rights in the USA

LITTLE ROCK CENTR

Black children being escorted into a 'whites only' school in Little Rock, 1957

special sections for blacks. This almost bankrupted the bus companies because most of their passengers were black! King also drew attention to the black cause by staging long marches through the South. Some of his supporters were attacked. There were even a few who were murdered. King did not give up and his slogan 'We shall overcome' gave hope to millions of blacks in the USA.

Meanwhile Eisenhower managed to get a Civil Rights Law passed by Congress (1957) which declared that obstacles put in the way of black people voting were illegal.

Kennedy and Johnson

In 1960, with Eisenhower due to retire from the Presidency, a majority of Americans still 'liked Ike'. But they did not necessarily like his Republican Party. For the election the Republicans chose Richard Nixon, a clever lawyer who had made his name in the days of McCarthy and had been Eisenhower's Vice-President. The Democrats chose **John F. Kennedy** who came of a rich Boston Irish family. The Kennedys had always been interested in politics. Kennedy's father, for example, had been US ambassador to Britain. Kennedy himself had become a war hero by saving the lives of some of his crew after their motor torpedo boat had been sliced in two by a Japanese cruiser. Nixon had also served in the US navy during the war.

Kennedy's speedy rise to presidential candidate was due to his influential family, his impressive personality and his unusual cleverness at politics. Even so, the battle with Nixon was a closely fought one. By the narrowest of margins Kennedy became America's youngest and first Roman Catholic President. He began by electrifying the nation. At the Inaugural Ceremony he proclaimed, 'Let the word go forth from this time and place, to friend and foe alike, that the torch has been passed to a new generation of Americans, born in this century, tempered by war, disciplined by a hard and bitter peace, proud of their ancient heritage'.

Like Roosevelt, the new President started with a Hundred Days of intense activity. Despite her richness, Kennedy knew that the USA was not using her full industrial potential. She was neglecting her natural resources, allowing the Soviet Union to train twice as many scientists and technologists each year, treating blacks as second-class citizens and letting poor children go hungry whilst surplus food rotted. He called his remedies for all this the '**New Frontier**' policy because he saw these problems as challenges to be overcome, just as the pioneers had beaten the old frontier with plough, axe and rifle.

President John F. Kennedy

The Kennedy programme sounded good. It suggested more foreign aid for poor countries, more houses, schools and free medical care at home. Kennedy himself warned Americans that they could not expect to remain the world's leading nation if they did not work harder and care more about the poverty and misery spread over half the globe. Yet there were contradictions in the policies worked out by the clever men Kennedy brought into government from business organisations and the universities. The new President promised to win the 'race in space'. This committed the USA to put a man on the moon before 1970, a purely prestige aim which was to cost enormous sums of money before it was achieved in July 1969. He began to send more 'advisers' to fight the Communists in Vietnam – a policy which was to lead to disaster and defeat after his death (see Chapter 27).

Quite early in his presidency Kennedy committed a dreadful blunder when he allowed the US **Central Intelligence Agency (CIA)** to organise an invasion of Cuba (see page 268). A mixed force of Cubans and a few Americans was to be landed in the Bay of Pigs (Cuba) where they would be joined by thousands who hated the rule of Fidel Castro. The landing was a disastrous failure. Castro knew of it in advance and the force was wiped out with no sign of the 'thousands' who were supposed to want to join the invading troops. Afterwards Kennedy remarked, 'All my life I've known better than to depend on experts. How could I have been so stupid as to let them go ahead?'

At home Kennedy never had enough time to do much. His suggestion of more free medical service, called Medicare, and his Civil Rights Bill were rejected by a Democratic Congress which distrusted the clever young man from Boston. Abroad, he made a much more lasting impression. The Cuban Missile Crisis, in particular, showed that he had the nerve and courage of a Churchill (see Chapter 26). Perhaps a clearer victory in the forthcoming 1964 Presidential Election might have allowed him to influence US development more permanently.

Lyndon B. Johnson, President after Kennedy's murder in 1962

'Buzz' Aldrin, 'man on the moon', 21 July 1969

With this in mind he was touring Texas to gain support when he drove into **Dallas** on the morning of 22 November 1963. He intended to deliver a speech which contained the words 'peace on earth, goodwill toward men'. The words were never spoken because he was murdered as he sat in his car, waving to the crowds.

Why Kennedy was assassinated is still not clear. A Communist, **Lee Harvey Oswald**, was arrested almost instantly. Unfortunately, Oswald himself was murdered a few days later and the matter never came to trial. Since that time there have been many suggested solutions to the mystery. Was Kennedy murdered by a racialist who disliked his Civil Rights policies? Was he murdered by someone mixed up in the Bay of Pigs disaster? Recently it has been suggested that more than one rifleman fired at him and that his assassins were in the pay of the Mafia, a criminal organisation. Certainly John F. Kennedy and his brother, Robert, had started a determined campaign against organised crime. And Robert was murdered in 1968, apparently by an Arab who disliked America's support of Israel. We shall probably never know the truth. Kennedy was the fourth US President to be murdered and the reasons for his death remain the most mysterious.

On the plane which flew back to Washington from Dallas, Vice-President **Lyndon B. Johnson** was sworn-in as the new President. No

greater contrast with Kennedy could be imagined. Kennedy was cultured, well-read and fond of intellectual company. Johnson was a blunt Texan who lived on a luxurious ranch and was little-known in the North. Kennedy had little experience as a Congressman. Johnson was famous for his skill at organising Congressional business. Kennedy knew a great deal about the outside world. Johnson knew very little. As one journalist remarked, 'The world and Lyndon B. Johnson were strangers on 23 November 1963'. Kennedy had talked of the 'torch' being handed on to the young. Now it seemed to have been given back to the old.

In fact, things were not as they seemed. Johnson showed just as much care for the poor as Kennedy, possibly because when young he had taught poverty-stricken Mexican children. His aim at what he called the **Great Society** was similar to Kennedy's, that is, better schooling, more housing and equal rights for blacks. Unlike Kennedy, however, his political skill allowed him to get more done. For example, he got Congress to pass a new Civil Rights Law. Nevertheless, after a smashing electoral victory over an unpopular Republican candidate, Barry Goldwater, in 1964, Johnson himself became unpopular with sections of the people. It was not just Northern intellectuals who delighted in making fun of him. The gradual involvement of the USA in the Vietnam War (see Chapter 27) divided the nation as it had not been split since the American Civil War (1861–5).

Many Americans, particularly students, believed the Vietnam War to be wrong and they blamed Johnson for sending US troops to fight in it. They condemned the heavy bombing raids being carried out by the US air force in Vietnam, saying the USA was waging an aggressive war. There were riots all over the USA. Men fled abroad or went to prison rather than be called-up for service in Vietnam. Johnson knew the cost of the war was rising all the time. He saw his 'Great Society' schemes threatened and did in fact push some of them through Congress before the true cost of the war was known. He felt that people were unfair to him. 'What do they want? . . .', he remarked once, 'I'm giving them boom times and more legislation [laws] than anybody else did and what do they do – attack and sneer!' But one of his favourite remarks was 'Don't they know there's a war on?' The trouble was that the American people did know there was a war on and, as the death-roll amongst US troops rose higher every day, Johnson became more unpopular.

The Protest People

The movement against the Vietnam War was only part of President Johnson's troubles. Economically, of course, he was right. The USA was going through 'boom' times with living standards rising dramatically. An opinion poll in the year Kennedy was murdered (1963) reported that over sixty per cent of Americans thought they were 'middle-class'. In the same year US corporations invested $80 billion in foreign countries, compared with $12 billion in 1945. But amongst the increased numbers of young people in America there was growing alarm at the

Anti-Vietnam War demonstration outside Capitol building, Washington, 1972

power of the US multi-national companies and the sophistication of US technology. They felt that as individuals they were in danger of being swamped; one protest group, for example, disliked computers. At a demonstration once, each marcher carried posters reading 'I am a Human Being. Do not Fold, Spindle or Mutilate'.

An extreme minority decided that they wanted nothing to do with the advanced technology of their country. These were the so-called 'hippies' who 'dropped out' of society, living in communes which tried to be self-sufficient by growing their own food and making their own clothes. Apart from such extremists, there were millions of American youngsters who behaved and dressed in a way which horrified their elders. The most sensational events connected with this revolt against established standards were probably the 'rock' festivals, held in fields instead of halls. In August 1969, for example, some rock music promoters decided to hold such a festival near the town of Woodstock in New York State. The festival was never held at Woodstock but the name stuck, especially after 400,000 people turned up instead of the expected 50,000! In spite of the rain, the audience thoroughly enjoyed listening to the music of their idols: singers like Joan Baez and Jimi Hendrix and groups such as Jefferson Airplane and the Family Stone.

The rock music which blared across the wet fields that day was often a 'protest song' about the Vietnam War or the conditions of blacks in

the USA. The problem of the blacks had now ceased to be exclusively a Southern one. Until 1940 some seventy-five per cent of blacks had lived in the South. But by the sixties there were large black communities in Northern cities like Baltimore, Detroit and Cleveland. These areas generated a violent type of 'Black Power' protest which rejected the peaceful ways of Martin Luther King. In the South blacks wanted the right to vote, to travel on buses and to eat in 'white' restaurants. In the North blacks already had such elementary rights. What annoyed them was what one black Congressman called the 'gut issue of who gets the money'. In other words, were blacks to get equal opportunities with whites for good, well-paid jobs?

From 1964 onwards blacks took to the streets and fought with the police. These riots led to many deaths and millions of dollars worth of damage. And, whereas King had dreamed of brotherly love between the races, one of the new Black Power leaders said, 'I don't care whether or not white people hate me. It's not essential that a man love you to live. But "the man" has to respect you.'

Another group who were beginning to demand equal pay and opportunities were women. Automation in factories and on farms

Scene after a race riot in Los Angeles, 1965

meant that physical strength was no longer so important in jobs. Women began to work in factories, to become lorry drivers and telephone engineers. By the late 1960s over twenty-three million US women had full-time jobs. And, beside this challenge to the male-dominated job market, came greater sexual freedom because of the contraceptive pill and easier access to abortion.

In the middle of all this protest Martin Luther King was murdered (1968), and a disgusted Lyndon Johnson decided not to stand for President again.

Nixon and Watergate

The 1968 Presidential Election was won by **Richard Nixon**, the man who had lost so narrowly to Kennedy in 1960. His victory meant that the Republicans were back in power. In his Inaugural Speech Nixon promised to 'bring the boys home' from Vietnam. 'We find ourselves rich in goods, but ragged in spirit', he said. 'The greatest honor history can bestow is the title of peacemaker'. By 1972 Nixon had kept his first promise. The USA brought her troops out of Vietnam (see Chapter 27). At the same time Nixon's Presidency brought a new style of diplomacy and a very new policy.

Nixon's Secretary of State, **Henry Kissinger**, travelled the world so often, trying to settle international disputes, that his style of diplomacy was called 'air shuttle'. It was Kissinger who negotiated the end of the American involvement in Vietnam. It was Kissinger and Nixon who visited the Soviet Union to try to establish more friendly relations between the two super-powers. And, most surprising of all, it was

President Nixon is shown the Great Wall of China

Kissinger who slipped into China in 1972 and arranged for President Nixon to visit Mao Tse-tung. The two arch-enemies of old were said to have talked of 'friendship' between the Chinese and American peoples. This was a long way from the days of the Cold War when American and Chinese troops had fought a bitter war in Korea (see page 224). Nixon's visit was denounced by the Soviet Union who claimed that China was entering into a 'dangerous plot with the ruling circles of the USA'. Soon afterwards the US government lifted the ban on trade with China which had existed since the Communist Revolution in 1949 (see Chapter 23).

Nixon regarded his peace-making in Vietnam and China as a great achievement. Perhaps he was right. But the 'ghost' of Vietnam still walked the United States and it led to disaster for Nixon and to one of the worst scandals in America's political history. It all began when an American newspaper, the *New York Times*, started to publish information about America's involvement in the Vietnam War, dating back to the days of Truman. Thousands of pages of 'secrets' appeared day by day and they became known as the 'Pentagon Papers', named after the headquarters of the US Armed Services in Washington.

The President became alarmed at such 'leaks' because they could only have been obtained from somebody working inside government. He gave orders for the telephones of suspects to be tapped and allowed break-ins at the apartments of people thought to be causing riots and disorder. His Special Investigation Unit became known as the 'plumbers' because of their attempts to close such leaks! Actually, it was soon discovered that the information had been stolen by an official named Daniel Ellsberg. He did not behave in a particularly secret way and went on television to state bluntly, 'There has never been a year when there would have been a war in Indochina [Vietnam] without American money'.

Nixon became obsessed with thoughts of traitors inside the government. Gradually the activities of his 'plumbers' grew more extensive and more illegal until they involved many high officials of his administration. As the 1972 Presidential Election drew near a Citizens' Committee for the Re-election of the President – known as CREEP – drew up plans to burgle the Democratic National Committee's headquarters in the **Watergate Hotel**, Washington. The idea was to find out exactly what the Democrats were planning for the election. In June 1972 men in the pay of the Republican Party did manage to get into these offices but they were discovered and arrested. Newspapers carried headlines like 'Five Charged With Burglary at Democratic Headquarters'. It seemed a fairly minor affair involving a few criminals. Actually, nearly every high official, including President Nixon himself, would soon be caught up in what became known as the 'cover-up'.

The fall of the President

Nixon won the election, almost certainly without any need for CREEP and its plumbers. But then, gradually, the truth came out. Nixon watched as, one by one, the most powerful members of his White

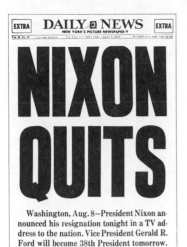

EXTRA DAILY NEWS **EXTRA**
NEW YORK'S PICTURE NEWSPAPER ®

NIXON QUITS

Washington, Aug. 8—President Nixon announced his resignation tonight in a TV address to the nation. Vice President Gerald R. Ford will become 38th President tomorrow.

Nixon is forced to resign because of the Watergate Scandal, 1974

President Jimmy Carter. He promised to 'clean up' US government

House staff were accused, convicted and sent to prison on charges connected with Watergate. During 1973 Nixon frequently assured the American people that he would co-operate fully with everybody investigating the affair. He behaved as though he was innocent. In fact, Nixon did not co-operate. In particular, he was reluctant to hand over tape recordings made with his own staff when he discussed Watergate. These would not have existed but for the President's mania for 'bugging' rooms and telephones. In October 1973 Nixon handed over seven tapes to a Washington District Court but said that he would not hand over any more. At the beginning of 1974 he told the nation, 'One year of Watergate is enough'.

But one year was not enough. In February 1974 John Mitchell, Nixon's chief law official, was brought to trial on charges of conspiracy, perjury and obstruction of the course of justice. By July the now discredited President released transcripts of the tapes running to 1,308 pages. They were put on sale to the public and became a best-seller. These tapes showed that Nixon knew all about the original break-in and the cover-up which followed. For example, the President said he did not know of any cover-up until 21 March 1973. The tapes revealed that he had discussed trying to stop the facts becoming public as early as 28 February. By this time the House of Representatives, acting in its role as a court, began to look into the possible trial of the President, known as impeachment. Only one US President had ever been impeached – Andrew Johnson in 1868 – and he had been found not guilty.

On 5 August 1974 President Nixon admitted that he had not been telling the truth about Watergate. He added that he did not think that his record justified 'the extreme step of impeachment and removal of a President'. Not many Americans agreed with him and, three days later, he resigned – the first US President ever to do so. A month later his successor, the Vice-President, **Gerald Ford**, decided to pardon Nixon for his offences. There was a storm of protest and this action probably helped Ford to lose the Presidential Election of 1976 to an almost unknown candidate, the Democrat, **Jimmy Carter**. Carter, an ex-navy officer and peanut farmer from Georgia, promised to clean up government.

Jimmy Carter's honesty did a great deal to wipe away the memory of Nixon and Watergate. But, being an 'outsider' from Georgia, he had none of the control of Congress for which Lyndon Johnson was famous. Indeed, Carter proved as unsuccessful as John Kennedy in getting bills passed by the Senate and the House of Representatives. This was shown by his relative failure to persuade the American people to save fuel. He spoke often of the energy crisis and often suggested fuel-saving measures. But the USA continued to use forty per cent of all the world's energy resources. The clear danger to overseas oil supplies posed by OPEC, the Iranian Revolution in 1979 and the Soviet invasion of Afghanistan in 1979–80 (see Chapter 31) may change American attitudes in the future. Meanwhile, Carter's greatest success remains the Middle East peace between Israel and Egypt, which was helped by Carter's promise of aid (see Chapter 24).

Timeline

1945	Truman decides to drop atomic bomb.
1947	Taft-Hartley Act.
1950–4	McCarthy 'witch hunt'.
1952	Eisenhower elected President.
1955	Martin Luther King leads movement to combat racism by peaceful methods.
1957	Trouble at Little Rock.
1960	Kennedy elected President. 'New Frontier' policy.
1963	Assassination of President Kennedy.
1964	Black Power protests in many US cities.
1965	Protests against US involvement in Vietnam. Civil Rights Law passed.
1968	Assassination of Martin Luther King.
1968–72	President Nixon gradually reduces American commitment in Vietnam.
1973–4	Watergate scandal. Nixon resigns.
1976	Jimmy Carter elected President.

Questions

1. 'The Committee meetings became tragic farces, with McCarthy waving sheets of blank paper supposed to contain the names of dozens of Communists.'

   a) How far did American attitudes to communism help Joseph McCarthy in his rise to power?
   b) What particular case convinced many Americans that the 'government was riddled with spies'?
   c) What were the main reasons for McCarthy's downfall?

2. Assess the successes and failures of President John Kennedy's Presidency, 1960–3.

3. 'The greatest honour history can bestow is the title of peacemaker' (Richard Nixon, 1969)

   In what ways did President Nixon try to achieve this great honour? How far was he successful?

4. Write short paragraphs on each of the following:
   a) Martin Luther King and the Civil Rights Movement
   b) the Watergate Scandal
   c) President Eisenhower
   d) Lyndon B. Johnson

29
Democracy and Dictatorship
Latin America

The continent of North America, first colonised by the British and French, from Canada to the Mexican border, is now industrialised and comparatively rich. The continent of South America, because it was settled by the Spanish and Portuguese whose languages were derived from Latin, has become known as Latin America. It has split up into twenty-two states, the majority of whose people are very poor. Some states are quite small, like Panama and El Salvador. Others, like Brazil, Argentina and Chile, are very large (see map on page 305). Brazil, for example, is the size of the whole of Europe apart from Russia. North America was colonised mainly by Anglo-Saxon people who were opposed by relatively few Red Indian tribes. The Spanish conquerors, however, found well-organised Indian empires like those of the Aztecs in Mexico and the Incas in Peru. Later, the Spanish settlers brought black slaves to some areas and to the Caribbean islands. Therefore today in Latin America there is a racial mix, with Indians, blacks and white descendants of the original Spanish and Portuguese settlers.

The British settlers in North America largely governed themselves from the start. Once they were free of British control altogether (1783), many Americans moved west. These pioneers were either given their land or bought it very cheaply. The Spanish and Portuguese settlers in South America came from countries ruled directly by a powerful monarch and dominated by a few wealthy families who owned most of the land. They brought this way of life with them. From that time until the present day this way of life has persisted in Latin America. Very few peasants own their own farms. They are tenants of rich landowners who take a share of their crops each year. Such landowning families use their profits to buy town property or even invest their money abroad; they rarely bother to improve their farms or the living conditions of the workers. Under such a system democracy is difficult. A man who depends on a rich landowner for a living is hardly likely to vote against the landowner's candidate in an election. In many cases, of course, the peasants have no voting rights.

When the settlers in Latin America broke free from Spanish rule in the early nineteenth century they formed separate states. These states were often ruled by generals who had led their armies in the wars of independence. This led to a tradition of personal rule, often by a soldier, which still exists in Latin America today. Such military men may have real power; there is a long history of dictatorships in many of these states. More often, they are the representatives of powerful ruling groups, usually rich landowning families. These families often supply the officers for the armies who, since they rarely have to fight a

war, spend a great deal of their time interfering in political affairs. Many officers regard their men as a sort of political party in uniform. They sometimes talk as though they have a right to overthrow a government which they do not like, usually claiming that it is 'for the good of the people'. Another strong influence in Latin America is the Roman Catholic Church, because most people are Catholics. In fact none of these ruling groups, except perhaps the Church, has done much to help the ordinary people in Latin American countries. The concentration of wealth in the hands of a few rich families creates misery and resentment amongst the poor who often have either no land or no work. Such people live in great poverty, in the countryside or in shanty towns on the outskirts of fine cities such as Rio de Janeiro (Brazil) and Buenos Aires (Argentina).

Although many Latin American states are rich in minerals such as copper, zinc and nitrates, industrialisation has been slow. Many governments either would not or could not finance industrial development. In many cases there is also a lack of a home market. Most Latin American people are too poor to buy manufactured goods in any large quantities. A great number of the factories and mines which have been developed there have got their money from foreign corporations. British businessmen were the first to invest in Latin American industry. The North Americans followed, to such an extent that in the 1930s the

The wealthy part of Buenos Aires

Latin America

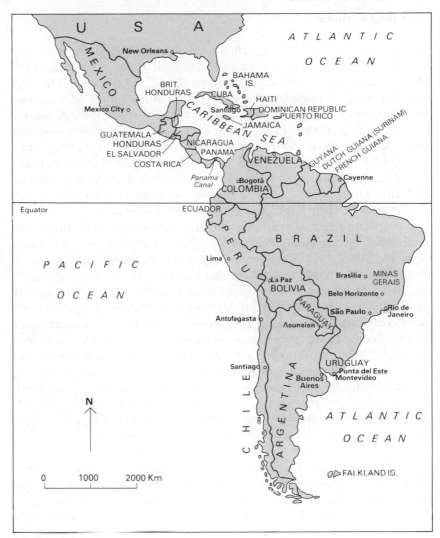

USA and Britain owned most of the investments in Latin America. In the case of the USA this led to political intervention in the affairs of some Latin American countries to protect US interests.

Those industries which did develop in Latin America helped the growth of trade unions. It was the trade unionists of the towns who first began to adopt political ideas which were different from, and very often violently opposed to, those of the ruling groups. Some workers became communists or socialists. Another influential political idea in Latin America was **populism**. A populist aims to form a single political movement of all the people – hence the name. This is no easy task in countries divided sharply between the very rich and the very poor. The enemy for Latin American populists is what they call **imperialism**. Imperialism is any form of foreign interference, whether economic or military. A populist also desires a sort of super-union of all Latin American states. This idea is known as **Pan-Americanism**.

'This land is yours'

The problem of land reform, that is the fair distribution of land, has only been tackled properly in one mainland Latin American state, Mexico. Even then it took years of bloodshed and disorder. This was not surprising because in the early nineteenth century Mexico had been notorious for the lawless ways of many of its people. A succession of weak governments failed to keep order. The countryside was pestered with *desperados* – bandits who roamed about stealing crops and killing peasants. The army was badly disciplined and often behaved in the same way; it was little more than a mob of bandits in uniform. The peasants existed in poverty, virtual slaves of the rich landowners on their large plantations (called *haciendas*).

Towards the end of the nineteenth century some sort of order was established by a soldier, Porfirio Diaz, who was President of Mexico from 1877 until 1911. Diaz formed *rurales*, a mounted police force, to patrol the countryside and to wipe out banditry. He reformed the army and used newly built railways to send soldiers into action quickly against trouble-makers. During his long rule Mexico prospered. Oil-wells were dug, and by 1910 Mexico was the world's leading exporter of petroleum. Silver also became a major export. But Diaz achieved this success by encouraging vast amounts of foreign investment and this annoyed the middle classes who felt that their country was losing its independence, particularly where the United States was concerned. At the same time the growth of a sugar industry caused the rich landowners to want even more land. This they seized, legally or illegally, from the peasants. As thousands of landless men were forced to earn a living in the sugar mills, the land problem became explosive.

Porfirio Díaz, dictator of Mexico for many years

In May 1911 Diaz was overthrown by discontented middle-class groups led by Francisco Madero. It soon became clear that this was more than a change of government. With Diaz gone, banditry again became a problem. In the north an outlaw nicknamed **Pancho Villa** started a revolution. Further south another revolutionary, **Emiliano Zapata**, began to burn the *haciendas* of the landowners and give the land back to the villagers. Madero was a democrat with high ideals. But he was not tough enough to control the Mexico of his time. When he met Zapata, the outlaw pointed a rifle at him and took his watch. That, he told Madero, was how a man got what he wanted! Madero could never agree with such violence and lawlessness.

Zapata, although a man of violence, was more than a mere bandit. His **Ayala Plan, 1911**, suggested that the land taken from the peasants for sugar-growing should be returned and that a third of each *hacienda* should be distributed amongst the people. Explaining this plan to Villa, Zapata said,

> The people have a great love of the land. They still can't believe it when one says to them 'this land is yours'. But as soon as they see that other people are getting a yield from those lands, they'll say, 'I shall ask for my own land and plant'.

Unfortunately, Zapata carried out his plan by killing landowners and

Symbol of the Mexican Revolution. Emiliano Zapata (right) and Pancho Villa (centre) in the Presidential Palace, Mexico City, 1914

burning down their houses. Furthermore, the plots of land he gave the peasants often proved too small for them to make a satisfactory living.

Before long, Madero was murdered and replaced by a group led by General Victoriano Huerta Both Zapata and Villa realised that Huerta represented the old ruling groups. So they joined forces and defeated the General's army. In December 1914 the two revolutionaries were photographed sitting in luxurious chairs in the Presidential Palace in Mexico City. It was a sight which symbolised the Mexican revolution. The two rough men had come in from the countryside with their army of ragged men and overthrown the rich, privileged and powerful. But the scene showed the violence and bloodshed which had been used to take the city.

Both Zapata (1919) and Villa (1923) died violently, murdered by their enemies. Of Villa there remains only a legend. Zapata's ideas, on the other hand, have lived on in Mexico. As early as 1917 a reformist government decided that all land, minerals and water were to be the property of the nation. We should say that they were 'nationalised'. At the same time the Church was forbidden to own land so as to reduce its political power. Gradually these laws were put into force. During the 1930s, for example, the government of President Lázaro Cárdenas redistributed over 20 million hectares of land amongst the peasants as well as setting up co-operative farms. In 1937 foreign-owned railways were taken over by the government. So the idea of '**Zapatismo**', of land for the people, became part of the Mexican way of life.

'Carry a big stick'

Relations between the United States and Latin America have never been very happy. In 1823 US President James Monroe announced the famous **Monroe Doctrine**, forbidding European nations to interfere in any part of North or South America. Although they agreed with its message, few educated Latin Americans were pleased because it was issued without consulting any government south of the Mexican border. Furthermore, it soon became clear that it did not apply to US interference! In 1848, after a successful war, the USA took New Mexico and California from the Mexicans. Fifty years later US troops arrived uninvited to help the Cubans in their war against their Spanish masters. Afterwards the USA kept bases on the island and claimed she had the right to intervene in Cuban affairs whenever she wished (see Chapter 5).

The US President, **Theodore Roosevelt**, who succeeded the murdered President William McKinley in 1901, took as his motto, 'Speak softly and carry a big stick'. He soon showed Latin Americans what he meant. With the cutting of the Panama Canal (completed in 1914), the USA became the dominant power in the Caribbean. Puerto Rico and Panama were reduced to little more than US colonies. When Venezuela refused to pay certain foreign debts, British and German warships blockaded her ports. Roosevelt persuaded them to go away by promising to collect the money for them (1902). This 'rent collecting' was also applied to the Dominican Republic. Again, in 1906, when a civil war broke out in Cuba, US troops invaded the island and established a government at first run by an American.

The USA waved the 'big stick' less after Theodore Roosevelt's time, but her businessmen took over more and more behind the scenes. President **Franklin Roosevelt** (1933–45) – a distant cousin of Theodore – started a '**Good Neighbour**' policy towards the Latin American states (see page 174). But the resulting welfare schemes, schools and technical assistance could not alter the resentment felt by a proud people. The USA is the chief buyer of Latin American products, the chief supplier of her goods, and, in recent years, the chief source of foreign aid. The educated Latin American knows this, but it only makes him dislike and distrust the USA more.

Since 1945 a new factor has increased US interest in Latin America. Leading United States politicians, particularly John Foster Dulles during the days of the 1950s Cold War with the Soviet Union (see Chapter 22), have feared that some Latin American states might 'go communist'. Consequently, the USA has done its best to overthrow reforming governments, as in the case of Guatemala in 1954, in case they developed along communist lines. Such action often left the USA supporting a near-fascist dictatorship in certain Latin American states.

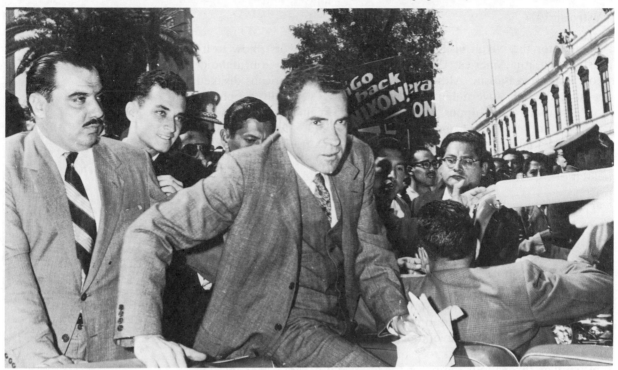

Richard Nixon during his troubled tour of Latin America, 1958

This has been deeply resented and has made the 'Colossus of the North', as the USA became known to Latin Americans, even more disliked in the southern continent.

This was shown very clearly in May 1958 when US Vice-President Richard Nixon went on a goodwill tour of eight Latin American countries – Uruguay, Colombia, Argentina, Paraguay, Bolivia, Ecuador, Peru and Venezuela. He did not expect trouble and, as always when abroad, he hoped to get a chance to show how rich the United States was, and how she had become, as he put it, 'closest to the ideal of prosperity for all in a classless society'. He intended to quote figures like, '44 million families in America own 56 million cars, 50 million television sets, 143 million radio sets, and 31 million of those families own their own home'.

The first sign that the people of Latin America did not take kindly to being told of US wealth and power was the sight of young men standing on street corners with signs reading, 'Racist', 'Son of a dog' and 'Imperialist'. But in Venezuela things got out of hand. A violent mob ambushed Nixon's motorcade repeatedly, spitting at the Vice-President and his party, throwing rocks and smashing all the windows of his car. At one point Nixon's car was nearly overturned and President Eisenhower, far away in the White House, ordered six destroyers, a guided missile cruiser and an aircraft carrier with marines on board to be prepared to rescue the Vice-President if necessary. By this time Nixon was safe. However, these hostile demonstrations had shown just how much hatred US wealth could inspire in a poor and down-trodden people.

'Castroism'

A year after the Nixon visit, the USA suffered the worst blow to its prestige in Latin America. Until 1959 Cuba was ruled by a brutal dictator, **Fulgencio Batista.** Although some individual Americans disliked his rule, the US government and 'big business' generally supported him. The main active opposition to the Batista régime came from terrorist student groups in Cuba. On 26 July 1953 **Fidel Castro**, a lawyer and son of a landowner, led an armed band which tried to capture the army barracks at Santiago (see map on page 305). The attack was beaten off. Castro was taken prisoner and sentenced to fifteen years in prison.

The young revolutionary was released quite quickly and allowed to go to Mexico. From Mexico he organised an invasion of Cuba in 1956. In a battle with Batista's forces all but twelve of Castro's men were killed. The remainder carried on a guerrilla campaign in the mountains. In 1958, more because of its own weakness than any military defeat, the Batista government collapsed. In 1959 Castro became dictator of Cuba, although he promised to give the people power. In fact, he ruled through a group called, first, the July 26th Movement, and later the Integrated Revolutionary Organisation (ORI).

Fidel Castro, Cuban revolutionary

The romantic side to Castro's lonely battle in the mountains made him popular throughout Latin America. Once it became clear that the USA wanted to overthrow him his popularity increased! The disastrous 'Bay of Pigs' invasion launched with the blessing of President Kennedy (see Chapter 26) caused Castro to turn to the Soviet Union for economic help. The Russians saw an opportunity to gain a foothold within 150 kilometres of the US coast. They promised to supply military and technical aid and to buy Cuba's main crop, sugar. Castro, in turn, moved towards communism, although it would be more accurate to call his brand of personal government 'Castroism'.

Castro has had some success, particularly in education where his schools have done a great deal to wipe out illiteracy in Cuba. Again and again he has called upon the Cubans to make great sacrifices to put the economy on a sound footing. In 1964 he asked for 10 million tonnes of sugar to be produced by 1970. When it became clear that this target was not going to be reached he announced 1969 as 'the year of decisive effort'. It was not, and both the Soviet Union and Castro were dissatisfied. Castro has often said that Cubans are lazy. Actually, some agricultural experts believe that the real trouble is that too much emphasis is laid on the amount of sugar-cane to be planted and not enough on the quality of the sugar produced. In addition, new sugar-growing areas started by the government often proved to have unsuitable soil. It became a Cuban joke to say, 'What a lot of sugar cane there is among the weeds this year'.

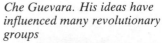

Che Guevara. His ideas have influenced many revolutionary groups

The fact that Cuba is economically and politically dependent upon the Soviet Union has gradually lowered Castro's prestige amongst Latin American reformers and revolutionaries. Yet the rise of Castro gave hope to the down-trodden and led to the growth of at least one legend. One of Castro's advisers was **Ernesto Che Guevara** (1928–67),

an Argentinian Marxist who worked with him from 1959 until 1965. In that year Guevara left Cuba to lead a guerrilla band in Bolivia, where he was killed. From a practical point of view, Che Guevara was a complete failure. His Bolivian adventure not only failed to get the support of the peasants, Guevara himself even ended up betrayed by a peasant! But his ideas have been very influential. Guevara believed that guerrilla activity would be needed to overthrow the Latin American ruling groups and their supporters, US business interests. He believed, moreover, that there was no need for these forces to have mass popular support. All that was necessary, Guevara argued, was a small, well-trained band of terrorists. Their violent activities would create 'a revolutionary situation' in which the ruling groups could be overthrown. The desperate state of the poor in many Latin American countries led them to follow such teachings and there were guerrilla wars in Panama, Guatemala and Nicaragua.

Brazil – the biggest!

Brazil is the largest and most populous country in Latin America (see map on page 305). It is in fact the fifth largest country in the world. Its history has been different from that of other Latin American states. Brazil was the only part of Latin America to be colonised by the Portuguese. When other states were fighting wars of independence against their Spanish masters, the Brazilians were receiving the Portuguese royal family as refugees after Napoleon's invasion of Portugal in 1808. Brazil had an emperor related to the Portuguese royal family until as late as 1889. However, in other ways Brazil was a typical Latin American state. During the nineteenth century power lay with the rich coffee planters of São Paulo and their supporters, the army. The bulk of the population lived without education or political rights, working as slaves on a starvation diet.

Because Brazil is so large, many of its provinces have at times been semi-independent or even in a state of revolt. The few peasants who were given voting rights found that they had to vote as the local political boss told them or they lost their jobs or their homes. This system is known as '**colonelismo**' because the local political boss, probably in the pay of the rich families, was often the colonel of the regional National Guard. The system has survived to the present day in many parts of Brazil. Another feature resulting from the country's size is the tendency of Brazilians to live on the coast. A visitor can fly for hours over wilderness before he sights one of Brazil's modern cities, Rio de Janeiro, São Paulo or Belo Horizonte. The size of these cities has created population problems which dwarf even those of India or China. São Paulo, with a 1979 population of 12 million, is the fastest growing city on earth. Rio de Janeiro's houses, flats and offices are spreading through the valleys and along a narrow strip of land between the mountains and the sea. Its city council is actually pulling down hills into the sea to make more room!

One city, **Brasilia**, is not on the coast. It was the idea of Brazilian President **Juscelino Kubitschek**, a man who came from Minas Gerais,

Crowded city. Rio de Janeiro, Brazil

the only landlocked region in Brazil. Kubitschek set out to prove that Brazil could have a wonderful city inland. Brasília is set on a flat, red plain. It is a city of startling beauty built to show the world Brazil's wealth and power. Some of the world's finest architects and artists worked on its construction. Brasília grew out of Kubitschek's determination to produce an economic 'miracle' in a country which he knew to be rich in natural resources. The military rulers who succeeded him have adopted the same policy.

How far has Brazil experienced a 'miracle'? There has been immense industrial activity. All sorts of goods, including cars and electronic equipment, are manufactured in Brazil for companies based in the United States or Europe. These goods can be produced more cheaply than in Europe, but only at the cost of suffering for the Brazilians. Since 1964 a military government has made sure that there are no strikes and has kept down wages. Yet prices have risen steadily, so cutting the living standards of the ordinary worker. Some people have made a fortune, but the shanty towns around the big cities house millions who live at starvation level. And because there is so little food for these people thousands of children die of malnutrition. In São Paulo, for example, an average of forty children die each day. They are buried in graves which are destroyed every two years to make way for more graves. The bodies which are dug up go into large pits.

It is, of course, easy to blame the government for these problems. In fact the growth of population all over Latin America and in other parts of the so-called 'Third World', not just Brazil, creates problems almost beyond the reach of any government. In Latin America the

Urchins living in the slums of Bogotá

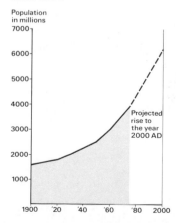

Growth of world population since 1900

Population
in millions

population is expected to double in the next twenty-four years. There are many reasons for this. The Roman Catholic Church is against artificial methods of birth control and most Latin Americans are Catholics. Also Latin American men feel that they must prove their masculinity by fathering large families. In any case, poor people aim to have many sons and daughters to look after them when they are old.

Certainly population growth in Latin America cancels out any benefits which might come from increased trade or industry. In the cities in particular this growth has been phenomenal. Bogotá, the capital of Colombia, had 33,000 inhabitants in 1938 and nearly 3 million in 1974. This might not matter if such town dwellers found work and lived well. But in Latin American towns, as in the cities of India, there is not enough work to go round. Over half the population of Bogotá live in shanty towns – clusters of wretched shacks made of wooden boxes, cardboard, petrol cans, straw matting and other materials. Such conditions make for an explosive political situation because sooner or later the poor will blame somebody for the conditions they live in. The most likely scapegoat is their government, or the rich nations of Western Europe and North America. Brazil, which had a population of 52 million in 1950 and 116 million in 1978, highlights a world problem of massive proportions.

Chile – the lost revolution

Fast growing population is one world problem seen most clearly in Latin America. Another is **inflation**. This occurs when the incomes people receive from the production of goods and services – in the form of wages, salaries, profits and rents – are greater than the actual amount of production. For example, if incomes go up by ten per cent in a year but there is only two per cent more national production the rate of inflation is eight per cent, that is, the difference between the two. To soak up this surplus spending power, prices rise. Of course, not all prices go up by the same amount. The inflation rate is an average figure. Nevertheless, once inflation starts it has a nasty habit of feeding on itself. Workers expect higher wages, manufacturers put up prices to maintain profits and the two chase each other in a vicious spiral.

Salvador Allende, Marxist ruler of Chile

In some countries inflation has accelerated to the point where it has become **hyper-inflation**. This happens when prices rise so quickly that people do not want to hold on to money. They try to exchange it for goods, whatever their prices. Hyper-inflation caused just such a 'spending spree' in Germany in the 1920s and the resulting political disturbances were a factor in Hitler's rise to power (see Chapter 16). More recently the political effects of hyper-inflation have been seen in Latin America, although we should not forget that many other factors have contributed to revolution and violence in that part of the world. It is no coincidence that when the military government seized power in Brazil in 1964 inflation was running at fifty per cent and the ruling groups feared trouble from the industrial workers in particular.

The problem of hyper-inflation has played an important part in the recent misfortunes of Chile, a country which had grown used to having a democratically elected President and Congress as well as thriving trade unions. In 1970 the Chileans elected, by a small majority, **Salvador Allende**, a Marxist, as President. This was the first time a Communist had gained power by democratic means and so it was seen by the outside world as a sort of test-tube experiment of how a Marxist system could control a democratic country. In fact, Allende did not head a purely Communist government. His support was of the Popular Front type, that is, he was supported by communists, socialists and trade unionists, as well as by an extreme revolutionary group, the MIR, which had been formed under the influence of Che Guevara in 1965. Allende was opposed by a powerful middle class, represented in Congress and in the membership of the Supreme Court, and to a certain extent by the army.

Allende set about reforms which had been the dream of Latin American revolutionaries for nearly a century. His government nationalised most industries, including the important copper mines, and began to carry out land reforms. Most experts seem to agree that he went too fast. By the autumn of 1972 the rate of inflation had reached 168 per cent whilst corn production and food supplies had dropped alarmingly. Allende's supporters blamed this situation on a drop in the world price of copper – one of Chile's chief exports – and the activities of US agents, both government and private, who sought to rally opposition against the President. However, large-scale strikes by workers protesting at rising prices and nationalisation showed that the trouble in Chile went deeper than a foreign plot.

The strikes failed to bring down the government. This was partly because certain key workers refused to join in and partly because the army remained loyal to the President. Allende showed his gratitude by bringing several leading generals into his Cabinet. This was unusual in Chile which had no tradition of military rule. Such moves angered the MIR who, according to their enemies, were now plotting armed revolution. They had already unofficially taken over the suburbs of Santiago, the Chilean capital (see map on page 305), whilst in the countryside some of their groups had given land to the peasants without waiting for the government's permission. The MIR was disliked by many of Allende's Communist supporters, not only by the ruling groups. The President clearly faced the danger of his own support breaking up into quarrelling groups. The MIR leaders, for instance, attacked him in their newspapers as a 'misguided reformist'. For some he was going too fast; for others he was much too slow.

In early 1973 Allende tried to introduce socialist teaching into schools. This annoyed the Church, which, as in most Latin American countries, ran the education system. Until that time clergymen had supported Allende's government because they saw it as a genuine reforming one anxious to help the poor but now many of the clergy turned against Allende. Worse was to follow. In April, 13,000 workers went on strike in one key mine and the President had to declare a state of emergency. By then Congress had decided to impeach (put on trial) leading members of Allende's Cabinet. At the same time, they asked the President to obey the laws of Chile which they claimed he was breaking. By midsummer MIR activists had seized a public building as a protest against the government's policies and a hundred soldiers with tanks staged an unsuccessful attack on the presidential palace in Santiago, La Monēda. Clearly extremists, enemies and so-called allies were on the move against Allende.

Santiago, Chile, becomes a battleground during the crisis leading to the overthrow of Allende's government, 1973

In September, with inflation running at 300 per cent and discontent everywhere, demonstrations and riots became a commonplace. Whilst youths armed with sticks and piles of stones built barricades to protect the presidential palace, the army leaders decided to act. Later they stated that the last straw for them was the news that the MIR might try to form an armed militia, that is, a rival army. Troops with tanks surrounded the presidential palace. Allende's guards surrendered but the President decided to fight on. Jet aircraft then bombed the building, and, when soldiers broke into La Monēda they found Allende's dead body seated in a chair. His widow claimed that he committed suicide with a machine-gun given him as a present by Fidel Castro.

The new leader of Chile was **General Augusto Pinochet**, the commander of the army. After the take-over he spoke of a secret plan hatched by the MIR and extreme Communists to kill top civilian and military leaders. Quite soon he was shooting 'suspects'. The numbers said to have been killed by the Pinochet régime vary wildly. Pinochet admitted to 1,500; Allende's widow spoke of a number between 15,000 and 800,000. What was certain was that Chilean democracy died with Allende in the smoking ruins of his palace. He was a genuinely tragic figure who may have been overthrown by foreign plotters but who was certainly not backed loyally by his own supporters. The question as to whether a Communist régime can rule democratically has still to be answered.

The Pinochet government has not solved Chile's problems since it came to power, even though it was given financial aid by the Communist government of China! The tank and the gun can keep a ruling group in power. They cannot solve the problems of inflation and over-population.

'The shirtless ones'

At their worst most Latin American dictators since 1945 have been fascist in their methods and beliefs, that is, they have believed in rule by a small group and the crushing of all opposition and criticism. And because of the existence of powerful Communist states like the Soviet Union and China they have been able to claim that they were 'saving' the country from Marxist rule. A slightly different type of military ruler was General **Juan Perón**, who was President of Argentina (see map on page 305) from 1946 until 1955. Perón, unlike many soldier rulers of the time, made a direct appeal to the people, particularly the industrial workers. He called these workers *descamisados* (shirtless ones) and, with the help of his beautiful wife, Eva (Evita), won their hearts. Perón nationalised many industries and bought out the investment of some foreign countries. However, he did little for the peasants, whilst his policies annoyed powerful Church and army leaders.

After the early death of Eva, Perón lost control and was driven from power (1955). But 'Perónista' ideas remained strong, both in Argentina and in other Latin American countries. After all, they contained populist and anti-imperialist theories dear to the Latin American heart. In Argentina there was so much popular support for Perónista

Eva Perón and her husband,
Juan, 1951

candidates that the military government refused to let them take part in elections. The Perónista reply was to refuse to vote – in millions. In 1972 public opinion forced the Argentinian government to allow the old dictator to return from exile in Spain. Soon afterwards a Perónista party, campaigning under another name, won both the Presidency and most of the seats in the Assembly. The leader of the victorious party asked Perón to become President once again.

Perón died in 1974, leaving his second wife, Isabel, to try to play the rôle once made famous by the lovely Eva – that of champion of the poor and oppressed. In the harsh world of the 1970s, with inflation, over-population and terrorism the main problems, such theatricals did not work. Isabel was overthrown in 1976 and Argentina went back to military rule.

What sort of revolution?

Following Vice-President Nixon's disastrous visit to Latin America (1958) and the coming to power of Castro in Cuba (1959), a new US President, John Kennedy, tried to go back to Franklin Roosevelt's policy of giving economic help to Latin American countries. In August 1961 a conference was held at Punta del Este, Uruguay (see map on page 305), between United States representatives and leading politicians from every Latin American country. Cuba sent delegates to take part in the discussions, although the resulting charter, named the **Alliance for Progress**, was not signed by them. The USA hoped by offers of increased help to persuade the Latin American states to change the way of life of the majority of their people. In return, the states were promised billions of dollars of aid over a ten year period.

Critics of US imperialism feared that this would be an excuse for more profitable deals by US companies, deals at the expense of the very workers and peasants whom the policy was supposed to help. In many cases they were proved right.

From the start the populist leaders in most Latin American countries refused to have anything to do with the US scheme. They were afraid of being labelled 'agents of American imperialism'. Military governments, such as those which came to power in Brazil in 1964 and Chile in 1973, were prepared to do deals with US 'big business'. But few of them had any intention of making changes in the way they ran their countries. Consequently, whether the Alliance leaders talked of reform or aid, or even of a Latin American 'Common Market' – as President Johnson did in 1967 – little money ever reached the people who toiled and suffered.

The constant power struggle between the ruling groups, the army, the trade unions and peasants continues throughout Latin America. As we have seen, their objectives often clash. Genuine attempts at social and political revolution, as in Chile, have led to disaster. Only in Mexico and Cuba have such attempts had any success. Revolutionaries armed with sticks and stones, such as those who tried to defend Allende's palace in 1973, learnt the grim truth that power lies with those who control the soldiers, tanks and aircraft. During the 1970s

Sandinista rebels in Nicaragua celebrate the overthrow of a right-wing ruler, President Somoza, 1979

revolutionary bands inspired by Che Guevara have been as unsuccessful as the man himself. In many countries they have become mere kidnappers, trying to force régimes to give them money or to release political prisoners. Meanwhile the real problems of Latin America, made worse by hyper-inflation and a growing population, remain to be solved.

Timeline

1823	Monroe Doctrine.
1877	Porfirio Díaz President of Mexico.
1901	Theodore Roosevelt's 'Big Stick' policy.
1911	Díaz overthrown by Francisco Madero.
	Revolution begins in Mexico, led by Villa and Zapata.
	Zapata's Ayala Plan.
1933	Franklin Roosevelt's 'Good Neighbour' policy.
1934–40	Cárdenas President of Mexico.
1946–55	Perón President of Argentina.
1956–61	Kubitschek President of Brazil.
1958	Vice-President Nixon's visit to Latin America.
1959	Batista government in Cuba overthrown by Castro. Castro becomes Prime Minister.
1961	Alliance for Progress.
1964	Military government seizes power in Brazil.
1967	Guevara killed during guerrilla fighting in Bolivia.
1970	Allende elected President of Chile.
1973	Allende government overthrown by army generals. Pinochet becomes President of Chile.

Questions

1. 'Many [Latin American] officers regard themselves as a sort of political party in uniform. They sometimes talk as though they have the right to overthrow a government which they do not like for "the good of the people"'

   What might such officers mean when they talked of 'the good of the people'? Choose one Latin American country and describe how the army officers overthrew the government.

2. a) Describe the events which led to the overthrow of the Batista government in 1958.
   b) Who became the new ruler of Cuba? Which foreign country gave him most support and why?

3. 'Meanwhile the real problems of Latin America . . . remain to be solved.' Give details of at least two of these 'real problems' and of the attempts made to solve them in Latin America.

4. Write short paragraphs on each of the following:
   a) the Monroe Doctrine, 1823 b) the Ayala Plan, 1911
   c) Ernesto Che Guevara   d) the Alliance for Progress

30
After Empire
The Dominions, India and Ireland since 1945

Of the chief countries of the Old British Empire (see map on page 128), Australia, Canada and New Zealand were colonised. India, Pakistan and Ireland, on the other hand, were conquered. This historical fact has made a great deal of difference to the attitudes of these countries towards Britain. To Australians, Canadians and New Zealanders Britain was the 'mother country'. To the Irish, Indians and Pakistanis Britain was a foreign power which at some time must be forced to give them their freedom. Furthermore, Australia, Canada and New Zealand were self-governing for most of the twentieth century. Only part of Ireland got Dominion status in 1921 and India and Pakistan had to wait until 1947.

Australia

The wartime ties between Australia and the USA (see Chapter 15) continued after 1945. When China went Communist in 1949 the leaders of the USA saw Australia as a stronghold of democracy in the Far East. During the Cold War between the Soviet Union and the USA successive US governments tried to involve the Australians in their 'crusade' against communism. In 1962, for example, the Australians allowed the Americans to set up a Polaris submarine control centre in their country. Perhaps more important, the USA persuaded Australian troops to fight with them in Vietnam. The military involvement in Vietnam led to an Australian anti-war movement, similar to the one which disrupted life in the USA (see Chapter 28). Young men ran away rather than join the army. There were student demonstrations and riots. In 1972 a new Australian Labour government, led by **Gough Whitlam**, showed that it was sympathetic to these attitudes. Men who had dodged army service were pardoned. At the same time, Whitlam opened up friendly relations with Communist China. Australia, he seemed to be saying, was not interested in taking sides in any Cold War.

If the Second World War forced a change of foreign policy upon Australia, breaking many of the old empire links with Britain, it also caused many Australians to alter their thinking about foreigners, particularly non-Europeans. The change took various forms. Under the so-called **Colombo Plan, 1951**, richer and more industrialised countries of the Far East, like Japan and Australia, offered to help less-developed countries with money, training and expert advice. As a result many Asian and African students graduated at Australian universities. The old, often racist 'White Australia' views, so common at the turn of the

Gough Whitlam; Labour Prime Minister of Australia

Queen Elizabeth II is greeted by crowds in Australia in 1977

century, were expressed less often. The threat of invasion and conquest by the Japanese during the war caused many post-war Australian governments to take a new attitude towards immigration. They realised that a large, relatively empty continent like Australia needed a larger population to defend it. Between 1945 and 1970 two-and-a-half million immigrants, mostly European refugees, were allowed to settle in Australia. A trickle of Asians got through illegally and, after 1972, it became official Australian policy to allow Asian immigration into Australia.

When Britain entered the Common Market in 1973 (see Chapter 31) some of the last imperial links between Australia and Britain were broken. The words, 'British Subject' were no longer printed on Australian passports and a song called 'Advance Australia Fair' replaced 'God Save the Queen' as the Australian National Anthem. However, when Queen Elizabeth II visited Australia in 1977 she was received by cheering crowds and only a few protestors. The ties of kinship and language may yet prove more important than treaties and statutes.

Canada

Canada was at first a French colony (see Chapter 4). It was taken from the French by British armies in 1763. There remained many thousands of French-speaking people in Quebec Province. As more

*'Long live a Free Quebec!'
President de Gaulle speaks to
French Canadians, 1967*

English-speaking settlers arrived in Canada, Quebec was surrounded and outnumbered by nine 'English' provinces – Newfoundland joined the Canadian Union in 1949. The French of Quebec felt they were being swamped both politically and culturally. They demanded that French be the second language of Canada and this was granted. They also began to press for a semi-independent Quebec within Canada.

French nationalists – as those who want such self-government are called – began what they termed 'a quiet revolution'. It was not particularly quiet because extremists staged bomb attacks as well as riots. Most French-Canadians were against violence. But most of them blamed the Ottawa-based government for Quebec's relative backwardness compared with other Canadian provinces. They also felt isolated in a continent of over 200 million English-speaking people. In July 1967 such feelings were inflamed further when Charles de Gaulle, the President of France, paid an official visit to Canada. Whereas some French nationalists had turned their backs on Queen Elizabeth II during a state visit in 1964, the French President received an almost royal welcome in Quebec province. Perhaps excited by this, de Gaulle made a speech ending with the words, 'Long live a Free Quebec!'. Lester Pearson, the Canadian Prime Minister, told de Gaulle not to interfere in Canadian affairs. The General left at once for France, without bothering to visit the Prime Minister in Ottawa.

The year after this visit, French nationalists formed a political party called *Parti Québecois* (Quebec Party). Its aim was to achieve independence for the province. A census held in 1971 showed that 67 per cent of Canadians spoke English, 18 per cent spoke French and 13 per cent spoke both languages. In May 1980 the people of Quebec voted decisively against independence in a specially held referendum. However, the Prime Minister of Canada, Pierre Trudeau, himself a French-speaking Canadian, spoke of the need for reform.

Jawaharlal Nehru

The slums of Calcutta

India

There was no more populated part of the British Empire than the Indian sub-continent, once described as the 'brightest jewel' in Queen Victoria's crown. After independence and partition (see Chapter 15) India was dominated politically, first by **Jawaharlal Nehru** and then by his daughter, **Mrs Indira Gandhi**. Whilst Nehru ruled, his Congress Party, which had led the opposition to British rule, made up the government, winning election after election. Nehru was a strange mixture. He had spent his early life trying to get rid of the British and had suffered imprisonment for his activities. Yet this rich, English-educated man once said, 'I looked upon the world almost from an Englishman's standpoint'. **Mahatma Gandhi**, the other leader in the struggle against the British, represented the age-old India. He lived the life of a Hindu holy man and loved village life with its handicrafts and peasant-style living. Nehru once said that in India there was a danger that poverty would be glorified. In a way Gandhi did this, and, after his murder in 1948, thousands of his followers, including members of the Congress Party, followed his example and his teachings.

Nehru, on the other hand, wanted to modernise India whilst preserving the best of its old way of life. The clash between these two points of view has continued ever since. India, as Mrs Gandhi has said, is 'the land of contradictions', a land where politicians can argue that India should be equipped with nuclear weapons as well as homes for old cows because the cow is a sacred animal to the Hindus. Nehru was determined to lift his country out of what he called 'the cow dung age'. He wanted state planning, new industries, scientific development and

birth control to limit India's teeming millions. He made a great deal of progress, partly because of his policies and partly because of his immense prestige. But India's greatest problem, poverty, has not been solved by Nehru or his daughter. Most Indian peasants manage to grow only the minimum food with which to feed themselves and their families. Such **subsistence farming** leaves no safety margin. More births, or the arrival of the monsoon rains late or early, can mean starvation. The crying need is for better irrigation of the soil and for more widespread use of modern agricultural methods.

Four out of five Indians live in villages. But since the end of the Second World War millions of starving poor have flooded into the cities. They build themselves makeshift huts, often at the sides of roads or railways on the outskirts of cities. City authorities regularly have these shanty towns destroyed but they are rebuilt almost as quickly. In one Indian city, Bombay, it is estimated that 1,500 extra people arrive to live every day. Houses, flats and modern skyscrapers are full up. By day the homeless walk the streets; at night they sleep on the pavements. Bombay's story is repeated in other large Indian cities, particularly in Calcutta. Despite thriving industries India's growing population often cancels out the benefits of such progress.

After Nehru, who?

The power and prestige of Jawaharlal Nehru was such that this question was often asked, both inside and outside India. People were afraid that the world's largest democracy would not be able to survive when Nehru's guiding hand was removed. Yet, when Nehru died suddenly in 1964, there was a peaceful take-over without riots or attempts to found a dictatorship. The new leader, **Lal Bahadur Shastri**, actually offered the post of Prime Minister to Nehru's daughter, Mrs Indira Gandhi. She refused and it was not until Shastri himself died in 1966 that there was a contest for the premiership. The two candidates were Mrs Gandhi and **Morarji Desai**, both members of the Congress Party. Mrs Gandhi won. This victory and her general election win the following year were a turning point in Indian politics.

The voting was 355 for Mrs Gandhi and 169 for Desai. For the first time since 1947 there was a split in the Congress Party. Once the party of protest and revolt against the British, by 1967 the Congress Party was looked upon by many as inefficient and even dishonest. Support for Mrs Gandhi was strong but equally there were those who resented the long dominance of the Nehru family in Indian politics. One opposition spokesman during the 1967 debates went so far as to call the Party 'the main enemy of the people'. In 1969 the split widened during a battle between Mrs Gandhi and her opponents. Smaller, opposition groups saw a chance at last of power if they combined against the Congress Party.

India, Pakistan and Bangladesh

Meanwhile outside events were having their effect upon Indian life and

*Sheikh Mujibur-Rahman,
ill-fated ruler of Bangladesh*

politics. During most of his seventeen years of power Nehru refused to let India become a satellite of either the Soviet Union or the USA. He accepted aid from both the West and the USSR but he refused to sign alliances with either power bloc. At international meetings and in India he tried to put the point of view of weak, developing nations. This **non-alignment** policy was nearly always peaceful; only against Pakistan and on the Kashmir question did Nehru mass troops and speak aggressively (see Chapter 15). Then came the border dispute with China and the Chinese army's brief attack on northern India in 1962. Nehru realised that he had been living in 'a fool's paradise'. He began to rearm the Indian forces.

In 1965 and 1971 India went to war with Pakistan. The existence of Pakistan had never been accepted by Indians. To them the reason for Pakistan's birth – the idea that Indian Muslims were a separate nation – was wrong. To a certain extent they were right. In any case the religious division is far from clear-cut geographically. Both India and East Pakistan (now Bangladesh) have large Muslim minorities. The language and culture of most East Pakistanis had more in common with the people of the Indian province of Bengal than those of West Pakistan. Consequently a movement for self-government, the so-called **Awami League**, led by **Sheikh Mujibur-Rahman**, developed in East Pakistan. Early in 1971 the League won an overwhelming electoral victory in the East. The military rulers of West Pakistan were not prepared to accept this. They sent large troop reinforcements to East Pakistan and arrested Sheikh Mujibur. Mujibur's supporters began fighting for an independent **Bangladesh** (Bengali land). It seemed a desperate and hopeless struggle against a well-equipped army.

Faced by an armed resistance movement, the Pakistani army began to massacre civilians. Millions of refugees fled across the border into India. India's own resources were soon strained by such extra numbers. Mrs Gandhi said it was an international problem. She toured Western capitals trying to get help. When these attempts failed, she decided to act. A general **Indo-Pakistan War** followed on both fronts (see map below). In Kashmir the West Pakistan army failed to break through. In East Pakistan a large Indian force overran the country, capturing Dacca, the capital, in December 1971. The Pakistani army surrendered and Sheikh Mujibur became President of a new, independent **Bangladesh**. These defeats led to the collapse of the military régime which had ruled West Pakistan almost continuously since 1947. **Zulfiqar Ali Bhutto**, a wealthy landowner with socialist views, ruled the country until he was overthrown by the army in 1978. **Mohammad Zia-ul-Haq**, the new military ruler, charged Bhutto with being involved in a murder plot. In April 1979 Bhutto was hanged on this charge. Zia promised elections but his ruthless rule, with savage floggings for both criminals and political opponents, made this seem unlikely.

Bangladesh, too, had an unhappy history. No change of government or name could alter the poverty of the region, or the effects of disastrous floods which drowned thousands. In March 1975 Sheikh Mujibur was murdered during a military take-over of the country.

India, showing the new state of Bangladesh

State of emergency

Mrs Gandhi had won a stunning military victory. But India's economy was strained by the war and also by a bad drought which followed it. During the early 1970s her opponents within the Congress Party, led by Morarji Desai, joined with other groups opposed to her style of government. This **Janata (People's) Front** agreed on little except their determination to overthrow Mrs Gandhi. In 1975 criticism of the Prime Minister came to a head when a High Court Judge ruled that Mrs Gandhi had behaved dishonestly during some elections. As a result she was disqualified from taking part in politics for five years. Mrs Gandhi's reaction was swift and devastating. She declared 'a state of emergency' and imprisoned hundreds of MPs who were opposed to her. She also ordered that all journals must submit their articles to a government department for censorship, an act which caused three magazines to cease publication.

Mrs Gandhi had gambled, relying on her massive support in the country and hoping that her policies would please the people. She announced a new programme of modernisation. It included the building of new power stations, more irrigation schemes and a promise to give more land to landless peasants. The programme also included a family planning scheme to limit India's population – by 1976 it had crossed the 600 million mark. Men and women were offered money if they agreed to be sterilised, whilst the minimum age of marriage was

Mrs Indira Gandhi speaks to a crowd in New Delhi during the state of emergency, 1975

set at 18 for women and 21 for men. None of this pleased the conservatives who regarded it as an attack on Hindu ways and customs. When it was alleged that Sanjay Gandhi, one of Mrs Gandhi's sons, was carrying out forcible sterilisation of men in certain provinces there was uproar. But Mrs Gandhi, confident she was still the most popular figure in Indian politics, decided to hold a general election in March 1977. The result was a landslide victory for the Janata Front. Morarji Desai became the new Prime Minister.

The Janata Front was just a loose coalition of different political parties. Its members soon started to quarrel with each other. Throughout 1978 Mrs Gandhi's supporters in the Congress Party won by-elections. Meanwhile, there were investigations of Mrs Gandhi's so-called 'misconduct' during the state of emergency. In December 1978 Mrs Gandhi was even sent to jail for a short time for refusing to give evidence to the courts examining her case. But her political strength was such that her section of the Congress Party was recognised as the official opposition. Desai's own cabinet ministers started to stage huge rallies to protest at his policies and to demand 'a better deal' for the peasants. In July 1979 Desai resigned and was replaced by one of his ministers, **Charan Singh**. The new Prime Minister promised a general election in 1980. Throughout the election campaign, Mrs Gandhi claimed that she alone could give India the firm government it needed. Sure enough, elections to the lower house of parliament in January 1980 gave her supporters a sweeping victory. Even her supposedly unpopular son, Sanjay, was elected an MP for the first time. The electors seemed to have grown tired of the quarrelling ambitious leaders of the Janata Front. Even a journalist once imprisoned by Mrs Gandhi remarked 'It is obvious that the non-governance of the Janata has weighed with people more than the misgovernance of Mrs Gandhi'. The 'Empress' of India, as some called her, was in power again.

Ireland since the war

In 1949 a new Prime Minister, **John Costello**, took Eire out of the British Commonwealth. Eire became a republic owing no loyalty to the British Monarchy and, in 1955, she became a member of the United Nations. Her government refused to join NATO because, as it stated, 'British forces occupied the six counties [Ulster]'. Britain, of course, was a member of NATO and as far as the new Irish Republic was concerned she was still an occupying power in Northern Ireland. So the old problem of the border remained. The IRA (see page 133) still plotted to drive the British out of Northern Ireland by force. Meanwhile, grievances felt by the Catholics in Northern Ireland led to a fresh explosion of violence.

Although Northern Ireland was ruled by a Protestant-dominated government based at Stormont (the name of the building) in Belfast, one-third of the people in Northern Ireland were Catholics. Many of these believed in a united Ireland; they wanted to join the south. Even more resented the way they were treated as second-class citizens in Northern Ireland. In certain electoral wards, for example, the voting lists were compiled in such a way that Catholics could not vote. Some ward boundaries were deliberately drawn so that Catholics were in a minority. There was also much discrimination against Catholics, particularly in housing but also in health facilities and transport. Above all, Northern Ireland was policed by two mainly Protestant forces, the **Royal Ulster Constabulary (RUC)** and a part-time organisation known as the **'B' Specials**. The 'B' Specials were particularly disliked by Catholics who accused them of unfairness and brutality.

In 1967 Catholics and sympathisers formed a Civil Rights Movement to march and protest against such treatment; a typical slogan was 'One man, one vote'. Their intentions were peaceful but bitterness between Protestant and Catholic extremists made this impossible. In October 1968 a march in Londonderry (see map opposite) roused the anger of Protestant 'Orangemen'. These are men who belong to 'Orange Lodges', a sort of freemasonry whose members are pledged to keep Northern Ireland as part of the United Kingdom. They get their name from William III of the Dutch royal family of Orange, who, when he became King of England, defeated a Catholic Irish revolt against him in 1690. The Londonderry march ended in riots and disorder. In May

An IRA bomb explodes in Belfast, 1972. Six people were killed and 146 hurt

Northern Ireland – scene of the troubles since 1969

1969 the Stormont Government announced that in future Catholics would be treated more fairly. It was too late.

By August 1969 street battles between Catholics and Protestants had reached such a pitch that the British government abolished the 'B' Specials and sent troops into Northern Ireland to keep order. At first even Catholics welcomed the soldiers as protectors against Protestant hooligans. The IRA, meanwhile, saw the troubles as an opportunity. They set themselves up as defenders of the Irish Catholic community. Bombings and riots continued, and, in February 1971, the first of hundreds of British soldiers was killed by an IRA gunman. Protestant groups, organised on a semi-military basis, reacted by killing Catholics. In January 1972 an already tense situation was made worse when British army paratroopers killed thirteen people during a Catholic civil rights demonstration in Londonderry. For a time certain Catholic districts in Belfast and Londonderry were run by the IRA, who put up barricades manned by gunmen. Such 'no go' areas, as they were called, were wiped out by the army in August 1972 with a massive display of force called **'Operation Motorman'**.

The 'Peace People'

In March 1972 the British had abolished the Stormont government. Northern Ireland was now ruled directly from London – a grievance for Protestants and, indeed, even Catholics. During 1973–4 the British tried a new kind of government for Northern Ireland. They announced that an Assembly would be elected on the basis of 'power-sharing' between the two communities. The Protestants claimed that this gave the Catholic minority more representatives than their numbers justified. They saw it as the thin end of the wedge towards union with the Irish Republic and their answer was decisive. A successful **General Strike** (1974) against the new scheme brought life in Northern Ireland to a standstill. Faced by Protestants who said they would 'eat grass' rather than accept power-sharing, the British government gave way. The idea of the Assembly was dropped and the British authorities went back to ruling Northern Ireland directly from London. A senior British cabinet minister was sent to Northern Ireland to direct the battle against the IRA.

The majority of Irish, both Catholic and Protestant, wanted an end to the violence. This was shown clearly in 1976 when Mrs Betty Williams and Miss Mairead Corrigan formed a **Peace People** organisation. Their decision to work openly for peace was a horrified reaction to the deaths of three young children, killed by a runaway car whose IRA driver had been shot dead by soldiers. Wherever the two women held a rally large crowds gathered to support them. They also toured Europe, telling audiences of the daily horrors of life in Northern Ireland. In 1976 they were awarded the Nobel Peace Prize for their work. In 1978 a journalist visiting Northern Ireland reported hearing remarks like, 'I'm a loyal Orangeman but by God I don't go along with this killing', and, from a Catholic, 'Well, I believe in a United Ireland but I think it's disgusting the way some people are going about it'.

Betty Williams (left) and Mairead Corrigan (centre) lead a peace march in Northern Ireland, 1976

Both the British and Irish governments are agreed on one thing – their dislike of the violent methods of the IRA. They know that the IRA wants to overthrow both governments in Ireland, replacing them with a 'workers' state'. After the killing of eighteen British soldiers at Warrenpoint (see map on page 329) and the murder on the same day of Lord Louis Mountbatten, Queen Elizabeth II's uncle (August 1979), fresh efforts were made to increase co-operation between the Irish Republic and Britain. Irish courts regularly deal out heavy sentences on IRA offenders but the ease with which gunmen and bombers can cross the border from Northern Ireland to the Irish Republic after a terrorist attack makes the British army's task more difficult. They want to pursue such men across the border but the Dublin government will not allow this. **Jack Lynch**, Prime Minister of the Irish Republic until December 1979, took a tough line with the IRA. He also went to the United States to explain to Irish Americans who support the idea of a united Ireland that the money they send to Ireland to help the 'cause' may end up in the hands of the IRA.

The deep divisions in Ireland help the IRA's cause, however much people condemn their murderous brutality. Catholics generally look towards the Irish Republic; Protestants towards Britain. The dispute about who should rule Northern Ireland is a quarrel in which both sides have an understandable point of view. Are the Protestants of Northern Ireland the 'last colonists' who should accept Dublin rule? Or are they right to remain loyal to Britain? If so, what of the Northern Irish Catholics who feel a loyalty to the Republic? The solution of such problems is hindered rather than helped by the tradition of the bomb and the gun in Irish politics.

Timeline

1947–64	Nehru Prime Minister of India.
1949	Newfoundland joins Canadian Union.
1951	Colombo Plan.
1955	Irish Republic joins UN.
1966–77	Mrs Gandhi Prime Minister of India.
1968	French nationalists in Canada form *Parti Québecois*.
1971	Awami League wins election in East Pakistan and civil war breaks out between East and West Pakistan. Indo-Pakistan War ends civil war and East Pakistan becomes independent of West Pakistan as state of Bangladesh.
1974	General Strike in Northern Ireland leads to collapse of British government's power-sharing scheme. Northern Ireland returns to direct rule from London.
1975–7	Mrs Gandhi declares 'state of emergency' in India.
1976	Northern Ireland Peace People formed.
1977	Janata Front wins election in India and Mrs Gandhi loses power.
1980	Mrs Gandhi re-elected Prime Minister of India.

Questions

1. What factors, both during the Second World War and since 1945, have caused Australian governments to seek close links with other countries besides Great Britain?

2. Why, and with what results, did India go to war with Pakistan in 1965 and again in 1971?

3. 'The "Empress" of India, as some called her, was in power again.'

   a) Who was called the 'Empress' of India?
   b) What policies had led to the defeat of the 'Empress' in the General Elections of 1977?
   c) What were the weaknesses of the Janata Front?
   d) When and how did the 'Empress' return to power?

4. Describe the troubles in Northern Ireland during the 1960s and '70s. How far are recent problems and grievances rooted in the past? (Refer also to Chapter 15)

5. Write short paragraphs on each of the following:
   a) Nehru's non-alignment policy
   b) Subsistence farming
   c) Orange Lodges
   d) the Irish Peace People, 1976

31
Defeat and Victory
Europe since 1945

The quarrels between different states in Europe during the twentieth century led to two world wars. After 1945 it was natural that men should consider ways of creating a united Europe. But politicians and peoples have differed about what sort of unity – military, economic or political – there should be. These arguments have been influenced by attitudes towards the two super-powers, the Soviet Union and the United States. In the early years after the Second World War it seemed to many Europeans that the overwhelming Soviet military presence in Eastern Europe presented a threat which only US power could counter. The outbreak of the Korean War (1950) showed that the Americans were ready, even eager, to challenge a Communist threat (see Chapter 23). The US government became anxious to form a European alliance against the Soviet Union. The **North Atlantic Treaty Organisation (NATO)** formed in April 1949 (see Chapter 22) took on a new life as a result. The Americans decided to rearm West Germany and began to form a truly anti-Soviet military force in Europe.

The French were not happy about a rearmed Germany. They suggested a European Defence Community (EDC) in which German units would not operate separately but would form part of a European army. In other words, there would be no German army commanded by German generals. They asked the British for support but instead Britain joined the USA in persuading the French to accept a rearmed Germany. At the same time the West German leader, **Dr Konrad Adenauer**, insisted that his country should have independent armed forces. But he promised that such forces would operate only as part of NATO and that Germany would neither make nor use atomic or chemical weapons. In 1954 the French parliament debated membership of the proposed EDC and it was rejected. The countries of France, Britain, Belgium, the Netherlands, Italy, Luxembourg and West Germany formed instead (1955) a much looser organisation called the **Western European Union (WEU)**. The British agreed to keep four army divisions and a tactical bomber force in Europe as a counter-balance to German power.

By 1958 the position had changed. A revived and vigorous France was led by **General de Gaulle**, by far the most famous French politician of the period. De Gaulle had his own ideas about the Soviet menace, which he thought exaggerated, and about American dominance, which he was determined to resist. Just as he had favoured tank power in the 1930s when other French soldiers still thought in terms of the old style infantry warfare, so now he claimed that France must be an independent nuclear power. It was, he maintained, a choice between

Konrad Adenauer, leader of postwar Germany

power and no power. However small the country, he believed that if she had nuclear weapons she would be listened to by the super-powers. He refused an American offer to supply France with such weapons. Instead, he surprised experts by showing that France was industrially strong enough to make her own.

De Gaulle did not favour a NATO overwhelmingly dominated by the United States. He thought that the development of long-range strategic weapons (rockets with nuclear warheads) meant that any American defence of Europe would be a scientific exercise in destruction, not an old style land war with US and Soviet troops fighting on the Continent. In 1959 he took all French warships out of NATO's Mediterranean Fleet. Seven years later France left NATO altogether. Since then the American defeat in Vietnam has caused many Americans to question and complain about their rôle as defenders of the non-Communist world. The chance of military confrontation in Europe seems less likely. Certainly the present power balance between NATO forces and those of the Soviet-organised **Warsaw Pact** countries (see page 267) means that only nuclear weapons could stop the Communist land forces from conquering Europe.

Modern warfare. US Army 'Lance' missile being tested in New Mexico

The Common Market

Just as de Gaulle played a major part in the arguments about European military unity, so he influenced the development of economic unity. After the Second World War Europe seemed set for a steady economic decline. Her share of world trade had dropped from fifty to forty per cent. On the Continent, border posts, different languages and currencies created barriers to free trade and more co-operation. There were also big differences of wealth and power between European countries. In 1948, for example, Britain was six times as rich as Greece. Italy could not be compared economically with West Germany. Some of the wealth Europe had obtained from her colonies had disappeared once they were granted independence.

Immediately after the war Europe was saved by the huge amount of aid supplied by the USA under the **Marshall Plan** (see page 212) Indirectly this helped point the way to more permanent recovery because it became necessary to co-operate in order to distribute the supplies fairly. The **Organisation for European Economic Co-operation (OEEC)**, which was set up to put the Plan into action, proved to be the forerunner of far more ambitious international groupings. In 1951 France, West Germany, Italy, Belgium, the Netherlands and Luxembourg (the last three known as the Benelux Countries) decided to share and develop their resources in a **European Coal and Steel Community (ECSC)**. The result was a twenty-five per cent increase in European steel production during the first three years of the ECSC's existence. In 1957 the same countries started a similar scheme of co-operation to produce atomic energy for peaceful purposes in the **European Atomic Energy Community (EURATOM)**.

However, the most famous and impressive achievement of these six countries was the forming of the **European Economic Community**

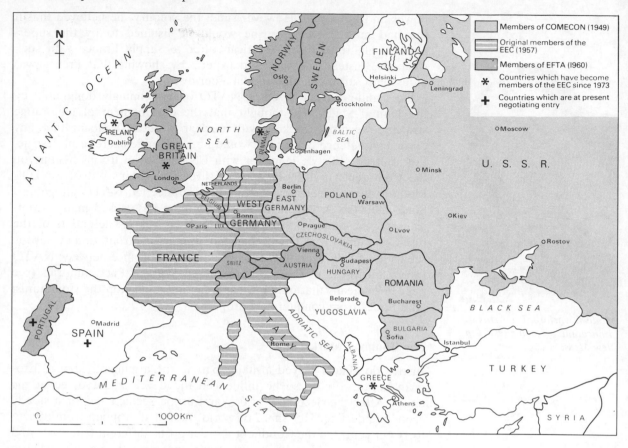

Europe since 1949

(EEC), popularly known as the Common Market, by the Treaty of Rome in 1957. Delegates of the six, representing 180,000,000 people at that time, decided to abolish all tariffs and other duties on trade between them and to introduce a charge on imports from outside. In this way artificial barriers between the six countries would be removed and the whole area developed as one economic unit. With every region specialising in its own products wasteful competition would cease and the general standard of living would rise for all. In a world of big economic groups, such as the Soviet Union and the USA, Europe would be able to compete on equal terms.

Such a development presented a problem for Britain. For two-and-a-half centuries Britain had been a sea power with possessions all over the world. Her first task had been to possess a powerful navy which could protect both her island home and foreign trade routes and colonies. Affairs in Europe were looked upon as a danger or a distraction depending upon the circumstances. Britain only intervened militarily in Europe if she felt that one nation was becoming too powerful. This she did in the eighteenth and nineteenth centuries, first against the France of Louis XIV and later that of Napoleon, and in the two world wars of this century against Germany. In 1945 she still had a large empire and what was regarded as a 'special' relationship with the USA because most of the early American colonies had been British. During the war

Churchill had told the British that they operated in three circles – the Anglo-American, the British Empire and the European. After 1945, with a Labour government intent above all on improving life for the British people, there was no doubt that the European 'circle' came a poor third.

Only gradually, as Britain gave independence to her Empire, starting with India in 1947, did her attitude towards Europe change. By 1956 the disastrous Suez adventure had shown that the old imperial Britain was only a memory (see Chapter 24). Weakened by war, slowed down by an out of date and inefficient economy, Britain had ceased to be a great power. When the EEC was formed, Britain refused to join because the Common Market tariff system would mean that she could not favour imports from the Commonwealth countries, particularly Australia and New Zealand. But Britain showed signs of a growing 'European' spirit by trying to form those countries not in the EEC into a free trade area. The **European Free Trade Association (EFTA)**, an economic alliance between Austria, Denmark, Norway, Portugal, Sweden, Switzerland and Britain, was formed in January 1960. It put Western Europe literally into sixes (EEC) and sevens (EFTA)!

In 1961 a Conservative Government led by Harold Macmillan decided to apply for British membership of the Common Market. The only EEC country likely to object was de Gaulle's France. In June 1962 Macmillan and de Gaulle met. De Gaulle favoured Britain's entry, providing that British military forces were integrated with European armies. In this way de Gaulle hoped to make Europe less dependent on the USA. He particularly disliked a NATO defence system dominated by the Americans. But, when the Americans stopped making a ground to air missile called 'Skybolt', leaving the British without a nuclear weapon, Britain agreed to buy the Polaris submarine missile from the USA. De Gaulle saw the cancellation of Skybolt as an opportunity for the British to join France and other European powers in making their own nuclear weapons. He was deeply disappointed about the Polaris deal and decided that there was no chance of Britain ever being truly independent of the USA.

The French leader was not prepared to let a Britain he regarded as dominated by America into Europe. In January 1963 he vetoed Britain's application for entry into the Common Market.

A wider Community

In 1967 Harold Wilson's Labour government again applied to join the EEC. The Labour Party was more split than the Conservatives upon this matter. Many Labour MPs were against becoming members of what they often referred to as a 'rich man's club', a club of capitalist countries. Nevertheless, Wilson knew he had enough support from all political parties to make entry possible. Personally, he had at first been against joining the EEC. The economic troubles between the USA and the Common Market during the 1960s had changed his mind. Wilson was afraid that Britain would be left isolated and weak if there was a

Britain's 1975 Common Market referendum. A rally in London against joining

serious trade war between the two economic giants. He told the British that the disadvantages of joining the Community were considerable, but he claimed that the long-term advantages far outweighed them.

Again there was the problem of France. Would the French veto the British application again? By 1969 de Gaulle had retired. New leaders, President Georges Pompidou in France and, from 1970, the Conservative Prime Minister, Edward Heath, in Britain, negotiated British entry this time. Pompidou was in many ways a follower of de Gaulle but he was not influenced by the old General's dislike of the USA – a dislike dating back to his quarrels with Roosevelt during the Second World War. Heath had always wanted Britain in the Common Market. Indeed, he was a firm believer in political as well as economic union between Britain and Europe as a way of avoiding future war. At the end of 1969, after de Gaulle's retirement, the leaders of the EEC had promised that they would let Britain in. Consequently Heath found a most favourable situation when he became Prime Minister in 1970. Negotiations went quickly and, by a treaty signed in January 1972, Britain, Denmark and the Irish Republic became full members of the EEC on 1 January 1973. Harold Wilson, soon to be Prime Minister again, complained that Britain could have got better terms. He promised that if he returned to power he would renegotiate the terms of entry.

By 1974 Wilson and the Labour Party were back in power. The new government managed to get new and better terms, mainly because other member countries were prepared to give Britain just enough to keep her in the Community. Then Wilson kept another promise, and, in 1975, gave Britain her first ever **referendum** on whether or not to stay in the Common Market. The situation was not as strange as it seemed because the Norwegian government had negotiated entry, only for it to be vetoed by the people in a referendum (1972). In Britain the result, after long debates in which Conservative and Labour politicians were often on the same side, was a resounding two to one vote to stay in. No doubt many voters were puzzled by the difficult, almost contradictory, arguments for and against membership. Probably many of those who voted 'yes' in 1975 thought it was too late to go back.

USA and USSR

Because of the Cold War between the Soviet Union and the United States, there was never a peace treaty to end the Second World War as there had been to end the First. Nobody was in any doubt about the frontiers between East and West, in Germany and elsewhere. But the Russians always hoped to get some sort of international blessing for the borders set up by force of arms in 1945 and, later, by a Communist take-over in Czechoslovakia in 1947. They got what they wanted at a conference held in Helsinki, Finland, between 1973 and 1975 (see Chapter 26). The confident American leaders who had faced the Soviet Union in the early days of the Cold War had been replaced by first President Nixon, disgraced by the Watergate scandal, and then President Gerald Ford, the only US President never to be elected to the office. The old crusading spirit which had led the USA to succeed in the Berlin Airlift (see page 213) and defeat a Communist attack in Korea (see page 224) had been replaced by deep disillusionment as one disaster followed another in Vietnam (see Chapter 27).

In these changed circumstances it is not surprising that America agreed, by the so-called **Final Act** of the Helsinki Conference, that existing European frontiers could not be changed. In return for accepting these Soviet conquests, the West was promised freer emigration from the Soviet Union for those who wished to leave, more freedom of speech for those who wished to criticise the Soviet system and better facilities for foreign journalists to find out about events in the USSR. The Final Act changed nothing. It merely showed that the USA was prepared to accept the existing situation in Europe. It had been obvious in Hungary in 1956 and in Czechoslovakia in 1968 (see Chapter 26) that she would do nothing to stop the Soviet Union taking an even tighter grip on her Eastern European empire.

The Helsinki *détente* (relaxation of tension) between the USSR and the USA was not a sign of friendship between the two super-powers. Both were still deeply hostile to each other as they moved into the last quarter of the twentieth century. On the other hand, they were both very much alone against the rest of the world. Communist China had by 1960 become an enemy of the Soviet Union (see Chapter 23), as the two powers quarrelled about different interpretations of Marxism, about spheres of influence in Africa and elsewhere, and even about their own borders. The 'buffer states' of Eastern Europe could be seen as a mixed blessing for the USSR. Could they be relied upon to fight for her? The Hungarian Rising of 1956 and the need to send Soviet armies into Czechoslovakia in 1968 did not suggest genuine friendship between the Soviet Union and her satellites.

Above all the Soviet Union, despite her bristling weaponry, was still the second, not the first, power in the world. She even had to accept economic aid from the West because her vast and costly armed services placed an almost unbearable strain on the Soviet economy. The United States, despite poor leadership and lack of success in Vietnam, was still very powerful. This was in spite of the fact that she was no longer the world's fastest growing country economically. This leading position was lost to Japan and some Western European countries during the 1960s and 1970s.

The Council of Europe

Churchill, even during the Second World War, had often spoken of the need for a united Europe. In September 1945 he asked for a European Assembly to be formed. Leading European politicians gathered at the Hague, Holland, in May 1948 and such an Assembly was formed in 1949. The **Council of Europe**, as it was called, consisted of Britain, France, Italy, the Irish Republic, the Netherlands, Belgium, Luxembourg, Denmark, Norway and Sweden. Later Iceland, Greece, Turkey, West Germany, Austria, Cyprus, Switzerland and Malta joined. The Council was not a parliament. It had no powers to make laws for its member states. Its representatives were appointed by each country's national parliament, they were not elected by the people.

The Council of Europe has remained for over thirty years a debating chamber where Europeans can meet and discuss their problems. From the start it promised to uphold human rights. A European Commission hears cases presented by member countries and its findings are examined by the European Court of Human Rights (set up in 1959), whose decisions can be binding. For example, in 1976 its ministers announced that terrorists should not be sheltered by a member state. During the same year they agreed with a claim by the Irish Republic that certain methods used by the British against IRA suspects in Northern Ireland amounted to torture. The British accepted this judgement but were angry because the Irish delegates continued to press the case long after the methods complained of had been stopped.

The European Community

In 1967 the three independent communities of the ECSC, EEC and EURATOM joined together to form a single European Community. Its Commission was in Brussels, its Court of Justice in Luxembourg and its Parliament in Strasbourg. A further move towards integration came in 1976 with the decision to hold direct elections to the European Parliament. In other words, people in each country should vote for their representatives just as they voted for members of their own parliaments. Such elections, cutting across national laws, had to be agreed to by each member country. This took some time, especially as it was stated that such elections should be 'equal, free, direct and secret'. Opponents of the European Community saw their own country losing its law-making powers to foreigners. They pointed out that the economic law-making powers of the EEC had led to a number of civil servants making a number of often complicated regulations and laws.

Opening of the European Parliament, 1979

Nevertheless the first British elections for the European Parliament were held in June 1979. Britain's share of members was 81 out of a total of 410, and the Conservative Party won 60 of them.

Neither the European Community nor the Council of Europe have altered the reality of power in Europe. Part of Europe is dominated by the Warsaw Pact system developed by the Soviet Union (see page 267). The western part, in the opinion of some, is too much influenced by the activities of US-owned companies. The frontiers of Europe, as we have seen, were 'frozen' by 1948. The chief irony was Germany, united by the sword in 1871 and divided by the sword in 1945. The wars which resulted in part from German unification had changed world history. Over a hundred years later mankind still faced the problems caused by the chain of events which began at Versailles in 1871.

Victory and defeat

Since 1870 the world has seen both Europe's defeat and her victory. The powerful Europe which went to war in 1914, a Europe dominated by a few great powers, has gone. Like Ancient Greece centuries before, its separate states weakened themselves in frightful wars. Their empires no longer exist; their fleets and armies no longer cause the world to tremble. Two super-powers, the Soviet Union and the United States, have replaced them. On the other hand, European influence, like that of Greece, lives on. Everywhere Europe's ways and customs, above all its industrialisation, seem destined to cover the earth, not because other people admire Europe but because its skills offer them the promise of higher standards of living.

There are serious and alarming faults in such a way of life. It is often noisy and ugly. It encourages people's greed. It has caused wars and

*Red Square military parade on
the sixtieth anniversary of the
Russian Revolution, 1977*

led to the use of nuclear weapons. Its scientific side-effects may even
threaten healthy life on earth by pollution of the atmosphere, earth
and sea. Yet there are great achievements, cultural as well as industrial, to its name. The technology which eventually put a man on the
moon points the way to a world of computers, lasers and other scientific marvels. It has also helped to remove hunger and starvation from
the lives of millions of people. But the mushroom-shaped cloud which
hung over Hiroshima in 1945 now hangs over mankind. Nuclear
weapons, stored in vast quantities by the Soviet Union and the United
States, could destroy life on this planet. In a troubled world any small
conflict might cause the super-powers to intervene and so lead to a
Third World War. In particular, the Arab-Israeli confrontation is in a
most sensitive area – almost in the centre of some of the world's
largest oil-fields.

The oil problem

The supply of oil has become a global problem. In 1870 most countries
produced their own fuel: wood, coal or farm waste (used extensively
until the 1940s). A hundred years later the situation had changed dramatically. Most industrialised and developing countries used great
quantities of oil. Only a few actually produced it. Not only were the
'have nots' of the oil world forced to buy it from the 'haves' but most
needed to buy it from North Africa and the Middle East. In 1970, of a
total supply of 2,200 million tonnes of oil needed by the non-
Communist countries, (the Soviet Union has her own oil-fields), nearly
half came from the Arab states of this area.

Until the early 1960s most North African and Middle Eastern Arab
states were controlled by Western powers and their business interests.

Middle Eastern oil. H₂S plant and separators on Das Island off Abu Dhabi

In the Middle East British, Dutch and American companies owned the oil-fields and saw to it that oil was supplied cheaply. But, as one Arab state after another gained its independence, their governments decided to take over and run the oil-fields themselves. One example was Iran which nationalised her oil industry in the early 1950s. Certain Arab leaders, angry at what they regarded as 'exploitation' by the Western powers of their natural resources, realised that oil offered them a powerful weapon. They could get the industrialised parts of the world to do what they wanted by stopping or slowing down oil supplies. Oil is the essential life-blood of Western industry. Any increase in fuel prices, for transport or heating, affects the cost of production and therefore the price of goods in the shops. So in 1961 leading Arab oil producers formed OPEC – the **Organisation of Petroleum Exporting Countries** – to agree on a standard price for oil. Their object was to get what they regarded as a fair price for their oil and at the same time to put political pressure on the West.

The problem was highlighted during the Arab-Israeli Yom Kippur War in 1973 (see Chapter 24). OPEC stopped, or reduced, oil supplies to countries friendly with Israel. Chief among these was the United States whose large Jewish population had made sure for many years that Israel did not lack military or other help. The result of OPEC's action was an energy crisis, particularly in the USA where huge 'gas-guzzling' cars and air-conditioning in most buildings use enormous amounts of fuel. At that time the USA imported only about seven per cent of the oil she needed from abroad, but losing even this percentage was enough to hit the economy hard. Britain, by contrast, was hoping to be self-sufficient in oil by 1981 due to her North Sea oil-fields.

*The Iranian Revolution.
Crowds march through the
streets of Teheran carrying
pictures of Ayatollah Khomeini,
1979*

A tanker every eight minutes

Since 1973 a series of oil price increases by OPEC took the price from $5 a barrel then to $23.50 a barrel in 1979. Industrialised economies, dependent upon oil, were soon showing signs of strain with much unemployment as firms went out of business because of steeply rising costs. In 1978 the pro-Western government of the Shah of Iran was overthrown and replaced by a 'revolutionary Islamic' government deeply hostile to the West in general and the United States in particular. Oil supplies were first disrupted by the Revolution, and then slowed down by the new government. Even an Arab state thought to be friendly towards the West, Saudi Arabia, deliberately limited its oil production for political and technical reasons.

There is an obvious danger in using oil supplies as a political weapon. How long will industrialised countries, particularly one as powerful as the United States, refrain from taking military action to protect supplies vital for their economies and high standard of living? Most industrialised countries get their oil from the Arab states; an oil tanker passes through the Straits of Hormuz (see map on page 227) every eight minutes. Yet, in the small Gulf States which control this coastline are Soviet advisers, tanks and other military equipment. As one observer remarked, 'Cut off that oil and the West would starve. NATO would be crippled. Japan would be in trouble within three months'. That the Soviet Union was prepared to act in the area was shown by her invasion of Afghanistan (December 1979). This clear threat to Middle Eastern oil supplies caused the USA to cut supplies of wheat and technical equipment to the Soviet Union. She also discussed possible defence moves with Pakistan and China.

As far as is known, the world's supplies of oil will begin to run out by the year 2000. In 1979 experts revised a forecast that oil production would be running at 45 million barrels a day in 1990, reducing it to 35 million a day. This they thought would be partly the result of the deliberate limiting of oil production by OPEC countries. But, whatever the cause, the world will need to find alternative fuels as soon as possible, preferably ones which cause less pollution than oil. As the troubled twentieth century draws to a close, Man's very intelligence, which gave him control of the earth, poses problems which could lead to swift destruction by nuclear warfare or slow destruction by pollution.

Timeline

1948   Marshall Plan.
1949   Council of Europe formed.
1951   European Coal and Steel Community (ECSC) formed.
1958   European Economic Community (EEC) and European Atomic Energy Community (EURATOM) formed.
1961   Organisation of Petroleum Exporting Countries (OPEC) formed.
1963   De Gaulle vetoes Britain's application to join EEC.
1967   Britain again applies to join EEC. EEC, ECSC, and EURATOM join together to form one single European Community.
1973   Britain becomes full member of EEC.
1975   Britain votes in its first ever referendum to remain in EEC.
1979   Direct elections to the European Parliament.

Questions

1. Outline the background to and the development of the Common Market. What problems faced Britain when she wished to join?

2. 'The Russians always hoped to get some sort of international blessing for the borders set up by force of arms in 1945 and, later, by a Communist take-over in Czechoslovakia in 1947.'

   How and with what results, did the Soviet Union get 'international blessing' for this situation at Helsinki in 1975?

3. 'Since 1870 the world has seen both Europe's defeat and her victory.' Explain this statement.

4. 'The supply of oil has become a global problem.'
   a) Describe the nature of this problem.
   b) Which countries are most dependent on outside oil supplies?
   c) How does the problem pose a threat to world peace?

5. Write short paragraphs on each of the following:
   a) EFTA
   b) EEC referendum in Britain, 1975
   c) the Council of Europe
   d) elections for the European Parliament, 1979

Index

Abyssinian War 156
Adenauer, Konrad 332
Africa, Scramble for 21–4
Afrikaners 256
Afrika Korps 185
Agadir Incident 50
Agricultural Adjustment
    Act (see New Deal)
Air Raid Precautions 180
Algeciras Conference 49–50
Algerian War 227–8
Allenby, General Edmund 83–5
Allende, Salvador 314–16
Alliance for Progress 317–18
Amiens, Battle of 85
Anarchism 165
Anglo-French Convention
    (1899) 20
Anglo-Japanese Alliance
    (1902) 47
Anschluss 93
Anti-Comintern Pact (1936) 174
Anzacs 73
Apartheid 256–7
Appeasement 157–9
Arab League (1945) 227
Arnhem, Battle of 191
Article 43 (UN Charter) 205
Arusha Declaration (1967) 250
Aswan High Dam 231
Atatürk, Kemal 72–4, 98–103
Atlantic Charter (1941) 175, 242
Auschwitz 204
Australia 25–7, 320–1
Austria-Hungary 11, 55–7
Axis, Rome-Berlin (1936) 156

Baden-Powell, Robert 33
Bakunin, Michael 165
Balfour Declaration (1917) 104
Balkan League 53
Balkan Wars 53–5
Bantustans 258–9
Bataan, defence of 194
Bangladesh 325
Batista, Fulgencio 310
Beatty, Admiral David 75
Beer-Hall Putsch 147
Belgium, invasion of (1914) 60
Belgium, neutrality 60
Benelux countries 210
Ben Gurion, David 228
Beria, Lavrenti 264
Berlin Airlift 213–14
Berlin, Congress of
    (1878) 14–16, 44

Berlin Treaty of (1885) 22
Berlin Wall 215
Bhutto, Zulfiqar Ali 325
Biafra 247
'Big Stick' Policy 308
Bismarck, Otto von 2–9
Black and Tans 135
Black Power 298
Black Thursday (1929) 121
Blitzkrieg 180
Bloody Sunday (Russia) 42
Bolsheviks 81–2
Boxer Rebellion 218
Braun, Eva 161
Brasília 311–12
Brazil 311–13
Breslau (German warship) 67
Brest-Litovsk, Treaty of
    (1918) 83
Brezhnev, Leonid 270, 273
Brinkmanship 267
Britain, Battle of 184
British Empire 25–7, 128–31
British North America Act
    (1867) 25
Broz, Josip (see Tito)
Brusilov Offensive 79–80
Bucharest, Treaty of (1913) 54
Buchlau meeting 52–3
Bulgaria 54
Bulge, Battle of the 191

Cabrinovic, Nedjelko 56
Cambrai, Battle of 81
Canada 25–7, 321–2
Caporetto, Battle of 83
Cape coloureds 256
Carter, President Jimmy 238, 301
Casement, Roger 133
Castro, Fidel 267, 310–11
Central African Federation 251
Central Intelligence Agency
    (CIA) 294
Chamberlain, Neville 158–60
Chiang Kai-shek 205, 219–21
Chile 313–16
China 216–22, 269, 277–81
Churchill, Sir Winston 181–2
Civil Rights Bill (USA) 291
Clay, General Lucius 213
Clemenceau, Georges 88–90
Cold War 210–11
Collective farming 113
Collins, Michael 133
Colombo Plan (1951) 320–1
Comintern 114
Common Market (EEC) 333–4

Communism 107–8
Communist Manifesto 107
Compiegne 87, 183
Confucius 216
Congress of Industrial
    Organisations (CIO) 288
Congress Party 323–4
Coral Sea, Battle of 195
Coronel, Battle of 68
Corregidor, defence of 194
Corrigan, Mairead 329
Costello, John 327
Council of Europe 338
Crete, Battle of 185
Crimean War 14
Cuban Crisis 267–9
Cultural Revolution 278–80
Curragh Mutiny 132
Curzon Line 92
Czechoslovakia 159, 269–70

Dawes Plan (1924) 147–8
De Gaulle, Charles 180, 183,
    228, 332
D (Deliverance) Day 189–90
Depression (Germany) 148–9
Depression (USA) 122
Desai, Morarji 324
Détente 271–4, 337
De Valera, Eamon 135–7
Díaz, Porfirio 306
Dien Bien Phu, Battle of 282
Disraeli, Benjamin 15–16
Dissidents 272–3
Doenitz, Admiral Karl 191
Double Tenth
    Revolution 218–19
Dowding, Air-Marshal Hugh 184
Dreadnought, HMS 47–8
Dual Alliance (1879) 44
Dual Entente (1893) 45
Dual Monarchy (1867) 11
Dubček, Alexander 270
Dulles, John Foster 266–7
Dunkirk Evacuation 182
Durham Report 25

East German Rising 265
Easter Rising (1916) 133–4
Eastern Question 12
Ebro, Battle of 170
Eden, Sir Anthony 231
Egypt 230–7
Egyptian-Israeli Peace Treaty
    (1979) 238
Eisenhower, General Dwight
    D. 189, 233, 291–2

El Alamein, Battle of 187
Ems telegram 4
Enabling Law (1933) 153
Engels, Friedrich 107
Enola Gay 199
Entente Cordiale (1904) 48
Enver Bey 52
European Coal and Steel
Community (ECSC) 333
European Free Trade Association
(EFTA) 335
European Recovery Programme
(ERP) 333
Extra-territorial rights 217

Falkland Islands, Battle of the 68
Fascist Party 114–16
Fashoda incident 18–20
Federal Emergency Relief
Administration (*see* New Deal)
Fenians, The 132–3
Fifth Regiment 168
Final solution 203–4
Fireside chats (Roosevelt) 123
Five Year Plans (China) 278
Five Year Plans (USSR) 111–13
Foch, Marshal Ferdinand 85
Food and Agricultural
Organisation (FAO) 208
Fourteen Points 88–90
France, invasion of (1940) 182–3
Franco, General 163–70
Franco-Prussian War 1–9
Frankfurt, Treaty of (1871) 8
Franz Ferdinand,
Archduke 56–8
Franz Joseph, Emperor 11
Free Corps 144
Frelimo 253
Front de Libération Nationale
(FLN) 227
Fuchida, Commander 176–9
Fuchs, Klaus 290

Gagarin, Yuri 266
Gallipoli Campaign 72–4
Gandhi, Indira 323–5
Gandhi, Mahatma 139–40, 323
Gang of Four 281
Gaza Raid 231
General Strike (N. Ireland) 329
Geneva Conference
(1954) 282–3
German Navy Law (1900) 46
Germany 1–9, 44–57, 213–15
Gestapo 153
Ghana 243
Giap, Vo Nguyen 282
Goebbels, Joseph 148

Goeben (German warship) 67
'Good Neighbour' Policy 174,
308
Government of India Act
(1935) 140
Gowon, General Yakubu 247
Grand National Assembly 98
Great Leap Forward 278
Great Society (USA) 296
Great Trek 27
Great Wall of China 216
Greece, invasion of (1941) 185
Guadalcanal, Battle of 196
Guam 193–4, 196
Guevara, Ernesto Che 310–11
Guernica, bombing of 169

Habsburg Empire 10–11, 55
Habsburgs, The 10
Hacha, Emil 159
Hammarskjöld, Dag 245
Harding, President Warren 119
Hearst, William Randolph 35–6
Herzl, Theodore 103
Himmler, Heinrich 153
Hindenburg Line 80
Hindenburg, Paul von 150
Hipper, Admiral Franz von 74
Hiroshima, bombing of 198–201
Hitler, Adolf 139–161
Hoare–Laval Pact 156
Ho Chi Minh 281–3
Holland (Netherlands), invasion of
(1940) 182
Home Guard 184
Home Rule (for Ireland) 131–2
Hoover, President
Herbert 119–21
Horst Wessel 146
'Hot-line' 269
Hungarian Rising 265

Ibarruri, Dolores 168–9
Ibo tribe 246
Imperialism 20–4
Imperial Preference 129
Imphal, Battle of 198
Inchon landing 223
India 137–41, 323–7
Inflation 313–14
International Brigades 168–9
Iranian Revolution 238, 342
Ireland 131–37, 327–30
Irish Peace Treaty 135
Irish Republican Army
(IRA) 135
Iron Curtain 208–10
Isandhlwana, defence of 28
Island-hopping strategy 196
Israel 228–34

Israeli-Egyptian Peace Treaty
(1979) 238
Italy 78–9, 114–17, 156
Iwo Jima, Battle of 198

Jameson Raid 31
Japan 38–43, 173, 193–201,
220–1, 275–6
Japanese surrender (1945) 201
Jellicoe, Admiral John 74–6
Jerusalem 84
Jewish Colonial Trust 103
Jinnah, Mohamed Ali 140–1
Joffre, General Joseph 63–4
Johnson Act (1921) 120, 172
Johnson, President Lyndon B.
284–5, 295–6
Jutland, Battle of 74–6

Kamikaze pilots 198
Kashmir 138
Katanga 245–6
Kellogg Pact (1928) 148
Kennedy, President John F. 268,
284, 293–4
Kenya African Democratic
Union 248
Kenya African National
Union 248
Kenyatta, Jomo 248–50
Kerensky, Alexander 82
Khrushchev, Nikita 263–7
Khmer Rouge 286
Kiaochow, capture of 67
King David Hotel 229
King, Martin Luther 292–3
Kissinger, Henry 299–300
Kitchener, General 18–20
Kluck, General von 63
Kolchak, Admiral 109
Konnigratz, Battle of (*see*
Sadowa)
Korean War 222–4
Kosygin, Alexei 237, 270
Kuomintang Government 219,
221
Kruger, Paul 30–3
Kruger telegram 31
Kubitschek, Juscelino 311–12

Lancaster House Conference
(1979) 255
Lateran Treaty and Concordat
(1929) 117
Latifundia 164
Latin America 174, 303–19
Lausanne, Treaty of (1923) 101
Lawrence, Colonel T.E. 84
League of Nations 94–5
Le Cateau, Battle of 62

Lend-Lease Scheme   174–5
Lenin, Vladimir Ilyich   82–3, 108–10
Leyte Gulf, Battle of   197
Lin Piao   280
Little Rock High School   292
Local Defence Volunteers   184
Locarno Pact (1925)   148
London, Treaty of (1913)   54
London, Treaty of (1915)   78
Long March   220
Los Alamos research   198–9
Lumumba, Patrice   245
Lusaka, Commonwealth Conference   254–5
Lusitania, sinking of   69
Luther King, Martin   (*see* King)
Lynch, Jack   330

MacArthur, General Douglas   196, 201, 223–4
McCarthy, Senator Joseph   289–90
Madrid, Battle of   168–9
Maginot Line   155
Maine, sinking of   35–6
Majuba, Battle of   28–9
Malawi   250
Manchu Dynasty (China)   217
Mao Tse-tung   219–22, 277–81
Marchand, Captain Jean   18–20
March on Rome   115–16
Marco Polo Bridge Incident   173
Marne, Battle of the   62–4
Marshall, General George   221
Marshall Plan   212, 333
Marx, Karl   107–8
Masurian Lakes, Battle of the   65, 78
Mau Mau rebellion   248
Megiddo, Battle of   84
Mein Kampf (My Struggle)   147, 157
Metz, Siege of   6
Midway Island, Battle of   195
Mobutu, Sese Seko   245–6
Mohammed, Brigadier Murtala   247
Molotov Plan   212
Moltke, General Helmuth von   2–9
Monckton, Lord   251
Monroe Doctrine (1823)   308
Mons, Battle of   62
Montagu-Chelmsford Reforms (1919)   140
Monte Cassino, Battle of   189
Montgomery, General Bernard   189

Morley-Minto Reforms (1909)   139
Morocco   49–50, 228
Mudanya Agreement (1922)   101
Mugabe, Robert   255
Mukden, Battle of   41
Mukden incident   172
Mulberry Harbour   190
Munich Agreement (1938)   158–60
Muslim League   140–1
Mussolini, Benito   114–17
MVD (Russian Secret Police)   262

Nagy, Imre   265
Napoleon III, Emperor   4
Nasser, Gamal Abdel   231–3
Nationalism   11, 226
National Recovery Act   (*see* New Deal)
National Socialist (Nazi) Party   145–6
Navarino, Battle of   12
Navy League   46
Nehru, Jawaharlal   323–4
Neuve-Chapelle, Battle of   69
New Deal   124–7
New Economic Policy (NEP)   111
'New Frontier' Policy   294
New York Journal   35
Nicholas II, Tsar of Russia   81–2
Nigeria   240, 246–8
Nine Power Treaty (1921)   171
Nixon, President Richard   285–6, 299, 309
Nkrumah, Kwame   243, 244
Non-Intervention Committee   167
North Atlantic Treaty Organisation (NATO)   211
Northern Ireland   135, 327–30
North German Confederation   3
Nuremburg Laws   153
Nuremburg Trials   203

Obasanjo, Olusegun   247
Occupation of Rhineland   156
Occupation of Ruhr   145
October Revolution (1917)   83
Oil problem   237, 340–2
Okinawa, Battle of   198
Omdurman, Battle of   18
'Open Door' Policy   171
Operation Barbarossa   185
Operation Yellow   182–3
Orangemen   328
Organisation de l'Armée Secrète (OAS)   228
Organisation for European

Economic Co-operation (OEEC)   333
Organisation of Petroleum Exporting Countries (OPEC)   341
Oswald, Lee Harvey   295
Ottawa Conference (1932)   129
Ottoman Empire (*see also* Turkey)   10–17

Pakistan   140
Palestine War   230
Panama Canal   37
Pan-Americanism   305
Panmunjom   224
Paris, Siege of   6–7
Patriotic Front   254
Peace People (Northern Ireland)   329
Peaceful co-existence   266
Pearl Harbour, attack on   176–9
Pearse, Patrick   131
People's Republic of China   222
Peron, Juan   316–17
Perry, Commodore Matthew   38–9
Philippines   194
Pinochet, Augusto   316
Platt Amendment (1905)   36
Plevna (Pleven)   14
Pluto pipeline   190
Poland   154, 161
Popular Fronts   114, 164
Population growth (Latin America)   313
Port Arthur, attack on   40
Portsmouth (USA), Treaty of (1905)   42
Potsdam Conference (1945)   213
Pretoria Convention (1881)   29
Princip, Gavrilo   57–8
Proportional representation   150
Proudhon, Pierre   165
Purges (Soviet)   113–14

Rasputin, Gregori   81
Realpolitik   8
Red Guards   279–80
Referendum (on Common Market)   336
Reichstag Fire   152–3
Reparations   94
Rhodes, Cecil   30–2
Rhodesia, Southern   (*see* Zimbabwe)
Röhm, Ernst   153–4
Rogers Plan (1970)   235
Roosevelt, President Franklin   123–7, 308

Roosevelt, President
Theodore   37
Rorke's Drift, defence of   28
Russia   81–4, 160–1, 185–6,
204, 208–12, 262–9
Russian Revolutions   81–4
Russo-Japanese War   40–1, 218

Sadat, Anwar   236, 238
Sadowa, Battle of   3
Sakarya, Battle of   100
Sanctions (Rhodesia)   252
Sand River Convention
(1852)   28
San Juan Hill   36
San Stefano, Treaty of (1878)   14
Sarajevo, murder at   56–8
Sarikamish, Battle of   67
Scheer, Admiral Reinhard
von   75–7
Schlieffen Plan   49, 59
Security Council (UN)   206
Sedan, Battle of   6
Self-determination   92–4
Serbia   55–6
Seven Weeks' War   3
Sèvres meeting (1956)   232
Sèvres, Treaty of (1920)   98–9
Seyss-Inquart, Arthur   157
Sharpeville shooting   257–8
Shastri, Lal Bahadur   324
Shimonoseki, Treaty of
(1895)   39
Singapore, fall of (1942)   194
Singh, Charan   327
Six Days War   234–5
Six Principles (Rhodesia)   252
Slave Trade   240
Somme, Battle of   71–2
South Africa   27–34, 255–8
South East Asia Treaty
Organisation (SEATO)   283
Soviets   82
Spanish Popular Front
government   165
Specialised Agencies (UN)   206
Splendid Isolation   47
'Sputnik'   266
Stalin, Joseph   111–14, 262–3
Stalingrad, Battle of   187
Strategic Arms Limitation Talks
(SALT)   271
Stresemann, Gustav   147
Sudetenland   157
Suez Canal   19, 231
Suez attack   232–3
Sun Yat-sen   218–19

Suppression of Communism Act
(1950)   257
Suvla Bay landing   74

Taft-Hartley Act (1947)   289
Tannenberg, Battle of   65, 78
Tanzania   250
Taoism   216
Tel-el-Kebir, Battle of   19
Tennessee Valley Authority
(TVA)   126–7
Test Ban Treaty (1963)   269
Thirty-eighth Parallel   (*see*
Korean War)
Three Emperors' League
(1872)   44
Tibbetts, Colonel Paul   199
Tito, Marshal   210
Tojo, General Hideki   176
Tokyo, bombing of   199
Transkei Bantustan   258–9
Treaty of Rome (1957)   334
Treblinka   204
Triple Alliance (1882)   44
Triple Intervention (1895)   40
Trotsky, Leon   110–11
Truman Doctrine (1947)   211
Truman, President Harry S.   198,
222
Tshombe, Moise   245–6
Tsushima, Battle of   42
Turkey, modernisation   101–3
Twentieth Congress Speech
(1956)   265
Twenty-One Demands
(1915)   171

Uitlanders   30
Ulundi, Battle of   28
Unilateral Declaration of
Independence (Rhodesia)   252
United Nations Charter
(1945)   205
United Nations Educational,
Scientific and Cultural
Organisation
(UNESCO)   208
United Nations General
Assembly   205
United Nations Organisation
(UNO)   206–7
United Nations Security
Council   205
United States of America   35–7,
119–27, 176–9, 193–201
USSR   (*see* Russia)

U Thant   206–7

Van der Lubbe, Marianus .   152–3
Venizelos, Eleutherios   53, 98
Verdun, Battle of   70–1
Vereeniging, Treaty of (1902)   33
Versailles, Treaty of
(1919)   88–96
Verwoerd, Dr Hendrik   258
Vichy Government   183
Vietnam   281–6
Villa, Pancho   306–8
Voortrekkers   27

Wailing Wall (Jerusalem)   104
Wake Island   193
War Guilt Clause (Versailles
Treaty)   148
Warren, Judge Earl   292
Warsaw Pact (1955)   267, 339
Washington Naval Conference
(1921)   171
Watergate Scandal   300–1
Weimar Republic   144–6
Western European Union   332
Westminster, Statute of
(1931)   129
Whitlam, Gough   320
William I, King of Prussia   1
William II,
Emperor-Kaiser   45–6
Williams, Betty   329
Wilson, Harold   335–6
Wilson, President
Woodrow   88–96
Winter War   180
World Health Organisation
(WHO)   207–8

Yamamoto, Admiral
Isoroku   177
Yom Kippur War   235–7, 276
Young Turks   52
Ypres, Battle of   65, 81

Zaïre (Congo)   244–8
Zambia   252
Zapata, Emiliano   306–8
Zhukov, General Georgi   186–7
Zia, General Ur-Rahman   325
Zimbabwe   251–5
Zimbabwe African National
Union (ZANU)   253
Zimbabwe African People's Union
(ZAPU)   253
Zimbabwe, ancient ruins   240
Zionism   103

Acknowledgements

We are grateful to the following for their permission to reproduce photographs:

Associated Press, pages 116, 168, 173, 322, 333; Anglo-Chinese Educational Institute, pages 221, 281 *above*; Barnaby's Picture Library, page 289; BBC Hulton Picture Library, pages 3, 4 *above*, 14, 15, 18, 19 *above and below*, 30 *above and below*, 36, 38 *above*, 42, 56, 57, 74, 80, 81, 83, 90, 99, 100, 107, 115, 132, 135, 143, 156 *below*, 159 *above*, 165, 182, 216, 223 *above*, 228 *above*, 306; Bettmann Archive Inc., page 126; Bildarchiv Preussischer Kulturbesitz, page 198; BP Photo. Courtesy SMBP Advertising Archive, page 341; Camera Press, pages 68 *below*, 108 (Tass/RBO), 111, 138, 178, 209, 227, 228 *below*, 231 (Portrait study by Karsh of Ottawa), 235, 243, 247 *below* (Photo: David Robison), 248 (Photo: Gerhard Cohn), 250 *above*, (Photo: Marion Kaplan), 250 *below* (Photo: Lawrence Alexandra), 253 (Photo: Jan Kopec), 254 (Camerapix), 255 *below* (Photo: Capa), 259 (Photo: John Seymour), 277, 279 (Photo: Rory Dell), 281 *below*, 283, 286 (Photo: David Hume Kennerly), 313 *above* (Photo: Paul Harrison), 314 (Photo: Christian Belpaire), 318 (Photo: FSLN soldier Emilio), 320 (Photo: Penny Tweedie), 323 *above*, 326 (Photo: Sarah Webb Barrell); J. Allan Cash Ltd., page 246 *below*; Culver Pics Inc., pages 95, 199; Daily News, page 301 *above*. Copyright 1974 New York News Inc. (Courtesy John Frost Newspaper Library); Jerry Doyle, page 124; John Hillelson Agency Ltd., pages 31, 170 (Photo: Robert Capa © Magnum), 189, 201 (Photo: Yusuhe Yamahata © Magnum); Imperial War Museum, London, cover and pages 47, 48, 60, 61, 71, 73, 76, 85 *above and below*, 86, 159 *below*; Keystone, pages 141, 146, 150, 166 *above*, 169, 175, 176, 184, 187, 194, 200, 214, 245 *below*, 249, 252, 258, 267, 270 *below*, 271, 272, 280, 284, 285 *above and below*, 290, 297, 301 *below*, 310 *above and below*, 317, 339; David King Collection, page 110; London Express News and Feature Services. Cartoon by David Low by arrangement with the Trustees and the London Evening Standard, page 161; Mansell Collection, pages 1, 2, 4 *below*, 6, 7, 11, 27, 28 *below*, 29, 35, 39, 46, 102, 103, 163, 218; National Library of Ireland, pages 133, 134; Peter Newark's Western Americana, pages 119, 123, 307; Novosti Press Agency, pages 112, 266, 273 (Photo: Y. Abramochkin), 340; Zimbabwe Department of Information, page 241; Walter Sanders/Life © Time Inc. 1948, page 213; Sony, page 276; Syndication International, page 328; Topham, pages 291, 294, 295 *above*, 298, 304, 312; Topix, page 139; Pacemaker Press Agency Ltd., Belfast, page 330; Popperfoto, pages 52, 82, 89, 105, 122, 136 *above*, 147, 153, 154, 181 *below*, 205, 210, 219, 233 (UPI), 255 *above* (UPI), 257, 263 (UPI), 264 (UPI), 270, *above*, 292, 315, 321, 325 *above*, 332, 336, 342 (UPI); Ullstein Bilderdienst, pages 45, 49, 88, 145, 148, 149, 152, 155, 157, 190 *below right*, 191, 203, 204; United Nations, page 323 *below*; USIS, pages 38 *below*, 196, 197, 268, 293, 295 *below*; UPI Photo's pages 65 *below*, 299, 309; H. Roger Viollet, pages 64 (Collection Viollet), 183 (Harlinque-Viollet).

We would be grateful for any information concerning the identity of the copyright holders of photographs on pages 80, 121, 229, 246 *above*.

We are also grateful to the following for permission to reproduce their adapted material:

Four maps from *The Anchor Atlas of World History Vol. II* by Herman Kinder and Werner Hilgemann, translated by Ernest A. Menze with maps designed by Harald and Ruth Bukor. Copyright © 1978 by Penguin Books Ltd. Reprinted by permission of Doubleday & Company, Inc. *The Penguin Atlas of World History Vol. 2*. Copyright © Deutscher Taschenbuch Verlag GmbH and Co. KG. Munchen (Deutschland), 1966. Translation copyright © Penguin Books Ltd., 1978 on pages 186, 212 *above and below*, 325 *below*; Times Books for map from *The Times Atlas of World History*, on page 84; United Nations for chart on page 207; George Weidenfeld and Nicolson Ltd. for maps from *American History Atlas* by Martin Gilbert on pages 172 and 267 *below* and *Recent History Atlas 1860–1962* by Martin Gilbert on pages 190 and 193.